Mastering
mental ray®

Mastering
mental ray®

Rendering Techniques for 3D & CAD Professionals

Jennifer O'Connor

Wiley Publishing, Inc.

Acquisitions Editor: Mariann Barsolo
Development Editor: Jennifer Leland
Production Editor: Christine O'Connor
Copy Editor: Kim Wimpsett
Editorial Manager: Pete Gaughan
Production Manager: Tim Tate
Vice President and Executive Group Publisher: Richard Swadley
Vice President and Publisher: Neil Edde
Assistant Project Manager: Jenny Swisher
Associate Producer: Marilyn Hummel
Quality Assurance: Shawn Patrick
Book Designer: Maureen Forys, Happenstance Type-O-Rama; Judy Fung
Compositor: James D. Kramer, Happenstance Type-O-Rama
Proofreader: Nancy Bell
Indexer: Robert Swanson
Project Coordinator, Cover: Lynsey Stanford
Cover Designer: Ryan Sneed
Cover Image: Pete Gardner/DigitalVision/Getty Images

For general information on our other products and services or to obtain technical support, please contact our Customer Care Department within the U.S. at (877) 762-2974, outside the U.S. at (317) 572-3993 or fax (317) 572-4002.

Wiley also publishes its books in a variety of electronic formats. Some content that appears in print may not be available in electronic books.

Library of Congress Cataloging-in-Publication Data

O'Connor, Jennifer, 1962-
 Mastering Mental ray : rendering techniques for 3D & CAD professionals / Jennifer O'Connor. -- 1st ed.
    p. cm.
 Includes bibliographical references and index.
 ISBN-13: 978-0-470-56385-4 (paper/DVD : alk. paper)
 ISBN-10: 0-470-56385-0 (paper/DVD : alk. paper)
 1. Computer-aided design. 2. Three-dimensional display systems. 3. Mental ray (Computer file) I. Title.
 T385.O28 2010
 620'.00420285536--dc22
                    2010003134

Dear Reader,

Thank you for choosing *Mastering mental ray: Rendering Techniques for 3D & CAD Professionals*. This book is part of a family of premium-quality Sybex books, all of which are written by outstanding authors who combine practical experience with a gift for teaching.

Sybex was founded in 1976. More than 30 years later, we're still committed to producing consistently exceptional books. With each of our titles, we're working hard to set a new standard for the industry. From the paper we print on, to the authors we work with, our goal is to bring you the best books available.

I hope you see all that reflected in these pages. I'd be very interested to hear your comments and get your feedback on how we're doing. Feel free to let me know what you think about this or any other Sybex book by sending me an email at nedde@wiley.com. If you think you've found a technical error in this book, please visit http://sybex.custhelp.com. Customer feedback is critical to our efforts at Sybex.

Best regards,

Neil Edde
Vice President and Publisher
Sybex, an Imprint of Wiley

I dedicate this book to my two wonderful children, Ryan and Catherine. They fill my life with love, wonder, and joy, and are the only things more interesting and endlessly fascinating than 3D technology.

Acknowledgments

Much thanks goes to Mark Gerhard for pitching this book to Wiley, for being a supportive mentor through this process, and for being my technical editor. Thank you to Mariann and Jen at Wiley for your patience, and for helping me through this process. I have learned a lot, and it has been a great experience.

Thanks to the many developers at mental images and Autodesk for producing a complex and interesting set of products which have occupied my time for endless hours, and hopefully will continue to do so for many years to come.

Thanks to my students at the College of Lake County and the members of the Chicago AAUGA for keeping me on my toes, and giving me an audience to work out my mental ray and 3ds Max presentations. Thanks for reading my early mental ray documents, and for encouraging me to produce this book.

As with all things, I stand on the shoulders of giants. There are a great number of people who produce books, tutorials, blogs, and give assistance on forums, which all add to our total knowledge and acquired experience. In particular, thank you to Zap Andersson for all of your great insight into the workings of mental ray, and Jeff Patton for his seemingly tireless work in mental ray and 3ds Max. And thanks to the wider mental ray community for every tip, technique, and troubleshooting tidbit that has helped me in my journey over these many years.

I feel very fortunate to be a part of this ever-evolving industry, and to have been able to watch it grow in incredible ways. It has given me an endless array of new things to learn, teach, and do with these incredible tools.

Learn. Discover. Teach. Repeat.

About the Author

Jennifer O'Connor is president and founder of 4D Artists, Inc. (4DA), an animation and rendering company formed in 1992 on the outskirts of Chicago. 4DA has experience on a wide variety of projects from conceptual 2D and 3D design and rendering, through to the production of complete turnkey sales and marketing videos for large commercial and residential developments, and everything in between. They work on projects from around the world, and for a wide variety of clients. This is Jennifer's first title with Sybex/Wiley.

In addition to her company, since 1996 Jennifer has worked as an adjunct college professor at the College of Lake County, teaching classes in 3ds Max Design for CGI, animation, and 3D Architectural Illustration, along with classes in AutoCAD, Revit, Inventor, and computer concepts.

Jennifer is the president and founder of the Autodesk Animation User's Group Association (AAUGA) for Chicago, a group focusing on 3ds Max/Design. The User's Group web site is at www.max3ds.com.

Jennifer's background is in computer science and engineering (i.e. a technology geek), and having grown up with Tron and Star Wars, has always had a passion for computer graphics from a hardware, software and user standpoint. She is an accomplished programmer in Assembly (Z-80 and Intel), PROLOG, Fortran, C, C++ and C#. She has designed and built working computer hardware from a pile of chips and wire, developed knowledge-based AI diagnostic systems, and several multi-tasking/multi-threaded distributed applications for a variety of purposes. She also has experience in designing, building and troubleshooting industrial controls and AC/DC drive systems, along with building, using and troubleshooting professional audio, video, and theater systems.

Jennifer has been an AutoCAD user since the mid '80s, and worked with the early 3D capabilities of AutoCAD and the first versions of RenderMan and Animator Pro. She started using 3D Studio for DOS back in 1992, and produced her early renderings and animations on 286-based computers rendered out to 8mm tapes. Her first commercial 3D project back then was with her good friend Emil McCauley, owner of TGWB Inc. Jennifer and Emil have worked through the evolution and use of 3D Studio and 3ds Max on a wide variety of projects ever since those very early days. Jennifer now works with her son Ryan, who started using 3ds Max when he was five, along with Emil and an array of friends and freelancers.

Jennifer currently resides in Lake County, Illinois, with her son Ryan and daughter Catherine.

Contents at a Glance

Contents

Introduction

mental ray within 3ds Max is a straightforward rendering choice for beginning users and also a powerful and sophisticated tool for serious artists and professionals. Its integration in a wide range of products means that users can use the knowledge gained in one application within many others. mental ray is mental ray no matter what the platform; however, the user interface will differ, as will the availability of certain features. In addition to being included in the 3ds Max product line, mental ray is included in Autodesk's AutoCAD, Inventor, and Revit products, and understanding how to efficiently use mental ray is of paramount importance to artists in many design fields. 3ds Max's close connections to these products and virtually free mental ray licensing makes it a cost-effective rendering tool compared to other third-party rendering technologies.

This book provides to-the-point practical information on using mental ray within 3ds Max and 3ds Max Design. Like me, busy architects, industrial designers, and other 3ds Max/Design users need to cut through the chaff and get to the essential tools and settings they need to get their work done, and this book is a practical and useful guide for that purpose. I also delve into the details of many aspects of mental ray for advanced users, and focus on the tools and techniques to optimize render time and to diagnose and troubleshoot problematic scenes.

Bonus material that didn't make it into the book is included on the book's DVD and also at www.mastering-mentalray.com. The DVD also includes all the project files mentioned in the book for your own experimentation.

The focus of this book is on producing realistic images using a modern workflow, including photometric lighting tools and energy-correct materials. Other techniques that might have been used in the past for an efficient workflow were usually developed to compensate for the limitations and slowness of computers and software. These techniques have now, in many ways, become both unnecessary and inefficient to use, are bad habits basically, and are generally a poor approach to producing realistic images. Certain legacy lights and materials, for instance, are still usable within mental ray, but they not only break the laws of physics but also tend to be more difficult for new users to control and thus are not recommended nor covered in this book.

I use 3ds Max/Design as a platform for explaining how to use mental ray, and in many ways this book is as much about 3ds Max/Design as it is about mental ray, and therefore some familiarity with 3ds Max/Design is assumed. Users of other applications will find a lot of common ground, and except for user interface elements and some terminology, mental ray is similar between applications.

Who Should Read This Book

Design Visualization, and the production of photo-real renderings, is becoming expected in this day and age. Clients are used to seeing photorealistic images in their daily lives, whether on TV, in print, or provided to them as part of design services. Artists from many design backgrounds are finding that their clients require realistic 3d images throughout the design process so that they can make informed decisions not only about the form and function of a design, but also about materials and finishes, and even lighting intensity and form. I have found over the years that design visualization often helps ensure that the client gets the building or product that they imagine.

The book is designed for a wide range of users, from intermediate to advanced, and covers a wide range of topics which will appeal to:

- Architects tasked with presenting their design to clients and the community, and for the production of marketing materials

- Architectural Illustrators looking to take advantage of this powerful rendering tool

- Industrial and product design professionals looking to enhance their skills

- Interior designers looking to create realistic representations of their designs

- Lighting designers looking to accurately evaluate and represent their designs

- CAD specialists tasked with visualization

- 3D enthusiasts looking to take advantage of more realistic tools

- 3ds max and mental ray educators

- And more…

If you are new to 3ds Max/Design, then this book will complement other resources to help you get up to speed. I will show almost every element you need to find to help reduce frustration in learning the user interface. I do assume, however, that you know how to make a light, transform objects, and work with modifiers. If you are still getting up to speed on 3ds Max/Design, then take a look at the excellent videos that ship with the 3ds Max/Design product before jumping into this book. That said, I trust that most users will be able to quickly use the information provided.

I provide many examples, including the end result of all step-by-step tutorials, so you can optimize your time and avoid lengthy renders if that is not practical for you. Looking at finished examples and playing with their settings is a great way to learn, and is encouraged.

What You Will Learn from This Book

This book covers the use of mental ray in 3ds Max/Design for production of photo-real renderings, and covers most features of mental ray in a comprehensive manner. The goal of this book is to discuss introductory through advanced tools and techniques, and to provide succinct real-world examples of each primary tool's use. We also provide projects that you can work through to reinforce and test your skills.

3ds Max/Design and mental ray are both vast subjects, and there are subjects we do not cover as extensively as we would like. We tried to touch on as much as we could within our limitations.

How to Use This Book

Although this book is designed to be progressive in its presentation of tools and techniques, each chapter is also intended to be stand-alone in its content, and experienced users should be able to jump around as needed to the topics that interest them most. When appropriate, we will direct you to the chapters that describe additional details beyond the essentials, or point you to where we cover the essentials when you delve into advanced information.

On the `www.mentalray4Design.com` web site, available for download and viewable on-line, is a searchable PersonalBrain Mind Map of much of the key concepts of mental ray and its use in 3ds Max/Design. This mind map allows you to randomly search and browse for mental ray information, and is a visual method of learning and relating information. See `www.personalbrain.com` for more on this technology. The "brain" for this book is the mental ray knowledge I have acquired over the years, and is the outline and structure used to build this book.

The web site also contains bonus material on advanced learning techniques, and I recommend a multi-pass approach to reading and learning this — or any other — complex material. I have found that the best way to start learning this material is to spend some time paging through the book, start to finish, to get an idea of the overall content, and repeating this often to build many thin layers of knowledge. This, combined with the Personal Brain, will help you in learning this material.

Conventions Used in this Book

This book uses some conventions and special formatting to easily communicate different commands, ideas, and concepts. Here is a look at some of the formats you will encounter:

◆ Items in *italic* generally are terms being introduced and defined. In some cases, italics are also used for variables or placeholders (as in *variable*) that suggest information you need to know or enter to work with a particular feature or application.

◆ Items in **boldface** generally are commands or text you can type, while lines of programming code, filenames, Internet addresses, and command-line entries appear in a `monospaced font`.

◆ Menu commands use a right-facing arrow to suggest the menu you should select, followed by the command. For instance, File ➢ Open means to click the File menu in the menu bar at the top of the screen and then click the Open command.

◆ Keyboard shortcuts often include special symbols and a plus sign (+) between them, such as Control+click or Shift+Tab. With keyboard shortcuts, you need to press all of the keys indicated simultaneously and then release them together.

You will find sidebars throughout the text that are designed to give you more information related to the current discussion. While sidebars often can be ignored, they are designed to offer interesting or helpful advice for going deeper into a particular topic. Real World Scenarios, sidebars identified by a special globe banner, are in-depth discussions of how the concepts relayed in this text bear upon day-to-day application of the software.

A Word about Software Versions

This book is written with the beta version of 3ds Max Design 2011 and mental ray version 3.8, and some features, screenshots, and details may change prior to final release of 3ds Max/Design 2011. Every effort was made to ensure the book was as accurate to the planned release as possible; since the book was completed several months prior to the release of 3ds Max/Design 2011 some differences may exist. Please see the www.mastering-mentalray.com site for any updates or errata.

Much of the material covered applies to 3ds Max/Design 2008 and newer. Most example scenes provided on the DVD are in 3ds Max/Design 2010 format, and files will have a "_2010" or "_2011" added to the file name to indicate versions. FBX export format files of many larger scenes may be available for backward compatibility and use in earlier versions, and users should ensure that they install the latest FBX plug-in from the Autodesk web site. The use of particular features discussed are dependent on 3ds Max/Design and mental ray versions. A 30-day demo copy of the latest version of 3ds Max/Design is available on the Autodesk web site, and students and teachers can get licenses for Autodesk software at http://students.autodesk.com with an .edu email address or invitation from their instructor.

There are two flavors of 3ds Max: plain vanilla *3ds Max*, and *3ds Max Design*. The only difference between the two is the addition of Lighting Analysis tools in 3ds Max Design, the availability of the Software Development Kit in 3ds Max, some different presets and a different focus of the tutorials that ships with each application. 3ds Max Design has primarily Architecture and Design-related tutorials, and 3ds Max has game and entertainment-related tutorials. 3ds Max Design's defaults are assumed throughout this book, and are detailed in Chapter 1.

The term 3ds Max/Design is used throughout this book to indicate features that apply to both the 3ds Max and the 3ds Max Design versions of this program. The exact term 3ds Max or 3ds Max Design will be used to indicate a feature only applicable to those versions.

3ds Max and 3ds Max Design require Windows XP, Windows Vista, or Windows 7 operating systems, either 32 or 64-bit. This book utilizes screen shots from 3ds Max Design 2011 running in the Windows 7 platform.

The Mastering Series

◆ The Sybex Mastering series: "By professionals for professionals" commitment. Mastering authors are themselves practitioners, with plenty of credentials in their areas of specialty.

◆ Hands-on practice: Skills are taught with step-by-step instruction in addition to narrative and background; then those skills are tested with real tutorials and by the "Bottom Line" wrap-up in each chapter (see below).

◆ Real-world scenarios: Every chapter includes at least one real-world example of how the skills and information apply to the reader's work. These range from case studies to interviews that show how the tool, technique, or knowledge presented is applied in actual practice.

◆ Skill-based training: Skills to be acquired are clearly listed and tested.

◆ Self-review test "Master It" problems and questions, so you can be certain you're equipped to do the job right.

◆ Every chapter ends with a section titled "The Bottom Line," where the skills learned are repeated, summarized, and tested.

How This Book Is Organized

Each chapter includes bonus material, including a video Chapter Overview, included on the DVD.

Chapter 1: **mental ray Essentials** shows you all of the core information you need to understand about what mental ray is, proper configuration of mental ray and 3ds Max/Design, and forms the groundwork for working with mental ray. We cover critical concepts such as File Scale, Gamma, and Aliasing, and move through the subset of tools you need to understand to control the basic quality and speed of your renderings. This chapter is for users of all levels.

Chapter 2: **Materials and Maps** focuses on the performance and quality settings of the Arch & Design series of materials, and the essential Map types that are used within the Design Visualization field. We cover Real-World scale for maps, the MetaSL shader, the use of the new node-based Slate Material Editor, and examine the impact of material and map setting on render time and image quality.

Chapter 3: **Light, Shadow, and Exposure Control** brings you through critical settings of the Photometric light objects that can optimize and improve renderings, including general strategies for lighting scenes. Chapter 3 covers performance and quality setting for different kinds of shadows and advanced mental ray tools for shadow reuse, and covers the use of the mr Photographic Exposure Control.

Chapter 4: **Rendering** takes you through critical settings for the mental ray renderer affecting speed and quality, covers techniques for reducing memory requirements, and details strategies producing both large images and lengthy animations with mental ray.

Chapter 5: **Indirect Illumination and Final Gather** explains the concept of indirect illumination using the Final Gather technology of mental ray, and shows advanced tools and techniques to use this feature to greatly improve the look and feel of your renderings. I cover the caching and reuse of Final Gather, and using Final Gather for large still images and lenthy animations.

Chapter 6: **Global Illumination and Caustics** covers these topics for exterior and interior renderings, which can greatly improve both rendering quality and speed.

Chapter 7: **Importons and Irradiance Particles** details these advanced rendering tools and techniques for optimizing Global Illumination, producing indirect illumination, and generating image-based lighting.

Chapter 8: **Effects** covers effects such as Depth of Field, Motion Blur, Lens, Volumetric and Environmental Effects.

Chapter 9: **mental ray for Architecture** covers the use of mental ray in scenes imported via FBX from Revit, the use of Light Meters and the Lighting Analysis tools, and creating non-photorealistic renderings using various mental ray tools and materials.

Chapter 10: **mental ray for Design** covers the creation and use of render studios to showcase your product renderings, the use of Render Elements for compositing in the new Autodesk 3ds Max Composite application, and the importing of design data from solid modeling programs such as Autodesk Inventor using the new SAT format.

Appendix A: **The Bottom Line** summarizes all of the "Master It" questions and Solutions presented in the individual chapters.

What Is on the DVD

We have included all sample scenes, organized by chapter and topic, into the \ProjectFolders folder on the DVD. Whenever possible, scene files are created for 3ds Max/Design 2010, and files will be labeled for versions.

For best results, copy the contents of individual chapter's project folders to a local hard or USB drive to allow editing and updating of the material. You will also need to set 3ds Max/Design's project to point to the chapter's project folder so that 3ds Max/Design can find the files it needs. This is explained in Chapter 1, "Essentials."

We have bonus screen-capture video overviews of each chapter in the \BonusVideo folder and at www.mastering-mentalray.com, to assist you in getting up to speed quickly on the content, and to help reinforce concepts and the Master It topics.

Bonus content is available in the \Bonus folder, including content from Dosch Design and Spheron VR.

How to Contact the Author

I greatly appreciate any feedback you may have on the book. There is certainly a lot more that can be said on the subject of mental ray and 3ds Max/Design, and you can participate in book-specific forums at the www.mastering-mentalray.com site, and also on mental ray in general at the http://forum.mentalimages.com, http://area.autodesk.com and www.vizdepot.com sites, where I tend to participate and assist users. You can contact me directly at jenni@mastering-mentalray.com.

Chapter 1

mental ray Essentials

mental ray by mental images is an advanced, Academy Award–winning rendering engine included with Autodesk's 3ds Max and 3ds Max Design applications. This industry-standard renderer is used in a multitude of productions ranging from the latest sci-fi and action movies to visually rich game cinematics to stunning renderings of vehicles, architecture, and products yet only imagined. mental ray is integrated in 3D applications from a variety of developers, most notably by Autodesk, and is the leading rendering application in the world.

In this chapter, I introduce you to a number of important topics for both Autodesk's 3ds Max/Design product and the mental ray rendering engine. This chapter ensures that you have a number of critical skills and all the valuable information that you will need as you move forward. In this chapter, you will learn to

- ◆ Set up mental ray
- ◆ Configure 3ds Max/Design
- ◆ Configure gamma settings
- ◆ Configure essential quality settings
- ◆ Adjust Final Gather presets

mental ray Overview

mental ray provides a number of high-end render features:

Bucket rendering   mental ray renders scenes in square areas of your image called *buckets* or tiles; each processor core in your machine takes a bucket and processes that portion of the rendering before moving on to process the next available bucket. Brackets appear around each bucket as it is processing, and when the bucket completes, mental ray jumps to the next easiest bucket to manage. Figure 1.1 shows completed buckets and four buckets that are in process on a quad-core machine.

FIGURE 1.1:
mental ray bucket rendering on a quad-core computer

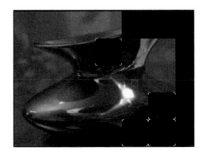

Distributed bucket rendering   Because mental ray subdivides the image into buckets, it can distribute the rendering of specific buckets to other machines, potentially allowing every computer on your network to work on individual buckets at the same time with some generous licensing limitations. Chapter 4, "Rendering," goes into more detail on this topic. For large installations, you can add mental ray–distributed rendering licenses by purchasing stand-alone versions of mental ray from your local reseller.

32-bit frame buffer   mental ray works in a 32-bit high dynamic range rendering environment, using floating-point engineering units for storing render data. The high dynamic range allows mental ray to represent color and light from the darkest black through the full spectrum of light to the full intensity and color of the sun and beyond. In addition to producing spectacular renderings, this capability is essential for accurate lighting analysis.

64-bit operating system support   64-bit support means access to as much memory as you can get into your computer, allowing you to render large and complex scenes. However, mental ray's advanced memory management tools also allow 32-bit machines with limited resources to successfully render large images.

High dynamic range, energy-accurate materials   The mental ray materials Arch & Design and the ProMaterials series are energy conserving, which means that the energy being reflected or refracted from or through a surface never exceeds the energy striking the surface. High dynamic range means a spectacular surface appearance and is essential for both realistic renderings and accurate lighting analysis.

Photometric lighting and indirect illumination   mental ray supports 3ds Max/Design's photometric lights and adds a few others to more accurately simulate the sun and sky and to assist with illuminating interior scenes. As you can see in Figure 1.2, the Indirect Illumination tools allow you to simulate the natural propagation of light through an environment to produce highly accurate images that account for all light propagation in an environment.

FIGURE 1.2:
Interior scene with photometric and indirect lighting

Lighting analysis tools   mental ray allows you to accurately simulate real-world lighting and create virtual light meters to measure the illuminence of surfaces to assist you in producing documentation for Leadership in Energy and Environmental Design (LEED) certification.

Hybrid, adaptive renderer   mental ray is a hybrid renderer in that it will use both ray tracing and fast scanline rendering of elements as needed. This hybrid approach gives you the highest-quality results with the most efficient use of time and can allow mental ray to render faster than the 3ds Max/Design's default scanline renderer for scenes that use ray-traced materials.

mental ray is also adaptive in that it will work harder on areas of your image that need more refinement, and it can quickly zip through areas that have less detail to resolve. You can define the quality settings mental ray uses, and you can tune exactly how much an image is refined as it renders.

In the next section, I cover some of the essentials of configuring 3ds Max/Design to use mental ray and setting mental ray as a default for all new scenes.

Enabling mental ray

In 3ds Max Design 2009 and newer versions of 3ds Max/Design, mental ray is the default rendering engine, and the materials in the Material Editor are, by default, mental ray's Arch & Design and ProMaterials. When editing legacy scenes, if you are using standard 3ds Max 2009 or are using earlier versions of 3ds Max/Design, you might need to select the mental ray renderer manually. In the sample scenes provided on this book's DVD, mental ray is selected as your rendering engine.

Choosing mental ray for an Existing Scene

To change an existing scene to use mental ray, first press F10 to open the Render Setup dialog box. Then, as shown in Figure 1.3, select the Common tab, expand the Assign Renderer drop-down section, and click the ellipsis button (...) to the right of Production to open the Choose Renderer dialog box. Select mental ray Renderer, and click the OK button.

FIGURE 1.3:
Selecting mental ray Renderer

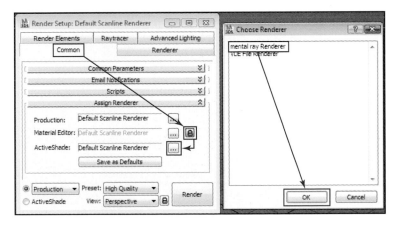

Click the Save as Defaults button to make this your new preferred rendering engine for all new scenes. To quickly switch to mental ray, you can also choose a preset from the bottom of the Render Setup dialog box that includes mental ray options, as shown in Figure 1.4.

FIGURE 1.4:
mental ray presets
from the Render
Setup dialog box

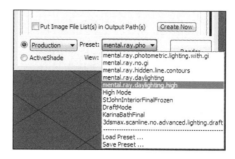

Your list of presets might vary from what is shown, depending on your 3ds Max/Design version and whether you have any user-defined presets. As with many presets provided with 3ds Max/Design, they can be a good starting point for many scenes. Creating your own presets for draft and final quality renderings is a good idea for every project. I provide some sample presets in the DVD's Chapter 1 project folder.

Setting mental ray Preferences and Using the Render Message Window

Selecting the Customize ➤ Preferences menu opens 3ds Max/Design's general Preference Settings dialog box, which includes the mental ray tab, as shown in Figure 1.5.

FIGURE 1.5:
mental ray Preference
Settings dialog box

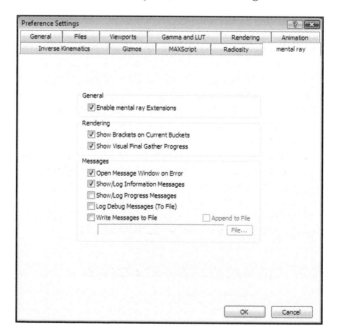

Generally I do not modify these settings; however, disabling the options for Show Brackets and Show Visual Final Gather will speed your renderings by a small percentage as mental ray will not use time to update the display during rendering. For machines used only for rendering, disabling these two options is a good idea as you will most likely not be monitoring the progress directly. For local rendering, I prefer these to remain enabled. In versions of 3ds Max/ Design prior to 2011, the mental ray preferences included options for controlling the mental ray Message Window, which streams useful render-time information from mental ray. These options are now found in the Rendering tab of the Preference Settings dialog box.

New in 3ds Max/Design is the Render Message Window, shown in Figure 1.6, which replaces the mental ray Message Window in previous versions of 3ds Max/Design. You can open this window from the Render ➤ Render Message Window option. It will also open automatically in the event of a render error.

FIGURE 1.6:
The Render Message window in 3ds Max/Design 2011 with right-click options shown.

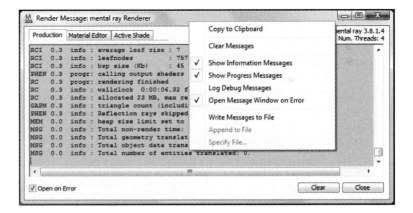

This new general purpose message window now works with other renderers such as the new Hardware renderer. In addition to preference settings in the Rendering tab of the Preference Settings dialog box, you can right-click on the Render message window to control message options, as shown in Figure 1.6.

The only setting I recommend changing at this point is to enable the Show Information option, which displays useful render-time information to the Renderer Message Window. Reviewing the Render Message Window at render time allows you to get a feel for what mental ray is doing behind the scenes; it may alert you to changes you need to make in render or object settings, and it can assist you in troubleshooting render issues. Messages might include warnings about incompatible features that are enabled, helpful status messages about connections to other computers, statistics about render time and memory use, and other details.

Next I discuss a number of key concepts and configuration options that contribute greatly to the successful production of accurate renderings.

Configuring 3ds Max/Design

Before you can begin to use 3ds Max/Design and mental ray efficiently and in order for your DVD sample scenes to work properly as you move through the book, you need to configure a few settings.

These settings include the following:

◆ mental ray and 3ds Max/Design defaults

◆ Project folders

◆ System units

◆ Gamma options

Exploring mental ray's Design-Related Defaults

3ds Max/Design allows you to customize the user interface and modify a number of default settings. I wrote this book using 3ds Max Design 2011 with the default light-colored 3ds Max UI scheme and certain other default settings related to 3ds Max Design. If you are using standard 3ds Max or different program defaults, then some examples in the book might not work as expected.

To change your defaults to the DesignVIZ.mentalray presets, from the top menus select Customize ➤ Custom UI And Defaults Switcher. Select the DesignVIZ.mentalray option, as shown in Figure 1.7, and click the Set button.

FIGURE 1.7:
DesignVIZ.mental-ray options selected

Within the dialog box, as you switch between various initial settings for tool options (on the upper-left side), you will see in the Overview window the default settings and behaviors that differ with each choice. Using options other than DesignVIZ.mentalray may potentially affect how book examples operate, and are not recommended at this point.

Clicking the Set button causes all new scenes to use these default settings; however, this does not modify render settings or change objects in existing scenes.

For standard 3ds Max, the UI and Default Switcher option Max is the initial default setting, rather than DesignVIZ.mentalray as it is with the 3ds Max Design version. With standard 3ds Max, you need to manually select the mental ray renderer for any new scenes that you create, as described earlier in this chapter. The UI Schemes options on the top-right side of the dialog box change your UI's color and icon style; this book utilizes the ame-light option. I tend to customize my UI quite a bit, and if you have previously customized your UI, then be certain to save your current UI from Customize ➢ Save Custom UI Scheme before you switch the UI scheme in this dialog box. This way, you can restore your last UI configuration settings, if required. Selecting Customize ➢ Customize User Interface allows you to save and recall individual files for keyboard shortcuts and other UI categories you may want to recall separately.

Using Project Folders

The purpose of the project folders is to keep assets related to a project within a specific group of folders, separate from other projects. The example files for the book are divided into separate folders on the DVD, divided by chapter number. For example, Chapter 1 uses the DVD folder \ProjectFolders\01_Essentials. For the sample projects to open and render properly, you need to set 3ds Max/Design's Project Folder option to point to the correct folder location and use the project configuration file located there. The project configuration file is a simple text file with the same name as the project folder and an .mxp extension.

UNIQUE PROJECT FOLDERS ARE USED IN EACH CHAPTER

Each chapter has a unique project folder that holds all of the chapter's scenes' bitmaps, rendered images, and other support files, and you will need to set 3ds Max/Design to use these project folders as you move from chapter to chapter. For the best results, copy the contents of the DVD's \ProjectFolders folder to your local hard drive, a network location, or a USB drive. After copying, you may need to clear the read-only properties of the files and folder by right-clicking the folder name, selecting Properties, and deselecting the Read-Only check box. This allows you to update files and add your own files and renderings to the folders.

Throughout the book I will refer to the \ProjectFolders location for sample files and will assume these are on a hard drive or USB drive and can be updated. You can open the "Browse for Folder" dialog box to select a project folder location from the far-right icon on the Quick Access Toolbar, as shown in Figure 1.8, or from the File menu.

If you select an empty folder for your project, Max/Design will create any subfolders necessary to hold project data and create an .mxp file to hold project-specific file paths. This is a simple text file that you can edit in Notepad, and you can also change it in the dialog boxes that open when you select Customize ➢ Configure Users Paths.

Because many scenes in this book take advantage of the bitmaps that ship with Max/Design, you will have to ensure 3ds Max/Design's map paths are included in your local bitmap paths within in the MXP file. For Max/Design 2011, this list typically includes the C:\Program Files\ Autodesk\3ds Max Design 2011\maps folder and subfolders, along with new path locations for the new Autodesk Material Library, covered in Chapter 2. Those maps may include paths such as C:\Program Files (x86)\Common Files\Autodesk Shared\Materials2011\assetlibrary_ base.fbm\1\Mats\. Map paths will change based on your installed version and whether you used the default folder paths for installing 3ds Max/Design.

FIGURE 1.8:
Selecting a project folder

This listing is from the MXP project file in the \ProjectFolders\01_Essentials folder for Chapter 1:

```
[Directories]
Animations=.\sceneassets\animations
Archives=.\archives
AutoBackup=.\autoback
BitmapProxies=.\proxies
Downloads=.\downloads
Export=.\export
Expressions=.\express
Images=.\sceneassets\images
Import=.\import
Materials=.\materiallibraries
MaxStart=.\scenes
Photometric=.\sceneassets\photometric
Previews=.\previews
ProjectFolder=C:\Users\Jenni\Documents\3dsMaxDesign
RenderAssets=.\sceneassets\renderassets
RenderOutput=.\renderoutput
RenderPresets=.\renderpresets
Scenes=.\scenes
Sounds=.\sceneassets\sounds
VideoPost=.\vpost
[XReferenceDirs]
Dir1=.\scenes
[BitmapDirs]
Dir1=C:\Program Files\Autodesk\3ds Max Design 2011\Maps
Dir2=C:\Program Files\Autodesk\3ds Max Design 2011\Maps\glare
Dir3=C:\Program Files\Autodesk\3ds Max Design 2011\Maps\adskMtl
```

```
Dir4=C:\Program Files\Autodesk\3ds Max Design 2011\Maps\Noise
Dir5=C:\Program Files\Autodesk\3ds Max Design 2011\Maps\fx
Dir6=.\downloads
Dir7=.\sceneassets\images
```

The .\ before a file path indicates that the folder location is relative to the project folder. For instance, if the project folder is D:\ProjectFolders\01_Essentials, then your scenes will be stored in the D:\ProjectFolders\01_Essentials\scenes folder. This allows you to store files specific to your project with the project, and 3ds Max/Design will know where to find them.

These are the folders you will use the most:

AutoBackup   All automatic backup files related to this project are stored in the .\autoback folder with file name AutoBackupXX.max, where the XX is a circular list of numbers. You can define the length of this list and other AutoBackup options from the Customize ➢ Preferences dialog box, and the Files tab.

Images   Place any custom bitmaps you will be using for this project in the .\sceneassets\images folder.

RenderAssets   Any render-time files generated for indirect illumination, the caching of scene data, and storage of mental ray Proxy files, are created and stored in the .\sceneassets\renderassets folder.

Scenes   All .max and .mac (container) files are created and retrieved from .\scenes by default.

[XReferenceDirs]   This group of folder contains paths to additional scene files used in your project. For instance, you might have subfolders in your Scenes folder for various components of your model or buildings in a development. Defining those subfolders in this section allows Max to quickly find all related scene files. Typically this will be subfolders of the .\scenes folder but might be model libraries used for that project contained on other drives or paths.

[BitmapDirs]   This section should list all folders that contain material bitmaps files used in your project. As you can see in the previous listing, the paths used for the book are the default bitmap installation folders for 3ds Max/Design 2011. I provide separate MXP files for 3ds Max/Design 2009 and 2010 in the project folders on the DVD, and you can drag the correct version into 3ds Max/Design to set up your project folders; however, you can edit the MXP file or rename the files if needed.

Keeping this list of map paths short helps 3ds Max/Design find what it needs quickly, without searching through numerous irrelevant folders. If the list is long, you might experience long delays when you open and render files.

AUTOSAVE AND PROJECT FOLDERS

In addition to keeping all your files together, one of the advantages of using project folders is that any automatically backed-up files (AutoBackupXX.max files) are saved only to that project's .\autoback. folder and will not overwrite backups from any other project. Setting the name used for your workstation's AutoBackup files to include your name or initials, such as Jenni_AutoBack, will separate your files from another user in a networked environment and prevent another user from overwriting your backup files. You set this filename by selecting Configuration ➢ Preferences and the Files tab. You can also edit the MXP file to point to a folder on your local computer to further isolate your backups from others and improve the speed of backing up files for large scenes.

Setting System Units

The *system unit* is the underlying generic unit of measurement that 3ds Max/Design uses to store data. It determines the floating-point accuracy of both geometry and Position/Rotate/Scale transformations, and setting it properly ensures that imported scenes are the correct size and will have the proper light decay over distance. To set the system units in your scene, select Customize ➢ Units Setup to open the Units Setup dialog box, as shown in Figure 1.9.

FIGURE 1.9:
Units Setup dialog box

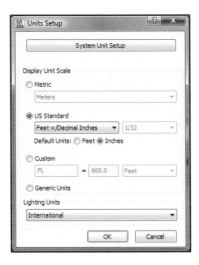

The Display Unit Scale settings specify how the system units are displayed in 3ds Max/Design's dialog boxes and spinners. You can change the display units at any time, and they can be completely different from the system unit; your display unit choice is simply a unit of measurement that is convenient for you, as shown in Figure 1.10.

FIGURE 1.10:
The US Standard drop-down list

You can change this value at any time, and it does not affect geometry, object translation, or rendering and lighting whatsoever.

The System Unit Setup button is at the top of the Units Setup dialog box; clicking it opens the System Unit Setup dialog box, as shown in Figure 1.11. In the United States, the units are, by default, set to 1 (generic) Unit = 1.0 Inches. For small objects with fine details, a setting of 1 Unit = 1 Millimeters may be appropriate to gain additional floating-point accuracy. For large Revit scenes, for instance, 1 Unit = 1 Feet or 1 Unit = 1 Meters might be appropriate. For planet-sized scenes, a setting of Miles or Kilometers may be required. The system unit setting is stored with the 3ds Max/Design file and may generate a warning when files with different system unit settings are opened. Once set, all new scenes created in your instance of 3ds Max/Design will use these system units.

FIGURE 1.11:
System Unit Setup
dialog box

SET SYSTEM UNITS FIRST

You must set the system units before you import or create any geometry, and you should not change the setting on an existing scene. If you need to change an existing scene, then consider merging the existing geometry into a scene with the proper system units. To maintain the accuracy of the imported CAD data, it is best to rescale the geometry in the CAD program that generated the data file and ensure that all data is as close to the origin as possible. This might mean creating an intermediate DWG file just for importing; however, the benefit in scene accuracy is significant and worth the additional effort. As you will see in Chapter 9, "mental ray for Architecture," the AutoCAD file import dialog box allows you to rescale CAD data on import. It does not, however, allow you to move data closer to the origin, and this is particularly critical in large civil projects.

If your scene comes in with the wrong units, you can also rescale your scene using the Rescale World Units tool, found on the Utility tab of the Command panel.

Setting Gamma Options

Gamma correction is an intensity adjustment applied to an image to compensate for nonlinearity in print and display devices. This nonlinearity can make material bitmaps render too bright in outdoor scenes or cause your rendered images to appear too dim on your monitor or printer. With gamma correction, you work in a what-you-see-is-what-you-get (WYSIWYG) environment, where a bitmap that goes into your rendering pipeline will look the same when it comes out as a rendered image. Gamma correction is generally required for all 8-bit images saved as JPEG and PNG, and not for images saved in floating-point formats such as HDR and EXR. For information on file formats, see Chapter 4.

Gamma is an essential setting, and you must properly configure it on your machine in order for example scenes in this book to render correctly. 3ds Max Design 2010 and later use a gamma-corrected workflow by default. However, in standard 3ds Max, in 3ds Max versions prior to 2010, and when working with legacy scenes, you must manually configure your gamma settings.

Figure 1.12 shows rendered output with gamma of 1.0 on left, 1.8 in center, and 2.2 on the right. As you can see, adding gamma (to the output of the file, in this case) greatly increases the brightness of your rendered image and makes it appear as if your lighting intensity is set higher. Without gamma correction, you may have instead reduced the exposure settings, increased lighting intensity, and perhaps added lights to the scene to boost illumination to acceptable levels. Your rendered images would appear too dark with incorrect output gamma, as shown on the left of Figure 1.12, and can result in surfaces that appear washed out in your rendering, particularly when using very bright daylight scene illumination.

THE GAMMA CURVE

A gamma correction factor is a simple numerical value that describes the shape of a correction curve applied to the intensity of an image. Gamma correction decreases the intensity of the midtones in the bitmap images you use in surface materials and increases the intensity of midtones in the files you save to your computer. A gamma of 1.0 gives no gamma correction (1 = 1 linear results), a gamma less than 1.0 darkens the midtones of an image, and a gamma greater than 1.0 brightens the midtones. Image brightness at the extremes, very dark or very light colors, are not affected significantly by gamma correction. The following graphic shows gamma curves and the increase or decrease in intensity output values vs. input:

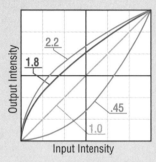

FIGURE 1.12:
Image gamma corrected (left to right) 1.0, 1.8, and 2.2

You can find all gamma-related settings by selecting Customize ➤ Preferences and going to the Gamma and LUT tab, as shown in Figure 1.13. These default settings for 3ds Max Design are a good starting point and might need only minor tweaking, particularly for your personal display.

FIGURE 1.13:
Gamma and LUT
settings

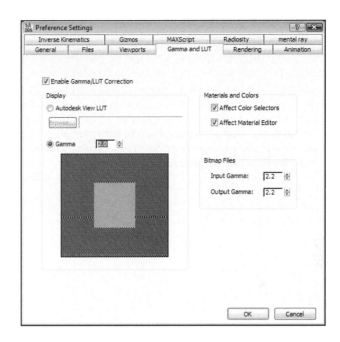

Referring to Figure 1.13, which shows the gamma settings for new scenes in 3ds Max Design 2010/2011, perform the following steps to adjust the gamma options within your installation of 3ds Max Design:

1. Select the Enable Gamma/LUT Correction check box, enabling the option.

2. Select the Gamma radio-button option instead of Autodesk View LUT.

3. Blur your eyes a bit, and adjust the Gamma value spinner until the inner and outer squares are about the same intensity on your monitor. (This value will differ from monitor to monitor.)

4. Select the Affect Color Selectors and Affect Material Editor check boxes. These critical settings give you a WYSIWYG color display in the material previews.

5. Set the Input Gamma and Output Gamma values to 2.2 each. These two settings ensure that images are read from (Input Gamma) and written to (Output Gamma) your bitmap files correctly and are described in the next section. The normal range for these values is 1.8 to 2.2, with 2.2 being the default.

As you can see in the dialog box in Figure 1.13, my monitor's Gamma setting is 2.0, and on my display the two squares look about the same brightness within 3ds Max/Design, yet in this book the two squares are very different. You will need different display gamma settings for each computer you use; however, the recommendation is to use 2.2 for all settings, including your monitor.

The inner square is 50 percent gray and the outer square contains a tiny black-and-white checkerboard giving the illusion of being 50 percent gray.; When the intensity of the two squares is the same, your monitor will have correct gamma correction applied to the display, and your renderings, bitmaps, and color selections will look brighter. Depending on your version of 3ds Max/Design, you might have to restart the program for gamma changes to take effect.

ENSURING CONSISTENT GAMMA CORRECTION

With 3ds Max/Design 2010 and newer, gamma settings are now preserved within the * .Max file; however, in legacy scenes only the gamma enabled on/off state is saved. With 3ds Max/Design and newer format scenes, you get a warning when you load a file that contains gamma settings different from your current settings, and you can accept the incoming settings or override the settings with your current settings, as shown here:

With these changes to 3ds Max/Design's file format, your scene's gamma now works consistently in Backburner network render jobs without needing to configure every server. For more information, see Chapter 4, "Rendering." With 3ds Max/Design 2009 and older, you must ensure that the gamma is set consistently on each workstation your artists use and also in each machine in your render farm.

If you keep your current settings when prompted by 3ds Max/Design rather than using the gamma settings in the incoming file, be aware that any bitmap that uses the Use System Default Gamma setting in its bitmap file settings will change the appearance of renderings produced with the alternate setting. If you need to ensure consistent renderings for a project, then adopt the settings or use the gamma override in each bitmap (as described in the "When Input Gamma Can Cause Problems" section later in this chapter) to ensure consistency no matter what the global gamma preferences.

If you open a legacy 3ds Max/Design scene, then you may only get a message to follow the gamma enable or disable states and not the input and output gamma settings.

Using Input Gamma Settings

The *Input gamma* setting, as found in the Customize ➢ Preferences and the Gamma and LUT tab, *de-gamma* corrects an image on your drive as it is brought into 3ds Max/Design, shifting the midtones downward so that the colors render correctly. It prevents bitmaps from appearing overly bright in your rendering. It compensates for images that were adjusted to look good on your monitor or when printed and makes them linear. This initial correction may be done automatically by some cameras or can be done in photo-editing software.

The Input Gamma setting is usually in the range of 1.8 to 2.2, and an Input Gamma setting of 1.8 seems to be most pleasing and may more closely match how a bitmap is stored by a camera or manually adjusted in Adobe Photoshop. An Input Gamma setting of 2.2 is the recommended default value from Autodesk and mental images, and 2.2 matches the sRGB standard developed by Microsoft and Hewlett-Packard and endorsed by Pantone, Corel, and others. I use 2.2 for both input and output gamma settings.

As you can see in Figure 1.14, the Input Gamma setting had a huge effect on the grass, brick, and wood bitmaps; however, it did not visibly affect the rendered colors on materials that are using a color swatch, such as the metallic paint on the center structure. The background environment and chrome teapot are also unaffected in this case.

FIGURE 1.14:
The left side has Input Gamma set to 2.2, and the right side has Input Gamma set to 1.0 (disabled).

When Input Gamma Can Cause Problems

The Input Gamma value can cause issues and undesired results in the following instances:

When a file already contains gamma information   TARGA is one of the few file formats that supports gamma information, and you may change the bitmap's option to Use Image's

Own Gamma in this case. This setting is found in the Select Bitmap Image File dialog box to specify maps used in your materials, and is shown in Figure 1.15. PNG files also support the use of gamma; however this is not always used consistently in 3ds Max/Design, and I tend to override the in-file setting. Some material libraries shipping with 3ds Max/Design may use the file's gamma values, and overriding the file's setting may improve your results.

When using high dynamic range Images   Images that are high dynamic range (HDR) 32-bit floating-point images will not look correct when gamma is corrected, and you will need to override the Input Gamma value to 1.0 for each HDR bitmap you use. Images that are 16 bits per channel may not require gamma correction, depending on the bitmap, and you can get a visual preview in the Select Bitmap dialog box. All low dynamic range (LDR) images, on the other hand, should be gamma corrected.

When using bump, normal, and displacement maps   For most purposes, the Input Gamma setting should be set to 1.0 when a bitmap is specifically for bump or displacement use. Otherwise, the bump/displacement will be artificially increased throughout the mid-range, which may not give you the expected results.

When using the mental ray Map Manager   In Chapter 4, I discuss translator memory settings, including the option called Use mental ray Map Manager. This option allows mental ray to store bitmaps. In some earlier versions of mental ray, this option ignores the bitmap's gamma override settings, and mental ray will use only the system gamma settings. In this case, use the Gamma & Gain map discussed next. This is not an issue with current versions of mental ray and 3ds Max/Design.

If you are experiencing issues with the default Input Gamma setting for a specific bitmap or have one of the situations listed where gamma correction would cause problems, you can override the Input Gamma option in the bitmap parameters using the Material Editor. You can find the Override option in the Select Bitmap Image File dialog box when you select a bitmap file on your drive, as shown in Figure 1.15.

FIGURE 1.15:
The gamma selection options for the Select Bitmap Image File dialog box

These options give you the opportunity to control or override the Input Gamma setting on a per-map basis. The Use System Default Gamma choice is typically used; however, I explain some of the exceptions to using this option in the next section. In 3ds Max/Design 2010 and newer, the preview thumbnail image will update its midtone brightness based on changes to the gamma setting.

USING THE GAMMA AND GAIN MAP

The Gamma & Gain (mi) map gives you image input gamma control over individual bitmaps to assist in overcoming limitations you might experience with the global Input Gamma setting. In 3ds Max/Design 2010 and older, this map was called the Utility Gamma and Gain map. The "(mi)" after a map or material name means that it is produced by mental images and is for use with mental ray. If you are *instancing* bitmaps in your scene (creating clones that are always identical), utilizing a noninstanced Gamma and Gain map where needed allows you to control specific bitmaps without affecting the other instances because only the bitmap, not the Gamma and gain map, will be instanced. These instructions are for the Compact Material Editor, formerly just the Material Editor; however with the addition of the ne Schematic material Editor (SME) the name has been changed. The new SME is covered in Chapter 2.

Perform the following steps to add the Gamma and Gain map wrapper to a bitmap:

1. From the settings of your bitmap, click the Bitmap button to open the Material/Map Browser, as shown in Figure 1.16 for the classic compact editor and as shown in Figure 1.17 for the new Schematic Material Editor (SME) version of the Material/Map Browser.

FIGURE 1.16:
Adding the Gamma & Gain wrapper to a map in the classic Material Editor

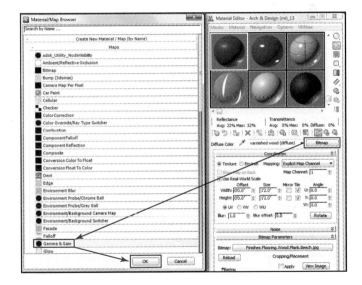

FIGURE 1.17:
The Gamma & Gain map shown connected to a bitmap and then a ProMaterial: Hardwood material in the SME

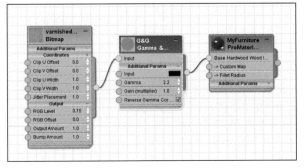

2. Make sure New is selected in the radio buttons on the left of the dialog box, and then scroll down and select the Gamma & Gain (mi) map.

3. Click OK.

4. You are asked whether you want to discard the old map or keep it as a submap; you will want to keep the map for this example. Your original map is now "wrapped" by the Gamma & Gain map, and the bitmap is processed by the Gamma & Gain map before being sent to the renderer.

Figure 1.18 shows the settings for the Gamma and Gain map. The Reverse Gamma Correction check box is selected by default and applies an inverse gamma correction to the bitmap, which in this case would be a gamma of approximately 0.454545 (1 ÷ 2.2). Be careful not to use gamma correction in the bitmap setting and in the Gamma and Gain map, because you will double-correct the image and end up with a very dark bitmap.

FIGURE 1.18:
Gamma & Gain settings to de-gamma an image

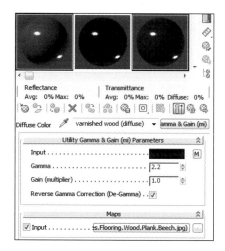

Unfortunately, there is little you can do to fix a rendered image with an incorrect Input Gamma setting, other than doing some Photoshop work on selected objects. This would need to be done on a per-material basis, provided you can mask those areas in Photoshop, and you would not gamma-correct a complete image because that would also shift rendered colors that would not have been normally changed in the gamma process.

Your best course of action, if you have the time, is to set the Input Gamma value correctly and rerender your image. Otherwise, use Photoshop to adjust regions of your image.

OUTPUT GAMMA SETTINGS

The Output Gamma setting shifts the midrange colors of a saved file upward to a range that will display well on other display devices. Output Gamma is different and independent of your display gamma and affects only the raw rendered image as it is transferred to a file.

🌐 Real World Scenario

PRACTICAL OUTPUT GAMMA

If your rendering looks fine within 3ds Max/Design but your client says the image looks too dark, consider turning up the Output Gamma setting in your preference settings or in the Output Gamma settings of your image's settings. A value of 2.2 is the default Output Gamma setting with 3ds Max/Design; however, you might want to set the Output Gamma value to be the same as your monitor's gamma value. Ultimately, you are compensating for your client's monitor or printer, and the default of 2.2 is usually sufficient.

Many users find a setting of 1.8 for Output Gamma looks best to them, but that might depend on the relative brightness of your scenes and your exposure settings, too. If you find yourself always adjusting the brightness of your renderings in photo-editing software, then you might want to consider using a different Output Gamma setting. An output value of 1.8 is fine for something that may be viewed on computer displays, but a setting of 2.2, the default, is common for video and matches the HP/Microsoft sRGB standard for monitors.

WHEN OUTPUT GAMMA CAN CAUSE ISSUES

The Output Gamma value can cause issues and undesired results in the following instances:

When saving to high dynamic range images   This includes formats such as HDR, EXR, and 32-bit TIFF. Gamma is necessary for low dynamic range images and should not be used for these file formats.

When saving alpha channel information   The gamma correction would change the transparency levels in the midrange of the alpha channel.

When using the logarithmic exposure control   The logarithmic exposure control adds a 2.2 gamma correction to your rendered image. See Chapter 3 for specifics on exposure control.

When using Backburner to render to strips   Rendering to strips allows multiple machines to render a large image, each taking a horizontal strip of the image. Two Backburner jobs are created: one for the strips and one for stitching the strips together into a final image. Both jobs add output gamma correction, and the image is corrected twice. For more information on network rendering, see Chapter 4.

In these instances, you should use an Output Gamma setting of 1.0 in your preferences, manually adjust the gamma in another application such as Photoshop, or control the gamma setting in the Render Output File dialog box for the saved image, as shown in Figure 1.19.

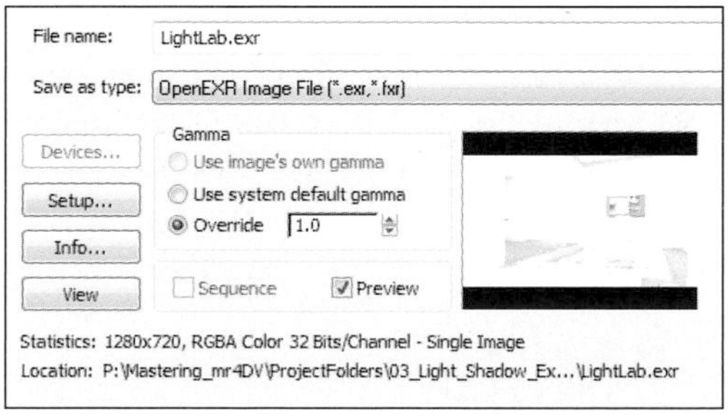

FIGURE 1.19:
Gamma override
options

Setting the Override value in the Render Output File dialog box is the most direct method of ensuring the output gamma is the value you desire, especially when working between multiple machines and in workgroups. As you will see in Chapter 4, using the Batch Render utility can also help ensure that output settings are always preserved.

If you need to correct the output gamma, open your image in Photoshop or a similar program, select Image ➢ Adjustments ➢ Exposure, and set the Gamma Correction value to somewhere between 1.8 and 2.2, as shown in Figure 1.20.

FIGURE 1.20:
Photoshop's Exposure dialog box

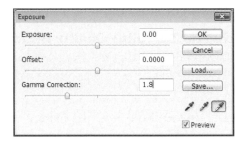

If your image was gamma-corrected twice, as with a Backburner Render to Strips job (see Chapter 4), then in the Gamma Correction field enter 1 ÷ *gamma value*, which for a 2.2 gamma is 0.454545. This shifts the image back into the proper range. Do not use any brightness or contrast settings to adjust the image until after gamma correction. After adjusting the gamma, it is also best not to use the Exposure or Offset options of this dialog box to adjust any 8- or 16-bit per channel images, because you can obtain much more direct and superior results by using the Curves tool (Image ➢ Adjustments ➢ Curves) of Photoshop.

In Autodesk Combustion, you need to add a Gamma/Pedestal/Gain node from the schematic view's right-click menu Add Operator ➢ Color Correction ➢ Gamma/Pedestal/Gain, placing it just after your file node and then adjust the gamma setting as shown in Figure 1.21. It works in an identical fashion to the Photoshop Exposure controls.

FIGURE 1.21:
Gamma correction adjustments in Combustion

In Autodesk's new 3ds Max Composite application — based on Autodesk Toxik — you can gamma-correct your images by adding the CC Basics node after your footage, as shown in Figure 1.22.

FIGURE 1.22:
3ds Max Composite's CC Basics node with its master gamma correction option set to 0.45454

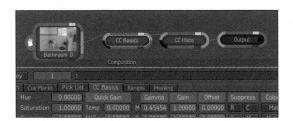

In the next section, I cover some of the critical mental ray settings and features that you need to get started using mental ray.

Quick-Start Render Settings

Although I delve into the mental ray render settings in detail in Chapter 4, it is important to take some time at this point to cover a number of settings that come into play in the examples in the next two chapters.

Introducing the Sampling Quality (Antialiasing) Settings

The Sampling Quality (Antialiasing) settings are a group of mental ray settings that include Sample per Pixel, Spatial Contrast, and Filter, and are the first few mental ray settings that are critical for you to understand. The settings are found in the Render Setup dialog box (press F10), and the Renderer tab. As the group name implies, these settings greatly impact the quality of your rendered image and as you will find, also impact the speed of your rendering.

DEFINING ANTIALIASING

Aliasing is missing or incorrect information in a rendered image due to an under-sampling of bitmaps and rendered elements. Simply put, it is the uneven edges in rendered images.

In Figure 1.23, you can see an under-sampled draft-quality rendering compared to a moderately antialiased and then highly sampled rendering.

FIGURE 1.23:
Low, medium, and high antialiasing settings in 3ds Max/Design

Under-sampling a rendering causes a distortion of the bitmap as the frequency of the checkerboard pattern increases into the distance. You will see jagged edges at pattern transitions, which is a high-frequency color transition, and aliasing shows up as very blocky areas rather than smoothed edges. Figure 1.24 shows four-times magnified images of the low and highly sampled images.

FIGURE 1.24:
Zoomed-in images of low and high antialiasing

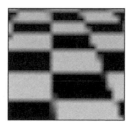

When images are properly antialiased, you gain image detail and reduce or eliminate undesired patterns in images, and you can reduce scintillation and image "crawling" in animations.

SAMPLES PER PIXEL SETTING

The Minimum and Maximum values for the Samples Per Pixel setting control how much effort mental ray is going to invest in rendering a pixel (or group of pixels) based on the composition of your scene, and they are the primary antialiasing controls.

On the Renderer tab of the Render Setup dialog box, you'll see the Sampling Quality drop-down list and the settings for Samples Per Pixel, as shown in Figure 1.25.

FIGURE 1.25:

The Samples Per Pixel settings in the Render Setup dialog box

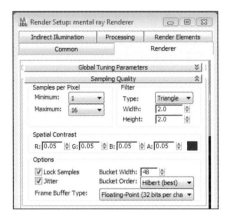

The Minimum setting allow mental ray to work quickly through easy areas such as environment maps and evenly colored areas and is the starting point for antialiasing your image. mental ray steps up through the Samples Per Pixel settings as more antialiasing is needed for an individual sample, and the Maximum setting is the upper limit for sampling.

The Image Precision setting in the Rendered Frame Window, as shown in Figure 1.26, gives you a convenient slider for choosing Draft through High preset settings for the Samples Per Pixel values. You can open the Rendered Frame Window from the Rendering ➢ Rendered Frame Window option, or from the toolbar.

FIGURE 1.26:

The Image Precision setting in the Rendered Frame Window

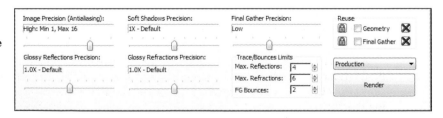

The Samples Per Pixel settings of Minimum and Maximum should be two to three levels apart from one another for efficient rendering. They should not be farther apart than four steps, and they should not be equal. A Samples Per Pixel greater than Maximum = 64 is rarely needed; in addition, do not use settings higher than 16 or 64 in your scenes unless you understand the render-time impact and have determined you need more detail. With a higher Samples Per Pixel value, you need to adjust the Spatial Contrast settings (described next) downward so mental ray will utilize the higher Samples Per Pixel settings.

SPATIAL CONTRAST

Spatial Contrast is a color that mental ray uses to compare adjacent samples to determine whether additional sampling is necessary. mental ray compares the current sample (whether groups of pixels or subpixels) with its neighbor samples, and if the difference (contrast) between the two is greater than the color of the Spatial Contrast setting, then mental ray will switch to a higher Samples Per Pixel setting and subdivide the pixels for greater detail.

In the example quality settings in Figure 1.27, each pixel would be sampled whole (Minimum = 1), and if the pixel next to it (another sample) had a color difference greater than 0.051, then it would subdivide that current sample into four new ¼-pixel samples.

FIGURE 1.27:
Spatial Contrast
settings of 0.051

A Spatial Contrast setting of 0.10 or greater will speed up draft renderings considerably, because mental ray will choose the Samples Per Pixel settings closer to Minimum more often as it renders your image. A setting of 0.02 or less produces higher-quality results and forces mental ray to subdivide samples toward the Maximum setting more often.

LOWER THE SPATIAL CONTRAST BEFORE YOU USE HIGH SAMPLE RATES

Often you can get a better and quicker render by reducing the Spatial Contrast setting rather than going to extremes for the Maximum value of the Samples Per Pixel setting. You can use a Spatial Contrast setting of 0.02 for higher-quality renderings, and you can even go a bit smaller to force more use of the Maximum value of the Samples Per Pixel setting. You should always consider lowering the Spatial Contrast value when you adjust Samples Per Pixel to higher sample rates; otherwise, mental ray will not utilize the higher settings.

A Spatial Contrast setting less than 0.015 is rarely needed, so leave it around 0.025 for most final renderings, 0.09 for fast draft renders, and less than 0.025 only if needed. Lower Spatial Contrast settings force the increased use of your Samples Per Pixel maximum, potentially causing the unnecessary use of high Samples Per Pixel levels, which may be inefficient for your particular rendering. I examine ways of visualizing and optimizing your Sampling Quality settings in Chapter 4.

Because human vision is less sensitive to green and blue colors, a Spatial Contrast setting of RGB 0.02, 0.04, and 0.06 can speed your renderings without a significant impact on the finished result.

FILTERS

Filters, as shown in Figure 1.28, take your raw rendered samples and turn them into final image pixels, blending between adjacent samples and pixels based on one of several filter algorithms. Filters are covered in more detail in Chapter 4.

FIGURE 1.28:
Filter options

Brief descriptions of each filter follow:

Box filter   A simple summing filter. This is the quickest sampling method with the roughest results. It is the default setting and should be changed for all production work.

Gauss filter   A blurring filter based on a bell curve. This is great for animations where you might experience flickering or scintillation.

Triangle filter   A filter that's fast and great for drafts. It filters samples in a pyramid pattern centered around the pixel being evaluated.

Mitchell filter   A sharpening filter using a steep bell curve. This is the best mode for most still images.

Lanczos filter   A bell curve–sharpening filter where samples farthest away from the pixel have less effect. This is great for final renders and the slowest method.

Filters can add significant time to your rendering. For any final-quality renderings, avoid the default Box filter and use a Mitchell or Lanczos filter. If you are rendering an animation, consider the Gauss filter with a 2.0 dimension. For draft-quality renders, use the Box filter or, for a little better quality, the Triangle filter.

Next, I cover some quick-start settings for Final Gather, a tool and technique that produces indirect illumination in your scene.

Introducing Final Gather

Final Gather (FG) is a method of collecting indirect or bounced illumination from your scene. It improves the realism and brightness of your rendered images and is a visible prepass process when rendering an image. In 3ds Max/Design 2010 and later, Final Gather is enabled by default for new scenes, and understanding a few basics and ground rules will help you get started using this feature. Final Gather is covered in detail in Chapter 5, "Indirect Illumination and Final Gather," and its use with other indirect illumination methods is covered in Chapter 6, "Global Illumination and Caustics."

The settings for Final Gather are in the Render Settings dialog box's Indirect Illumination tab and also in the Rendered Frame window, as shown in Figure 1.29. Final Gather is easy to use, and you simply need to enable it (you can do this with the Image Precision slider in the Rendered Frame window), choose the Draft, Low, or Medium setting, and add one or two diffuse bounces. It is rare that Final Gather settings greater than Medium are needed for a scene.

FIGURE 1.29:

Final Gather settings in the Rendered Frame window

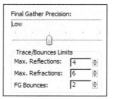

FG is ideal for almost any rendering and is often combined with global illumination for highest-quality indoor renderings and is used alone for outdoor scenes.

 Real World Scenario

RENDER, TWEAK, REPEAT: PLAYING WITH MENTAL RAY

One of the most time-consuming aspects of learning and using mental ray is creating test-renderings of a scene. You render, examine, tweak settings, render, compare, tweak, render, and repeat. It takes a lot of time and a lot of experimentation, and the trick is not having this experimentation eat up all of your time when you should be making progress on a project. Most people do not have the time or the inclination to spend countless hours rendering scenes to figure this all out — and that is why you have this book. Much of the focus of the book is to help reduce your test-renders and experimentation time while achieving quality results. I discuss a lot of features and settings throughout the book that all combine in various ways to give you the speed and quality you need, and I stress what is important to understand as you go along.

I have seen many people, my students and professionals alike, become frustrated with this wonderful renderer because of long render times or low-quality results, when simply understanding and adjusting a few settings could make their experience faster, make it more enjoyable, and make their final images a much higher quality. Sometimes the issue is their expectations of how long it should take to render an image. I get mildly amused when people are shocked at 10- to 15-minute renders when I routinely dealt with 24-hour renders in the early days. These days, I may even have my render farm burning away for several hours on final renders for a large project.

When people ask me what the best way is to learn mental ray, my first response, albeit somewhat tongue in cheek, is for them to get another computer they can use for the render-tweak-repeat process. Getting additional hardware is not always practical for my readers, of course, so throughout the book I provide rendered image samples to highlight differences and show render times so you can benchmark the results. I have a farm of 64-bit quad-core computers at my disposal, which makes it much easier to play with and explore mental ray. Providing sample renders and detailing render times in the book should both help reduce the amount of testing you must do to understand the concepts and help you make decisions about the settings for your own scenes without having to invest time in extensive experimenting.

That said, the best way to learn is to do, and if you are like me, you will most likely open up one of your own scenes and begin playing with whatever features are discussed. Doing hands-on experimentation — *playing* — with scenes is an important part of the learning process. I do a lot of playing, and I certainly encourage you to do the same. However, remember that just because a setting goes to Very High doesn't mean that this setting is practical to use, that it will generate the results you need, or that it will render in the time frame you require.

Start low with the draft settings discussed in the book, and then work your way up. In addition to utilizing draft-quality settings, making liberal use of 3ds Max/Design's Area To Render options to render only what you need to test will save you significant time during the iterative process of learning and testing. Utilize additional hardware if you can, and read Chapter 4 to learn additional render strategies for optimizing your settings, using additional machines, and using tools to queue jobs to render when your machines are idle.

You have already been briefly exposed to the mental ray settings you will work with the most: the quality settings (including antialiasing) and Final Gather. You have also learned some critical 3ds Max/Design settings such as Gamma and Scene Scale. I recently provided training at a large architectural firm in Chicago with offices worldwide and worked with some of the designers who produce images for clients that are constructing some of the tallest and most expensive buildings ever conceived. Simply covering the topics in this chapter got a good portion of their rendering issues ironed out and gave them a conceptual platform to start building more knowledge about mental ray — a good starting point from which to move forward.

Armed with these first few settings in Chapter 1, you should now create at least two render presets for quickly retrieving these settings within your scenes: one preset for fast draft-quality renders and another for final high-quality renders. These presets will give you a good starting point for working with both the sample files for the book and your own projects. Presets allow you to quickly switch between draft and final settings, minimizing test-render time and helping reduce mistakes in final settings.

Perform the following steps to create draft-quality render settings:

1. From the Quick Access Toolbar, set 3ds Max/Design to use the project folder for Chapter 1, `\ProjectFolders\01_Essentials`.

2. Open the `QualitySettings2010.max` file from the project folder's `\scene` folder. (There is an alternate 3ds Max 2009–compatible file in the folder, too.)

3. This file purposely has gamma disabled, and if you are using 3ds Max/Design and have gamma enabled, you should get a warning dialog box for the gamma setting. Accept the incoming settings.

GAMMA IN SAMPLE SCENES

Unless otherwise indicated, you want to ensure that gamma is enabled for all scenes used for this book and that you are using a value of 2.2 for the Input Gamma and Output Gamma settings. Opening the example scenes in the book will bring in the correct settings as needed, provided you accept the incoming file's gamma. If necessary, select the Rendering ➤ Gamma And LUT Setup menu to reconfigure the values.

4. Open the Render Setup dialog box (press F10), and on the Common tab, open the Assign Renderer drop-down menu. Click the Choose Renderer button to the right of Production to set mental ray as the rendering engine.

5. Set your output size to 800×600.

6. On the Renderer tab, set the Samples Per Pixel settings: Minimum=1/16 and Maximum=1.

7. Set the Spatial Contrast RGBA settings by clicking the color swatch and adjusting the Value number to 0.09.

8. Set Filter Type to Triangle.

9. On the Indirect Illumination tab, ensure that Final Gather is selected, choose the Draft preset, and set Diffuse Bounces to 1.

10. Open the Rendered Frame window, and optionally set Glossy Reflections Precision, Soft Shadow Precision, and Glossy Refraction Precisions to a Low or Disabled state (move slider to the far left to disable the feature).

11. In the Rendered Frame window, choose the Save Preset option in the Render Preset drop-down list. It should default to the \renderpresets folder of your current project.

12. Click Save in the Render Preset Save dialog box; a list dialog box opens. Hold down the Ctrl key and highlight the Common, mental ray Renderer, Processing, and Indirect Illumination options. Then click Save.

13. Render the camera view, and note the render time.

These settings are a good starting place for a new scene and do not take up much rendering time as you test and tweak. Turn down the Minimum and Maximum values for Samples Per Pixel if you still need better performance from more complex scenes, albeit with a grainier image. Other strategies for faster draft render times are covered in Chapter 4.

On the DVD, in the \ProjectFolders\01_Essentials\renderpresets folder, you'll find a mental ray draft-quality preset you can use, called DraftQuality.rps.

Perform the following steps to create a high-quality render preset:

1. In the Render Setup dialog box, on the Common tab, set Output Resolution to HDTV 1920×1080.

2. On the Renderer tab, set the Samples Per Pixel settings as such: Minimum = 1 and Maximum = 16. If more detail is needed, settings of Minimum = 4 and Maximum = 64 or Minimum = 1 and Maximum = 64 work well, too. (Hint: Use the Rendered Frame window's Image Precision slider.)

3. Set the Spatial Contrast RGBA settings to between 0.025 and 0.015 each. Lower numbers mean higher image refinement but potentially longer render times.

4. If you are producing an animation, set Filter to Gauss, and set Width and Height to 2 each. Use the Mitchell filter for sharp still-image renderings.

5. On the Indirect Illumination tab, set the Final Gather preset to Low or Medium, and set Diffuse Bounces to 2.

6. In the Rendered Frame window, set the Glossy Reflections Precision, Soft Shadow Precision, and Glossy Refraction Precision settings to a Medium 1.0x or higher state.

7. Save your preset to a new file.

Your available time to render and the unique needs of your image are always the biggest determining factors in what settings to use. As you gain more experience with these settings, you will know where to start for most scenes. As you can see in Figure 1.30, there is considerable difference between the results of the draft and high-quality settings.

FIGURE 1.30:
A RAM player split-screen comparison of the draft (left) and high (right) rendering results at 800×600

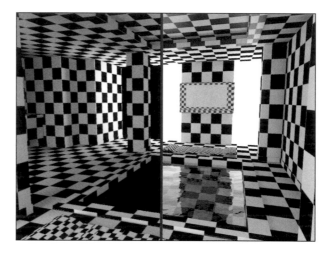

On a single 2.44GHz quad-core computer, this 3ds Max/Design 2011 scene with draft settings took 1 minute 52 seconds, whereas the same scene with the high settings took 42 minutes 25 seconds. This is a huge increase in rendering time for a seemingly uncomplicated scene, certainly; however, a lot of factors go into why the draft render was so fast, including the ability in 3ds Max/Design 2010 and newer to easily override and disable reflection, refraction, and shadow settings. I present a number of factors that go into render time throughout the remainder of the book.

The rendered images are in the \renderedoutput folder of the Chapter 1 project folder, and preconfigured draft and high-quality sample scenes are in the project's \scenes folder.

The Bottom Line

Set up mental ray There are relatively few global mental ray preferences for mental ray, and they primarily affect the visibility of render buckets and the functionality of the mental ray Messages window.

Master It Change the mental ray preferences to allow logging of render-time information.

Master It Enable mental ray for your current scene.

Configure 3ds Max/Design   3ds Max/Design 2011 is preconfigured with mental ray as the preferred rendering engine for all new scenes and has other internal presets to assist artists and designers specifically manage imported CAD data, among other things. Proper configuration ensures that sample files and imported data operates correctly.

Master It   Configure 3ds Max/Design to use the DesignVIZ.mentalray preset template and ame-light user interface.

Master It   Set your project folder to the Chapter 1 location.

Master It   Configure your system units to use millimeters for all scenes.

Configure gamma settings   Gamma is an intensity adjustment made to an image to compensate for nonlinearity in display and print devices and is necessary for low dynamic range images.

Master It   Enable gamma correction, and adjust its preferences.

Configure essential quality settings   mental ray adaptively samples your scene as it renders, subdividing portions of the image into smaller and smaller parts, to produce the final image. Controlling the sampling has a great impact not only on the quality of your rendered image but on the amount of time it will take to render.

Master It   Choose settings for a fast draft-quality rendering and save as a render preset.

Adjust Final Gather presets   Final Gather is one of several methods of calculating indirect, or bounced, illumination in your rendering. It is enabled by default in 3ds Max Design as a draft preset and must be enabled manually in legacy scenes and other flavors of 3ds Max/Design.

Master It   Enable Final Gather, and choose medium-quality settings.

Chapter 2

Materials and Maps

A number of settings within mental ray, 3ds Max/Design, and their individual materials not only affect the quality of your final rendered image but can greatly affect the speed at which your image will render. Learning how to manage these settings can help you eliminate memory and image issues and get the results you need with the minimum amount of render time.

You should have a basic understanding of how to create and apply materials, including the use of the Material Editor and the basic functionality of mental ray materials. This chapter focuses on advanced render features related to maps and materials and the performance and quality settings within the primary mental ray material type, Arch & Design. In 3ds Max/Design 2011, ProMaterials have been discontinued and we now have a new material type, the Autodesk material.

In this chapter, you will learn to

◆ Use the new Slate Material Editor mode

◆ Control performance options for bitmaps

◆ Adjust material and map settings that affect render quality and speed

---

MATERIALS, MAPS, AND SHADERS

The term *shader* is often used interchangeably for both materials and maps. In 3ds Max/Design, a shader more often is used to describe a map and is a component that is used within a material such as a noise map, or is used for producing effects such as the Glare effect or the mr Physical Sky environment.

Introducing the Slate Material Editor

The Slate Material Editor (SME) is a new feature for 3ds Max/Design 2011 and is a powerful tool for creating, testing, and manipulating materials using a node-based methodology. The SME gives you a quick, straightforward, and graphical way to work with both maps and materials by simply connecting related input and output node connections.

Figure 2.1 shows the SME for the scene in your DVD's Chapter 2 project's scenes folder (\ProjectFolders\02_Materials_Maps\scenes) called Material_Samples_2011.max and is shown with the right-click menu for a material header, specifically the *brushed metal* scene material. On the left side of the dialog box is the SME's version of the Material/Map Browser that allows you to browse existing maps and materials, create and apply new ones, and maintain material libraries. The upper-right corner shows a Navigator area, and below that is the Parameter Editor for the current map or material, each of which can be toggled on and off via the hotkeys N and P, respectively, or via buttons on the toolbar.

FIGURE 2.1
The Slate Material Editor user interface

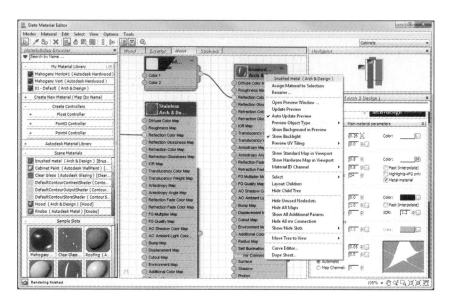

The SME is fully compatible with mental ray and other third-party materials. The classic Material Editor, which is now called the Compact Material Editor (CME), is the default for 3ds Max Design 2011, and the SME is the default for 3ds Max 2011. You can toggle back and forth between the two new editors via the Modes menu option in the CME and SME, via the new flyout Material Editor button in 3ds Max/Design's toolbar, or with the Rendering ➤ Material Editor menu option.

USING CHAPTER PROJECT FOLDERS

All files referenced in this chapter are included on your book's DVD in the \ProjectFolders\ 02_Materials_Maps folder. For best results, copy the\ProjectFolder\02_Materials_Maps folder to a location on your computer or a USB drive. Set 3ds Max/Design's project folder to the new location for the\02_Materials_Maps folder whenever you work with the example scenes in this chapter. I covered the use of project folders in Chapter 1, "mental ray Essentials."

Using the Slate Material Editor

You will find that many operations in the SME allow you to drag and drop, and many functions include right-click functionality that you need to explore to become proficient at using the SME. Here are a few tips:

Switching between the Slate Material Editor and Compact Material Editor   When you click and hold the Material Editor toolbar button it will now fly out to show two options, one for the SME and one for the CME. The top fly out image and default for 3ds Max Design 2011 is the CME, and in 3ds Max 2011 it is the SME; however, 3ds Max/Design remembers the last editor you used in your current session and changes the Material Editor toolbar button to match your choice. You cannot have both editors open at the same time and opening one editor will close the other. You can toggle between the two at any time, nondestructively, by choosing a different editor.

Using the Material/Map Browser   On the left of the SME is the new Material/Map Browser; the old Material/Map Browser found in legacy versions of 3ds Max/Design has been completely replaced by this new tool, including within the CME and anywhere in 3ds Max/Design where you need to choose a material or map. This new tool is very powerful to use, takes a little getting used to, and therefore needs some explanation.

The first item to point out is the Search By Name feature and the drop-down menu at the top of the Material/Map Browser, as shown in Figure 2.2.

FIGURE 2.2

The Search By Name feature and drop-down menu of the Material/Map Browser

The new Material/Map Browser can hold a lot of materials, maps, and material libraries; therefore, I find that the quickest way to find anything in the browser is to begin to type its name in this search box. A short list of materials or maps that match the typed text will appear below the text as you type. The search list will include new and existing items including materials currently in your scene. Drag an item into an SME view to create a new material and to edit an instance of an existing material; in the case of materials, you can also drag them from the Material/Map Browser onto objects in your scene to assign the material.

The drop-down menu shown in Figure 2.2 is activated by clicking the chevron to the left of the Search By Name input area. The chevron drop-down menu includes items for creating groups and libraries, for opening libraries, and for controlling what classes of items are visible in the Material/Map Browser, shown as check marks next to a menu item.

Controlling groups and libraries   A *group* is a collection of material libraries, and you can create as many groups and material libraries as you like. Libraries and groups are persistent in the SME's Material/Map Browser between 3ds Max/Design sessions on the same computer and user. Groups and libraries are both created from the chevron drop-down menu shown in Figure 2.2. The right-click menu for groups and libraries allows you to control how groups and libraries are displayed in the Material/Map Browser, as shown in Figure 2.3.

In the Group right-click menu, the topmost option shows the library's name and submenu items allow you to reload, save, or "save as" the library to another file or location. Unlike previous versions of 3ds Max/Design, the material libraries are not saved with your project, and instead they are local to your username and are saved at C:\Users\<username>\AppData\ Local\Autodesk\3dsMaxDesign\2011 - 64bit\enu\SME\Libs (in the instance of 3ds Max Design 2011 installed on a 64-bit computer). In earlier versions of 3ds Max/Design material libraries were stored by default in a project's .\materiallibraries folder; now if you want a library saved with a project, you must perform a Save As operation and save it to the new location.

FIGURE 2.3
Material/Map
Browser display
options shown
with right-click
menu for a mate-
rial library

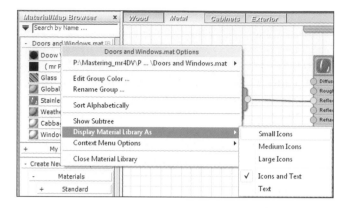

To add a map or material from a view into a material library, drag its output nodeslot into the library in the Material/Map browser. Nodeslots are the small circles on the left or right of a material or map node.

Each group and library is expandable and collapsible by clicking on the header, and you can rename, sort, and reorganize items with drag-and-drop to keep your most important tools within reach. Groups can be color-coded to make identification easy and library content can be displayed as icons of varying sizes, as icons and text, or simply as text, all independent of other groups. The default display mode is to show library content as a small icon with the material's name. Also shown in Figure 2.3 are options for sorting the list, showing submaterials/maps (Show Subtree) for Multi/Sub-Object and other compound materials, and closing the library.

You can drag materials, libraries, and groups virtually anywhere within your own groups and libraries; however, you cannot add your maps or materials to the groups Create New Material/Map, Create Controller, Autodesk Material Library, or Scene Materials. These either are fixed lists based on your 3ds Max/Design installation or are automatically populated based on your scene contents.

Using sample slots   In the CME, all editing revolves around the 24 sample slots, typically displayed as spheres at the top of the editor. The Material/Map Browser in the SME also has a group called Sample Slots that contains material instances consistent between the SME and CME. You can therefore "send" a material to the CME from the SME by dragging a material's output node onto a sample slot in the Material/Map Browser, and access the CME's materials in the same manner.

Creating and using views   The center section of the SME is the multi-tabbed *view* region used for connecting map and material nodes. One of my favorite features of the SME is the ability to create multiple views (tabs) to categorize and organize materials in complex scenes. Figure 2.4 shows the tabbed views with four custom tabs from the Material_Samples_2011. max scene included in the Chapter 2 project folder.

FIGURE 2.4
The interface with
custom tabs

In this scene, I've created views for different logical groupings of materials: Wood, Metal, Cabinets, and Exterior. The default view tab in your scenes is simply labeled "View1" unless you change it. You can create new views by right-clicking a tab and choosing Create New View. You can create as many views as you need, and if necessary, left-right navigation arrows will appear to allow scrolling to expose any hidden views. At the upper right of the SME is a drop-down list that allows you to quickly switch between views. Views can be renamed, deleted, and shifted via a right-click menu. You can also rearrange views by clicking and dragging the tab to a new position.

Adding materials and maps to views   You add materials to views by dragging them from the Material/Map Browser into a view or by using the eyedropper tool. Materials and maps can exist on multiple tabs at the same time as instances. An instance in one view is the same as an instance in another; however, each view can have only one instance of a material. You can quickly populate the current view with all the materials in a scene by using the Material ➢ Get All Scene Materials menu option. To move a material to a different view, right-click a material's header within a view, and choose the Move Tree To View menu option.

With the eyedropper tool in the SME toolbar, you can quickly bring a material from an object in your scene into the current view. If the material already exists in the current view, the view will shift to the selected material. If the material exists in a different view in the SME, then an instance clone of the material appears in the current view.

Finding material/map nodes   In the lower-left of the views area is a search tool. As you type, the text will remain bold when the text you enter matches something in the current view. The search tool includes a Zoom To Results button to find your material result(s) within large views.

Opening the Parameter Editor   The Parameter Editor is the dialog box with the options and values for a particular material or map, and in the CME this is always open for the selected material or map. In the SME, its use is entirely optional. Double-click a material/map's header or press P to open the Parameter Editor for a selected node. Only one Parameter Editor can be open at a time.

In the SME, many material and map options are adjustable directly in a view; you may need to open a material or map's *Additional Params* to see the full list of options, as shown in Figure 2.5. Using the parameters within a view is much faster than waiting for the Parameter Editor to switch to the selected material or map and load values.

FIGURE 2.5
SME nodes showing additional parameters available for the new Autodesk Generic material

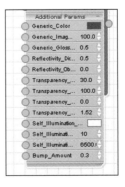

The parameters shown in Figure 2.5 are editable directly by typing in values or by using the up/down arrows, or you can attach an appropriate animation controller to the input node (see the "Using animation controllers" item later in this list). Animating a value automatically adds an animation controller.

Rearranging SME dialog boxes   You can drag the header of the Material/Map Browser, Properties dialog box, and Navigator dialog box window off the SME and make each into a floating dialog box, allowing you to resize and place them anywhere. This undocking capability is not available for the tabbed views. To redock a dialog box, drag it back into the SME, and drop the header onto one of the arrows that appears as you drag the dialog box window over the SME.

Using nodes   Nodes are materials, maps, and animation controllers. To create a new material for your scene, you drag a new material from the Material/Map Browser into a view, right-click, and select Rename to give it a unique name, modify some parameters, or add map nodes to the material inputs. Then you drag from the output nodeslot of the material and drop onto an object to assign the material to that object. As in the CME, if you have an object selected, you can also use the Assign Material To Selection toolbar button at the top of the SME dialog box. You can also drag materials directly from the Material/Map Browser onto objects in your scene.

Connecting nodes   Attaching map, material, and controller nodes to one another is a simple matter of dragging the output nodeslot of a map into the input nodeslot of a material or another map, such as the Gamma & Gain map. The SME not only allows you to edit materials and maps but also allows you to create and connect animation controllers to set and animate parameters. Controllers include floating-point single-value controllers, Point3 controllers for XYZ and RGB control, and Point4 controllers for RGBA color values.

Optimizing your view space   Pressing the H key toggles whether unused nodeslots are visible on a material or map. You can also right-click a material or map header and select the Hide Unused Nodeslots option. Also in a material's right-click menu are options for hiding individual nodeslot categories: Map, Additional Params, and the mr Connection nodeslots.

If an entire category of nodeslots is hidden, you can bring back specific items via the right-click menu and the Show/Hide Slots menu option. Alternately, double-clicking a material or map header will open the Parameter Editor and give you access to all parameters.

Moving parent and children nodes together   Holding down Ctrl+Alt while clicking a node allows you to drag the node and its children, or you can enable the Move Children toolbar button to toggle this functionality.

Adjusting the material/map sample   Double-clicking the sample at the top of a material or map node causes it to toggle its size from small to large; double-click again to return to small. At the lower-right of each node is a resize handle that you can drag to make the sample any size you like if the sample is in its large state. Press H to eliminate unnecessary nodeslot inputs from the view.

You can open a resizable floating sample by right-clicking a material or map header and choosing the Open Preview Window option. Figure 2.6 shows the floating sample sphere.

FIGURE 2.6
A floating sample
sphere

You can also dock this floating sample sphere within the SME by dragging it to an edge; a docking arrow will appear and releasing over an arrow docks the sample sphere. The sample sphere can be switched either to automatically show the sample for the currently selected material or to a specific material via the drop-down menu at the bottom of the sample (in Figure 2.6, the drop-down is showing the Mahogany Horiz material). You can also set the floating sample to update manually by turning off the Auto check box. When you view sub-materials and maps, you can disable the Show End Result icon at the top of the floater to see only the current level.

Converting one material type to another   3ds Max/Design keeps tracks of materials by their names, so replacing a material with a new material is simply a matter of creating a new material with the same name as the old material and then assigning the new material to an object in your scene. You will get a warning about replacing the material; choose Replace It, and the new material now exists in your scene. With the SME and the switch to the new node methodology, you do not have a Put button to automatically assign a material with the same name to objects in your scene.

To convert a material *type* in the CME you can bring an existing material into a sample slot, click the type of material (Standard, for instance) to open the Material/Map Browser, and just choose a different material type to change the current material to that new type. The material name is preserved, as is the connection to the scene geometry. Be sure to save any maps or color swatches to another sample slot or the Color Clipboard on the Utility tab of the Command panel as you will lose those items.

The SME works well for converting materials if you want to preserve maps and colors for that new material. With the SME you need to drag the new material into a SME view along with the existing material, connect the maps from the old material into the new material, and then copy and paste any color swatches between the two. If you assign the same name to the new material and assign it to an object, then the old material is replaced in the scene but still exists in the SME's view. As with the CME, materials assigned to objects in the scene will appear with small triangles in the corners of the sample to show that any changes to the material will affect the scene.

Using animation controllers   One distinct benefit of the SME is that it allows you to easily use and adjust animation controllers directly in an SME view. As soon as you animate a parameter in a material it is assigned an appropriate animation controller; for a simple value it may be a Bezier controller, for instance. With the SME, when you animate a parameter, an animation controller appears in the view attached to that parameter's input nodeslot, provided that parameter is not on a hidden nodeslot. Figure 2.7 shows a Transparency value animated on an Autodesk material and the corresponding Bezier controller automatically assigned to the parameter.

FIGURE 2.7
Animation controllers in the SME

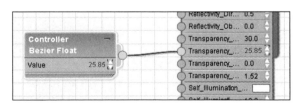

You can delete a parameter's animation by deleting the animation controller. You can assign specific animation controllers of different types (Linear or Noise, for instance) from the Track View or by using the animation controllers listed in the Material/Map Browser. In the Material/ Map Browser is the group Create Controllers with libraries of controllers for floating-point values, Point3 controllers for RGB and XYZ control, and Point4 controllers for RGBA and XYZW.

Double-clicking a controller does not open anything in the parameter view; all animated values are adjusted within an SME view, or you can right-click the controller node and open the animation in the Dope Sheet or Curve Editor from the right-click menu. The SME will not allow connections between incompatible types, such as a floating-point output to a bitmap input. If you are familiar with parameter wiring in 3ds Max/Design, then you are familiar with this behavior.

In the next section, I cover techniques for managing materials and maps for your scenes.

Working with Bitmaps

To speed performance, 3ds Max/Design keeps bitmaps in memory between renderings. This takes up valuable memory that cannot be reclaimed without restarting 3ds Max/Design. Because maps are never updated during a session, you might need to use a bitmap's Reload feature, as shown in Figure 2.8, to force the update of files modified during your 3ds Max/Design session.

FIGURE 2.8
A bitmap's Reload option in the bitmap settings

The general size of bitmaps can greatly affect the overall performance of 3ds Max/Design and impact the performance and memory use of mental ray. Manually resizing overly large images (perhaps larger than 1024 pixels square) will reduce your overall 3ds Max/Design memory footprint and reduce memory allocation issues with mental ray.

You need to be aware of three key bitmap-related settings when you work with mental ray and 3ds Max/Design:

◆ Bitmap Proxies

◆ Bitmap Pager

◆ mental ray Map Manager

These three options can affect memory use and performance when you work with large scenes and/or large bitmaps.

The first setting I cover is Bitmap Proxies.

Using the Bitmap Proxies Option

The Bitmap Proxies feature of 3ds Max/Design is a mechanism for caching and automatically downscaling large bitmaps. You'll find the settings on the Render Setup dialog box's Common tab. Click the Bitmap Performance and Memory Options' Setup button, as shown in Figure 2.9.

The bitmap proxy system is disabled by default, and when enabled, the default option is to keep the images at full resolution and store them in memory between renders, as set by the Render Mode drop-down menu shown in Figure 2.10.

FIGURE 2.9
Bitmap proxy settings in 3ds Max/ Design 2010 SP1 and newer

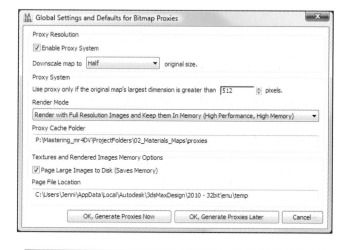

FIGURE 2.10
Bitmap proxy's Render Mode options

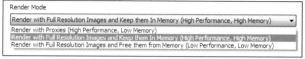

When the Render Mode setting is set to Render With Proxies (High Performance, Low Memory), 3ds Max/Design automatically rescales bitmaps based on the Size threshold and saves the newly resized map to your project folder's `.\proxies` folder. The third Render Mode option sets 3ds Max/Design to not store bitmaps between render sessions, saving memory. This causes a delay at render time but can improve 3ds Max/Design's editing performance between renders when memory is an issue. It is always a good idea to ensure that bitmaps are a reasonable size before using in a scene, no matter what the proxy option. Bitmap size is almost always an issue when dealing with Autodesk Civil3D projects that utilize large aerial photographs.

Using the Bitmap Pager Option

Bitmap Pager is another bitmap caching option. This option is off by default in 3ds Max 2009 and older and is enabled in 3ds Max/Design 2010 and newer. The Bitmap Pager option can reduce memory requirements with scenes that have very large bitmaps, with scenes that have a large quantity of maps, and when rendering large images. It allows machines with limited memory to render images much larger than previously possible.

Bitmap Pager is a setting that might cause render-time performance issues with certain scenes, and if you are experiencing delays when you start to render, then try disabling this feature. In 3ds Max 2009, you can find the settings on the Preferences dialog box's Rendering tab, as shown in Figure 2.11, and in 3ds Max/Design 2010 SP1 and newer, the settings are included along with the bitmap proxy settings as "Page Large Images to Disk (Saves Memory)", as shown earlier in Figure 2.9.

FIGURE 2.11
Bitmap Pager set-
tings for 3ds Max
2009 and earlier

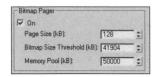

In 3ds Max 2009 you have the option of setting the memory amount used and thresholds for map size, whereas 3ds Max/Design 2010 SP1 and newer only allows you to enable or disable the setting, and memory use is managed automatically to adapt to your scene's and computer's unique memory needs. For 3ds Max 2009, the Page Size (kB) parameter defines the size of the paging file used to store bitmaps. The Bitmap Size Threshold (kB) parameter is the minimum size of a bitmap before 3ds Max/Design will begin paging the file. Memory Pool (kB) is the amount of computer memory used to hold all active bitmaps; all pages remain in memory until this limit is reached. 3ds Max/Design will work to keep bitmaps that are used most often within memory to help reduce transfer time.

Using the mental ray Map Manager

You can find the mental ray Map Manager translator options on the Processing tab of the Render Setup dialog box under Translator Options. This setting allows mental ray to manage bitmap memory use, unloading bitmaps when not needed and selectively reloading bitmaps as needed by a particular bucket. When it's turned off, 3ds Max/Design sends color data directly to mental ray as required, and when it's turned on, mental ray reads maps directly from disk and can remove them from memory when space is needed. For large scenes that have limited memory, this option can reduce memory allocation issues; however, the render time can be longer because maps are repeatedly reloaded when needed. mental images recommends always using this feature when using distributed bucket rendering, because only the maps needed by the remote renderers are transferred through the network.

For 3ds Max 2009 and older, this option might cause gaps in the seams of tiled bitmaps that use the Blur option within bitmap settings. In this instance, the seams will work as expected if you reduce or eliminate the Blur option. Figure 2.12 shows an extreme blur setting causing large black seams in the otherwise seamless flooring.

FIGURE 2.12
An extreme
example of seams
when using Blur
and the mental ray
Map Manager with
legacy mental ray

One common issue you might confront is the need to work both in the office on the networked systems and also on laptops and systems at home. Each machine will invariably have different paths for files, and in the next section I outline some tools to assist you with varying paths.

Using Bitmaps When Working Remotely

3ds Max/Design has the following useful tools to assist you when you work remotely, away from your main machine or network:

- Project folders (covered in Chapter 1)
- Relative paths and the Resource Collector
- Asset Tracking
- Bitmap/Photometric Path Editor
- The Application button's Save As ➤ Archive (entire project Zip compression) feature

Using Project Folders

For project folders, I use different project .mxp files for remote work and at the office; this allows me to have separate paths within each project .mxp file for each location, which helps 3ds Max/Design find the files it needs at each location and can eliminate long delays when rendering and opening scenes. The .mxp file extension stands for MaX Project and is covered in Chapter 1. Without correct paths in the .mxp file, 3ds Max/Design might search for any missing files on nonexistent paths, including network shares with long timeout values. You can edit the existing project file in Notepad or change it using 3ds Max/Design's Customize ➤ Configure User Paths menu. Change paths to point to folder locations on your remote machine, and then use Save As to create a new filename.

The easiest way to load a specific .mxp file is to drag and drop it from Windows Explorer into 3ds Max/Design and then choose the Load option. If multiple .mxp files exist in a project folder, then 3ds Max/Design only loads the project file with the folder's name when you use the Quick Access Toolbar's Project button to change your project folder. In this instance, 3ds Max/Design displays a warning that multiple project files exist and shows you which .mxp file is loaded.

USING PROJECT MXP FILES WITH *MASTERING MENTAL RAY*

The project folder provided on the DVD comes with versions of .mxp files for 3ds Max/Design 2010 and 2011 with the default project being configured for 3ds Max/Design 2011. For best results, move unneeded projects to another folder or delete them. You might also need to edit the MXP files for your particular system to ensure that 3ds Max/Design can find the files it needs.

Having different path configuration files for different situations helps; however, some files, such as XRef scenes, bitmaps, and render resources, are oftentimes in the same location relative to the project folder's location. The Relative Paths option makes those resources available no matter where the project folder is located.

Using Relative Paths and the Resource Collector

Even with project folders and adding paths to your MXP configuration, 3ds Max/Design might still not find your bitmaps and other resources if they have a file path hard-coded into the file's name or if the file does not exist on your disconnected machine. To fix these issues, you can set 3ds Max/Design to use relative rather than absolute file paths and then move all project bitmaps into the project folders using the Resource Collector. The Convert Local File Paths To Relative option is enabled on the Files tab of the Preference Settings dialog box (Customize ➤ Preference Settings), as shown in Figure 2.13.

FIGURE 2.13

The Convert Local File Paths To Relative option

With this option enabled, rather than storing the complete path to a scene file as `C:\Users\<username>\Documents\3dsMaxDesign\scenes\MyFile.max`, for instance, it stores the filename as `.\scenes\MyFile.max`. For network file paths, instead of looking to a specific drive letter or universal naming convention (UNC) path, such as `\\servername\sharename\folder`, 3ds Max looks to the project folder's `.\sceneassets\images` folder for bitmaps, the `.\scenes` folder for `.max` files, and so on. The `.\` prefix causes 3ds Max/Design to look in folders relative to the local project folder, not a drive letter or UNC path, so the project can exist anywhere.

You might experience issues with this option when using Backburner and the Split Scan Lines option and with the Video Post option (Rendering ➤ Video Post), specifically it may not be able to find the files with a relative path. Just be aware of possible issues with 3ds Max/Design finding files if you use these features. Split Scan Lines is covered in Chapter 4, "Rendering."

The 3ds Max/Design utility Resource Collector moves any bitmaps used in your scene into a folder you choose, typically your `.\sceneassets\images` folder, and optionally Resource Collector can update the material bitmaps to point to that folder instead of the original location. You can access the Resource Collector by going to the Command panel's Utility tab (click the More button).

Perform the following steps to collect the bitmaps in your project and change their file paths to relative:

1. Open the Preference Settings dialog box by selecting Customize ➤ Preferences.

2. Switch to the Files tab.

3. Enable the Convert Local File Paths To Relative option. Close the dialog box.

4. On the Command panel's Utility tab, click the More button, and then choose the Resource Collector option. The Resource Collector menu is shown in Figure 2.14.

5. Click Browse, and select `.\sceneassets\images` folder for your project (it will show the full path in the settings).

6. Select Update Materials.

7. Click Begin to collect (copy) all bitmaps used in your scene into your project's folder and change their file paths to relative.

8. Open the Configure User Paths dialog box by selecting Customize ➤ Configure User Paths, and be sure that the relative path `.\sceneassets\images` is listed. Click Save As, and save the configuration to the project's MXP file, as shown in Figure 2.15.

FIGURE 2.14
The Resource Collector utility moves assets used in your scene into a new folder and optionally updates the material's file path.

FIGURE 2.15
The Configure User Paths dialog box, which shows the file paths used for Chapter 2, including the relative path for `.\sceneassets\images`

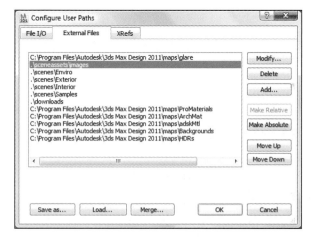

Despite using relative paths, some materials stored in libraries and merged scenes may have full paths in their filenames, which in addition to loading delays can cause network render jobs to fail. In the next sections, I cover the Asset Tracking tool and Bitmap/Photometric Path Editor for finding and resolving these issues.

MULTIFILE MATERIAL MANAGEMENT

It is rare for a project to consist of a single scene file that contains all 3D assets for the project. My typical architectural projects have, at minimum, three files that are in development simultaneously: the building, the site, and the landscaping. Each one is an external reference (XRef) into the next, and they combine to create a complete model for final renders. An XRef is a 3ds Max/Design scene that exists outside your current scene. When a scene that references an XRef is loaded, 3ds Max/Design also loads the geometry of the XRef. XRefs help to keep file sizes to a minimum, because only a placeholder to the XRef needs to be maintained in the current scene.

You can attach XRef scenes to objects in a scene (typically to a dummy object) to allow for controlling the position, rotation, and scale of the XRef scene. XRefs are added by clicking the quick-access M icon (Application button) and then selecting References ➤ XRef Scene or by selecting the File ➤ XRef Scenes menu. You can also add XRrefs by dragging and dropping a scene from your drive into a 3ds Max/Design viewport using Windows Explorer. This is my preferred method of adding XRefs because it automatically attaches the XRef to a new dummy object.

For product design projects, you may have the product scene (a car for instance) as an XRef into another scene with reflective environment geometry, lights, and cameras. Alternately you can XRef a pre-made environment scene into a product scene to quickly provide a consistent environment for multiple products; the use of these "render studios" is covered in Chapter 10, "mental ray for Design." XRefs allow you to more easily create and edit geometry and perform test-renders without having to include lights and geometry in every XRef scene you will be testing. As much as XRefs can help to organize and maintain files, XRefs can cause issues when working to maintain common materials across scene files. The XRef *material* type allows you to use materials from objects in external scenes within your scene. For many projects, I will create a file called Material Samples.max where I can adjust materials for all related scenes. If I have a number of buildings with the same brick, roofing, trim, etc., I can have each XRef the materials in the one scene file making it easy to modify all scenes at once.

Next I cover the Asset Tracking tool that allows you to see bitmaps on your current scene and all XRef scenes, and edit file definitions and paths. It is my primary tool for finding and fixing missing maps.

Using the Asset Tracking Tool

The Asset Tracking tool, as shown in Figure 2.16, is a more complete and advanced form of the Bitmap/Photometric Path Editor, described in the next section, because it also includes in its listing both XRefs scenes and the XRef's bitmaps, and it optionally works with Autodesk Vault for storing and opening files related to your project.

FIGURE 2.16
The Asset Tracking dialog box for a Chapter 5 sample scene

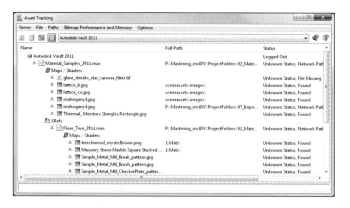

Open the Asset Tracking dialog box by clicking the Application button and selecting Manage ➢ Asset Tracking or by selecting the File ➢ Asset Tracking menu item for legacy 3ds Max/Design. Right-clicking bitmaps in the CME's or SME's Parameter Editor (the hotkey P in SME) gives you the menu item Highlight Assets In ATS Dialog, which is the Asset Tracking tool.

Looking down the list in Figure 2.16, you'll find that the glare_streaks_star_camera_filter.tif file is missing, and a little farther down there are two copies of the mahogany4.jpg image, one that is using relative paths and the other with a full path definition. Selecting a bitmap from the list and right-clicking to bring up its Quad menu, as shown in Figure 2.17, allows you to strip the path (in the case of the duplicate map with the full path) or to browse for the missing file to define its location, in the case of the glare map.

FIGURE 2.17
The Asset Tracking tool's Quad menu. Many of the grayed-out items are specific to Autodesk Vault.

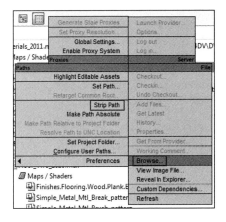

Stripping the path on both `mahogany4.jpg` files will combine them into one line and force 3ds Max/Design to search the user path definitions in the project `.mxp` for the file.

Also in the Quad menu are options to set your project folder location and open the Configure User Paths dialog box. The Asset Tracking tool is an excellent resource to check before you submit network render jobs to ensure that all bitmaps are available in all related files.

Accessing the Bitmap/Photometric Path Editor

This tool assists in maintaining paths for your scene maps, including easily finding and replacing incorrect paths or removing paths so that 3ds Max/Design will search your project's paths. You can access it from the Material Explorer's Tool menu or from the Command panel's Utility tab using the More option. As you create materials, the full path to the bitmap may be stored, and as you can see in Figure 2.18, this particular scene has many maps that reference S: (for scenes) and M: (for maps) drives on our servers.

FIGURE 2.18
With the Bitmap/ Photometric Path Editor, you can find and correct problems with missing files.

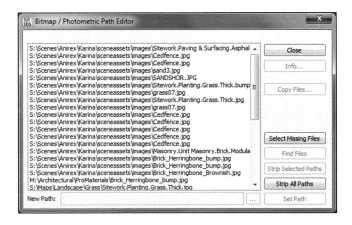

If you notice a long delay when you start your renders, check that the bitmap's file paths are correct in this tool, and also minimize the length of your project's path list in the MXP file. Full path names might be faster at render time, when they are correct and 3ds Max/Design does not need to search for a file; however, the full path names might also cause long delays when working from machines with different drive paths. An alternative to using project folders and relative paths is to put all needed files into the same folder as your 3ds Max/Design scene file; 3ds Max/Design should then find everything.

Editing XRef Paths for Maps and Scenes

Using XRefs is not helpful if 3ds Max/Design cannot find the files, and there is one last setting that can affect your own work and the use of the samples in this book: XRef paths. XRef paths are additional locations that 3ds Max/Design searches for missing scene files.

You can find the XRef path settings in the User Paths dialog box and within your project's MXP file, and you can edit the definitions in either location. In the MXP file, the paths are listed under the [XReferenceDirs] heading, which includes the Dir1=.\scenes path by default. Additional paths can be added to help 3ds Max/Design find the XRefs used for your project.

Perform the following steps to edit your XRef paths within 3ds Max/Design:

1. As described previously in this chapter, ensure that the Convert Local File Paths To Relative option is enabled on the Files tab of the Preference Settings dialog box.

2. Open the Configure User Paths dialog box (Customize ➤ Configure User Paths).

3. Switch to the External Files tab. This contains the bitmap paths specified in your MXP project file.

4. Ensure that .\sceneassets\images is in the list, along with correcting any other paths important to the current project. The default project MXP files that ship with the book are configured to 3ds Max Design 2011. However, you might be using a different version and will need to modify these paths or use an alternate file.

5. Switch to the XRefs tab.

6. Click the Add button to browse folder locations and add a new path to the list.

7. If you modify this list, be certain to click Save As to store your new paths to your MXP project file.

Now that you know how to manage and manipulate maps, materials, and paths, I examine the specifics of the primary mental ray materials, the new Autodesk material, ProMaterials and Arch & Design.

RESOLVING MISSING BITMAP ISSUES

Despite your best efforts in configuring the MXP file for your computer's paths, 3ds Max/Design may still not find bitmaps for materials with built-in maps, such as the brushed finish used in the Autodesk Metal material, or the bump in Autodesk Concrete, particularly if you move from computer to computer. These maps are typically located in the .\maps\adskMtl folder of your 3ds Max/Design installation, and copying them to your .\sceneassets\images folder will help resolve these issues.

For new Autodesk materials, introduced later in this chapter, you can find the bitmaps included in the Autodesk Material Library in subfolders of `C:\Program Files (x86)\Common Files\Autodesk Shared\Materials2011\assetlibrary_base.fbm\`.

Working with Materials, Maps, and Colors

There are two main mental ray material types included with 3ds Max/Design 2011, the new Autodesk material series and the Arch & Design (A&D) material: ProMaterials are still usable in legacy scenes and Revit FBX imports, but are not available for new materials in 3ds Max/Design 2011. All mental ray materials are *energy conserving*, meaning they have real-world interaction with scene lighting and the environment and they utilize floating-point numbers for color selection. They follow the laws of physics, so the energy leaving a surface is never more than the energy entering a surface. Energy conserving also means that as transparency increases, the diffuse results decrease accordingly.

The mental ray materials produce high dynamic range results and are essential for best results if you are rendering to a high dynamic range file format or working with lighting analysis. The Arch & Design materials also provide 3ds Max/Design with additional Render Element options that allow you to separate the components of a rendered image into individual channels such as reflections, diffuse, opacity, and so on. These elements can be used in applications such as 3ds Max Composite to combine and adjust these into a final image. The additional render elements give you the ability to adjust and control many aspects of the final result without having to render the image. 3ds Max/Design 2011's expanded OpenEXR support now allows all layers to exist in one file and is covered later in the chapter. Render elements and the use of 3ds Max Composite are covered in Chapter 10, "mental ray for Design."

Next I cover the new Autodesk material series, a set of advanced materials with a streamlined interface to provide quick setup for many design projects.

Introducing the Autodesk Materials

The new Autodesk materials in 3ds Max/Design 2011 are a series of finish-specific materials similar to and replacing ProMaterials, however with a very streamlined interface. The Autodesk material is part of Autodesk's Common Material Library and the material types and settings of materials are identical between Autodesk applications such as Revit and 3ds Max/Design. They are an excellent way to quickly build new materials with a specific finish, and the materials have just the controls needed for that finish. The Ceramic material, for instance, does not need settings for self-illumination or transparency, but it does have presets related to real-world ceramic materials such as High Gloss, Satin, and Matte, as well as a Wavy bumpy surface. In the new Material/Map Browser, you can find the Autodesk under the Create New Material Map (By Name) group, the Materials sub-group, and the *mental ray* library. Figure 2.19 shows the Parameter Editor setting for the Autodesk Generic material, showing some of the simplified sliders and options typical in these materials.

The potential downside of the Autodesk materials is that your options for adjustments are limited, and you may not agree with the look provided for a particular predefined finish. With the Autodesk materials, in contrast to ProMaterials or Arch & Design, you do not have the ability to enable special effects such as ambient occlusion or round corners or have access to advanced settings such as reflective and refractive glossy samples. These settings can often make the difference in the quality and speed of your renderings. To compensate for the lack of settings in the individual materials, you can control the overall reflective and refractive properties in the mental ray settings in the Rendered Frame Window dialog box's Trace/Bounce settings, and you can adjust the quality of the glossy reflections and refractions through the Rendered Frame Window dialog box's Glossy Reflections Precision and Glossy Refractions Precision sliders. These global adjustments adjust all materials in the scene.

FIGURE 2.19

The Autodesk
Generic material's
parameters

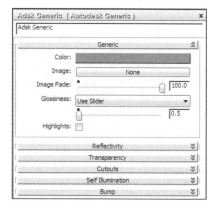

In some cases, the Autodesk materials take longer to render than materials created from the Arch & Design materials, covered later in this chapter, and some of this is because of additional behind-the-scenes features added to the Autodesk materials and the inability to tune performance options. For instance, the Autodesk Water material appears to include a submerge feature to tint objects below the waterline, which increases realism but significantly increases render time. If you find that an Autodesk material does not give you the flexibility or speed that you need then, consider switching to the Arch & Design material.

My experience with the Autodesk materials is that they produce spectacular results, and the render times for many materials are slightly faster than their corresponding ProMaterials and unoptimized Arch & Design materials. I tend to use ProMaterials and (now) Autodesk materials for most materials where I have a definite need to achieve a specific look quickly, and they are brilliant for most purposes. However, the Autodesk materials' lack of special effects and the inability to control glossy samples per material means that the Arch & Design material must be used for most critical materials.

Introducing the Autodesk Material Library

3ds Max/Design 2011 now includes an extensive library of Autodesk materials known as the Autodesk Material Library (AML) included as a separate component installed with 3ds Max/Design 2011. The library contains about 2,000 bitmaps and related materials in a wide variety of classifications, and replaces the ProMaterials material libraries in previous versions of 3ds Max/Design. With this new library comes a new method for organizing bitmaps used in the materials; instead of maps being stored in a subfolder of the .\maps folder of your 3ds Max/Design installation, they are installed in a common folder area, specifically, C:\Program Files (x86)\ Common Files\Autodesk Shared\Materials2011\assetlibrary_base.fbm\ in the subfolders

`.\1\Mats`, `.\2\Mats`, and `.\3\Mats`. Your paths may differ depending on your installed options, and adjusting your project's folder paths may be required.

The Autodesk Material Library will display as a separate group within the Material/Map Browser and contain a series of libraries for material categories such as Asphalt, Brick, Ceiling, Ceramic, and so on. You cannot modify these libraries. Bitmaps used in these materials use a new Autodesk Bitmap shader which includes minimal controls.

As I discussed in Chapter 1, bitmaps generally require gamma correction to be properly viewed in 3ds Max/Design and rendered properly in mental ray. The Autodesk Material Library and the bitmaps in each material are set to use the image's gamma for each bitmap, and will render correctly with this setting. In 3ds Max/Design 2010 and earlier some ProMaterial libraries are also set to use the images gamma value and may not render correctly. Setting the bitmap to use the correct gamma value will fix this issue.

The next mental ray material, Arch & Design, gives the artist the most flexibility in creating surface finishes within a structured tool. It includes templates for getting started quickly on your own materials, and it includes advanced settings for self-illumination, detail enhancement through ambient occlusion, and optimized glossy and reflective effects.

Introducing the Arch & Design Material

The Arch & Design (A&D) material is feature-rich general-purpose material that should be used in place of legacy component materials for mental ray, such as the Diffuse/Glossy/Specular (DGS) material. The A&D material contains extensive features required for controlling the quality and speed of rendering. Figure 2.20 shows the Arch & Design material's main user interface.

FIGURE 2.20

The Arch & Design type

Understanding the Arch & Design Templates

The Arch & Design materials include a Template drop-down menu that contains a number of material presets and fully configured materials to help get you started on your own materials. The Template drop-down menu has the following five groups:

- Appearance & Attributes
- Finishes
- Transparent Materials
- Metals

◆ Advanced Tools

The items in this drop-down list are controlled by the file `mrArchmaterial.ini` located in the User AppData folder path, which is typically at `C:\Users\<Username>\AppData\Local\ Autodesk\3dsMaxDesign\2011 - 64bit\enu\plugcfg\` for your specific user. The INI file defines the contents of the template's drop-down list and the specific actions for each list item. Each item in the list calls a MAXscript or loads a material from a library.

The Appearance & Attributes section of the Template drop-down menu contains selections for Matte, Pearl, and Glossy finishes, and selecting an option runs a corresponding script in the `C:\Users\<Username>\AppData\Local\Autodesk\3dsMaxDesign\2011 - 64bit\enu\ plugcfg\mrArchMaterialTemplates\Attributes\` folder. There is a separate script for each finish, and you can modify the script files to change the effects of this template selection. Running this script will not replace your material; it will only adjust settings related to reflectivity and glossiness.

The next three option groups — Finishes, Transparent Materials, and Metals — completely replace your current material with a material from the `mrArch_DesignTemplates.mat` file, found in your 3ds Max/Design installation's `\materiallibraries` folder. Be sure to copy or save any materials you want to preserve to another sample sphere in the Samples area of the SME (or CME) before you choose this option, or you will lose your current material's maps and settings. Modifying the `mrArch_Designtemplates.mat` material library changes the preset's effect. Materials are selected by the script from the library by their name.

The last two options under Advanced Tools run script commands to enable or disable ambient occlusion detail enhancement in the current material. Ambient occlusion settings are found in the material's Special Effect menu section, which is shown in the examples later in the chapter.

UNDERSTANDING THE ARCH & DESIGN SETTINGS

There are a number of settings within the Arch & Design material type that I would consider critical to understand. When adjusting material settings for a scene, I am most concerned with quality and speed, and that will be a central theme in this chapter and throughout the book. Oftentimes you cannot achieve high quality without reduced speed; however, in this section I cover some of the settings that can assist you in balancing both these quantities.

Diffuse The first setting you will probably set is the color of the Diffuse setting, or you'll assign a bitmap to the material. Figure 2.21 shows the Diffuse settings.

FIGURE 2.21
The A&D material
Diffuse settings

Materials are the color that they reflect, and the Diffuse Level setting shown on the left scales the brightness and apparent reflectivity of the diffuse color or an assigned map. Clicking the color swatch brings up the Select Color dialog box; with mental ray materials the color selections are a decimal value between 0.0 and 1.0 rather than the integer 0 to 255 values of legacy materials. This decimal color selector is necessary to give you an infinitely variable color space.

USING THE DECIMAL COLOR SELECTOR

With legacy materials such as Standard and Architectural, clicking a color swatch brings up a color selection dialog box where the RGB values are integers in the range of 0 to 255, which is the value range for an 8-bit integer. However, with mental ray materials, the RGB color values are infinitely variable decimal numbers in the range of 0.0 through 1.0, as shown here.

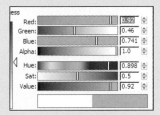

The new decimal values are essential in a high dynamic range workflow. Using mental ray and the high-dynamic range (HDR) capabilities of the materials, the renderer allows you to make excellent use of HDR images both as input for materials and environments and for output for later compositing and image processing. You can right-click and copy and paste color swatches freely between decimal and integer color swatches and use the Utility tab's Color Clipboard to hold either color type. If you are used to (or have been provided) RGB integer (0 to 255) values, you will need to do a little math to get a corresponding decimal value. 3ds Max/Design gives you a method to perform math in dialog boxes, the Numerical Expression Evaluator dialog box, as shown here.

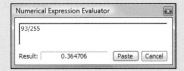

Click in the number box for the RGB value you want to calculate, and press Ctrl+N to open the Numerical Expression Evaluator. For an integer color conversion, enter the 1 to 255 color value you need to convert (such as 93), the divide symbol (/), and 255; then click Paste to enter the new value.

Realistic materials are never 100 percent pure white, completely black, or 100 percent saturated no matter what the color. When assigning a color value, it is important to keep the HSV *Value* setting at or below 0.85. Many real world surfaces are at or below 0.50, and most are in the range of 0.20 to 0.70. Many paint samples include light reflectance values (LRV) codes, which a manufacturer measures from an actual paint sample. The LRV numbers are in the range of 0 to 100 and equate to a Value setting of 0.0 to 1.0 for a color swatch. Using the LRV number can assist you in creating an accurate lighting simulation for an environment. You can view a 3ds Max/Design material's reflectance values within the Compact Material Editor by enabling the Display Reflectance & Transmittance Information option on the Preference Settings dialog box's Radiosity tab.

Reflection and BRDF The next critical settings are in the Reflection section of the Main Material Parameters. Figure 2.22 shows the reflection options.

FIGURE 2.22

The Arch & Design material's Reflection options

One key to realistic materials is to avoid exceptionally high Reflectivity values, unless the material truly is a highly polished or mirrorlike surface. The Reflectivity setting determines the maximum reflectivity of the surface, but another critical setting, BRDF, determines the actual reflectivity of the surface based on the camera's angle to the surface. Figure 2.23 shows the settings for BRDF.

FIGURE 2.23

The Arch & Design material's BRDF settings

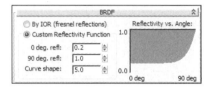

BRDF stands for Bidirectional Reflectance Distribution Function and controls the interaction between light and the surface. A classic example of BDRF is when you stand directly in front of a storefront; your angle is perpendicular to the surface (a 0-degree angle of incidence and parallel to the surface normal), there is little reflectivity (returned light), and you can see into the store. As your viewing angle becomes closer to parallel to the surface (a 90-degree angle of incidence or perpendicular to the surface normal), the surface becomes more mirrorlike and approaches the maximum Reflectivity value. In the new Autodesk material, BRDF is represented by two simple sliders for 0- and 90-degree reflectivity.

The BRDF settings allow you to use the material's index of refraction (IOR) to automatically control reflectivity, or you can directly control reflectivity based on angle. For critical materials, a designer may want to measure real-world surface properties using calibrated equipment called a *gonioreflectometer* that measures reflectivity in a hemisphere around a surface, although these measurements tend to be time-consuming and difficult, and mental ray only takes values for a 90-degree arc across the surface. If you are not certain where to set these values, then using the IOR setting in the Refraction settings and finding a material's IOR will work well.

Again, the Reflectivity parameter sets the maximum surface reflectivity that is then scaled by the BRDF. Because the final rendered result of a particular pixel is dependent on the diffuse color, reflectivity, transparency, and translucency, changes in reflectivity across the surface of an object will produce an interesting and realistic representation of an object. Trying to simulate automotive paint, for instance, with the legacy Raytrace material creates an evenly reflective and odd-looking surface, whereas a material using BRDF allows you to see the underlying color at the proper angles.

For surfaces such as a polished floor, you may have a Reflectivity setting of 0.5 to 0.7, and the 0-degree reflectivity may be around 0.02 with a 90-degree setting of 1.0, or 100 percent of the Reflectivity value. The BRDF Curve Shape parameter is typically left at 5.0; however, I have used lower and higher settings to adjust the reflectivity of a surface from a particular camera view.

MARVELOUS METALS

Although we don't always think of opaque materials like metal as having an IOR, using the BRDF's *By IOR* setting and setting a high IOR value in the Arch & Design's Refraction settings can produce spectacular results with metal and other opaque materials. Metals tend to be reflective across the entire range of angles unlike dielectric materials such as plastic or glass, and they require high settings for 0-degree reflection in BRDF. A dielectric or non-electricity-conducting material is most reflective at glancing angles and typically has low settings at 0-degree reflectivity.

For reflective metals, many experts recommend using an IOR value of 8.0 to 25.0 or more, which sets the BDRF to generate a high level of reflectivity across the surface with a dip in reflectivity just before 90 degrees. An IOR of 8 gives a 0-degree reflectivity around 0.6, whereas 25 gives a value around 0.90. The default template settings for Arch & Design materials in 3ds Max Design 2011 now use an IOR of 25 for the Chrome and Brushed Metal material templates and use an IOR setting of 40 for Copper. The exact number to use really depends on your artistic eye and the result you believe works best. As with all materials, having a reference photograph to help evaluate and compare results helps.

The realism of metal materials can also be enhanced by using a Falloff map in the diffuse color with a slightly darker material for the backside and by further varying the reflectivity of the surface through a noise map.

The next setting, Glossy Samples, controls the quality of glossy reflections and highlights on surfaces.

Glossy Samples   The Glossy Samples setting greatly affects the quality of glossy specular reflections on surfaces. A setting of 0 creates a mirrorlike finish. Figure 2.24 shows a Wood material with the default Glossy Samples setting of 8.

FIGURE 2.24
Arch & Design material with the default Glossy Samples setting of 8

The default Glossy Samples setting of 8 is very low, and the result is evident in the spotty appearance of the surfaces. This problem is most evident in interior scenes like this where there is a bright outdoor daylight component (visible through an off-camera window) and/or high intensity photometric lights. To create glossy reflections, mental ray shoots random rays out into the scene from each rendered sample (controlled by the Sampling Quality render settings), and the quantity of rays shot is the Glossy Samples setting. In these scenes, some of the rays randomly see the very high intensity light sources and produce bright speckles.

PRACTICAL GLOSSY SAMPLES

To reduce the speckled finish, you might need to set the Glossy Samples setting to 24, 32, 48, or more. Because the setting is technically Glossy Samples per rendered sample, increasing the Samples Per Pixel settings in the Render Setup dialog box or increasing Image Precision in the Rendered Frame Window can reduce the size of the speckles and improve the image. Be sure to test your Glossy Samples settings with your final quality render settings to avoid overly high Glossy Samples settings and long render times.

Figure 2.25 shows the same materials with the Glossy Samples setting set to 64 for the wood and the stainless steel countertop.

FIGURE 2.25
Arch & Design materials with the Glossy Samples setting set to 64

Choosing the correct setting to use in a scene, 64 glossy samples in this instance, was determined through trial and retrial until the desired effect was achieved. As a point of reference, going from 32 to 64 samples for this scene did not significantly change the render times. For most surfaces I will change the Glossy Samples setting to 16 or 24 and higher if artifacts appear in the surface. The default setting of 8 works for many slightly reflective surfaces and where there is an even lighting level.

The Render Setup dialog box and the Rendered Frame Window both include settings for a global Glossy Reflections Precision effect that acts as a multiplier for the Glossy Samples setting for all materials. Although this is convenient, I find that adjusting Glossy Samples per material produces faster renderings because materials that are not experiencing issues will not get the additional rays. The Arch & Design and ProMaterials allow per-material settings for Glossy Samples; however, the Autodesk materials do not. Your choices with Autodesk materials are to either increase the global settings for Glossy Samples or convert to Arch & Design.

In some situations you might find that increasing the Glossy Samples value will not get you the results you need with a reasonable render time, particularly for animations. In this case, you might need to use the Highlights+FG setting, which I cover next.

Highlights+FG   This setting resolves issues that cannot be cleaned up by increasing the Glossy Samples setting and will greatly improve the speed of rendering by producing simulated glossy reflections. Figure 2.26 shows the same scene as Figure 2.25, this time with the Highlights+FG setting.

FIGURE 2.26
The interior wood finish that uses the Arch & Design Highlights+FG setting

This image with the Highlights+FG option rendered from two to eight times faster than renderings that used Glossy Samples, depending on the Glossy Samples setting used for comparison. The results are definitely more diffuse across the surface and do not fully reflect the environment. For surfaces that are particularly problematic and would otherwise require exceptionally high glossy settings or for surfaces where accurate glossy reflections are not critical, this option can save you considerable render time.

Fast Glossy Interpolation   The Fast Glossy Interpolation setting accelerates the process of creating reflections on a flat surface. When the Fast (Interpolate) check box is enabled in the Reflection settings, the settings shown in Figure 2.27 are used to control the resolution of the reflections.

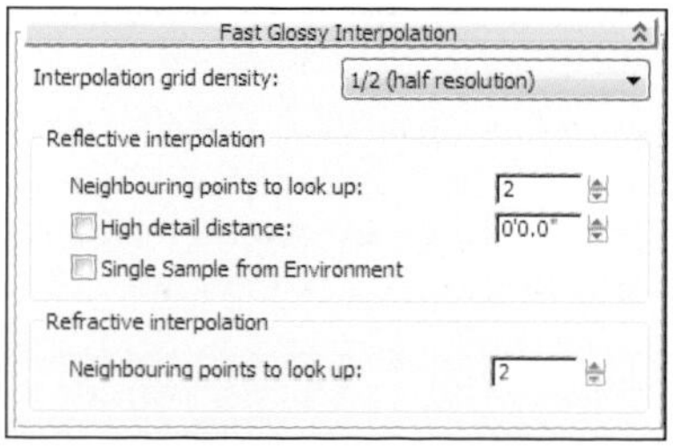

FIGURE 2.27
The Fast Glossy Interpolation Arch & Design settings

This feature works by calculating glossy reflections across the rendered image, not on the surfaces themselves; therefore, Fast Glossy Interpolation is most useful on large flat reflective surfaces such as flooring and is not useful on curved surfaces such as furniture because it cannot follow the curvature of the surface. Figure 2.28 shows a flooring surface without the Fast Glossy Interpolation option on the left and with Fast Glossy Interpolation on the right.

FIGURE 2.28
An interior floor without (left) and with (right) the Fast Glossy Interpolation option

The effect is most noticeable in the reflection of the column. The Fast Glossy Interpolation image rendered in less than half the time of the scene without Fast Glossy Interpolation. The setting used for the left side was 32 Glossy Samples and for the right side was Fast Glossy Interpolation set to ⅓ (third resolution) and Neighboring Points To Look Up set to 4. The options for resolution are 2, 1, ½, ⅓, ¼, and ⅕ the render resolution. Higher Neighboring Points To Look Up settings tend to blur the surface considerably. I have used the Fast Glossy Interpolation feature on surfaces where they are already rather diffuse but I desire a reflective effect, such as on asphalt streets, semipolished concrete, or epoxy floors. The example in Figure 2.28 uses a modified Glazed Ceramic Tiles preset in the Arch & Design Material and represents a surface where I would not generally consider using this feature and prefer increased Glossy Samples instead.

Self Illumination (Glow)   The Self Illumination (Glow) setting in the Arch & Design material differs from the Standard material's self illumination in that this can produce diffuse illumination in the scene when using Final Gather and can use real-world lighting units. Figure 2.29 shows the settings for Self Illumination (Glow).

FIGURE 2.29
Self Illumination (Glow) settings

If you need a material to glow a particular color, then generally I use a D65 Illuminant preset (same as 6500 Kelvin) and set the Filter color to the color I want the material to appear as; without a filter color, the materials wash out to white despite a diffuse color or bitmap. If you have an actual light source within a light fixture, then generally you would not use the

Illuminates The Scene option. The illumination produced by this effect, because it is an indirect illumination process, is very diffuse and will not produce sharp shadows. It is terrific for neon glows and other diffuse lighting effects.

The next two settings, found in the Special Effects roll-down, are particularly important to architectural design visualization work.

Special Effects   The Special Effects roll-down in the Arch & Design material includes two material options: Ambient Occlusion and Round Corners. The Ambient Occlusion option adds darkness to surfaces based on how much geometry is blocking (occluding) the surface from ambient lighting. It is generally used to add contact shadows between objects and to add shadow details in renderings that have been lost, washed out essentially, through the averaging of indirect light over features in your scene. The Round Corners option adds highlights along edges in your objects, similar to a bump effect, to help define and highlight edges of objects.

Figure 2.30 shows the settings for Ambient Occlusion and Round Corners.

FIGURE 2.30
The A&D material's
Special Effects options

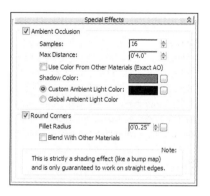

Ambient Occlusion is a detail enhancement option that darkens rendered pixels based on how much of the surface is blocked from ambient light. The Ambient Occlusion option also helps create contact shadows between objects and darkens crevices in areas that might be washed out with indirect illumination. Figure 2.31 shows a rendered sample, in blue, and 16 random AO samples (green rays) radiating out 4″, which is the default Ambient Occlusion distance settings. Only a couple of rays strike the red object, which results in just a small amount of additional darkening for that rendered sample.

Looking closely at this image you may be able to see how the surface gets slightly darker as it progresses under the red surface.

The settings for Ambient Occlusion include the following:

Samples   This is the number of rays cast out into a scene from a rendered sample. Sixteen rays is the default and is usually sufficient. Values up to 64 are good when fine detail and additional accuracy are needed albeit with much higher render times. Remember that this is AO sample rays per rendered sample across the entire visible surface of objects that contain this material. Rendered samples may be groups of pixels, pixels, or fractional pixels. Higher Image Precision/Samples Per Pixel settings may mean that lower ambient occlusion samples can be used with good results.

FIGURE 2.31
A rendered sample in blue and the ambient occlusion rays used to determine occlusion

Max Distance   This is the distance that each ray will look out into your scene for an occluding surface. Too high of a value might waste render time and result in overly dark areas in areas not naturally affected by ambient occlusion, and too small of a value might significantly reduce the effect.

Use Color From Other Mats (Exact AO)   This option adds light bleeding from surfaces, including self-illuminated surfaces, and can correct for excessive darkening. Without Use Color From Other mats (Exact AO) enabled, a nearby self-illuminated object will produce a darkening effect on an adjacent surface, as shown in Figure 2.32 under the sphere on the left, rather than collect self illumination, as shown on the right.

FIGURE 2.32
The glowing sphere on the left shows shadows because of ambient occlusion used on the floor. On the left the Exact AO option was used.

Figure 2.33 shows side-by-side images of a detailed cabinet with a simple white, semigloss Arch & Design material, with and without the Ambient Occlusion option enabled.

The surfaces on the right are darker not only in the crevices and details of the cabinet but also in the areas behind the drawer knobs, helping to set those apart from the drawer fronts. I find the Ambient Occlusion option to be an essential tool that must be used selectively for the best effect and minimal impact in render time. It does increase render time because each rendered sample must send out ambient occlusion rays to compute the additional shading of that point.

FIGURE 2.33
The left side shows
rendered image
without the Ambient
Occlusion option, and
the right side is with
Ambient Occlusion.

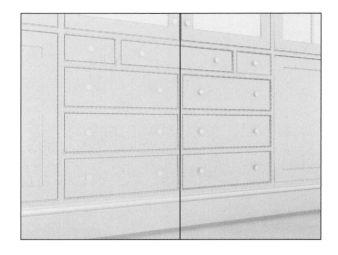

The Round Corners option has two parameters, one for the radius at the edge of the surface and another one to enable blending with adjacent surfaces. The Round Corners option takes virtually no additional render time but can play a significant part in adding realism to your scenes. In the past, I would take the time to painstakingly chamfer the edges of objects that would benefit from highlights along the edge or objects where the lack of contrasting colors and shadows caused the edges to disappear. There is also something very "artificial feeling" about a rendering that does not have some highlights and softness along the edges, because almost no manufactured objects are without a slight radius along an edge and a corresponding visible highlight. Figure 2.34 shows an image where the left side is without round corners and the right is with round corners.

FIGURE 2.34
Cabinet without
round corners on
left and with round
corners on the right

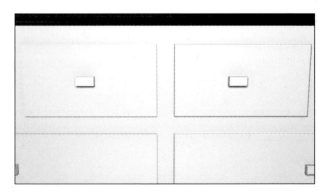

In Figure 2.34 both sides are using the Ambient Occlusion option; without the Ambient Occlusion option, the image on the left would show almost no detail at all, because this is a basic box-model object with no chamfering. The A&D Round Corners option has saved countless hours of chamfering and adjusting of geometry to create highlights. That said, it is not ideal for all surfaces, in particular most walls in imported Revit models. Figure 2.35 shows an extreme example of a Wall material with a very large radius value. If the wall joint is not edited to meet at the corner, then a radius highlight and shadow will occur where the two walls meet. In this figure, all walls and floors should join evenly and instead have a radius.

FIGURE 2.35
Revit geometry with an exception-ally large Round Corner radius

Without the Round Corners option, each surface fits together perfectly; with the Round Corners option, it looks disjointed. If you need the round corners effect on some areas, consider detaching surfaces into planes to disable the effect on the edges, or use a Multi/Sub-Object material where appropriate.

BACKFACE CULLING AND THE TWO-SIDED MATERIAL

Every face of an object has a *surface normal* that is an invisible vector pointing directly out of the center of one side of the face. This normal is used to control effects such as automatic smoothing and other mesh operations and is also used to determine which side of a face is generally renderable. By eliminating from consideration any faces whose normals are 90 degrees or greater away from the current view, a renderer may be able to speed calculation; those faces are simply discarded or culled. This process of eliminating the faces pointing backward is called *back face culling*. You can find the Back Face Culling option in the Arch & Design material in the Advanced Rendering Options roll-down.

Arch & Design materials are, by default, two-sided materials with the Back Face Culling option turned off. This is in contrast to the legacy Standard and Architectural materials which require you to enable the two-sided option. ProMaterials and the new Autodesk materials, like the Arch & Design material, automatically produce two-sided results. For the purposes of ray tracing, the need to use the Back Face Culling option is greatly reduced because other optimizations are used to sort faces. See Chapter 4 and BSP for more information.

The next material type I cover is the ProMaterials series, which has been replaced by the new Autodesk Material in 3ds Max/Design 2011.

Introducing ProMaterials

Autodesk introduced the mental ray ProMaterials in 3ds Max/Design 2009 as a streamlined alternative to the Arch & Design material, and like the new Autodesk material type ProMaterials have finish-specific versions for Ceramic, Concrete, etc. The ProMaterials have some advantages over the new Autodesk materials in that you can access the Ambient Occlusion and Round Corners options, and adjust the reflective and refractive glossy properties of the materials. ProMaterials have been discontinued in 3ds Max/Design 2011, however FBX models and legacy scenes may still use ProMaterials on the existing and newly imported geometry.

Although the general use of ProMaterials is fairly straightforward, there are several settings I point out in this section that affect the speed and quality of these materials. Figure 2.36 shows the ProMaterials: Generic material's user interface for the Performance Tuning Parameters section of settings.

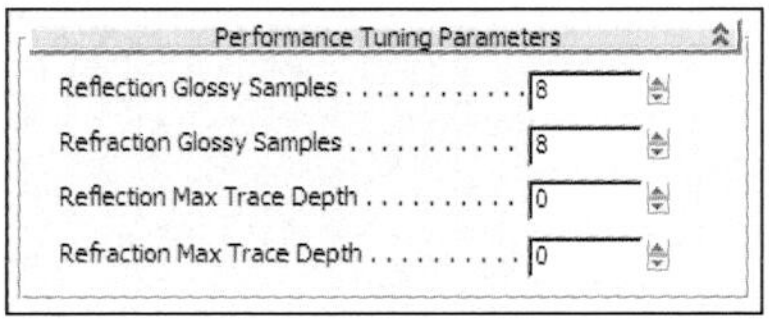

FIGURE 2.36
ProMaterials:
Generic settings in
the Performance
Tuning Parameters
section

Although different ProMaterials contain different groupings of these settings depending on their need, usually they have at least the two Reflection parameters. The two Glossy Samples settings affect how many rays are cast to fine-tune the highlights on the surface. If you are seeing speckles on the surface of your materials, then try increasing the Reflection Glossy Samples setting to 32 for most scenes; however 64 Glossy Samples or more may be required to resolve the highlight for difficult scenes. As covered in the Arch & Design material, indoor scenes that have high-intensity lights or have the very bright daylight visible in the scene often suffer from speckles because of inadequate glossy samples.

The Trace Depth settings, however, are different from what you find in the Arch & Design material and are set to 0. This means that the material will use the mental ray Trace Limits setting for the material, which is a default of four reflections. Setting this value to 1 can speed rendering when using glossy and reflective ProMaterials.

Introducing the MetaSL Material

Another addition to 3ds Max/Design 2011 is the ability to create *MetaSL* materials directly within the Slate Material Editor. A MetaSL material is a series of low-level shaders that can be combined to create nearly limitless materials that will work in a number of applications; mental images describes MetaSL as the "universal shader language." MetaSL was introduced with 3ds Max/Design 2010 and required you to compile shaders in the mental images application *mental mill* and then use the DirectX material within 3ds Max/Design to load the material and apply it to your objects. A basic version of mental mill, the Artists Edition, came with 3ds Max/Design 2010. The more advanced mental mill Standard Edition allows access to lower-level components of shaders and debugging, and it adds Maya, 3ds Max/Design, and Softimage exporters for better integration. An extensive library of precompiled MetaSL materials is available at `http://materials.mentalimages.com`, and mental images also provides a Shader Pack, downloadable from its forums at `http://forums.mentalimages.com`, which will help you get up to speed with mental mill. In addition to the new MetaSL material, the SME includes the menu option Material ➢ Export metaSL to create an `.xmsl` file that can be read in mental mill.

In the next section, I cover using a script to convert legacy materials to Arch & Design.

Converting Existing Materials to Arch & Design

There are many benefits to converting legacy materials to the newer Arch & Design, ProMaterials and Autodesk materials, including the ability to get high dynamic range results, the ability to self-illuminate the scene with Final Gather, the ability to control reflectivity based on your angle to the surface (BRDF), rounded corners, and detail enhancement via the Ambient Occlusion option.

Manually converting legacy materials to Arch & Design materials can be tedious and error-prone. The SME can make the manual process of converting easier because you can connect maps from existing materials to the input nodeslot of new material and easily copy and paste colors.

Fortunately for us, our friend Zap Andersson, mental images software engineer and blogger at `http://mentalraytip.blogspot.com`, and PF Breton of Autodesk have provided an automated converter, the mr Arch Design Tools. This script file, `Macro_mrArchMtlTools.mcr`, is included on your book DVD in the `\Scripts` folder and also on Andersson's blog. A similar script ships on 3ds Max/Design's Samples DVD but does not include the material conversion routine.

Perform the following steps to install and use this script:

1. Drag and drop the script file from the `\Scripts` folder of the DVD into a 3ds Max/Design viewport. This installs the script in 3ds Max/Design and makes it available to use.

2. Select Customize ➤ Customize User Interface.

3. Switch to the Menus tab.

4. Change the Category drop-down menu to the "mental ray" category. The Action list is now filtered to only show the scripts in the mental ray category.

5. Click the New button above the tree view of menu items, and create a new menu called mr. It will be added to the Menus listing at the bottom-left of the dialog box.

6. Scroll the Menus list, find the new mr menu, and drag it into the menu tree view on the right, between MAXScript and Help, as shown in Figure 2.37.

FIGURE 2.37
The Customize User Interface dialog box with the new 'mr' tree menu at right, shown with several sub-menu items

7. Click the + symbol next to the mr menu item to expand the menu.

8. Drag the mr Arch & Design action item into the mr tree view below mr.

9. If desired, drag other mental ray action items into the mr menu.

THE RETURN OF THE FILE MENU

For 3ds Max/Design 2010 and 2011, the File menu has been replaced by the large letter *M*, dubbed the *Application button*, on the Quick Access Toolbar located at the upper left of the program. This Application button functionality is consistent across newer Autodesk applications, and the new Application button's file history for recent documents is particularly useful in the new menus. Many users, however, find that the legacy File menu is faster and more direct to use than the Application button menus. You can restore the File menu to your copy of 3ds Max/Design by dragging the File menu from the Menus list at the bottom left of the Customize User Interface dialog box into the tree view on the right. Figure 2.37 shows the restored File menu at the top of the menu tree.

---

10. Optionally, click the Save button to save just the menu items to a file. I like to save the individual sections of the UI to files in case I need to use them if 3ds Max/Design is reinstalled or I need it for another machine. UI files are typically stored in the `c:\Users\ <username>\AppData\Local\Autodesk\3dsMaxDesign\2011 - 64bit\enu\UI` folder.

11. Close the dialog box, choose Customize Save Custom UI Scheme, and save the menus to the `MaxStartUI.ui` file to ensure your changes are all saved.

12. Select the mr ➤ mr Arch & Design Tools menu option to open the dialog box, as shown in Figure 2.38.

FIGURE 2.38
The mr Arch &
Design Utilities

The bottom button, Convert Materials To mr Arch & Design, automatically steps through each material in your scene and creates a replacement Arch & Design material with similar settings including the same material name, general settings, and bitmaps used in the original material. The script converts VRay, mental ray DGS, Architectural, and Standard materials. You might need to adjust some Arch & Design settings once conversion is completed, because this tool cannot take into account all the surface options of their source materials and rendered results will differ.

Next I cover options for creating glazing for architectural models.

Creating Glazing Materials

The glazing-specific materials provided as ProMaterials: Glazing and Autodesk Glazing provide a quick and effective method of producing a realistic glass effect without the overhead of the refraction of light. Both materials are a glass material with no Index Of Refraction setting and thus no bending or distortion of light as it passes through the surfaces. They are intended for flat surfaces utilizing thin geometry, usually a plane or boxlike surface that represents glass in a window. The surface can have a color defined by a preset drop-down menu or can use a custom color from a color swatch or a bitmap. For the Custom Color swatch or map to have an effect, you need to change the Color drop-down to the Custom option. The Value setting of the color swatch's color affects the apparent transparency of the object (a higher value = more transparent).

Figure 2.39 shows the user interface for the new Autodesk Glazing material.

FIGURE 2.39

The Autodesk Glazing material settings

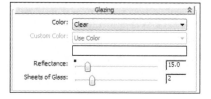

The Sheets Of Glass setting in the Autodesk Glazing material is the same as the ProMaterials: Glazing's Refraction Levels setting. These settings compensate for windows modeled with multiple panes of glass and will reduce the opacity of the glazing so that the total transparency through all panes equals the color swatch's Value setting. The Sheets Of Glass/Refraction Levels setting of 2 is correct for glazing modeled as a box and can be set to 1 for glazing modeled as a single plane. For multipane glass, you set your color swatch's Value setting to the total transparency of the window and set the Sheets Of Glass/Refraction Levels option for the total polygons a ray of light will pass through. The color of each sheet will be reduced so that the total color through all sheets of glass will be the value selected.

The Reflectance value is 0.1 by default in the ProMaterial, which means it is on average 10 percent reflective, and it has a setting of 15 in the Autodesk Glazing material, or 15 percent. The Reflectance setting is the maximum reflectivity and will produce different amounts of reflection based on your angle to the surface, just like BRDF in the Arch & Design material. Glazing produces near mirrorlike reflections when you are nearly parallel to the surface and are seeing reflections at a glancing angle. As you approach being perpendicular to the glazing, looking straight into a storefront, for instance, the surface has very little reflection.

The ProMaterial: Glazing material includes performance-tuning settings for both Reflections and Refractions. With insufficient Refraction levels, transparent objects render as black once the ray limit is hit; as you see through more panes of glass, you eventually see black, as shown in Figure 2.40. Too high of a setting impacts performance.

FIGURE 2.40
Glass can turn black when looking through multiple panes.

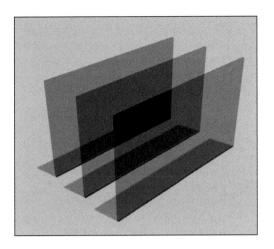

USING GLAZING IN 3DS MAX/DESIGN 2011

In 3ds Max/Design 2011 mental images has improved how the glazing and transparent Arch & Design materials operate, and rays will pass straight through to the environment or to the first solid object rather than returning black once trace depth limits are reached. Setting trace depth to reasonable values will produce the best results, but you will not experience ruined renders if trace depth is too low.

You can also create glazing using the Arch & Design material, and there is a template called Glass (Thin Geometry) that has an IOR of 1.5 but has the Advanced Rendering option Thin-Walled (Can Use Single Faces) option selected and does not bend the rays passing through the material. The IOR setting controls the BRDF surface reflectivity only. In the Arch & Design material, you may need to adjust the Max. Trace Depth For Reflections And Refractions setting to allow adequate depth. In versions of 3ds Max/Design prior to 2011, you might need to adjust the Max Refractions settings on the Render Setup's Render tab to allow rays to pass through all sheets of glazing.

In the next section. I look at some of the particulars of the use of high dynamic range (HDR) image formats.

Using Low and High Dynamic Range Image Formats

Dynamic range in images refers to the range of color values that the bitmap can represent. Low dynamic range images (LDRI) are most common and include JPEG and PNG 24-, 32- and 48-bit images. In these image file formats, the RGB color data is stored in as integer numbers with values from 0 to 255 per-color channel for a 24-bit image, and 0 to 65,535 per channel for a 48-bit image. High dynamic range images (HDRI) include the Radiance Image File and OpenEXR (EXR) formats. All HDRI data is stored in a floating-point format and is able to represent RGB values of any number.

LDRI images used in a material should always be gamma corrected, and HDR images should not be gamma corrected for file input or output. Some image formats, such as PNG, may contain gamma information stored with the images. This may or may not be valid, depending on how the image was originally processed, and you may need to manually override the gamma value in 3ds Max/Design to achieve the desired results.

HDRI are often used as spherical environment maps, giving brilliant color to reflections in rendered objects. You can use HDRI to produce image-based lighting (IBL) effects, accurately replicating the lighting of the scene where the HDRI was photographed by adding it to a standard Sky Light object or by using an HDRI environment with Irradiance Particles. These techniques are covered in Chapter 3, "Light, Shadow, and Exposure Control," and in Chapter 7, "Importons and Irradiance Particles." 3ds Max/Design ships with sample HDR images in the .\maps\HDRs folder of your 3ds Max/Design installation, and sources for additional HDR environments are provided at www.mastering-mentalray.com. Sample HDR images from Dosch Design and Spheron VR are in the Bonus folder of your DVD.

Using HDRI formats for saving renderings allows you to precisely edit and control the color and exposure of an image within another application, such as 3ds Max Composite, allowing for finer adjustment than adjusting an integer-based LDRI format. Using HDRI in 3ds Max Composite can prevent banding effects that LDRI may suffer from when adjusting brightness and contrast.

CONFIGURE THE FRAME BUFFER TO OUTPUT HDRI

To render and output HDR images, you must ensure that mental ray's frame buffer is set to 32-bits per channel. You cannot make a HDR image if the frame buffer is 16 bits and the 32-bit frame buffer is required for use with lighting analysis covered in Chapter 9, "mental ray for Architecture."

The 32-bit frame buffer is the default for new scenes with 3ds Max Design but not for 3ds Max, and legacy scenes may be set to the 16-bit frame buffer option. This setting is in the Render Settings dialog box, the Renderer tab, and Options section.

The original file format for holding high dynamic range images is the Radiance format that uses the .hdr file extension.

USING THE RADIANCE IMAGE FORMAT (HDR)

The HDRI Load Settings dialog box, as shown in Figure 2.41, for the HDR (Radiance) file format contains an image preview, image exposure adjustments, and bitmap storage options.

Autodesk recommends that you set the Internal Storage option to 16 Bit/Chan Linear (48 bpp) unless you specifically need to use a different internal format; however, mental images says that the Real Pixels (32 bpp) option is correct for use with mental ray. I also recommend using the Real Pixels format and using the Def. Exposure option for most HDR images. Turning off the Def. Exposure option enables the Black Point and White Point settings and their corresponding lines within the histogram chart. The Exposure histogram chart shows the range of color intensity within the HDR image, with the darkest colors to the left and brightest to the right. You can use just a portion of the light range of the HDRI or scale the range of colors by adjusting where absolute black occurs (Black Point) and where the brightest color occurs (White Point). Moving Black Point into the color range of the Exposure histogram causes any colors below that point to clamp to black. Similarly, turning the White Point down so it is within the HDRI color range causes bright colors to clamp to white and perhaps look overexposed in renderings. A Whitepoint well above the visible range of the Exposure histogram will darken the resulting HDR image. In the center, below the histogram, you'll find the Measured Min/Max values for Black Point and White Point within the selected image, and this gives you a reference for setting your own values. Again, using the Def. Exposure option is best for most images.

FIGURE 2.41
Input dialog box for
HDR file formats

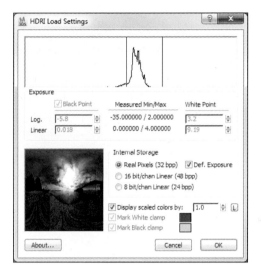

Using the Autodesk-recommended 16-bit/channel mode compresses the incoming data. To compensate for this compression, you should set the RGB Level setting for the HDRI bitmap, as shown in Figure 2.42, to match the Linear White Point value of the HDR settings, thus uncompressing the image.

FIGURE 2.42
The bitmap RGB
Level value set to
match the Linear
White Point value
of the HDR image

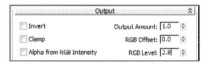

When you use the 16-bit per channel option, the HDR dialog box's thumbnail preview image may show the bitmap with cyan and magenta highlights in the image preview. These are areas where the Exposure settings for the bitmap are out of range and colors are clamped (forced) to black or full white, respectively. You are losing color data when clamping occurs and should adjust the dialog box's Exposure values to encompass the range of the Exposure histogram without any visible clamping. Clamp colors work only on 16- and 8-bit/channel images and not with 32-bit Real Pixel images. The Display Scaled Colors By option increases the brightness of the preview but does not affect how the image is used within 3ds Max/Design.

To adjust the brightness in your rendering, use the HDR map within a Gamma & Gain map (formerly Utility Gamma & Gain). The use of Gamma & Gain and HDRI maps for environments is covered in Chapter 10, "mental ray for Design."

The newest and preferred HDR file format is the OpenEXR format developed by LucasFilm for use in film production. 3ds Max/Design 2011 has extended the functionality of the EXR format for use with compositing applications such as the new 3ds Max Composite application.

Using the OpenEXR Image Format (EXR)

3ds Max/Design 2011 now supports the ability to save and read additional channels of render data, called *render elements*, as layers within an OpenEXR-formatted image. This reduces the need to use separate render element files to store raw render data and z-depth, for instance. Figure 2.43 shows the new OpenEXR Configuration dialog box with render elements shown as embedded channels and listed in the drop-down menu.

FIGURE 2.43
New OpenEXR Configuration dialog box for 3ds Max/Design 2011

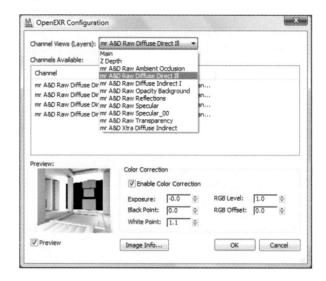

I cover the use of render elements in Chapter 10. In the next section I cover using real-world scale for controlling the size of bitmaps used for materials.

Applying Real-World Scale

Real-world scale (RWS) allows you to specify the physical size that a bitmap represents within the bitmap settings, as shown in Figure 2.44, giving you one point of control for all materials using that map. For instance, when you use an image of brick, you can estimate the real-world size the image of brick represents, enter those values into the bitmap's RWS settings, and all objects with that material will have consistent map sizes. To adjust the size of the brick, simply open a material editor and change the size values.

FIGURE 2.44
Texture coordinates with real-world scale enabled

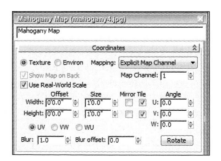

Without RWS, the rendered size of the bitmap is controlled by parameters within a UVW Map modifier you need to add to each object. UVW are the three letters in the alphabet before XYZ and mean basically the same thing, three different axes; however, these directions are local to an object and can vary depending on the configuration of the UVW Map modifier. The UVW Map modifier controls the size, shape, and placement of maps applied to objects and, for 3ds Max Design, is set to automatically use the RWS option. All newly created parametric objects in 3ds Max Design and geometry imported from Revit use RWS by default, and the new Autodesk Material Library uses RWS for all of its materials. Unless I need a bitmap spread across an entire object, then I will use RWS.

When RWS is enabled in the bitmap settings, as shown in Figure 2.44, the bitmap tiling values change to match the display units of the scene, which are inches in this case instead of a decimal tiling value. Switching between RWS and tiling can leave tiny numbers in the tiling value; set this to 1.0 if reverting from RWS. The use of RWS is enabled by default in 3ds Max Design, and this feature is controlled by an option in the Preferences dialog box's General tab.

RWS gives you a single place to quickly and consistently set the mapping size and eliminates the need to instance mapping modifiers between objects to obtain a consistent appearance. Objects should either have mapping coordinates with the RWS enabled or have a UVW Map modifier with RWS enabled or use the Map Scalar modifier. The Map Scalar modifier allows you to control the size of a bitmap on an individual object and is explained in detail in the bonus video `Mapping.mov`, located in your DVD's `\BonusVideos` folder.

As you can see in Figure 2.45, mapping issues will occur if the bitmap settings for RWS do not match the object's RWS setting. The sphere has a material using RWS, but the object has the option disabled.

FIGURE 2.45
Rendered sphere on left has RWS disabled, which results in a mismatch in RWS between the object and the bitmap's settings.

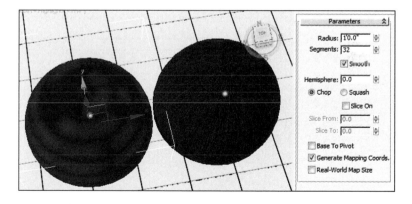

The new Autodesk Material Library materials all use RWS. Objects imported from Revit FBX files typically use RWS but may need adjustments. All new parametric objects created in 3ds Max Design use RWS by default, and is a check-box option in the Modify tab. The ProMaterial materials that use bitmaps, such as Brushed Metal, Concrete patterns, Wavy patterns, and so on, use RWS. Some material libraries supplied with 3ds Max/Design have RWS configured correctly, like the ProMaterial libraries, and other classic libraries may not use RWS or may have the size set to 1″ by 1″, which need to be rescaled to render correctly. In this case, adding the MapScalar modifier (Object Space or World Space Modifier version) to the affected objects and setting a scale factor often works well. The MapScalar setting will have an initial value of 1″, which is equal to 100 percent RWS. Figure 2.46 shows the modifier stack for a Box object.

FIGURE 2.46

A Box object with a MapScalar (WSM) modifier, adjusted to give 250 percent scaling to the object's bitmaps

The modifier will show as "Map Scalar Binding (WSM) within the stack, but the modifier is "MapScalar (WSM)" in the modifier drop-down list. Figure 2.46 shows a MapScalar (WSM) modifier is applied to the box's stack and set to scale the maps 250 percent, as shown as 2.5". Here, 1.0" equals 100 percent scaling. You can also adjust the position of the mapping to correct for misalignments between objects using the U and V Offset values.

For more information on RWS and strategies for mapping objects, see the Mapping.mov video on the DVD in the \BonusVideos\ folder. In this video, I also cover critical concepts such as the Map Scalar modifier, the use of the XForm modifier, and the effect of mapping when scaling objects.

The Bottom Line

Use the new Slate Material Editor mode The SME is a powerful new node-based visual tool for creating, managing, and editing materials and maps.

> **Master It** How do you create an Arch & Design material for use on a wood kitchen island using the SME?

Control performance options for bitmaps 3ds Max/Design and mental ray have a variety of options for storing and using bitmaps, including holding maps in memory, caching and resizing to disk, and managing map paths.

> **Master It** How do you enable the rescaling of large bitmaps, disable the Bitmap Pager option, and enable the mental ray map Manager?

Adjust material and map settings that affect render quality and speed The default settings for bitmaps and materials are not always the best choice for your scene, and it is important to understand the options and how they affect both image quality and render time.

> **Master It** How do you adjust the Ambient Occlusion, Round Corners, Glossy Samples, and Reflection Trace Depth settings to add detail, eliminate surface speckles, and trim render time?

Chapter 3

Light, Shadow, and Exposure Control

Lighting is, arguably, one of the most important aspects of your scene. Great materials and wonderful geometry will all be for nothing if you have a poorly lit scene. Despite its importance, all too often the task of lighting a scene is left for the end of a project, where little time and attention can be afforded to creating a quality lighting solution and properly testing both light settings and render options. A great rendering is rarely created on the first try after simply throwing in lights and clicking Render. Lighting and rendering your scene can be a time-consuming process, and the process typically takes a lot of tweaking to adjust settings for each unique scene.

To produce the highest-quality images in the least amount of time, you need to understand both how the lights operate and the techniques to effectively control and balance your lighting. Because the rendered results of the direct lighting produced by light objects is heavily influenced by indirect illumination tools, I'm saving the large sample projects for Chapter 5, "Indirect Illumination and Final Gather," and Chapter 6, "Global Illumination and Caustics."

In this chapter, you will learn how to

◆ Configure exposure control settings for varying conditions

◆ Optimize and control photometric lights and shadow quality

Using Material Override

As you test-render scene lighting and eventually make adjustments to indirect illumination, you might find that rendering with all the maps, materials, and the overhead of reflection and refraction takes a lot of time. Fortunately, mental ray provides a method to speed test-renders by replacing all of your materials with a single material using the Material Override option. You'll find this feature on the Render Setup dialog box's Processing tab; you would typically set it to a matte white paint material.

The advantage of this matte white Material Override is that your renders will take much less time than they would with full materials and effects, and Material Override is used on scenes throughout the book. The downside is that all objects will be opaque if this one Material Override material is opaque, which is typically the case. An opaque Material Override material will block light from outdoors and adjacent rooms and from light fixtures with filters and globes and will not give you a good representation of all lighting sources. As long as you can isolate objects, turning off shadow casting for those transparent objects helps, as shown in Figure 3.1, which is an image rendered from the Chapter 3 project's .\scenes\LightLab\LightLab_Override_Start.max scene file. This scene rendered in 6 percent of the time of the original without the Material Override option selected.

To get around this opacity limitation, you can use a Multi/SubObject (MSO) material in place of a single material and assign one material channel to a transparent Autodesk or ProMaterial Glazing. An MSO material with three materials, the first two as a white Wall Paint and the third as Glazing, will allow 3ds Max/Design's parametric doors and windows to remain transparent for the panels that are typically glass. Any other glass or transparent objects in your scene would need either their material IDs edited or a Material modifier added to their stack and set to ID number 3.

Obviously, any objects that have something with a material ID of 3 will have the Glazing material, including nonglass objects, so a little forethought in material IDs might be necessary if you need to have more accurate transparency in these test-renders. Figure 3.2 shows the scene `LightLab_Override_Finish.max` with a three-item MSO material as the Material Override, with item 3 as ProMaterial: Glazing. The water and all glazing objects have a Material modifier with ID 3. This scene rendered in 11 percent of the time of the original scene.

FIGURE 3.1
Material Override scene with shadow casting turned off for clear objects

FIGURE 3.2
LightLab scene with a three-part MSO material

Next I cover exposure controls, which in mental ray work in the same manner as exposure settings in a single-lens reflex camera.

Introducing Exposure Controls

An *exposure control* is a tool for converting raw rendered pixels into an appropriate brightness range for display and print; it's also referred to as *tone mapping*. Like the iris of a real-world camera, the exposure control's purpose is to limit the amount of light coming in through your virtual camera lens, and it determines the brightness of your rendered scene. Internally, mental ray renders your scene in a high dynamic range, which is able to produce any range of light and color. Because your computer display and most file formats are low dynamic range, the rendering must be converted from HDR to LDR to be viewable. In 3ds Max/Design, there are five types of exposure controls that are accessible in the Environment and Effects dialog box (press the 8 key to open): Automatic, Linear, Logarithmic, mr Photographic, and Pseudo Color exposure controls.

The Automatic and Linear exposure controls are not supported in mental ray. The mr Photographic exposure control should be your choice unless you have a compelling reason to use the Logarithmic exposure control. The Logarithmic exposure control has been replaced by the mr Photographic. However, versions of 3ds Max prior to 3ds Max 2008 did not have the newer control, so Logarithmic was the only correct option with mental ray. If you have a legacy scene using the Logarithmic control, I recommend that you switch to the mr Photographic, provided you do not need to match any existing renderings.

The first exposure control covered in this chapter is the Logarithmic exposure control, a legacy tool that is still compatible with mental ray and is supplanted by the mr Photographic.

The Logarithmic Exposure Control

This feature has a simple set of controls and is needed when you use the Render To Texture tools in 3ds Max prior to 2010. The advantage to the Logarithmic control is that it is faster than the mr Photographic exposure control. One of its disadvantages is the inability to animate and control the Exterior Daylight option, making it impossible to produce animations going from a bright daylight to a dim interior environment. This leaves you having to light the interior as an exterior, or vice versa, in order to have the exposure consistent between the two environments. You should not use the Logarithmic exposure control with the Lighting Analysis tools, because Lighting Analysis was designed for use with the mr Photographic Exposure Control.

Another disadvantage is that the Logarithmic exposure control does such a good job of shifting your rendering into a usable brightness range that it is easy to produce a greatly overlit or underlit scene without realizing it. Overly bright lighting ends up pushed down to a moderately bright range, and an underlit scene is shifted up to the visible range. Inexperienced users tend to drop in lights with default intensity settings and away they go; and default photometric lights are too bright for use in a small interior, a fact that this exposure control can hide. With the mr Photographic exposure control, however, you set the exposure to something that relates to the real world, such as Interior Daylight, and then set your lighting into realistic ranges. With this workflow, it is difficult to mask problems due to out-of-range scene lighting.

The Logarithmic control adds a 2.2 gamma to the output of your image and should not be used with an Output Gamma setting. You can use the Override option in the File Save dialog box and set the file gamma to 1.0, or you can change your preferences for the Output Gamma setting. See Chapter 1, "mental ray Essentials," for more details on gamma correction.

The mr Photographic Exposure Control

The mr Photographic is the preferred exposure control to use with mental ray and photometric lights. It includes camera-like exposure controls such as f-stop, ISO, and shutter speed, as well as a simple exposure value that is the end result of combining the other three variables. There is a Preset drop-down menu where you can choose from settings such as these:

- Physically Based Lighting Outdoor Daylight, Clear Sky
- Physically Based Lighting, Indoor Nighttime
- Non Physically Based Lighting

Presets are an excellent starting point for many scenes.

3ds Max 2010 (and newer) includes the ability to use exposure controls within your viewports to get a more accurate idea of the effects of your lighting. This is enabled from the viewport labels, as shown in Figure 3.3. If your equipment can handle hardware shading with your current scene, selecting the Illuminate With Scene Lights option and the Enable Exposure Control In Viewport option can greatly speed up the process of lighting your scenes.

FIGURE 3.3
The Enable Exposure Control In Viewport option in the viewport menu

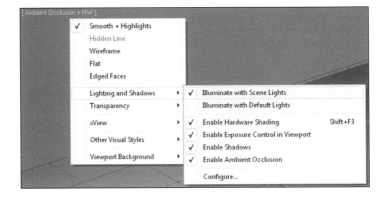

The mr Photographic control, like the Logarithmic control, will add a gamma of 2.2 to your rendered output. However, unlike the Logarithmic control, it will disable its own gamma correction and use the global gamma settings if they are defined. The use of global gamma correction settings is encouraged with the mr Photographic control and discouraged with the Logarithmic control, at least for output gamma.

PRESETS

The Preset drop-down list gives you some common scene lighting scenarios, as shown in Figure 3.4. Choosing a preset provides an exposure setting to get your scene in the right exposure range. As you will see throughout this chapter, using settings that relate to real-world values and real-world ranges gives you a realistic starting point for your scenes.

FIGURE 3.4
Exposure preset settings for the mr Photographic exposure control

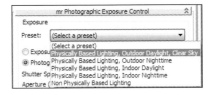

EXPOSURE VALUE

The Exposure Value (EV) setting is the easiest way to adjust your overall exposure; it has a range of –6 to 16. Each whole number change doubles the brightness (with a lower EV number) or cuts the brightness in half (with higher EV numbers), and adjusting in increments of 0.5 or less is a reasonable approach. EV is the result of computing the Shutter Speed, Aperture, and Film Speed values, discussed in the next section. If you are trying to match the exposure of a background image, try the Photographic group of settings; otherwise, use EV. The mr Photographic control's setting can be animated, which is great for animations that go between different lighting levels (outdoors to indoors, for instance). Animating the EV will create individual animation keys for the Shutter Speed, Aperture, and Film Speed settings, and not the EV setting itself.

For exterior daylight scenes using the default Daylight System settings, you might want to use an EV of 14.75 to boost the brightness a bit. However, some details might be too bright and lost; see the mr Photographic setting Highlights (Burn), described later in this chapter.

For an interior scene without daylight, your EV might be between 1.0 and 8.0, depending on the brightness of your lights. An EV of 10 or slightly more is common for a bright interior that includes an exterior daylight component. If you find you are going to extremes in EV settings, much beyond one or two numbers of a preset, you might want to look at the brightness values of your lights to ensure they are in a normal range for the type of illumination you are simulating and look for things such as duplicate Daylight Systems, including within XRefs and container objects.

Looking Outside from Inside

One common issue I hear from clients and users alike is that they cannot see the outside daylight when they are looking at the world from inside their scene. They expect that the renderings should work like their perception of brightness, but there is a simple explanation as to why this is not the case.

The human eye, when you look from your inside environment to outdoors, will adjust your eye's "exposure" to handle the bright light, and you do not notice that everything in the periphery is now dimmer as a result. You only see the now correctly exposed exterior, and as your eyes return to the interior, they instantly adjust again, and you do not notice the now overexposed exterior.

A camera, in contrast, looks at a wide area, and we are forced to choose an exposure that either works for the interior illumination or works for the exterior illumination. If exposure is set for being able to see outdoors, then the interior will be dark, and if it's set for the indoors, then the exterior will be overexposed. The image shown here is a split image where the right side was set for an interior exposure and the left side was set for an outside environment.

For clients who need to be able to see inside and outside in their images, there are two approaches: either light the interior and exterior to the same brightness of light or render the exterior separate from the interior and composite the two in a product such as 3ds Max Composite or Adobe Photoshop. If your goal is a correct simulation of daylight in interior lighting, then obviously the second option is best because you maintain the correct values of your lighting.

A number of projects I've had over the years, including animations, have had to be produced via compositing because the client wanted to see outdoors. The advantage with separate images is that you can balance the brightness of each separately in 3ds Max Composite and get the look your client needs. Rendering to an HDRI format and compositing in the new 3ds Max Composite application is covered in Chapter 10, "mental ray for Design."

PHOTOGRAPHIC EXPOSURE

These settings simulate the controls and properties of a single-lens reflex (SLR) camera and film. Unless you are trying to simulate a specific setting, the EV setting is the simplest way to control the brightness of your rendering. The camera-like settings for the mr Photographic include Shutter Speed, Aperture (f-stop), and Film Speed (ISO):

Shutter Speed   This is the amount of time the virtual shutter is open, exposing the "film" of mental ray. Unlike a real camera, this has no relation to the settings for motion blur. Typical camera settings are 1 (the most light), 2, 4, 8, 15, 30, 60, 125, 250, 500, and 1000 (the least light). Each typical setting shown represents a halving or doubling of the light reaching the rendering, and mental ray allows any speed value.

Aperture (f-stop)   This is the size of the opening to allow light into the virtual film. In the real world, the Aperture setting affects the depth-of-field (DOF) lens effect; however, this Aperture setting has no effect on DOF. Typical f-stop settings are 1.4 (the most light), 2, 2.8, 4, 5.6, 8, 11, 16, and 22 (the least light). Each typical setting shown represents a halving or doubling of the light reaching the rendering, similar to the typical shutter speed settings in a camera, and mental ray allows any value to be used.

Film Speed (ISO)   This is the speed of the virtual film. Lower numbers (such as 100 and 200) produce darker images compared to higher typical settings of 400 and 1000. ISO 100 is best for outdoors, and 400 is better for indoor photography because of the sensitivity of the film. mental ray does not simulate the graininess of film, so you would need to add film grain as a post-process.

IMAGE CONTROL

The Image Control section of the mr Photographic settings includes the more subtle adjustments required to fine-tune the look of your image. The section provides an interactive graph to show how the controls affect the image brightness, as shown in Figure 3.5, and at the upper right in the graph you can see a curve that represents the effect of the Highlights (Burn), Midtones, and Shadows settings. The graph in Figure 3.5 is not linear from lower left to upper right and peaks before the end of the graph, which indicates that the image is pushed to 100 percent brightness by the Highlights (Burn) feature before it reaches full brightness.

FIGURE 3.5
Image Control settings
for the mr Photographic
control

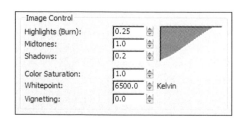

Highlights (Burn)   To simulate a natural photographic effect, this feature pushes bright areas of the rendered image to white, as shown in Figure 3.6, and as you can see in comparing these images, it can affect your entire image. The default is usually fine; however, for some renderings, the blown-out pixels might be undesirable, particularly if you lose details in product renders and outdoor scenes, for instance. For outdoor scenes with water, it can add nice bright highlights that follow the peaks of the waves. Setting Highlights (Burn) to 0.0 will slightly speed up rendering, and for the two images in Figure 3.6, it was approximately 15 percent faster.

FIGURE 3.6
Comparison of no highlights (top), default 0.25 (middle), and settings at 0.50 (bottom)

Midtones   With a default setting of 1.0 (no effect), the Midtones setting can shift the rendered image's midtone color range brighter (a setting greater than 1.0) or darker (a setting less than 1.0). Slight variations in this value can help to bring out details in renderings with many dark regions or can bring down a light render without affecting the brightness on the high end. Remember that gamma correction also affects midtones, so set that correctly before you determine a need to adjust this value. Figure 3.7 compares different Midtones values.

FIGURE 3.7
Comparison of Midtones setting at 0.5 (left), 1.0 (middle), and 1.5 (right)

Whitepoint   A value in degrees Kelvin, this corrects for tint in light sources and is similar to the white balance setting on cameras. In general, this should be set to match the color of the lighting in your scene to make the colors render as white light.

The default of 6500 Kelvin is perfect for exterior daylight scenes and when using interior lights with the D65 lighting reference color. For interior scenes, Autodesk recommends a Whitepoint setting of 3700K. You can make slight adjustments to the Whitepoint setting to help add "warmth" to an otherwise sterile-looking image.

As Figure 3.8 shows, for incandescent light templates, the rendering is very yellow when you use the default 6500K Whitepoint setting.

Vignetting   There is a darkening around the edges of this image that can make the image appear photographic in nature. This effect is usually attributed to inexpensive lenses and not high-end equipment, and like with lens flares in Photoshop, you should use them sparingly. Figure 3.9 shows the Light Lab scene with Vignetting set to 20.0.

Notice in Figure 3.9 how the exposure darkens toward the outside of the image and allows you to see the outdoor scene through the right windows despite the center windows being overly bright. The image has a "flash effect" feel, as if the lighting were focused into the center of the field of view.

Next I cover Physical Scale, which allows you to work either in a photometric environment where lighting uses physical units or in a unitless environment where standard lights can be scaled into a photometric range.

FIGURE 3.8
Scene with incandescent light preset and using the default Whitepoint setting of 6500K (above) and again with a 3000K Whitepoint setting (below)

FIGURE 3.9
The Light Lab scene with Vignetting set to 20.0

PHYSICAL SCALE

The Physical Scale setting has two modes of operation: Physical Units and Unitless. The Physical Scale setting should be left in the default Physical Units setting when using exclusively photo-metric lights, Daylight Systems and the mr Physical Sky feature. High Dynamic Range Image (HDRI) background images, when properly calibrated to Candela/m^2, will appear correctly in your environment when you use the Physical Units option; however, Low Dynamic Range Images (LDRIs) and some HDRI will need either a Gamma & Gain wrapper map added as a par-ent to the background bitmap, the bitmap Output value increased, or the Unitless option used to scale the image brightness.

The Unitless setting is similar to the Logarithmic control's Physical Scale setting, and it acts as a candela multiplier for the intensity setting of standard lights, environment/background images, and self-illuminated materials. If used, it is typically set to the intensity of your bright-est light source.

For a scene with a Daylight System the Unitless value should be 90,000 to 100,000 for scaling lights into a sunlight range or 3500 for scaling just an environment map. For an exterior night or interior scene, Unitless can be anywhere from 25 to 3200 or more. You can find a scene that dem-onstrates these settings in the `\ProjectFolders\03_Light_Shadow_Exp\scenes\` project folder on your DVD; the file is called mr `PEC_HDRI_Max2009.max`.

The last exposure control I cover is the Pseudo Color exposure control, which allows you to use a scaled gradient across your rendered image to represent the brightness striking or reflected from surfaces represented by the image pixels.

The Pseudo Color Exposure Control

This exposure control allows you to visualize the *luminance* (light reflection from a surface) or *illuminance* (light striking a surface) within your scene. In 3ds Max/Design 2010 and newer, the Pseudo Color Exposure Control gives you a real-time preview of these values on your geometry within your viewport when using Hardware Viewport Shading and the Enable Exposure Control options, described later in this chapter.

To assist you in exploring this feature, I have provided a sample scene on the DVD in the `\ProjectFolders\03_Light_Shadow_Exp` folder. For the best results with all the examples on the DVD, copy the contents of the project folder to a local hard drive for editing.

Perform the following steps to configure this scene for use with the Pseudo Color exposure control:

1. Open the file `.\scenes\LightLab\LightLab_2010.max`.

2. Press 8 to open the exposure control settings.

3. Choose the Pseudo Color option.

4. Set the maximum value to 1500.

5. Render the exposure control's preview window to evaluate the settings, and adjust if necessary.

6. Press Shift+F3 to enable hardware shading.

7. From the viewport menus at the upper left, select the Illuminate With Scene Lights and Enable Exposure Control In Viewport options. You should now have a color approximation of the results of the Pseudo Color exposure control in your viewport.

8. Render the view to see the actual results. With 3ds Max/Design 2011, in addition to your rendered view, you also get a separate rendered window that includes the color scale for the image, as shown in Figure 3.10.

FIGURE 3.10

Pseudo Color illuminance (lx) rendering

The complete scene is available in the Chapter 3 project folder as `.\scenes\LightLab\ LightLab_PseudoColor_2010.max`.

Set your exposure to match your target scene, such as Interior Night or Exterior Day, to give you a good starting point for determining the settings for light in your scene. In the next section, I cover some general rules and tips for adjusting and using photometric lights.

Working with Light Objects

There are two basic classes of lights in 3ds Max/Design: standard and photometric. Other than some shadow modes and settings, mental ray fully supports these lights. The photometric lights use real-world parameters such as lumens, candela, lux, and foot-candles to represent the intensity of the light, and they always follow the laws of physics for the natural decay of light over distance, namely, the inverse-square law. For a modern, photorealistic workflow, it is recommended to use photometric lights for almost all purposes; they are required for physically accurate results, they are required when using the Lighting Analysis tools, and they produce energy-accurate rendered results when combined with the Autodesk ProMaterials and Arch & Design materials.

Photometric lights can optionally use manufacturer-supplied photometric web files to reproduce accurate intensity and distribution of light from a specific bulb or fixture. This can greatly simplify your lighting setup, because you are working with a representation of real-world light objects that will behave just as their physical counterparts. Not only is this easier to set up, but it enhances the realism and accuracy of your rendering. All photometric lights can act as area lights, including 2D and 3D shapes, whereas you must use the mental ray standard lights to get area effects.

Standard lights use multiplier values to control the intensity of the light and, by default, do not decay over distance; standard lights might optionally use a linear decay or the natural inverse-square decay options. The default of No Decay renders fast; however, this allows the light to travel forever unless you enable shadows and you block the light with some geometry or unless the light is limited by the Far Attenuation setting. The Linear decay setting is faster than the inverse-square but does not produce realistic results. Figure 3.11 shows a standard light with default options for decay and a photometric light of a similar intensity.

FIGURE 3.11
Interior scene with default setting for a standard spotlight at left and a photometric spotlight of the same intensity on right

The light on the left is at full intensity all the way to the floor and produces a lot of reflected light from the floor onto the surrounding walls. The light on the right decays quickly and naturally and results in the correct illumination at the floor and no excessive reflected light. Standard lights do have the advantage that they can evenly light an area when no decay is used and allow the use of negative multiplier values, which can remove light from an area and allow you to project shadow images. This negative-light capability allows you to turn off shadow casting for objects such as trees and instead project its shadow image onto the ground. This renders much faster than calculated shadows; however, overlapping shadows tend to be darker within overlapped regions of negative light.

Standard lights are not the focus of this book because they can break the laws of physics and affect the accuracy of not only your renderings but also lighting analysis. Refer to books such as *Mastering Autodesk 3ds Max Design 2010* for more on standard lighting techniques.

MIXING STANDARD AND PHOTOMETRIC LIGHTS

As a general rule, you should never mix standard and photometric lights in a scene if the goal is an accurate lighting simulation with predictable results. If you have issues with lighting or rendering and are not sure why, look for standard lights mixed with photometrics and replace the standard lights.

Before I cover the settings and use of Photometric lights in 3ds Max, I next cover a few ground rules for lighting any scene.

Eight Simple Rules for Lighting Your Scene

Half the battle when lighting a scene is understanding the tools at hand, and the other half is having an efficient workflow to help simplify the lighting process. These rules — guidelines really — are the things I consider as I work with lights within my scenes, and they might assist you with the process of lighting.

Start in Darkness…

…and work with lights in isolation. This is the number-one rule, particularly for interior scenes. Your test-renders will be faster, you can evaluate the effect that one individual light will have on your scene, you can better evaluate shadow quality, and you will be able to tweak settings for light Attenuation and Shadow Samples without having to contend with the confusion of multiple light and shadow sources. After one light is adjusted, turn it off, and then work with the next light in isolation. It is also important to set a reasonable exposure control EV that's representative of the scene you are lighting (Indoor Night or Exterior Daylight, for example) before you add and adjust any lights.

TROUBLESHOOTING PROBLEM LIGHTING

When I am confronted with a scene that has lighting issues, it is usually because the artist began lighting their scenes by immediately adding lights everywhere they were indicated in the plan and then tried to make various adjustments to all the lights at once.

Or, when faced with unsatisfactory results, they just kept adding lights in an attempt to improve the unacceptable render. The additional lights just made it more difficult to control scene illumination. The first thing I do is return to darkness — turn all the lights off but one — and work in isolation. If there is still illumination with all lights off, then I ensure that XRef scenes and containers are not bringing in unwanted illumination.

With the use of photometric lights for architectural scenes, adding many lights at once is perhaps not as disastrous as it once was, because you are now working with physical values for the lighting intensity. This is the case with imported Revit scenes, where all lights are photometric and set to values related to the fixture specified. However, with all lights in place, you still deal with long renders, and it will make it harder to see the effect of changes to individual settings.

One additional thing to keep in mind is that you might not need every light in your scene that is specified by the designer or within a fixture, and you might be able to eliminate or limit the effect of some lights that do not contribute much to the rendered image beyond additional render time (see the "Far Attenuation" section later in this chapter). Replacing a set of lamps in a group of stadium lights with a single point or area light can significantly reduce render time.

Use Photometric Lights

For realistic and easily controllable lighting effects, the exclusive use of photometric lights (combined with real-world exposure controls) produces the best results in an understandable and controllable manner. There are certainly times where a standard light comes in handy, for instance, if you need to evenly illuminate a surface and do not want the inverse-square effect of decay or want a directional substitute for ambient light. In these instances, you probably understand the results you are trying to achieve and the pitfalls of working with standard lights. As a general practice, however, you should avoid standard lights and not use the None option for decay.

Related to this rule is a tip to use a Light Meter helper object to determine the brightness of surfaces in your scene. With the Pseudo Color exposure control, you have already seen one method for determining lighting levels on all your surfaces. In a similar way, placing Light Meter objects at floor or tabletop level gives brightness values that can be used to determine whether you have acceptable light levels. Figure 3.12 shows the Light Lab scene with a Light Meter helper, which shows the resulting illumination from a single light source.

FIGURE 3.12
Light Lab scene with a Light meter measuring total illumination at the floor. Red indicates 700lx in this case.

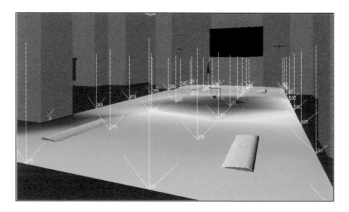

Each arrow on a light meter shows a sampled lux value. You can create light meters by selecting Lighting Analysis ➤ Create ➤ Light Meter. With the Light Meter objects, you can work backward from desired floor light levels to then adjust your light's intensity values.

Use Shadows

Shadows create depth in your scene, add contrast to set objects apart and define edges, help to connect your objects to their surroundings, and define relative scale. Without shadows, you cannot tell whether something is tiny and floating right in front of the camera or is large and far away. In the Defaults And UI Switcher dialog box, covered in Chapter 1, there are four default options — two options for 3ds Max and two for DesignVIZ. The two options for 3ds Max have all newly created lights with shadows disabled by default, and as it says in the dialog box, this is done for placing highlights and adding fill lights. This need for shadowless lights is certainly a potential requirement in the DesignVIZ field, too; however, most lights should have shadows enabled.

Use Hardware Viewport Shading to Preview Lighting

One of the best ways to previsualize your lights and shadows is to use the viewport Hardware Shading mode available in 3ds Max/Design 2010 and newer. The use of a high-performance workstation-class video card such as the NVIDIA Quadro series combined with Hardware Shading mode can simplify and greatly speed the process of lighting your scene. Because hardware shading works with your exposure control, it gives you real-time feedback of lighting adjustments that closely match the direct lighting of your final rendering.

Hardware-shaded viewport performance for orbiting and moving in a large scene might be an issue for you, depending on your video hardware and scene, and does not replace nonhardware legacy smooth or hidden-line shading for fast interaction with your scene. This technology is seeing rapid development at both Autodesk and mental images; mental ray 3.8 now supports the iray interactive lighting technology with global illumination (perfect for design visualization), and 3ds Max/Design 2011 continues to improve the features and speed of hardware shading, particularly with mental ray materials. See www.mastering-mentalray.com for my blog on the latest technology.

To enable hardware shading, press Shift+F3 or click the third viewport configuration button in your view, and then choose the Lighting And Shadows menu option. Select Illuminate With Scene Lights, Enable Exposure Control In Viewport, and Enable Shadows.

Use Light Assemblies

An *assembly* is a combination of Geometry and Light objects, similar to a group object or container, which allows you to create a single object that is easy to place and adjust in your scene. An assembly encapsulates the light and geometry and provides a simple dimmer-like Multiplier value on the Modify tab, together with a color swatch for a filter. For an assembly to work, you must create a Wired parameter connection from the light's Multiplier (standard light) or Dimmer parameter (photometric light) to the Assembly object's Dimmer parameter.

You can find the menus for creating and controlling an assembly in the Group ➤ Assembly top pull-down menus. I discuss the light's Dimmer options in the upcoming "Intensity" section. Several bonus assembly example files and instructions for creating assemblies are provided for you on the DVD in the \ProjectFolders\03_Light_Shadow_Exp\scenes\Assemblies\ folder.

Use Instance Lights with Common Properties

When you create clones of an object (you hold down Shift while transforming objects to create a clone), selecting the Instance clone option creates a two-way connection between the original and the new cloned object(s). Changing one instanced clone's parameters changes all others. Any time you have a light or assembly that has the same parameters as another in your scene, consider using the Instance option. In the Light Lister (Tools ➤ Light Lister), the lights are then grouped together with a single set of parameters, making it easy to adjust your scene.

Before you clone any object, it is good practice to first name the object based on its purpose or designation in a plan. For a light or assembly object, shorten names to, for instance, PL-F12-01, which in this case would mean "Photometric Light Fixture type 12 object number one." The shortened name helps with readability in the Light Lister when displaying the light name within the dialog box. Be sure to add the -01 to the suffix so the process of cloning does not change the F12 to F13, and so on.

As always, work with a single light in isolation whenever possible prior to cloning. I will often delete cloned lights, adjust one light in isolation, and re-create the clones. Using placeholders at light locations and the Clone And Align tool assists with this process. Currently, scenes imported via the FBX (Filmbox) format from Revit models will not have instanced lights despite using the same fixture within Revit. Using the Clone And Align tool in 3ds Max/Design can assist in placing new instanced lights.

Avoid Ambient Light

Ambient light refers to light that comes from all directions and affects all surfaces. In the bad old days of computer graphics, adding this omnipresent light helped compensate for the lack of any indirect illumination tools, and it brightened areas that did not receive any direct lighting whatsoever. You can find the Ambient setting in the Environment And Effects dialog box (press 8 to open the dialog box).

Older version of 3ds Max shipped with Ambient set to a brightness of 11 (out of 255), and 3ds Max/Design currently ships with this setting at a value of 0. Ambient illumination in 3ds Max/Design is an Environment option; press the 8 key to toggle the Environment Settings dialog box, and select the color swatch to change the ambient light value.

You should never use the Ambient setting to increase the brightness of your scene, because it reduces contrast, "flattens" the appearance of your renderings, takes away control from scene lights, and lightens shadows. I have seen users use this to help light a scene, adjusting it as if they were adjusting a scene light, and it always produces poor results. Just say no. If you need to boost the illumination of your scene, then adding small spherical or spot-shaped lights to specific areas makes the additional light more controllable and natural-looking in your rendering. Just like lighting a set for a television show or movie or setting up lighting for a professional architectural photo shoot, you *can* have lights that do not have a representation in a physical object in your scene, and depending on your goals, you can add lights to improve your overall lighting as needed. Just remember to adjust in isolation!

Use the Light Lister to Manage Lights

This is more of a tip than a rule. The Light Lister is another often-overlooked tool that can assist you when you work with numerous lights; you can find it by selecting Tools ➤ Light Lister. In the Light Lister dialog box that opens, shown in Figure 3.13, you can select lights in your scene by simply clicking the far-left button (the currently selected light object is shown with a blue button), and you can easily toggle the On/Off state of the lights via the On check box for working in isolation.

FIGURE 3.13
The Light Lister
dialog box

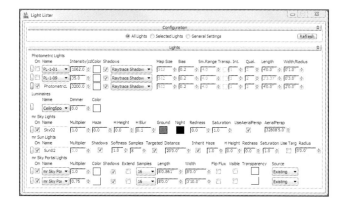

Any changes made in the Light Lister are reflected in the scene immediately; however, any Command Panel changes are not updated here automatically, and you need to click the Refresh button to reread the settings from the scene. The Light Lister will show any instanced lights as one light with a drop-down list, as shown for PL-1-09 in Figure 3.13. Keeping the light name short helps you find the light you need within the Light Lister.

Now that I have set some ground rules for lighting scenes, I cover some of the settings of the photometric lights.

Understanding Photometric Lights

In the photometric light user interface in the command panel, the first section provides a drop-down menu to choose a preset template, as shown in Figure 3.14.

FIGURE 3.14

Light presets (templates) for many common lamps

You can modify and extend this list and the parameters returned by editing the `Photometric LightTemplates.ini` file in your user's local configuration at `C:\Users\<username>\AppData\Local\Autodesk\3dsMaxDesign\2011 - 64bit\enu\plugcfg\`. The INI file contains a short description and a call to a script in the `\PhotometricLights` subfolder, which then sets up the light. The INI files are where you add or remove items from the Templates drop-down list, and the individual scripts are where you would change parameters for a particular light. Always make a backup of any file before you make changes; however, originals are in your local 3ds Max/Design installation at `C:\Program Files\Autodesk\3ds Max Design 2011\plugcfg`.

These presets will change not only the intensity of your light to match the wattage shown in the drop-down list but also the light color temperature and distribution pattern. I will usually tweak these to some degree after choosing a template.

In the next section, I cover the use of shadows in mental ray, including shadow maps, mental ray shadow maps, and ray traced shadows.

Understanding Shadow Types

The available shadow types for both photometric and standard lights are Advanced Ray Trace, mental ray Shadow Maps, Area Shadows, Shadow Map, and Ray Trace Shadow.

Although there are five types of shadows listed in the Shadow drop-down list, only the mental ray Shadow Maps, Shadow Map, and Ray Traced Shadows options are supported by mental ray. You can select the other options, but mental ray will render those as ray-traced shadows regardless of the setting and show a warning in the Render Message dialog box.

SHADOW GLOBAL SETTINGS

When the Use Global Settings check box is selected (it's on by default), any changes you make to the shadow settings for this light will affect all other lights that have the Use Global Settings check box selected. Be certain to deselect the Use Global Settings setting in order to change only the current light.

It is important to note that for photometric lights, the ray-traced shadows are generally the best choice for high-quality renderings. Using the Use Global Settings option allows you to choose fast shadow maps for test-renders for all lights and then switch to higher-quality ray-traced shadows for production. The mental ray Shadow Maps option should be used only in certain circumstances, as with hair and fur and when producing motion blur.

There are three types of shadows that mental ray supports: shadow maps, mental ray shadow maps, and ray-traced shadows.

SHADOW MAPS

A *shadow map* approximates a shadow by tracing a rough outline of the geometry in your scene onto a bitmap, from the point of view of the light creating the shadow. The advantage to shadow maps (as compared to ray-traced shadows) is that they are quick to compute and give soft edges to shadows via the Sample Range setting. They can also be cached (stored) and reused via mental ray settings in the Render Setup dialog box (the Shadows and Displacement settings on the Renderer tab). The disadvantage to shadow maps is that they consume memory at render time, do not produce sharp shadows without high settings, and do not handle transparent objects — all objects are seen as opaque.

USING SHADOW MAPS IN MENTAL RAY

I do not recommended using Shadow maps with mental ray unless there is a specific reason to use them. All lights using shadows maps are seen as spherical by mental ray for purposes of creating the shadows, even if it is a spotlight, and generally require very high Size settings to produce good results. 3ds Max defaults to Shadow Maps whereas 3ds Max Design defaults to Raytraced. Any scene using mental ray in 3ds Max should consider switching the Global Setting to Raytraced. If you see unexplainable splotches and poor shadows on your rendered images, examine your shadow settings in the Light Lister.

Size The default dimension for the shadow bitmap is 512×512 pixels. This setting is adequate, for instance, for shadows in a relative small area from a spotlight and is most likely much too small for uniform diffuse (hemispherical) and especially uniform spherical lights.

In mental ray all shadow mapped lights are seen as omnidirectional and the default single 512×512-pixel map is wrapped in a sphere projected in all directions. As a result it will look very blotchy because there isn't enough resolution to adequately represent the shadows. Doubling or quadrupling the value is reasonable, but remember that doubling the size quadruples the bitmap area because you double in two dimensions (2 times the width × 2 times height), and it also quadruples the memory used by these maps. Quadrupling the map to 2048×2048 gives you 16 times the memory use (4×4). Each pixel of the map takes up 4 bytes of memory, making the map 2048×2048×4=16 megabytes of RAM.

If you have many lights that use shadow maps, then this can add up to considerable memory use. Running out of memory causes Windows to use virtual memory, which is an order-of-magnitude slower than RAM. Ray-traced shadows are generally recommended for use with photometrics because of the large shadow map size a photometric light would need for accurate shadows.

Bias   Bias is a shadow offset based on the size of your scene, moving the shadow slightly away from the object creating the shadow. The default setting is 1.0. How far the shadow is actually moved is determined by 3ds Max/Design based on the extents of your scene, and different size scenes will get different values for what Bias = 1.0 actually offsets. For many large scenes, the default of 1.0 can offset the shadows off your model, and you will have missing shadows under window ledges, overhangs, and so forth, as well as a disconnect in the shadow where objects rest on other surfaces.

If you use shadow maps, try turning down the Bias setting to 0.1 or less, and do some tests with your scene to see the effect. What value to use depends on the scale of your scene, the shadow map settings, and angles between lights and objects, and it may take experimentation. Too small of a value can cause shadow *leakage*, where shadows are seen on the lit side of objects, and can result in moiré patterns and streaking. Too high of a value can cause shadows to be disconnected.

The 3ds Max/Design help documentation states that the Bias setting is ignored when using mental ray, but that is not the case in 3ds Max/Design 2010 and newer. Bias is always ignored for ray-traced shadows, however.

Sample Range   Sample Range is blurring of the shadow map to take out the blockiness that otherwise results from the low resolution of the map. This can make the shadow appear larger than the area it actually represents.

Absolute Map Bias   This forces the Bias value to use 3ds Max/Design units rather than an offset value automatically determined by the scale of your scene. This might give more consistent shadow results if you are animating objects that would change the extents of your scene.

2-Sided Shadows   mental ray always renders two-sided shadows for shadow maps. This is important for thin-shell objects, where the interior of the shell needs to create shadows.

EXCLUDING AND INCLUDING OBJECTS

A light's Exclude/Include option either ignores certain objects (Exclude) or affects only certain objects (Include) for light and/or shadows. This is a terrific feature for highlighting important objects in your scene or boosting illumination on an object without creating shadows.

Excluding a light from shadow-casting does not work when you use shadow maps with mental ray. Use ray-traced shadows instead. You can find the Exclude/Include option by pressing the Exclude button in the light's settings within the command panel

---

The next shadow mode is the mental ray shadow map, which adds capabilities to the simple shadow map.

MENTAL RAY SHADOW MAPS

The mental ray shadow map (also called a *detail shadow map* in the mental ray world) has an advantage over the standard shadow map in that it supports transparent shadows, can contain color information, and in many cases is the preferred shadow mode to use whenever rendering hair and fur or when producing motion blur. Figure 3.15 shows the parameters for the mental ray shadow maps.

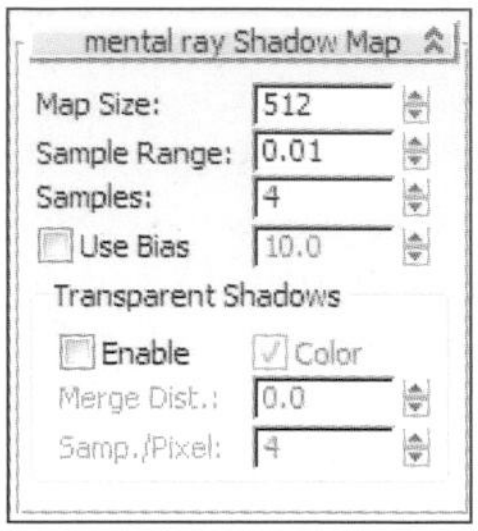

FIGURE 3.15
The "mental ray
Shadow Map" settings

The mental ray shadow maps, combined with the Fast Rasterizer rendering option, may generate rendering artifacts when using ray-traced effects such as reflections and refractions and is thus not ideal for architectural interiors and product renderings.

RAY-TRACED SHADOWS

Ray-traced shadows are created by casting a ray from a sample being rendered back into the scene to a rendered surface and then on to light sources. Figure 3.16 shows the parameters for ray-traced shadows.

FIGURE 3.16
The Ray Traced
Shadow Params
settings

Anywhere a light ray is blocked from a light source, a shadow is generated. Ray-traced shadows are very crisp and do not have soft edges without using area lights. Their advantages are that they are accurate, support transparency, and take little memory at render time. Their disadvantage is that they take more time to calculate than the approximated shadow maps. Ray-traced shadows are the default shadow type for 3ds Max Design's DesignVIZ defaults and should be used for most purposes, particularly with uniform spherical and uniform diffuse light distribution.

The settings for ray-traced shadows include Ray Bias, 2-Sided Shadows, and Max Quadtree Depth.

Ray Bias   This is ignored with mental ray. Normally this would offset the shadow from its objects, similar to a shadow map bias setting.

2-Sided Shadows   This is ignored with mental ray and ray-traced shadows; they're always one sided. Use a two-sided material, which is also the default setting of Backface Cull = Off for an Arch & Design material. ProMaterials are two-sided by default.

Max Quadtree Depth   Slightly larger values can improve ray trace times at the expense of memory use and a slight increase in the time needed to generate the quadtree. What values to use for a particular scene depends on the geometry and is not intuitive; each scene requires experimentation. For complex scenes, setting this value to 9 may greatly speed ray-traced shadow calculation.

Light distribution types, which I discuss next, allow you to control and optimize the area that a light influences.

ADDITIONAL SHADOW CONTROLS

In addition to the individual shadow types used by lights, there are three shadow-processing modes in the mental ray Renderer tab in the Render Settings dialog box: Simple, Sort, and Segments. See Chapter 4, "Rendering," for more information on these settings, which can affect your rendering and potentially optimize your shadows.

Working with Light Distribution (Type) Settings

Photometric lights have the ability to distribute the light in a variety of patterns, and you control the direction of illumination via the Light Distribution drop-down menu, located in the light properties on the Modify tab of the command panel. Each type has an impact on render time, and different shapes will give you vastly different illumination levels in a scene.

There are four light distribution types:

Uniform Spherical This default distribution type is an omnidirectional light source, and mental ray must calculate light and shadows in every direction from that source.

Uniform Diffuse The Uniform Diffuse setting provides a hemispherical distribution and renders slightly faster than the spherical distribution because geometry behind the light can ignore the light. Test-renders on an array of nine lights gave this a speed approximately 9.5 percent faster than the Uniform Spherical setting and provided half the illumination.

Spot Spot is a good option because you can control where the light and shadows are placed, minimize the area used for the shadows, and achieve crisp results with minimum time and memory. The speed for this light, for my test, was approximately 7 percent faster than Uniform Spherical.

Photometric Web This is the best method for accurately simulating a specific bulb or fixture; it has the drawback of always being a point source and never an area light. This point effect is most noticeable at the light source and in shadows. This light type rendered the slowest in my testing — 18 percent slower than Uniform Spherical.

The next portion of the photometric light parameters are the Color, Intensity, and Attenuation settings, as found in the command panel.

Working with Light Color, Intensity, and Attenuation Settings

The Light, Color, and Attenuation series of controls allow you to replicate real-world bulbs and fixtures by simulating the natural color of specific bulb technologies, specify intensity in real-world units, and additionally limit the light's influence to reduce render time. To simulate natural and artificial lighting, you can choose the color of the light from a list of bulb presets and also as a specific color defined in degrees Kelvin.

COLOR AND COLOR PRESETS

The drop-down list of presets for Color has a number of choices for common bulbs, as shown in Figure 3.17. Incandescent lights are yellow orange, lights that are cool have a shift more toward blue, and warm lights have a shift toward red.

FIGURE 3.17
Color presets

The color of lights greatly affects the color of your rendered surfaces, and the colors of your surfaces are always the combination of the light color and surface properties. If you are not concerned that your light represents a real-world bulb technology, then choose one of the two Reference White presets; D50 is calibrated to 5000K, and D65 is set to 6500K.

COLOR TEMPERATURE AND DEGREES KELVIN

The color of a light source is often described as a value in degrees Kelvin, and this color value refers to an object called a *blackbody radiator* — an object that does not reflect any light energy at all, like the obelisk in *2001: A Space Odyssey*. If you heat a blackbody radiator object, however, it radiates light of a color that depends directly on the temperature of the blackbody object. Warm temperatures are below 3200 Kelvin and are shifted toward yellow and red. Cool color temperatures are shifted toward green and blue and are above 4000K. Colors between 3200K and 4000K are considered neutral-color light. Manufacturers typically supply the color temperatures of their lamps, and as you can see in Table 3.1, the color temperature might vary quite a bit for a given description or lamp technology.

TABLE 3.1: Common Color Temperatures

LIGHT SOURCE	COLOR TEMPERATURE
Match flame, candle	1500K–1850K
High pressure sodium, heat lamp	2200K–2450K
40W Incandescent lamp	2680K
100W incandescent lamp	2800K–3000K
200W incandescent lamp	3000K
100W tungsten halogen, warm white fluorescent lamp	2850K–3000K

LIGHT SOURCE	COLOR TEMPERATURE
Sunrise/Sunset, warm (3K) metal halide, quartz stage lights	3200K
Photoflood lamps, tungsten professional lamp, projector, fluorescent lamp	3400K
Metal halide (Sky Clear), carbon arc lamp	4000K
Cool white fluorescent, moonlight, xenon arc lamp, morning	4100K–4300K
Daylight at horizon, D50 Reference White, natural white metal halide	5000K
Average noon daylight, electronic flash	5300K–6000K
"True Daylight" color-match tubes, D65 Reference White	6500K
Overcast daylight, daylight fluorescent lamp	6300K–7100K
Outdoor noon shade	8000K
Blue sky	9000K–20000K
Lightning	30000K

Twenty-two renderings, each using a different photometric light color preset, are provided for your reference in the ProjectFolders\03_Light_Shadow_Exp\renderoutput\Lights_Kelvin folder of the DVD. These images are white-balanced to 6500K.

WHITE-BALANCING IMAGES

Because videographers and photographers may "white-balance" or color-correct images and video, you may not see the color tint from a light in the final product from these professionals. Talk to your client, and unless your client is looking for a warm image, choosing a D50 or D65 Illuminate for your color temperature will give them what they imagine their space or product will look like. You may need to consider how lighting would be done for a professional photograph, rather than how a point-and-click photo would turn out in the real environment.

As mentioned previously in the section "The mr Photographic Exposure Control," you can white-balance your images in the mental ray Photographic exposure control by adjusting the Whitepoint setting.

INTENSITY

Light intensity for photometric lights is expressed in the following real-world units:

Lumens (lm)   This is a measurement of overall output/power of a light (*luminous flux*) in all directions. Imagine a sphere around the light collecting all the energy and measuring the result. A 60-watt bulb generates about 900lm.

Candela (cd)   This is a measurement of the maximum luminous intensity of the light in a particular direction, like you may measure in the real world with a light meter. A 60-watt bulb is about 70cd.

Lux (lx)   Measured at a specific distance (defaults to 1 meter), this is a measurement of the illuminance that passes through or strikes a surface. Lux is lumens per square meter. At 1 meter, a 60-watt bulb is 70lx, and daylight at ground level is 80,000lx.

These are international units, and in the Units Setup dialog box (Customize ➢ Units Setup), you can change lux to the American unit foot-candles. A lux is about 10.76 times the value of foot-candles.

Each unit represents a different way in which light is measured and what is being measured (power vs. intensity vs. illuminance), and you can switch between the units as needed at any time. Which set of units to use for a particular application depends entirely on the lighting values you are given from the designer or the values you can look up from a lamp manufacturer.

Setting the intensity to a reasonable value is important, and starting with a preset, or values from a manufacturer or this book, is a great place to start. The default intensity for a photometric light is 1500cd, which may be a rather bright light source for a small interior. In comparison, a 100-watt incandescent lamp is 139cd, and a 4′ pendent fluorescent lamp is 649cd (per the templates).

You can determine the intensity value for a specific wattage of bulb if you have the efficacy of the lamp, as specified by the manufacturer. This number, specified in lumens per watt, can be multiplied by the desired wattage to determine the lumens intensity for your light.

Table 3.2 shows a list of intensity values of some common light fixtures, in lumens per watt.

TABLE 3.2:   Lamp Lumens per Watt

LAMP TECHNOLOGY	LUMENS PER WATT
Fluorescent lamp	35–100
compact fluorescent	44–80
Halogen	12–36
Infrared	6–9
Incandescent	10–17
LED	30–60
LP sodium	90–180
Mercury vapor	50–140
Metal-halide	60–125
HP sodium	60–140
Theoretical maximum for a lamp	225

With this table, you could set your Intensity value to the lm (lumens) scale, as shown in Figure 3.18. Then set the value to the average for the kind of bulb you are using (such as 35 to 100lm/watt for fluorescent), and finally set the multiplier to the wattage you desire (times 100 because it is a percentage).

FIGURE 3.18
Example of using
lm/watt

The example in Figure 3.18 shows a 40W lamp at 35 lumens/watt × a dimmer value of 4,000 (4,000 = 40W * 100 for conversion to percentage) at the low end of the lm/watt scale for a fluorescent bulb, which gives a Resulting Intensity value of 1400.0lm. (As soon as you select the Multiplier check box, the lm intensity setting becomes disabled.)

For a 4′ 40-watt fluorescent tube, 3200lm is more typical and comes to 80lm/watt, closer to the maximum lm/watt range listed in Table 3.2.

You can combine dimming with the Incandescent Lamp Color Shift When Dimming option to give a real-world effect to a dimmed light; as it gets dimmer, the color becomes warmer, shifting toward red. If you just want to change the intensity as a percentage, then leave the color shift off (the default). A lighting designer typically chooses lamps of a specific technology to get a distinct color temperature and chooses wattages of lights to get a certain level of illumination without dimming, avoiding a shift in the color; if you need 100 watts of light, you do not choose a 200W light and dim it to 50 percent if you still expect it to be the correct color.

FAR ATTENUATION

The Far Attenuation feature allows you to control how far the light will travel; the settings are shown in Figure 3.19. This can considerably lower render times and should be used for a majority of photometric lights in your scene.

FIGURE 3.19
Far Attenuation
settings

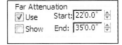

At the Start value, the light is at its normal intensity (including decay) and then performs a linear fade to black between Start and End values, in addition to the natural inverse-square decay. After the End distance, 3ds Max/Design ignores the light and does not generate shadows, speeding up rendering as mental ray ignores the light after the Far distance.

It is also another reason to adjust lights in isolation, because you can see how far the useful range of an individual light may be and can reduce the Far Attenuation value to optimize your render time without negatively affecting the image.

Because shadow casting doesn't happen after the End value, Far Attenuation assists greatly when adding fill lights with shadows that you want to affect your objects but not cast light or shadows on the surrounding environment. By controlling the spread of light and shadow, you can greatly reduce the occurrence of confusing shadows.

Shape and area shadows are for defining whether a light is a point shape — a 2D point in space with no area — or a 2D or 3D area light with dimensions and soft shadow effects. I discuss these in the next section.

Understanding Shape and Area Shadows

Photometric lights are, by default, infinitely small points in space and do not produce the soft shadows you have with real-world lights and fixtures. In the real world, all bulbs have some length and width and produce shadows with edges that gradually fade away as surfaces approach full illumination. With lights represented by points, however, the shadows have a sharp edge at the transition from shadow to light. Figure 3.20 shows the contrast between point and area lights.

FIGURE 3.20

A comparison between point shadows (shown on left) and area shadows (shown on right)

The area light version of this scene shows a gradient of light along the columns and a soft diffuse lighting effect along the ceiling. The area light image also took 6.5 times longer to render.

SHAPES

In addition to being a point in space, photometric lights can be a variety of 2D and 3D shapes, as shown in the drop-down list in Figure 3.21.

FIGURE 3.21

Shape/Area Shadows choices

Because all lamps in the real world have some dimension to them, an area light gives you the highest quality and feel to your images, including graduated lighting and soft shadows. Enabling shapes other than the default Point setting can greatly increase render times and might require an adjustment of the Shadow Samples setting for acceptable results. The more complex the light both in shape and samples, the more time it will take to render. The Point shape is the fastest; then come the 2D shapes of Line, Rectangle, and Disc and finally the 3D shapes. For test-renders on an array of nine lights (with a uniform spherical point light as a baseline of 100 percent), Line, Rectangle, and Disc shapes were approximately 165 percent the time of Point, and cylinder and Sphere were slightly slower at approximately 170 percent. A scene with scene states for your own testing is provided in the Chapter 3 project folder as `.\scenes\LightLab\LightLab_Shapes_2010.max`.

Area lights, despite the high impact on render time, can make a significant positive impact on your rendered image.

Shadow Samples

The Shadow Samples setting is only for the area lights, and the higher the number, the higher the quality of your shadows. The default setting is 32 samples, which generally gives good quality and performance. The quality of area shadows is affected by the settings for Samples Per Pixel (SPP), and with higher-quality SPP settings, you can often get away with moderate Shadow Sample settings.

You can adjust Shadow Samples on a global basis from the Soft Shadow Precision setting in the Rendered Frame window. One lighting workflow strategy is to set your light's individual Shadow Samples settings relative to one another (less important lights at 16, more important lights at 32, and higher-detail lights at 64) and then adjust them globally up or down from the Soft Shadow Precision settings. Figure 3.22 shows the Shadow Sample results from a single 24"-square spotlight at 2, 8, and 32 samples.

This scene is available for your own testing as `.\scenes\LightLab\LightLab_ShadowSamples_2010.max`. There are scene states for various configurations you can try. Full-size images are provided in `.\renderoutput\ShadowSamples`, with a chart of settings and render times for each shadow setting.

With the default setting of 32 samples as a 100 percent baseline render time, the test scene with light set to two samples had a 262 percent longer render time and was almost the slowest to render. Sixteen samples were 117 percent of the baseline, and 64 was 96 percent; with samples at 128, the time was only 102 percent of 32 samples. As I moved to very high settings, 512 samples were 178 percent, and 1,024 samples were 286 percent to baseline, which was the slowest render time. Because this scene has a single area light, more complex scenes with multiple light sources may experience additional render time increases. In a scene with many overlapping lights, very high Shadow Sample settings are rarely required because the shadows are softened by the direct illumination of other light sources. If you are using high SPP settings, then you can typically use moderate Shadow Samples settings, as shown in Figure 3.23.

Now that I have covered the core settings of a photometric light, I cover a special-case photometric light — the Daylight System.

FIGURE 3.22
Areas shadows with
Shadow Samples set
at 2, 8, and 32

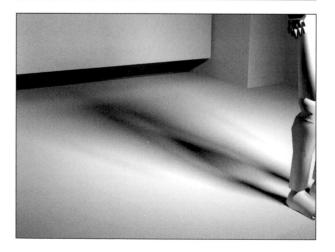

FIGURE 3.23
Area Shadow Samples
at 8 and SPP presets
at Medium, High, and
Very High

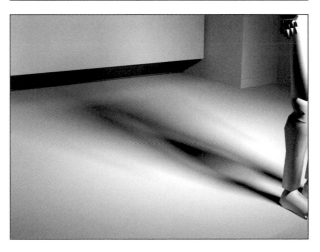

Introducing Daylight Systems

The Daylight System is a complex assembly-like object that combines two lights that simulate the direct illumination of the sun and diffuse illumination of the sky, simulating a particular place, date, and time, as defined in the Motion tab of the command panel. The Daylight System greatly simplifies the setup of outdoor lighting and produces exceptional results when combined with the mr Physical Sky environment map and the mr Photographic exposure control.

With the Daylight System, you can animate time and date to produce sunlight studies and show the position of the sun and building shadows over the course of days, weeks, or months. An example of an animated Daylight System is provided for you in the Chapter 3 project folder on your DVD in .\scenes\Daylight_Progression_2010.max. A Daylight System can use weather data files from the site http://apps1.eere.energy.gov/buildings/energyplus/cfm/Weather_data.cfm to produce accurate illumination from collected sky measurements, which is particularly useful for re-creating conditions for forensic animations.

The Daylight System supports three sky models, which are different ways that the mr Sky object produces illumination.

SKY MODELS

A *sky model* is the method in which the sky produces illumination. There are three sky models available with the mental ray mr Sky light:

Haze Driven   This model produces a nice blue sky and is great for beautiful architectural renderings. However, it is not intended for lighting analysis or for true physical accuracy. It does have a 24-hour usable time range, unlike the Perez and CIE models.

Perez All-Weather   The Perez All-Weather sky model is a physically accurate sky model that is recognized as an industry standard. It is good for daytime renderings and is not for twilight or night renderings. Use this sky model when you use Lighting Analysis tools on a day-lit interior scene because the tools are calibrated for this sky model. For exterior scenes, you might want to reduce the EV of the exposure control when you use this sky model. Use the Haze Driven sky model for twilight or night renderings because the Perez sky model is a daylight-only setting.

The CIE sky model   The CIE sky model is another industry-standard physically accurate sky representation. CIE stands for Commission Internationale de l'Eclairage and is an international organization charged with coordinating lighting standards. The CIE sky model has settings for a diffuse overcast sky (the default) and a clear sky. Be sure to enable the Clear Sky option for a much brighter rendering. With the CIE sky model, you might want to reduce the EV in the exposure control to between 13 and 14. This is a daylight-only sky option and does not work for extreme sunrise/sunset or for night renderings. Use the Haze Driven sky model in these cases.

THE MR SKY SETTINGS

Although the default settings for the mr Sky are correct for most scenes, there are three settings for the mr Sky that can cause issues in some renderings:

Height   This setting is the vertical position of the horizon line, which affects not only its appearance in the sky but also the position at which the sun "sets." A slight negative value (−0.1) can minimize the horizon in most renderings, and increasing the Blur value will help soften the sometimes harsh horizon line.

Ground Color   This setting should be set to an average color for your ground plane. It represents the "floor" of your environment and affects the color of the horizon line. If you do not have geometry for a ground plane in your scene, this color is visible in the environment below your objects; it generates reflected illumination and affects the lighting and color of your scene.

Aerial Perspective   This setting is the fuzzy horizon that is added to your background image at the horizon line, and when using the mr Physical Sky, it is rarely noticeable. This effect will not look correct if you have a bitmap for an environment, however, and you might need to turn this off. Reducing this value based on the scale of your scene can help add a natural haze effect to your rendering. Too small of a small distance value can make your rendering look hazy to the point of being foggy.

Introducing the mr Sky Portal

The mr Sky Portal brings light from an outdoor Daylight System into your interior space through an opening in the geometry. The mr Sky Portal vastly improves the quality and accuracy of interior day-lit renders, while also reducing the need for high Final Gather settings. It is a rectangular area light object, placed just outside your window or opening, and generally requires an active Skylight object, mental ray Skylight object (part of the mental ray Daylight System), or Standard Skylight object to function.

Without an mr Sky Portal, a rendering of an indoor scene that includes daylight illumination through an opening will oftentimes be unnaturally dark and, when using indirect illumination, will produce splotchy results. As shown in Figure 3.24, even with high Final Gather and Global Illumination settings, you might not achieve smooth results.

FIGURE 3.24
Day-lit Interior scenes without (top) and with (bottom) the mr Sky Portal

This scene is available as `.\scenes\LightLab\LightLab_mrSP_2010.max` in your Chapter 3 project folder and has scene states with and without the mr Sky Portals. You can recall scene states by right-clicking in a viewport and selecting the Restore Scene States quad-menu option.

Adding an mr Sky Portal allows you to use much lower settings for indirect illumination, allowing you to avoid adding unnecessary lights to even out the interior rendering. Although the mr Sky portals have some overhead themselves, your render times can be significantly reduced because of the ability to use much lower Final Gather settings.

You can also use the mr Sky Portals when you render an outdoor scene, where an indoor area looks unnaturally dark as seen from outside. In this case, you might want to turn off shadows for the mr Sky Portal to save rendering time. This topic and the use of the mr Sky Portal in renderings are covered further in Chapter 5.

In the next section, I examine the settings of the mr Sky Portal, including the critical Shadow Samples setting.

UNDERSTANDING THE MR SKY PORTAL SETTINGS

The primary settings you will use with the mr Sky Portal are the Multiplier value, the From "Outdoors" check box, and the Shadow Samples settings.

Figure 3.25 shows the command panel and default settings for the mr Sky Portal parameters.

FIGURE 3.25
The mr Sky Portal
Parameters

Multiplier   This scales the amount of light entering from outdoors, and larger portals create more light than smaller portals, just as a larger window brings in more light than a smaller one. Values for lighting can be very subjective, and your exposure control settings can play a big part in what light values you choose; however, I generally keep the value between 0.25 and 1.5. I have seen recommendations from others to increase this to 5.0 and greater, but 1.0 gives you realistic results. Your goal in this case should be to use values close 1.0 and to balance your interior lights and exposure values to give you the results you need.

From "Outdoors"   This option brings shadows from outside to the inside scene. Leave it deselected (the default) unless absolutely necessary, because it greatly increases render times.

Shadow Samples   I covered Shadow Samples in the section on photometric light shadows, so give that a look for details on this setting. The default setting is 16 samples, but for many scenes, a setting of 32 or 64 gives better refinement of the shadows, as I examined in the section "Understanding Shape and Area Shadows." If you are using mr Sky Portals to help illuminate an interior area in an outdoor rendering, consider turning off shadows completely.

Setting the Color Source and Using the mr Sky Portal as an Area Light

In normal use the mr Sky Portal is placed across windows, skylights, and other openings to bright light into an interior space. The mr Sky Portal can also be used as an area light when set to use a custom light Color Source, located in the Advanced Parameters settings for the mr Sky Portal. The great advantage to using the mr Sky Portal as an area light as opposed to a photometric light is that it is a true soft area light; photometric area lights, as I will show, do not produce the same soft illumination. Figure 3.26 shows the Advanced Parameters drop-down menu for the mr Sky Portal, which allows you to make the light visible to the renderer, control the transparency, and change the color of the illumination produced.

FIGURE 3.26

mr Sky Portal Advanced Parameters roll-down menu

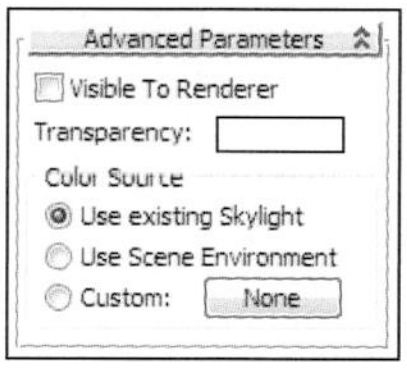

Typically with a mr Sky Portal you would use the default option Use Existing Skylight in combination with a Daylight System and the mr Physical Sky environment shader, and not need to change mr Sky Portal settings for most scenes. Without a Daylight System, however, the mr Sky Portal will not produce light. If you are using an HDR environment image, then the Use Scene Environment setting would be appropriate, and light will be produced matching the color of the environment (see the file `mrSP_Use_Environment_2010.max` in the Chapter 3 project folder).

You can use the mr Sky Portal as a simple area light by choosing the Custom color source option and then simply changing the Multiplier value to the Lux value (candelas per meter squared) that you need for the light. You do not have to choose a custom shader to use the mr Sky Portal as an area light; just leave it blank. Rescaling the size of the light and adjusting the Multiplier both change the brightness of the light. The scene `mrSP_Area_Light_2010.max` demonstrates this technique.

Introducing the Kelvin Temperature Color Shader

In 3ds Max/Design 2011 Autodesk added a new shader (or map) type, the Kelvin Temperature Color shader. This shader can be used anywhere you need to set a color based on Kelvin degrees, however is most likely to be used in the Advanced Parameters and Custom Color setting in a mr Sky Portal to create an area light. The Kelvin Temperature Color shader has one parameter for color and another parameter for intensity in lux (candelas per meter squared). Because intensity is in lux the amount of light produced is directly proportional to the size of the mr Sky Portal; a 1′ square mr Sky Portal has 1/9th the light of a 3′ by 3′ mr Sky Portal.

When Kelvin Temperature Color is used as a diffuse map it makes objects appear to glow based on color and intensity (similar to the Self Illumination settings), and therefore can be used in ProMaterials and Autodesk Materials that normally would not glow, like ceramic. It does not produce illumination in this case, unlike the Self Illumination settings of the Arch & Design material. Open the `Kelvin_Ceramic_Teapot.max` file in this chapter's project, and try the scene with and without light, and with and without Final Gather.

To change the mr Sky Portal into an area light, simply choose the Custom radio button from the Advanced Parameters menu, click the None button to bring up the Material Pool (Material/Map Browser), and add the Kelvin Temperature Color shader. You need to drag the new map into the new Slate or classic Compact Material Editor to edit the parameters. The Kelvin Color Temperature map has two parameters: one for the color temperature in degrees Kelvin and one for intensity in lux (candelas per meter squared). Figure 3.27 shows the Advanced Parameters drop-down list with a Custom color source selected. At the left are the settings for the new Kelvin Temperature Color map.

FIGURE 3.27

The mr Sky Portal Advanced Parameters drop-down list with the Kelvin Temperature Color map assigned for the custom color source

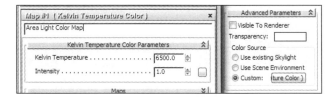

In 3ds Max/Design 2010 and older, however, advanced users can enable additional shaders to use with the mr Sky Portal by editing both the `base.mi` and `base_max.mi` files in Notepad. The files are located in the `c:\Program Files\Autodesk\3ds Max 2010\mentalray\shaders_standard\include` folder on your 3ds Max installation. In `base_max.mi`, find the text `gui_mib_cie_d`, and place a hash mark (#) in front of the `hidden` declarations for that item and the next, the `giu_mib_blackbody`. The section should look like this:

```
gui "gui_mib_cie_d" {
    control "Global" "Global" (
      # "hidden"
    )
  }

  gui "gui_mib_blackbody" {
    control "Global" "Global" (
      # "hidden"
    )
  }
```

In the `base.mi` file, find the text `Light utils`, and add a comma, a space, and the word `texture` after the words `apply light` in two locations. It should now look like this:

```
#----------------------------------------- Light utils

declare shader
  color "mib_cie_d" (
    scalar    "temperature",
    scalar    "intensity"
  )
```

```
    version 1
    apply light, texture
  end declare

  declare shader
    color "mib_blackbody" (
      scalar    "temperature",
      scalar    "intensity"
    )
    version 1
    apply light, texture
  end declare
```

Restart 3ds Max/Design to accept the changes. For the custom color source, you can now choose the mib_blackbody or mib_cie_d shaders to provide you with controls for color in Kelvin and intensity in lux (candela per meter squared). You must first drag the map from the command panel to the Material Editor to edit the settings. The smallest color value for the blackbody shader is 1000K.

MR SKY PORTAL INTENSITY VS. SIZE

Resizing the mr Sky Portal light, in addition to adjusting the Multiplier and Intensity values of the Kelvin Temperature Color map, change the amount of light cast into the scene. The intensity is always in lux (candela per meter squared) and varies based on size.

A sample scene that demonstrates the use of the Blackbody map is provided as .\scenes\ mrSP_Blackbody_2010.max in your Chapter 3 project folder; however, it first requires the modifications of your mental ray include files, described earlier. The other shader I exposed is the mib_cie_d shader, which is intended to represent natural daylight and has a color range of 4000K to 25000K. A good default for a bright daylight color is 6500K. The sample scene .\scenes\ mrSP_CIE_D_2010.max is in the Chapter 3 project's .\scenes folder. Figure 3.28 shows two mr Sky Portals configured instead as area light sources and no mr Physical Sky to control their illumination.

FIGURE 3.28
The mr Sky Portal as an area light (right) compared with a photometric area light (left).

Real World Scenario

GPU Accelerated Lighting Workflow

One of the areas of intense development in the 3D world is in graphics processing units (GPUs). This development is driven in large part by the game market; however, in recent years there has been accelerated use of GPUs for not only game and viewport rendering purposes but also for supercomputing using both stand-alone products such as the NVIDIA Quadro cards and complete systems such as the NVIDIA Tesla GPU-based personal supercomputers. Because of their ability to handle massively parallel computing processes, GPUs can handle the unfolding of proteins, the simulation of biochemical processes, the analysis of weather patterns, and the visualization of volumetric effects, among many other things. Also, movie studios are using GPUs to accelerate the computation of fire and fluid effects, and several companies are producing rendering engines based on GPUs, including Autodesk's Quicksilver hardware rendering, mental images' iray, and ART VPS's Shaderlight. mental images also produces a GPU-based rendering technology and development kit called OptiX to allow third-party companies to add GUP-accelerated renderings to their products.

At this point, many of these products are about improving feedback to you, the artist, so that you can make intelligent choices about lighting, materials, and render settings prior to using your renderer of choice. Final-frame renderers such as Shaderlight, iray, and Autodesk's new hardware renderer in 3ds Max/design 2011 are coming of age and will only improve over time. Some of the difficulty in getting renderers such as mental ray to be GPU-based is that not all computing processes lend themselves to parallel computing, and not all features developed over the years for an existing rendering engine are easily ported to a completely new hardware and computing platform. mental images is bridging that gap with their MetaSL technology, a universal shading language that works on both hardware and software renderers.

Between the time this chapter was written and the books hit the shelves, no doubt a number of interesting and important products have arrived on the scene. Someday I will look back at this book and think about how slow, cumbersome, and quaint technology was back then, because there is always something new and faster, and that is what keeps this field exciting. Meanwhile, visit www.mastering-mentalray.com for the latest news on mental ray and GPU-based rendering.

The Bottom Line

Configure exposure control settings for varying conditions   An exposure control maps the high dynamic range of the frame buffer into a low dynamic range for viewing and printing.

> **Master It**   How do you assign an mr Photographic exposure control and adjust it for different times of the day for an interior scene?

Optimize and control photometric lights and shadow quality   There are key light parameters that can have a great impact on rendered image quality and render time.

> **Master It**   How do you adjust shadow samples for high-quality results and adjust light parameters to minimize render time and control light distribution?

Chapter 4

Rendering

Producing a rendering should be simply a matter of clicking the Render button and waiting for your beautiful image to complete. That day may not be too far off, but for the moment it is not always that easy! Getting a project rendered and out the door can sometimes be the most stressful part of the job particularly when the renderings are taking too long for you to meet a deadline. Understanding what the render options do for you will potentially help speed your renderings and also solve problems that you encounter. This chapter focuses on critical render settings, but it also focuses on the tools and render strategies that help you get the job done.

In this chapter, you will learn to

◆ Strategize rendering scenes, including Batch Render and Backburner network rendering

◆ Understand the memory management features of mental ray to reduce memory issues, including using mental ray proxy objects

◆ Use visual diagnostic modes to configure the Samples Per Pixel and BSP options

Introducing Backburner Network Rendering

Backburner is a set of programs that allows you to render your still images and animations on multiple computers at the same time. Each computer takes a frame of the animation or a portion of the image (a *strip*). As soon as a computer finishes its frame or strip, Backburner assigns the next available portion of the job until it is completed. One license of 3ds Max/Design gives you up to 9,999 computers that you can use as render servers, each one with a render-node license of mental ray. This virtually limitless licensing makes it possible to create an affordable mental ray render farm with as many computers as you can network and also provides a convenient method to queue multiple jobs on a single machine.

One computer on the network must run the Manager application, and each render computer then runs the Server application. The server machines can be set to automatically search for a manager machine, or you might need to enter the network name or IP address of the computer running Manager. A single machine can run both Manager and Server.

Enabling Render Output to Backburner

To assign a render to Backburner, enable the Net Render option in the Render Output dialog box, and click Render. The Net Render option is in the Render Output section of the Common tab, as shown in Figure 4.1. Both the Net Render option and the file output specified under Save File is ignored if you are in Iterative render mode, so you must have Production selected, as shown in the lower-left corner of the Render Output dialog box in Figure 4.1.

INTRODUCING BACKBURNER 2011

Shipping with 3ds Max/Design 2011 is Autodesk's next-generation network rendering system, Backburner 2011. Although it has functionally similar to previous incarnations of Backburner, this version is not compatible with versions of 3ds Max/Design prior to 3ds Max Design 2011, and 3ds Max Design 2011 is optimally designed to work with Backburner 2011. Existing render farms, if switched to exclusively Backburner 2011, will not be able to render using 3ds Max 2010 and older. The new version of Backburner can exist in a network that also runs legacy Backburner, and each version of Server 2008 and 2010 then communicates to its own Manager application.

At the time of this writing, the details on Backburner 2011 are still preliminary. More complete information on how to install and use this application is available from Autodesk and also at www .masteringmentalray.com. It is expected that 3ds Max/Design 2011 will support Backburner 2008 for use with legacy versions of software; however, support for Backburner 2008 might end with this release cycle.

FIGURE 4.1
The Net Render and Render Output options in the Render Output dialog box

After you enable the Net Render option and click Render, the Network Job Assignment dialog box opens, as shown in Figure 4.2, which completes the assignment of the job to the network manager. The Network Job Assignment dialog box contains a few important settings to assist you when you render large images and when you choose which servers to use.

Each job must have a unique name; current jobs are listed in the lower-right quadrant of the dialog box where they show the job status and priority level. Jobs with a lower-priority number are rendered first; the closer to priority 1, the higher the priority. All servers that are registered to the Backburner's Manager application are listed in the upper right. Machines with yellow marks are working on a job, green marks indicate idle machines, and gray marks indicate machines that are registered to the manager but not currently online. You can close the server application when you do not want it available for rendering, or ideally you can schedule times that machines are unavailable within the Monitor program. The Monitor program is the third program along with Manager and Server that comprises Backburner. Monitor connects to Manager to control and monitor servers and jobs and is covered later in this chapter. In Monitor, right-click a server name to define the week schedule for that particular machine.

It is important to note that 3ds Max and 3ds Max Design are seen as different applications with different render plugins for Backburner. If you submit a job from 3ds Max Design, you will not see machines that only have 3ds Max installed, and vice versa. If your render farm supports one application, open your scene in that application to submit it to Backburner.

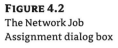

FIGURE 4.2
The Network Job
Assignment dialog box

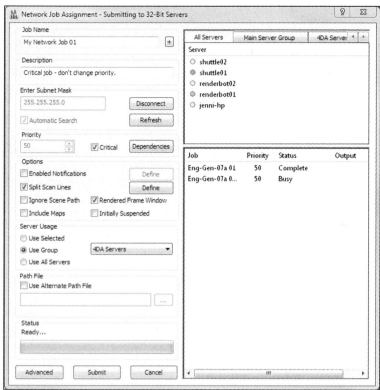

In 3ds Max/Design 2009 and older, you need to manually configure gamma correction on all server machines to ensure they are all set the same. With these earlier versions of 3ds Max/Design, gamma settings are not stored with the scene; only the Enable/Disable setting and therefore local configuration are required on each machine. In 3ds Max/Design 2009 and older, the Input Gamma and Output Gamma settings are stored in the `3dsmax.ini` file in your local user folders, for instance at `C:\Users\<username>\AppData\Local\Autodesk\3dsmax\2009 - 64bit\enu`. To edit the file or to copy the file for pasting into render servers, first be sure that your folder settings (in the Windows Control Panel, Appearance and Personalization category, and the Folder Options dialog box) allow you to see hidden files and folders. 3ds Max/Design's INI files are text files that you can edit in WordPad.

For 3ds Max Design 2010 and newer, gamma and many other settings are stored in the `DesignVIZ.mentalray.ini` file, located in your local user's files. Change it to `C:\Users\<username>\AppData\Local\Autodesk\3dsMaxDesign\2011 - 64bit\enu\defaults\DesignVIZ.mentalray\`, open the `CurrentDefaults.ini` file in WordPad, and go to the end of the file to adjust the gamma settings.

Using Split Scan Lines

In the middle-left section of the Network Job Assignment dialog box, as shown earlier in Figure 4.2, is the Split Scan Lines option and its Define button. The Split Scan Lines option takes a single-image rendering job and splits it into multiple rendering jobs of individual horizontal strips, each typically 10 percent of the height of your full image.

This splitting of the image into 10 jobs instead of one has three benefits. First, it allows multiple computers to work on the individual portions of your rendering without needing to use distributed bucket rendering, effectively giving you unlimited cores for processing a single image. *Distributed bucket rendering* allows your copy of 3ds Max/Design to connect to other machines to render individual buckets. I cover this topic in detail later in this chapter. Distributed rendering has licensing limitations, and the crash of any one computer can ruin a long render. It is tenuous for critical and long renders.

This multimachine, single-image rendering can be performed on other machines while you continue to work on your machine (as long as Server is closed), which is something you cannot do with distributed bucket rendering because your local cores are always used. Be certain that distributed bucket rendering is not enabled before you submit a network job, or every machine with a distributed bucket rendering configuration file (a *rayhosts* file) will try to use distributed rendering.

The second advantage to using the Split Scan Lines option is that each portion of your rendered image is saved after each job is completed, and any machine crashing or losing the connection to the Manager application will affect only the one strip that was rendering. It will not affect the already completed work or other computers that are rendering other strips. Split Scan Lines is my preferred method of rendering any large or time-consuming images.

The third advantage of Split Scan Lines is that it reduces the memory required to render a scene because just the smaller strip image is managed by 3ds Max/Design and mental ray, not the memory and overhead of a frame buffer for a full-sized image. Larger renderings that previously would not render on machines with limited resources might work fine with this option.

Clicking the Define button opens a small dialog box where you can specify the number of horizontal strips via a percentage or a pixel size value, as shown in Figure 4.3.

FIGURE 4.3
The Strips Setup
dialog box

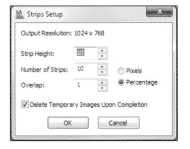

If the strips are large, then slower computers might take an exceptionally long time to render compared to faster machines, and the entire job will wait for those slower machines. To reduce this possibility, I typically keep the number of strips between 10 and 20 (10 or 5 percent), depending on the pixel height of the image. Certain strips might just naturally take more time than others if they include more reflective and refractive elements than other strips, and choosing more strips (a smaller percentage) can allow individual machines to finish quicker and reduce the number of machines potentially stuck on long renders. Deselect the Delete Temporary Images Upon Completion option in the Strips Setup dialog box to keep both the individual strips and the final stitched image.

When you create a Split Scan Lines job, two jobs are created in the Backburner queue: one for the strips, which render as multiframe crop renders to separate files (images labeled _STP0001_ FileName.png, for instance), and another job that combines the strips into a final frame. The second job is dependent on the first job completing. Figure 4.4 shows the Backburner Monitor program and a single, large-image job using the Split Scan Lines option.

FIGURE 4.4
Backburner Monitor showing a Split Scan Lines job and the resulting render assignments

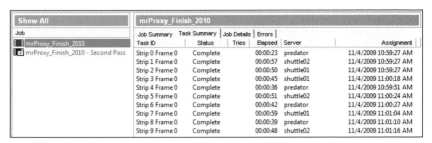

You should be aware of the following issues when you use Split Scan Lines:

♦ Ensure that all render servers have the same gamma setting if you are using 3ds Max/Design 2009 or older.

♦ When you use output gamma correction for file output, as you should for any low dynamic range image file format, then gamma correction will be applied twice to the image — once for each strip and again when the strips are reassembled into the final image. You will need Adobe Photoshop or 3ds Max Composite (formerly Toxik) to reverse-gamma-correct the image. When saving to high dynamic range images, you should not have output gamma correction applied and thus will not have a double gamma correction issue.

♦ Split Scan Lines might have difficulty producing an image with proper transparency when outputting to the TIFF format.

♦ Split Scan Lines will not be able to reassemble the image when using the Relative Paths file option in Preferences. Define the full path to the file in this case, or disable the Relative Paths option and redefine the file path. The strips are preserved if they cannot be assembled, and then you can assemble them in Photoshop by pasting them into a blank image.

♦ When rendering with multiple machines, ensure that all file paths are commonly accessible on a network shared drive, not a local drive.

♦ Image formats that contain additional channels might have issues when being reassembled.

♦ To conserve render time and ensure accurate results, precompute and set to read-only (cache) your Final Gather and Global Illumination files prior to sending a Split Scan Lines render job. I explain precomputing and the reuse options (Final Gather and Global Illumination Disk Caching) in Chapters 5, "Indirect Illumination and Final Gather," and Chapter 6, "Global Illumination and Caustics."

Correcting Gamma with Split Scan Lines Images

Both the first and second jobs of a Split Scan Lines job will apply output gamma to the image, which results in double gamma correction if the output gamma is not equal to 1.0. In this case, you can edit the second Backburner job to not use gamma, or you can manually apply an inverse gamma value to the image in Photoshop or 3ds Max Composite. Applying an output gamma of 2.2 twice will then require an inverse gamma of 0.454545 to be applied to the image for de-gamma correction.

PRECOMPUTING INDIRECT ILLUMINATION FOR NETWORK RENDER JOBS

I generally precompute indirect illumination before I submit a network job, particularly for Split Scanline jobs. First, it ensures that there is no duplication of effort for computing the global illumination; computing the global illumination is a scene-wide process, so if not precomputed (cached) and locked (set to read-only), then each Split Scan Lines strip would need to compute the global illumination for the entire scene, thus duplicating effort and wasting render time.

Second, you can save time by precomputing the Final Gather image at one-half image resolution with a higher Final Gather setting and then lock the solution prior to network rendering. The Final Gather quality still remains high but computes faster overall. Each strip reads the cached files from the .\sceneassets\renderassets folder of your project and skips all indirect illumination processing. You can read more about the reuse options(Final Gather and Global Illumination Disk Caching) in Chapters 5 and 6.

In Photoshop, you can change the gamma in an image in the Exposure dialog box (select Image ➤ Adjustments ➤ Exposure). You can also change an image's gamma in 3ds Max Composite (formerly Toxik) or Combustion. In 3ds Max Composite, add the CC Basics operator to the output node of your footage, and adjust the master Gamma value, as shown in Figure 4.5. In Combustion, simply add a Gamma/Pedestal/Gain operator after your imported file, and enter your gamma value.

FIGURE 4.5
3ds Max Composite
program and the
CC Basics opera-
tor shown with the
Gamma master value
set to 0.45454

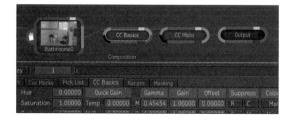

Next I cover some of the network job settings accessible by clicking the Advanced button in the Network Job Assignment dialog box.

Adjusting Network Rendering Advanced Settings

Clicking the Advanced button (at the bottom left of the Network Job Assignment dialog box) opens the Advanced Settings dialog box shown in Figure 4.6.

Two settings might require your attention. The first setting is the Per Job Timeouts. By default it is disabled, and Manager uses its own timeout values of 20, 600, and 10 minutes, respectively, for each frame or strip of a render job. Disabling this option does not mean that timeouts are disabled; it just means that global timeouts are used. If you have a render that might take more than 600 minutes, be sure to use the Per Job Timeouts option and enter a new value for Wait For MAX To Render that is large enough for your longest anticipated render time. Using Split Scan Lines technique greatly reduces the possibility of hitting the default 600 minute timeout, but using Split Scan Lines is not always practical for you to use depending on your output format and whether you need additional render channels, and is not generally useful for animations. In those cases changing the timeouts in this dialog box for long renders is essential.

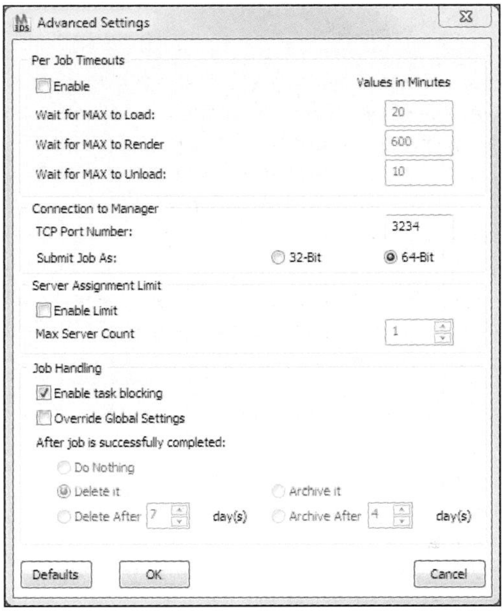

FIGURE 4.6
Network job
assignment's
Advanced Settings
dialog box

In the middle of the dialog box in the Connection To Manager section is the Submit Job As option for 32-bit and 64-bit machines. No matter what 32-bit or 64-bit version of 3ds Max/Design you are using, you can change the target version of 3ds Max/Design. Changing this option might change the list of available machines in the Network Job Assignment dialog box if a particular machine does not have both 32-bit and 64-bit versions of 3ds Max/Design installed. Using 32-bit is necessary, for instance, if you are using certain video codecs and formats that are not supported in a 64-bit program, such as the Cinepak codec and Apple QuickTime format; this lack of 64-bit support is true for both reading and writing those video formats. Because of this limitation, I generally install both 32-bit and 64-bit versions of 3ds Max/Design on a 64-bit machine.

Next I cover the Monitor application for Backburner, which allows you to monitor and control network jobs and servers.

Using the Backburner Monitor

The Monitor program allows you to manage jobs and computers, as shown in Figure 4.7. Server machines may be controlled based on the time of day to limit render times, and you can manually add and remove jobs as required. Right-click on a server name to define its Week Schedule. You can create local render groups, such as Renderfarm or Office so you can quickly assign jobs to particular machines from the Network Job Assignment dialog box. Also, you can have multiple Monitor applications running on the network, but only one can be the queue controller; you can request control using the Request Queue Control menu option in Manager.

FIGURE 4.7
Backburner application dialog box

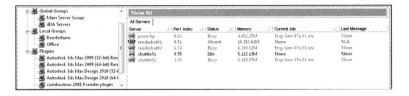

In the All Servers tab in the lower-right quadrant of the Monitor application is the list of render servers that are registered to the Manager application as well as the status of each server. You can select a job in the Job list, as shown earlier in Figure 4.4, and then right-click a server name to add or remove it from that job. You can see the optional *Perf. Index* and *Memory* statistics in Figure 4.7; you can add these and other server statistics by selecting the Servers ➤ Column Chooser menu or by right-clicking the columns and choosing the Column Chooser menu option. The performance index shows the relative speed of each computer and can help identify machines with performance problems; however, those machines might have just been assigned to render more difficult frames or strips. Right-clicking a machine name allows you to reset its index.

Next I cover the Batch Render utility, which allows you to automate the rendering of a series of camera shots, each with potentially different render and scene settings.

Using Batch Render

The Batch Render utility allows you to preconfigure a series of camera shots and quickly queue multiple images for render. Batch Render can work with or without Backburner, and using it without a network allows you to render several images in sequence without having to manually manage and start each render. You can simply define your camera shots and filenames and click Render, and each image is rendered one after the other. You open the Batch Render utility, as shown in Figure 4.8, by selecting the Rendering ➤ Batch Render menu option.

FIGURE 4.8
Batch Render dialog box showing scenes with scene states and presets per job

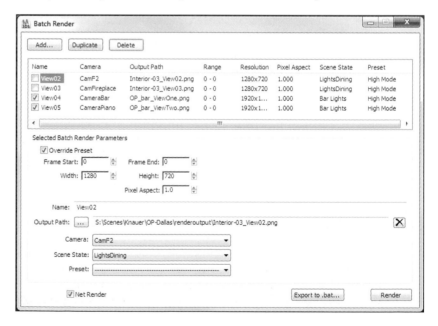

This tool is terrific for automating the production of draft and high-quality renderings and managing numerous camera shots that all require different filenames and potentially different resolutions or render quality settings. As you will see in Chapter 5, Batch Render can help automate the creation of Final Gather passes for high-resolution images and animations.

BATCH RENDER BLUES

Certain versions of 3ds Max and BackBurner might not handle multiple-batch render jobs correctly when submitted all at one time. If this happens, submit the jobs one at a time to BackBurner.

Next I cover the mental ray proxy object, which is a placeholder object for geometry that has been cached to your drive.

Introducing mental ray Proxy Objects

The mental ray *proxy object* is a lightweight placeholder for preprocessed scene geometry. Use it to reduce mental ray and 3ds Max/Design memory use and improve viewport performance. Objects are converted into a .mib file format and stored on the drive for use at render time, leaving a simple stand-in object in your scene, as shown in Figure 4.9.

FIGURE 4.9
Original and mental ray proxy object with 256 cloud points

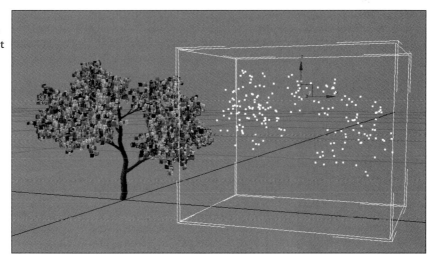

During rendering, only the placeholder is transferred to mental ray, and the geometry behind the mental ray proxy objects (the .mib files) is not loaded until a bucket needs that specific geometry. The benefit is that proxy geometry can be unloaded from memory when no longer needed, whereas typically geometry must remain in memory throughout the render process. Using proxy objects can significantly speed your rendering if memory is an issue and can reduce the incidence of memory errors; however, it does not make your object any easier to render. A difficult object to render will still be a difficult object.

mental ray proxies are frequently used for high-polygon objects, particularly if they are cloned and used several times in a scene, and they are also ideal for use with any object that might be cloned numerous times, whether it is a high or low polygon-count object. Figure 4.9 shows an Xfrog tree object (available for free from http://seek.autodesk.com both as its original 3D object and as a mental ray proxy). You can create a forest of high-polygon trees without excessive memory overhead when the trees are proxies. In scenes where an instance of a proxy object is always in view, your scene may not benefit any more than simply instancing the original polygon objects; however your viewport performance may improve with the mr Proxy.

Converting an object to a mental ray proxy creates a `.mib` file in your `.\sceneassets\` `renderassets` folder, together with a thumbnail image in BMP format. If you are converting an animated object, then one MIB file is created for each frame that you specify. One advantage to having the external `.mib` file is that it gives you the ability to update the `.mib` and then update all scenes that use that `.mib`.

To easily create proxy objects, this book's DVD includes a script from Zap Andersson's blog at `http://mentalraytips.blogspot.com`, the script `mental ray-mrProxyBake.mcr`, which provides semi-automatic conversion of one or more objects. This is an improved version of the script that ships with 3ds Max/Design and allows multiple objects to be converted into multiple proxies all at one time.

Perform the following steps to add this script to a menu:

1. Drag this script from the DVD into your 3ds Max/Design editor to install it.

2. Select Customize ➢ Customize User Interface, go to the Menus tab, and set Category to mental ray.

3. Drag the Convert Object(s) to mental ray Proxy action to the Create node of the mental ray tree view on the right. Be sure you have the script with the plural "Object(s)" in its name to use the latest script. Close the dialog box, and save your new custom user interface.

If you want to manually create mental ray proxy objects, perform the following steps:

1. Set your project to the Chapter 4 project folder, and open the scene `mrProxy_Start_2010` `.max`, which is a gazebo scene by Ryan O'Connor of 4D Artists, Inc.

2. If you want to convert several objects into a single proxy object, you must first combine all the geometry into a single mesh or poly.

3. Select the `Gazebo_Base` object, and perform a Collapse All operation on the stack to convert it into an Editable Mesh object.

4. Click the edit mesh's Attach List button, and select all the unfrozen objects in the scene. In the next Attach Options dialog box, select the Match Material IDs To Material option to allow the automatic changing of IDs where needed.

5. Rename the object to `Gazebo-01`. In the Compact Material Editor or SME, load the gazebo's new multi/subobject into the editor, and rename the material to **Gazebo**. If you manually create mental ray proxy objects without Zap's script, then you must preserve the material so you can reassign it to the new proxy object.

6. Because Zap's macro deletes the original object, be sure to save your scene under a new name or select Save Selected to save just the gazebo object.

7. With the gazebo object selected, run your new menu item Create ➢ mental ray ➢ Convert Object(s) to mental ray Proxy. When you are prompted for a filename in the `.\sceneassets\renderassets` folder, enter **Gazebo**, and then click Save. When you see the mental ray Proxy Creation dialog box, accept the defaults. A `.bmp` thumbnail rendering of your object is created together with the `.mib` gazebo geometry.

CREATING A MENTAL RAY PROXY LIBRARY

If you want to turn your mental ray proxy objects into a library object that you can easily reuse, copy the `.mib`, `.bmp` thumbnail, and any material bitmap files to a shared network location. On the Modify tab, change the filename for the mental ray proxy to point to the new location, and select Save Selected to save the new mental ray proxy object to the network share. You can then merge this with scenes to add the new proxy object. For objects like Xfrog trees, you can have a library of individual 3ds Max/Design files that contain mental ray proxy objects for a specific plant, which you can quickly drop into scenes and then instance when you need them.

Next I cover the mental ray render settings in the Render Setup and Rendered Frame Window dialog boxes.

Understanding Render Settings

Quality almost always comes with a price; the higher the settings, the better the result. However, oftentimes there is a seemingly logarithmic increase in render time. The render settings discussed in this chapter are just part of the equation, and as you will discover throughout the book, a number of factors always go into the amount of time a rendering takes. Understanding how individual settings for the renderer, lighting, and materials can all affect render times is critical to achieving both good and fast results.

You might need different settings for animation and still images, because with animations you might see *scintillation* (shimmering) at the edges of objects or on bumpy surfaces that require higher Samples Per Pixel settings, lower Sample Contrast settings, Gauss filtering, or an adjustment to your materials or geometry. This scintillation would not exist in a still image, obviously, but may be visible as a jagged edge or missing details. Scintillation in an animation happens primarily along long horizontal and vertical edges, as with stairs and balusters. You can reduce some scintillation by adjusting camera paths to add motion in another axis, such as moving vertically as well as to the side.

Determining the settings you need for animations usually requires you to render a segment of your animation with your final settings and play it back at full speed, looking for scintillation in the edges of objects and for coplanar faces that might flash on surfaces. Do not settle on the settings for an animation until you are certain, and do some tests. For any scene, knowing what values to start with comes from gleaning the experience and knowledge from this book and from your personal experience.

If you are rendering an image for print, you might find that a small amount of jaggedness on rendered objects will be blended by the natural mixing of ink droplets on paper, and extreme settings are rarely necessary. Using the computer screen to proof your images might result in using settings higher than necessary, and knowing what settings to use is a simple matter of testing on the print medium.

Next I cover the settings on the Common tab that affect render time in mental ray.

Modifying Common Tab Settings

Although not specific to mental ray, one Common tab setting that can help save you considerable render time is the Area Lights/Shadows As Points check box, as shown in Figure 4.10.

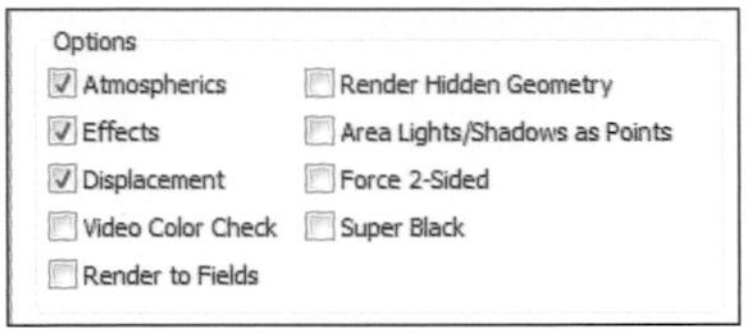

FIGURE 4.10
The Area Lights/Shadows As Points option in the Render Setup dialog box

This option disables the area light's shadow samples and might be necessary to use when you perform draft-quality renderings or when you are using area lights and later determine that they take too long to render. You might find for projects that require both still images and animations that area lights might take too long to render for the animation but are necessary for the quality of the still images, so you toggle this setting as needed. If you move the Soft Shadow Precision slider all the way to the left in the Rendered Frame Window dialog box, it disables the Shadow Samples option and turns on the Area Lights/Shadows As Points check box in the Render Setup dialog box. As you saw in Chapter 3, "Lights, Shadow, and Exposure Control," the quality of shadow samples is directly related to Samples Per Pixel, and if you are using moderately high Samples Per Pixel settings, then you might be able to use the Rendered Frame Window dialog box's slider to turn down shadow samples rather than turning them off completely.

Defining File Output Options

A majority of our work is rendered to 48-bit PNG files using the mental ray Photographic exposure control. This low dynamic range image format gives you an uncompressed, readily usable image with a reasonable dynamic color range if further adjustments are needed. The JPEG format, in contrast, is 24-bit, and its compression technology is *lossy* — you always have some compression artifacts and a loss of detail. Most simple animations are rendered to PNG and compiled into ANI or MOV format within Premiere or Combustion. You can also use the RAM Player to produce animations by loading the images and then saving to another format; however, the RAM Player is really intended for draft-quality use and has some issues with handling gamma correction. If you need a simple method of compiling frames into an animation, look at the Video Post feature of 3ds Max/Design, or use an image sequence as a background image and rerender as an AVI or MOV file. Gamma will be corrected as the file is imported and corrected as it is saved out to the animation.

Animations that require effects such as Depth of Field, fog, motion blur, and compositing will use the RPF format if going to Combustion, or the OpenEXR format if going to 3ds Max Composite. These formats support a high dynamic range and additional render channels such as Z Depth and render elements such as reflections.

Saving your rendering to a high dynamic range image format and then performing exposure control in 3ds Max Composite or Photoshop gives you the ability to make fine adjustments to the exposure and color of your scene. When you save to a high dynamic range format, be certain that your mental ray frame buffer type is set to 32 bits on the Rendered tab — the default for 3ds Max Design — and not to 16 bits — the default for 3ds Max. Otherwise, you will not create a high dynamic range image. As shown in Figure 4.11, exposure control and gamma correction are not used for high dynamic range images, and what you will see in the Rendered Frame Window dialog box might appear overexposed.

FIGURE 4.11

The Sponza scene by Marko Dabrovic, rendered to a high dynamic range OpenEXR format, as shown in the Rendered Frame Window dialog box without exposure control

The OpenEXR image format, developed by Industrial Light & Magic, gives you support for a variety of bit-depth and compression formats, allows the embedding of g-buffer effects channels, and — new for 3ds Max/Design 2011 — allows render elements to be embedded within the file rather than stored as separate files. You can find more information on the OpenEXR format at www.openexr.org.

3ds Max/Design 2011 has a completely new dialog box for the OpenEXR output format, as shown in Figure 4.12. This was also available to subscription customers for 3ds Max/Design 2010.

With this dialog box and the updated OpenEXR format, you now have the ability to store render elements as layers within a single OpenEXR file, and you do not need to save your render elements individually from the Render Elements tab of the Render Setup dialog box. In the OpenEXR dialog box, enable the option Automatically Add/Remove Render Elements From Render Dialog in the Render Elements section. Otherwise, the additional channels will be both stored in the OpenEXR file and saved as individual render element image files, as defined in the Render Setup dialog box and the Render Elements tab. Currently, mental ray does not support the use of the mental ray Map Manager option and the additional render element layers.

G-buffer channels store information about your scene geometry in a graphical manner, either as a color region or as a grayscale value, and they are used to represent either the property of an object (such as material ID or mapping coordinates) or a value in the scene (such as depth or velocity). A material ID g-buffer channel contains, for instance, a black background and a unique solid color where surfaces contain a material with that ID, as shown in Figure 4.13.

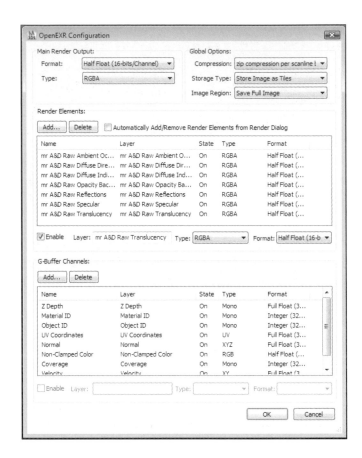

Your post-processing application can then use that additional channel data to, for instance, produce glow effects around that material or to color-correct just that material within an application like Combustion or 3ds Max Composite. Compositing scenes and using render elements are covered in Chapter 10, "mental ray for Design." Figure 4.13 shows the famous Sponza Atrium scene, donated to the public by Marko Dabrovic of RNA Studios, which is a classic scene for testing global illumination techniques. This scene is available on the DVD in the Bonus folder and is used as examples in later chapters. Next I cover the primary mental ray settings on the Renderer tab of the Render Setup dialog box.

Understanding the Renderer Tab Settings

A primary focus of this book is to help you get the best quality with a minimum amount of time. Understanding how individual settings for the renderer, lighting, and materials can affect render times is critical to achieving both good and fast results. A number of factors always go into the amount of time a rendering takes, and so far you've seen the impact of the Sample Quality settings, different shadow types, and different materials and lighting. The settings discussed in this chapter are just another part of the equation.

FIGURE 4.13
The Sponza scene rendering that shows the g-buffer for the node ID

The main Sampling Quality settings include Samples Per Pixel, Spatial Contrast, and Filter, which were covered in Chapter 1, "mental ray Essentials." In this chapter I cover additional Renderer tab settings. I address additional common settings and then present production scenes in the chapters to follow. First I cover the sample rate visual diagnostics mode that allows you to visualize how mental ray is processing your rendering.

SAMPLE RATE VISUAL DIAGNOSTICS

To help visualize what is going on "under the hood" with the Samples Per Pixel settings, mental ray provides a visual diagnostics mode that overlays your rendered image with information about how mental ray is creating your rendering. Figure 4.14 shows the settings for visual diagnostics that you can find in the Render Setup dialog box and the Processing tab.

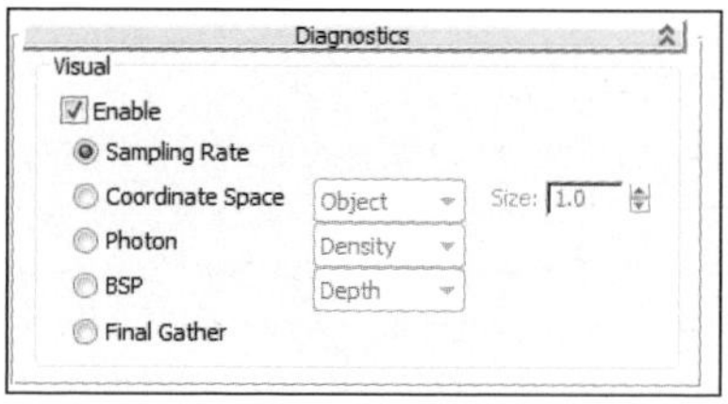

FIGURE 4.14
Visual diagnostic options

Figure 4.15 shows a visual diagnostics mode rendering using the Sampling Rate option, which gives you an indication where mental ray puts its effort into this scene. The scene is a sample that ships with 3ds Max/Design.

FIGURE 4.15
This diagnostic sample rate image where dark areas represent Minimum = 1/64 and light areas are Maximum = 1

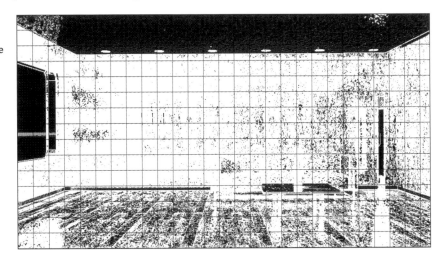

This diagnostic render has Samples Per Pixel settings of 1/64 and 1 and a Spatial Contrast setting of 0.52, which are fairly low settings. This image generated in 21 minutes on a Core 2 Quad machine at 2.4 gigahertz (GHz). In this image, the brighter an area is, the more mental ray found adjacent samples that have comparatively high contrast and subdivided samples to achieve better antialiasing. The red grid is the boundary of the buckets.

Because the Samples Per Pixel settings were low, there is a lot of white in the image, which indicates that much of the effort was placed on the higher Samples Per Pixel setting of Maximum = 1 to render this image, and very few areas are using the lower settings between 1/64 and 1 (black areas). This might indicate that you need to increase your Minimum and Maximum settings and perhaps adjust the Spatial Contrast setting downward.

Figure 4.16 is the same scene with sample rates of 1 and 16 and a Spatial Contrast setting of 0.02, which are moderate settings. This image rendered in 2 hours 34 minutes on a Core 2 Quad at 2.4GHz, which is considerably longer than the previous image, but the nondiagnostic rendered image was much improved.

The overall coverage is gray instead of black. Every pixel gets sampled once because Minimum was 1. Areas that need more detail are sampled successively higher up to the Maximum = 16 subdivisions per pixel; those areas are progressively brighter in this image, and white pixels are where the Samples Per Pixel setting's Maximum value was used. Because there are more gray areas than the earlier image, this shows that more work is being done at the lower and moderate Samples Per Pixel setting before jumping to a higher sample subdivision, which is ideal. You want mental ray to use the highest Samples Per Pixel setting only where it needs additional detail for a great picture and not waste time on areas that are relatively flat looking.

FIGURE 4.16
Visual diagnostic image with Minimum = 1 and Maximum = 16, completed in 2 hours 34 minutes

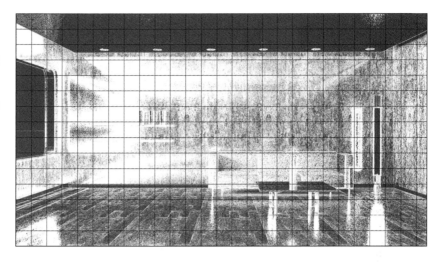

SAMPLING QUALITY OPTIONS

Figure 4.17 shows the Sampling Quality options of mental ray, including options for bucket size and alignment from frame to frame, together with the frame buffer bit depth.

FIGURE 4.17
Sample quality options

Under most circumstances these settings do not need to be modified; however, there are certain times, such as when rendering animations, when using contours, or when producing high dynamic range images, where understanding these settings can improve your rendered results. The settings in the Options section include the following:

Lock Samples The Lock Samples option allows for repeatability in sampling from image to image and refers to area light sampling, not pixel sampling. It is recommended that you turn this off for animations.

Jitter The Jitter option refers to the random shifting of the center used for a pixel sample. This option can help reduce aliasing along edges and points of objects. It should not be used for contour renderings.

Bucket Width The Bucket Width option is the pixel size of the rendered bucket. If you have renders with complex objects or regions, occasionally you will find that a few buckets seem to get stuck at the end of the render, particularly on multicore machines and also with distributed rendering; therefore, all the cores of your machine(s) sit and wait for those last buckets to complete before working on the next image or returning control of 3ds Max/Design. Reducing the Bucket Width setting reduces the time spent on any one bucket and can make better use of multicore machines because more cores can work on all regions of your image.

Too small of a value might increase rendering overhead; however, I usually see a slight increase in speed with setting this to 24 on multicore machines. If you have images getting stuck, then try 24 or go down to 12 on scenes with particular problems.

Bucket Order   The Bucket Order option sets the method that mental ray uses to march buckets across your image. The seeming random Hilbert method (the default) determines which bucket is the easiest to begin next and must be used when the translator option Use Placeholders is used. The other options are for your convenience if you perhaps need a specific pattern for a faster image preview.

Frame Buffer Type   For 3ds Max Design, the floating-point 32-bit frame buffer is the default and is required whenever outputting images to an HDR format. The default in older versions of 3ds Max Design and in standard 3ds Max is the 16-bit integer-based frame buffer. It might take less memory, but it cannot produce images that are high dynamic range no matter what output file type you select.

RENDERING ALGORITHMS

mental ray can use three methods to render a surface: scanline, ray tracing, and the Fast Rasterizer. Because mental ray is an adaptive rendering tool, it will use the faster scanline rendering method when possible and the more time-intensive ray trace rendering technique when needed. This gives you, potentially, the best optimization of render time. The Fast Rasterizer is a special-case option for use with motion blur. Figure 4.18 shows the settings for the scanline rendering algorithm.

FIGURE 4.18
Scanline settings

Scanline   This option does not produce reflections, refractions, shadows, depth of field, and indirect illumination, and mental ray automatically ray-traces for those features. There are occasions where the Scanline option will cause issues in your image and where the Scanline option prevents certain effects from operating properly. If you are starting to get memory issues, disabling the scanline renderer not only can improve memory usage, but in many scenes the forced use of ray tracing might also be faster than with Scanline as an option. Disabling the Scanline option also disables the Fast Rasterizer.

I recommend turning off Scanline or using the Use Fast Rasterizer option when rendering exceptionally high-polygon scenes because it reduces memory requirements.

MOTION BLUR AND SCANLINE

If you have a moving camera when using global illumination or caustic photon maps and are producing motion blur, I recommend disabling the Scanline option to improve the speed of ray tracing and to improve the quality of the global illumination results.

Use Fast Rasterizer The Fast Rasterizer can produce soft, fast-motion blur effects. Enabling this setting disables the primary Samples Per Pixel and Spatial Contrast settings, and instead this feature's Samples Per Pixel and Shades Per Pixel (contrast) settings are used. This option is grouped with the Scanline option and requires Scanline to be enabled to enable Fast Rasterizer; however, it really is not related. The Samples Per Pixel setting here has one setting, and not a min/max range as with Samples Per Pixel; therefore, it's therefore always doing maximum sampling across the image.

In general, this option can give you superior image results, particularly when you are producing motion blur. However, it's at the cost of speed. Ideally, you need to use the RAM Player to compare images to ensure that you are getting the overall image quality that you expect at reasonable sample rates.

The Fast Rasterizer can reduce memory load when rendering scenes with exceptionally high polygon count.

> **Samples Per Pixel** Samples Per Pixel defines the number of subpixels, starting at 1 (a whole pixel), then 4 (2×2 array of sub-pixels), 9 (3×3), 16 (4×4), and so on. Samples cannot be larger than a pixel, and every pixel is always subdivided by the same amount. As a fixed subdivision value, it obviously does not adaptively subdivide samples, and therefore the visual diagnostic tools are not available.

> **Shades Per Pixel** This option controls the number of shading calls per pixel. Higher numbers give more accurate results, and the range is from 0.1 to 10000, with a default of 2.0.

Ray Tracing You must have the Ray Tracing option enabled (the default) to get any indirect illumination, reflections, refractions, ray-traced shadows, and depth of field in your renderings. You might want to turn this feature off when generating quick test-renders where you do not want to override the materials of a scene (see the Processing tab and Translator Options in this chapter) and still need some basic material information. Figure 4.19 shows the ray tracing algorithm settings.

FIGURE 4.19
Ray tracing settings

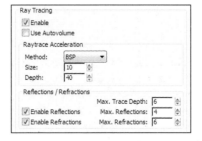

The primary ray tracing settings include Enable and Use Autovolume, BSP, and trace depth settings to control how many times rays can reflect or refract through a scene.

> **Use Autovolume** This option (off by default) is required if you have overlapping volumetric effects, effects within effects, or your camera goes inside a volumetric effect. In this case, you must turn off Scanline, enable ray tracing, and set your shadow mode to Segments (see "Shadows & Displacement" in this chapter).

Raytrace Acceleration: BSP (Binary Space Partitioning)   For mental ray to produce a rendered sample, it must cast a "ray" from the camera into the scene along the line of sight of the camera — an *eye-ray*. Potentially, it must test the path of that ray against all geometry in your scene to see whether that ray intersects any face. However, testing all geometry would take an extraordinarily long amount of time. To simplify things, mental ray will divide geometry in the scene into small partitions, and then a ray only needs to be checked against the small partition of faces that it intersects. This process is called *binary space partitioning*. mental ray has two BSP options, the default BSP and BSP2.

The newer BSP2 mode is recommended for large and complex scenes. It does not have any settings, and mental ray manages partitioning automatically. For smaller scenes, you might notice a slight drop in rendering performance compared to BSP mode, in which case the default settings for BSP are usually adequate. Properly adjusting BPS settings takes some trial and error and can reduce render times significantly, perhaps by hours for complex scenes. Changes in the BSP setting only affect memory and render time and do not affect the quality of your rendered image.

There is a diagnostic mode to visualize how the BSP works, which is a mode that is not usable for the BSP2 mode. To assist with determining a setting for BSP the Render Message Window dialog box gives statistics on BSP depth and leaf size for the last rendering.

Figure 4.20 shows the depth and arrangement of BSP partitions. Red indicates faces that are at the top of a partition tree and faces in the partition closest to the view, and lighter colors are progressively farther away. An ideal image would have predominantly midrange colors of yellow-orange, and considering the geometry of this scene, it looks good. A partition tree consists of faces that are generally pointing the same direction, within +–90 degrees, and as many faces as the Size parameter permits. A ray striking part of the partition tree is compared with the rest of that tree.

Knowing what settings to use with BSP is based on two guidelines (discussed in a moment) and your own tests with a particular scene. The default option, BSP, has two parameters, Size and Depth. Increasing the Size value reduces memory consumption; however, it may significantly increase render time because more triangles are managed in each partition, and each ray would need to consider all the faces in the partition. A larger partition Size requires fewer partitions, requires less Depth, and may reduce memory consumption.

Decreasing the Size parameter means more partitions, more Depth required, and more memory consumed. The benefit is that there will be fewer triangles per partition and potentially a speed-up in ray-tracing performance. Too small of a value, and you may experience some delay because additional partitions must be created and managed.

Increasing the Depth value can reduce rendering time for large triangle-count scenes; however, mental ray will use more memory and render preprocessing time. Large values may also negatively affect render time in scenes using motion blur, which often relies on many partitions when rendering the effect. If Windows or mental ray runs out of memory and starts to swap to the disk, there is a significant drop-off in render speed, so use large Depth values with caution.

Figure 4.21 shows a visual diagnostics image for BSP size; different size partition trees are in different colors (a final rendered image of this scene is in the book's image gallery).

FIGURE 4.20
Visual diagnostic mode for BSP depth

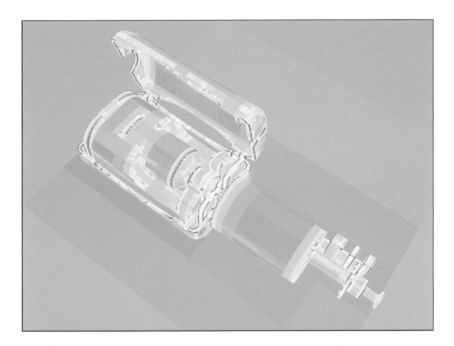

FIGURE 4.21
A BSP visual diagnostic image that shows low settings for BSP that result in a large increase in render time

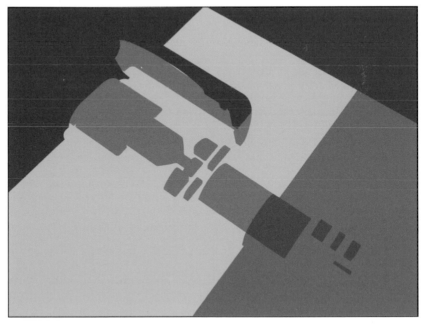

This image shows BSP settings that are too low, namely, a Size setting of 20 and a very low Depth setting of 10. The BSP calculation time took 40 times longer than with default settings of Size = 10 and Depth = 40. For this particular scene, increasing Size from the default dropped render time slightly, whereas larger Depth values did not have a measureable impact. For scenes that are taking a long time to render, particularly animations, try a Depth setting of 50 or more. When troubleshooting long renders, play with BSP values without using visual diagnostics to determine the fastest settings. However, for most scenes, the default settings, or using BSP2, are usually sufficient. The time difference between using BSP and BSP2 for the scene in Figure 4.19 gave a 9 percent decrease in render time with BSP2.

Reflection/Refractions   The Trace Depth settings, as shown previously in Figure 4.19, can greatly affect both render time and the quality and quantity of reflections in your scene. It is important that you increase these settings if you are getting black areas inside transparent objects, yet keep them to a minimum to prevent long render times.

Max Trace Depth   This value controls the total number of reflections and refractions that a ray can take, which is an upper limit for combined reflect/refract. If this setting is 6, for instance, then you can have two reflections and four refractions, five reflections and one refraction, and so on, depending on the needs of your scene.

Max Reflections and Max Refractions   As their names imply, the Max Reflections value caps total reflections for a ray, and Max Refractions caps the refractions. Even though between the two they typically add up to more than the Max Trace setting's Depth value, no ray can have its total reflections and refractions greater than the Max Trace setting's Depth setting.

REFLECTIONS AND REFRACTIONS

If you are seeing too few reflections or black areas where you should see transparency, then consider increasing these global Trace Depth settings. The mental ray A&D material and the ProMaterials have their own limits for reflections and refractions, and you need to ensure that both the renderer and materials have enough trace depth. ProMaterials uses a zero for its Depth settings, which means that it will instead use the global limit setting in the Render Setup dialog box. You can gain a lot of render speed while also keeping global reflect and refract trace depth where you need them by limiting the trace depth per material rather than by limiting the global setting.

Subset Pixel Rendering   This option, as shown in Figure 4.22, causes only the pixels on the selected object(s) to be rendered. It differs from Area To Render's Selected option in the Render Frame Window dialog box in that it renders the object within the full context of your scene, leaves the current frame buffer intact, and gives you full reflections and shadows on the selected objects; however, the rendering is limited to the outline of the selected objects.

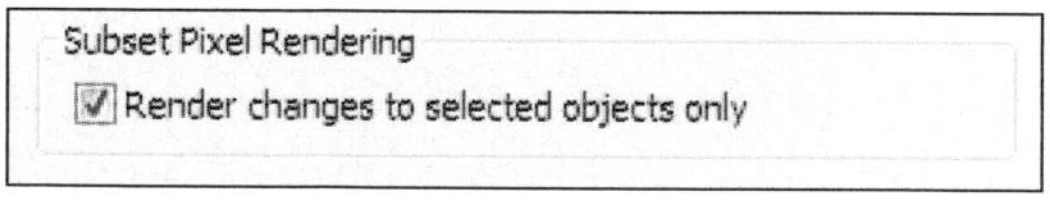

FIGURE 4.22
The Subset Pixel
Rendering option
on the Render
Setup dialog box's
Rendering tab

Subset Pixel Rendering
☑ Render changes to selected objects only

I use Subset Rendered Pixels when I refine renderings and when I produce option images for clients. This option allows you to change an object's material, for instance, and render different versions of your scene without having to render the entire scene. The only issue you might find with this option is that any reflections of the new material visible in other surfaces of the scene will be incorrect. Figure 4.23 shows the Render Subset icon in the Rendered Frame Window dialog box. There are no options beyond selecting an object, enabling this button, and clicking Render.

FIGURE 4.23
The Render Subset option in the Render Frame Window dialog box

In Figure 4.24 you can see an image that was fully rendered; then the object colors were changed, and those objects rerendered with the Render Subset option. Notice that the reflections in the ground plane are now wrong for that changed object, that the plastic shell behind the glass vial did not change color despite the change in material, and that there is a black edge around the rerendered shell. The black edge is the biggest issue I have with this feature. Certainly, this is a difficult case; however, for things such as wall and carpet colors for an interior, for instance, this can work very well and save a considerable amount of rerendering time.

FIGURE 4.24
Objects rerendered with Render Subset option

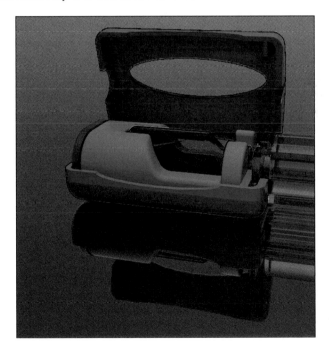

An alternative to this Render Subset option is covered in Chapter 8, "Effects," and is the *Render Subset of Scene/Masking* lens shader. It works in a similar way to Render Subset but has additional options to reduced artifacts along edges by antialiasing against a pre-rendered background; however the rendered subset in this case must be composited with an external compositing application.

In the next section, I cover the last grouping on the Renderer tab: the Shadows & Displacement settings.

SHADOWS & DISPLACEMENT

The settings shown in Figure 4.25 control the way shadows are calculated for a particular ray and allow for the caching of shadow maps to the hard drive for quick reuse.

FIGURE 4.25
Shadows & Displacement settings

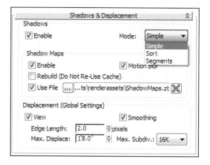

The options in the Mode drop-down list control how shadows are calculated in mental ray. Typically you can keep this at Simple; however, you might see messages in the Render Message Window dialog box that suggest other settings.

Simple   This option is the default shadow mode and calls shadow shaders in a random order.

Sort   This option causes mental ray to call shadow shaders as a ray traverses your scene. It is provided for use by third-party shadow shaders and not used in other instances.

Segments   The Segments mode is one you will probably see mentioned in the Render Message Window dialog box, particularly if you are using A&D materials. It is primarily intended for use with volume shaders and might cause issues in your scene where shadows are treated as if within a volumetric effect when they are not.

This next group of settings in the Shadow Maps section of the Shadows & Displacement settings controls whether motion blur is supported by shadows and controls the optional caching and reuse of shadow maps. The Motion Blur setting should not be enabled here if it is also enabled as a camera effect. Use the camera effect only in this case.

Rebuild and Use File   The Rebuild option — on by default — causes shadow maps to be generated on each frame. Disabling this option and specifying a file in Use File creates a series of `.zt` files in your `.\sceneassets\renderassets` folder, one file for each light using shadow maps. For an animation, this will potentially save render time; however, once the shadows are created, they are static and do not change if objects are animated or if you change your scene. Rebuild the files for each frame in that instance. The light shadow option *mental ray Shadow Map* does not create maps that can be cached using the Use File option.

The last group of settings includes global settings for displacement effects. Displacement works by subdividing a surface and then displacing the tessellated surface a distance defined by the Max. Displace value and the intensity of the pixels in the bitmap. The surface must have a bitmap in the Displacement channel of an Arch & Design material.

View   The View check box toggles whether the displacement Edge Length is in pixels (the View option selected) or in scene units.

Smoothing   This option, as it name implies, smooths the results of the displacement. This setting is not for use with height map displacement because it affects the displaced geometry.

Edge Length   This setting allows you to specify the smallest subdivision possible in the tessellated and displaced surface. The default is 2 pixels.

Max. Displacement   This setting is a distance in scene units to limit the total displacement of all surfaces. Black pixels will have no displacement, and white pixels will displace the surface to this distance. Pixels between black and white will displace a varying amount based on their brightness.

Max. Subdiv.   This setting is the maximum number of subdivisions a surface mesh triangle can be subdivided into to create the displacement needed by the image. Subdividing is a recursive process, and mental ray will tessellate each triangle repeatedly to create the desired displacement, not to exceed this maximum value.

In the next section I cover the Processing tab settings, which can help optimize memory use and which contain the visual diagnostics tools and the settings to control distributed bucket rendering.

Understanding the Processing Tab Settings

The Processing tab of the Render Settings dialog box (press F10) contains settings for the translator, visual diagnostics, and distributed bucket rendering. Visual diagnostics mode was covered earlier in this chapter for the Sample Rate settings and is also covered in Chapters 5 and 6. Visual diagnostics allows you to see a rendered color overlay that represents the behind-the-scenes values for indirect illumination and other internal processing values to assist you in making adjustment to mental ray settings.

Understanding Translator Settings and Memory Settings

The Translator is the portion of mental ray that converts your scene into a format that mental ray can render, allows you to override materials and cache geometry, and also manages memory and hard drive use for the renderer.

One of the biggest issues that users had in earlier versions of 3ds Max/Design is out-of-memory errors when rendering with mental ray and the render subsequently crashing. When this happens, a warning dialog box opens indicating that mental ray cannot allocate memory. In this instance, it is advisable to close and reopen your scene in order to reliably continue editing and rendering your scene.

When you do not have enough memory in a machine to hold your rendering, then that memory limitation can have a huge impact on the speed of your rendering; when not enough memory is available, your computer will start using the hard drive to swap parts in and out of your scene as needed. Hard drives are an order of magnitude slower than DRAM, and swapping to the drive greatly impacts rendering speed. For instance, a rendering that might be 15 minutes on a machine with 4GB might be several hours or more on a machine with only 2GB. When you run out of memory resources, physical and virtual, then mental ray will crash. Using 64-bit operating systems and a minimum of 4GB or 8GB of memory will help with many problematic scenes. Memory is cheap, your time is not.

To greatly help with this issue, mental ray in 3ds Max/Design 2010 and newer handles memory management itself and does not require a lot of user interaction to function well. Even 32-bit computers with relatively limited resources can render high-resolution images that would not be possible before. Memory management is controlled in the Translator Options, and Figure 4.26 shows the Translator Options in 3ds Max/Design 2010 and newer, which are discussed in detail in the following sections.

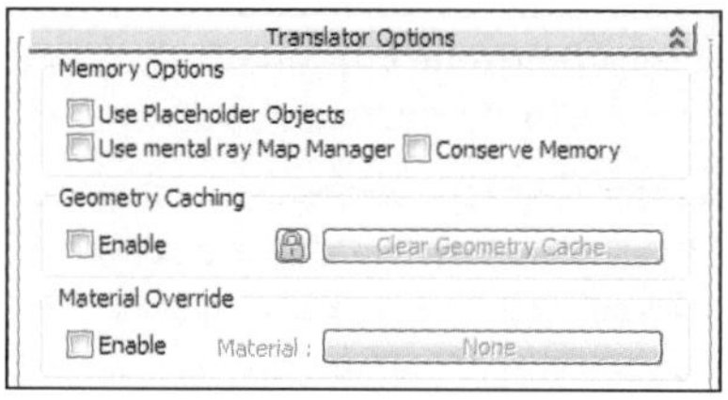

FIGURE 4.26
Translator Options settings can greatly affect memory use.

Having adequate physical DRAM is still essential to efficiency; however, the new technology in 3ds Max/Design 2010 and newer helps those with limited resources get the job accomplished. That said, minimizing polygon count and minimizing the size of bitmaps used in your scenes can result in faster renders and a more stable experience with 3ds Max/Design and mental ray.

Use Placeholder Objects   This option allows mental ray to manage your individual geometry objects as empty bounding boxes — placeholders — until that geometry is needed by a bucket being rendered. It allows the Translator to swap geometry in and out of your scene to conserve memory and can reduce network utilization in distributed rendering.

mental images says that this is a "must use" option whenever you use distributed bucket rendering. Distributed bucket rendering will work without this, but your network utilization might be higher with this option off, because all machines get a full copy of the scene geometry, and consequently the memory requirements at remote machines may be higher because they will need to hold the entire scene in memory rather than just the geometry they need to render.

Use mental ray Map Manager   This option causes mental ray to read bitmaps from disk only when they are needed. It then converts them into a mental ray bitmap format, and they are held in memory; the advantage is that mental ray can remove the map from memory when space is needed.

Turning this option off prevents mental ray from off-loading unneeded bitmaps, and bitmaps are then managed by 3ds Max/Design. The default for 3ds Max/Design is that all maps are held in memory, even between rendering sessions, which can impact your available free memory. Having this option off can be faster for rendering if you have the resources, because the bitmaps will be immediately available at render time. Just keep in mind that this can also use up a lot of memory that may be needed for editing scenes and running other applications. In 3ds Max/Design 2010 and newer, 3ds Max/Design provides options for adjusting bitmap caching, accessible from the Render Setup dialog box's Common tab, and you can control whether 3ds Max/Design stores bitmaps between render sessions.

Because using this option may affect the bitmap and the filtering applied, be certain that your image looks correct when rendered. In some versions of mental ray, the mental ray Map Manager will appear to put "seams" in some bitmaps that have a Blur setting enabled. Lower the Blur setting to 0.01, apply Blur manually to the bitmap on the hard drive using a photo editor, or do not use the mental ray Map Manager feature. An alternative to this feature is to use the 3ds Max/Design Bitmap Pager if you need to better manage bitmap memory.

In some versions of mental ray, the mental ray Map Manager feature ignores any Gamma Override settings you might have on your bitmaps and only uses the global values specified by selecting Customize ➤ Preferences. To override gamma on a per-image basis, you need to wrap your bitmap in the Gamma & Gain shader, discussed in Chapter 1, or manually apply correction to the bitmap image on your drive.

Memory Limit (legacy setting)   This setting, as shown in Figure 4.27 is not shown in Figure 4.26 because this setting applies only to 3ds Max/Design 2009 and older. 3ds Max/Design 2010 and newer no longer have a Memory Limit setting, and RAM memory limits are automatically managed by mental ray based on your computer's resources.

FIGURE 4.27
3ds Max 2009's
Memory Limit and
Translator settings

The Memory Limit setting specifies the total memory that mental ray will use in your system, and is the set point where one or more of the other Memory Options settings begins to manage memory, swapping geometry and bitmaps out to the hard drive. The default is 640MB, but mental images recommends 20 percent less than the maximum memory available. 32-bit systems have an upper limit of 3GB, and for 64-bit systems, there is effectively no upper limit to the setting. You are, of course, limited by your available physical memory and the memory remaining after loading your operating system, 3ds Max/Design, and other applications.

Too low of a Memory Limit value will cause poor performance, because mental ray needs to take time swapping out the old and bringing in the new when the limit is hit and would leave memory unused. Physical memory is an order of magnitude faster than virtual memory, so having enough physical memory is critical to efficient rendering.

Conserve Memory   This option causes mental ray to work harder to minimize memory use, at the expense of additional time spent managing placeholder objects and reading/translating maps from your drive. If you are getting memory allocation errors with mental ray, try this option.

OTHER MEMORY OPTIMIZATIONS

Many other things go into memory use and avoiding memory problems, and I will cover those issues throughout the book. These issues include the quantity of lights in your scenes, the type and settings for shadows, the polygon count, indirect illumination settings, and much more.

Geometry Caching This option can speed up repeated renders by saving your preprocessed translated geometry to the hard drive for fast reuse. Any changes to objects, materials, and position/rotation/scale will update the cached data. Turning on the Lock icon should prevent subobject changes from being updated. Clear the cache to reload with new data.

You can find the option for caching geometry on both the Processing tab of the Renderer Setup dialog box, as shown in Figure 4.26, and in the Reuse section of the Rendered Frame Window dialog box. As an alternative to the Material Override option, the translator provides a Skip Maps And Textures check box, which does just what it describes. Unlike the Material Override option, the underlying surface color and surface properties such as gloss, reflection, and transparency are maintained.

Material Override The Material Override option allows you to replace all materials in your scene with a single material. It is typically used for accelerating test-renders when used with a diffuse white material and is also used when rendering images with ambient occlusion for later compositing.

In the next section, I cover distributed bucket rendering, which allows you to utilize the computing power of other networked computers to render your images.

Using Distributed Bucket Rendering

As mentioned earlier, distributed bucket rendering (DBR) is the process of using CPU cores on remote machines to assist in rendering an image. The render job is distributed across the machines, where each local and remote CPU core handles a bucket. All buckets are managed through the network by your one copy of 3ds Max/Design. Being able to harness the power of remote machines is a significant advantage over the default scanline renderer.

At the remote computers you need to have either a copy of the same version of 3ds Max/Design installed or the correct version of the stand-alone satellite version of mental ray. 3ds Max/Design does not have to be running at the remote machines to use distributed bucket rendering; it just needs to be installed. You enable distributed bucket rendering on the Processing tab and the Distributed Bucket Rendering drop-down section, as shown in Figure 4.28.

FIGURE 4.28
Distributed rendering options

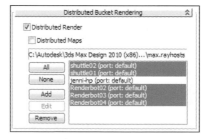

You first need to add the name or IP address of all remote machines to the local "max.rayhosts" list by clicking the Add button. In this figure I have six of my machines listed with five selected for use (in blue), giving me six machines that will be used for the render (the five selected plus my local machine). The CPU cores on the local machine are always used. If you are running 3ds Max/Design on a 64-bit machine, then the target machines must also be x64. I will generally install both x32 and x64 versions of 3ds Max/Design on any machines that can support both versions. Generally, distributed bucket rendering is not used with Backburner rendering.

The Distributed Maps option allows mental ray to load bitmaps from drive paths local to the distributed machines, potentially saving render time. The drive paths must be the same as the main host machine, and using either 3ds Max/Design's local installation and `.\maps` folder or another local drive is preferable to a network drive.

THE TRANSLATOR AND DISTRIBUTED RENDERING

According to the mental ray documentation with 3ds Max/Design, you must turn on Use mental ray Map Manager and Use Placeholder Objects under Translator Options on the Processing tab (see Figure 4.26) when you use distributed bucket rendering. Although it will work without these options, performing a few test-renders ensures that you are not losing speed or seeing artifacts in your bitmaps. For more information on this option, see the "Understanding Translator Settings and Memory Settings" section earlier in this chapter.

The network bandwidth used with distributed bucket rendering can get heavy, especially when dealing with complex geometry and large bitmaps, and gigabit network equipment can speed distributed bucket rendering. The Use Placeholders translator option will help reduce network traffic significantly, as will the Distributed Maps option. The Distributed Maps option forces remote machines to use local drives for retrieving bitmaps, and all machines must have the same path to the bitmaps. This is preferably a local hard drive rather than a network resource.

I tend to use a Backburner network render to remote machines rather than use distributed rendering for final renders, and I use Backburner's Split Scan Lines option for any large images. This way, multiple machines still work on the one image, and progress is saved along the way in the form of individual strip files. If there are issues with a server machine or 3ds Max/Design, any completed strips are safe.

USING RPC WITH DISTRIBUTED RENDERING

Archvision RPC content might show up as red boxes if you use distributed bucket rendering. In this case, use the Split Scan Lines option during Backburner network rendering to use the other computers to render images rather than distributed bucket rendering.

DISTRIBUTED BUCKET RENDERING LICENSING

There are some limitations to the number of processor and processor cores you can use with 3ds Max/Design and mental ray. Without the purchase of additional licenses of mental ray, here is a list of the current licensing and processor capabilities of mental ray within 3ds Max/Design (from Autodesk):

◆ *Number of mental ray satellite (distributed) CPUs (defined as a chip in a socket, not cores):* Eight CPUs

◆ *Local processing core limit (any number of CPUs):* Eight cores

◆ *Network rendering computers via Backburner:* Unlimited

◆ *Architecture:* 32 and 64-bit architecture (you must install both versions of 3ds Max/Design on 64-bit machines for use of x32 and x64)

Assuming four-core CPUs, this gives you up to 32 distributed cores (eight satellite CPUs at up to four cores each) plus your local eight cores, for a total of 40 cores possible during a distributed render without purchasing additional licenses. The newer Intel i7-based CPUs show up as eight cores, and still qualify as a single CPU for licensing purposes.

If you render via Backburner, typically you would not use distributed bucket rendering and would have up to eight cores per machine and an unlimited number of machines.

 **Real World Scenario**

SPEEDING UP RENDERS

In a recent large project for a new client, I sent them, at minimum, daily renderings both to show the client the progress I made on the various parts of the project and so they could evaluate the scene at every stage. Work-in-progress renderings allow you to get feedback from the client as early as possible on materials and lighting to avoid surprises later. They also give you an opportunity to find problems in materials, lights, and settings and let you gauge what your final render times will be for that scene. Many of the examples in this book are designed to show potential problems and solutions and are the kinds of things that will hit you at the last minute if you don't test scenes early. New clients often need a lot more information to get them up to speed on the 3D process and more in-process images so that they know what to expect from your renderings. It is usually best to avoid high settings and area shadows for initial renderings unless you know that your final rendering will use those settings.

Potentially the most stressful parts of a project are the final steps of getting the lighting, materials, and render settings all balanced and optimized so that you can get the rendering accomplished in the time you have available and at the quality you need. Through many years of experience with using the original 3D Studio, then 3ds Max, and now 3ds Max Design and mental ray, I've found that testing a scene early and testing often is the key. Every scene is different, every client's expectations are different, and the more you can experiment with your scene to tweak settings and understand their impact on that scene and the more work-in-process images you can share with the client, the more prepared you will be when the time comes for the final renderings that the more accurate your clients expectations will be. You can better gauge your available time, and you can gauge how far you can push the settings for your target render time, and there will be fewer surprises.

Whether you are learning new rendering tools or need to tweak a project's settings so you can get it out the door, it is imperative that you spend some time doing test-renders and playing with the software prior to committing to a final image or animation. So that you don't waste your time watching your computer render, utilize break and lunch times, after-work hours, or better yet another machine, to do your test renders. The earlier you can do this in a project, the better, and the more enjoyable the rendering experience.

Next I cover some tips and techniques for optimizing your render times, particularly for the testing phase of a project.

Accelerating Test Renders

This testing and discovery process can, and will, take up a lot of computer time, but you can use a few techniques that will speed up this playing phase. Your results will vary, and it depends on your scene and computer speed whether you need to do some of the following:

Use network rendering and a different computer for test renderings   Although not a requirement, this one is pretty important if your time is tight. It both frees you up for more work while the render is burning and gives you extra computer resources when you need to do your final renderings. It is the number-one thing you can do to be more productive when using 3ds Max/Design and mental ray and while you are learning these tools.

One benefit of network rendering is that it does not require you to own additional copies of 3ds Max/Design; any networked computer with a good CPU and adequate memory can render most images. If you have an additional 3ds Max/Design license, then you can also keep your test scene up on the other computer, load the current scene, and render. To justify the expense, look at the time lost waiting for test renders and what billable time you could use for something else. Computers are cheap, network rendering is free functionality, and your time is valuable.

Use the Subset Pixels (Of Selected Objects) option   Detailed in this chapter, this setting can be used, for instance, when you change an object's material and you just need to show the change and update the rendering in the current Rendered Frame Window dialog box, which saves a lot of test-render time. It has issues with some scenes but is terrific for test renderings. As this can cause artifacts, also look at the *Render Subset of Scene/Masking* shader in Chapter 8, "Effects".

Enable the Area Lights/Shadows As Points option   Area lights are a big time killer, and this check box should be enabled (Lights As Points) unless you are prepping for final renders and have more time available to render. See Chapter 2, "Materials and Maps," for information on area light options.

Use Draft mode for Final Gather   This gives you a quick idea of what your lighting and materials will look like without a lot of overhead. The FG feature in 3ds Max/Design 2009 and newer is more intelligent than earlier versions, and you can get better results at lower settings than you saw in 3ds Max 8 and 2008.

Use the Final Gather pass as a quick preview tool   …and cancel when the render begins or you have seen enough. You get a good idea what your lighting and materials will look like just from the Final Gather data. With 3ds Max/Design 2010 and newer, a canceled Final Gather pass is preserved in the Rendered Frame Window dialog box, and not cleared as in previous releases.

Keep your Samples Per Pixel setting to 1/4 and 4, or less   Unless you are doing a final render, having higher settings usually just consumes your time. You will have small jagged edges on objects in your render but can save a lot of time.

Set Spatial Contrast to 0.9 for RGBA   The Spatial Contrast setting is the contrast (color) difference 3ds Max/Design needs to see between pixels and subpixels before it jumps to a higher sample rate. Keeping this high (0.52 is the default) speeds up your test rendering considerably, because the lower Samples Per Pixel rate is almost always chosen. Choose 0.05 or lower for final renderings.

Use the Material Override option As discussed in Chapter 3, this is a technique that allows you to replace every material in your scene with a single material and speeds up test-renders by replacing maps and materials with one simple material. It is usually a white matte paint. It also helps you to focus on the geometry and not the materials when evaluating the composition of your scene.

Keep the rendered image size to a minimum Doubling an image size quadruples the amount of space for the rendered image, since you double in two dimensions. Use a small size, and make liberal use of the Region and Crop render tools to render only those areas you need to examine.

Precompute and save Final Gather and Global Illumination files, and freeze them for instant reuse The Final Gather pass can take longer than the rendering itself, so reuse that information as much as possible. If you make a lot of changes or see splotches in your render, then delete the Final Gather .fgm file and make a new one. Always precompute for animations, computing every few frames rather than every frame.

I often compute the Final Gather file on a reduced-sized render image and freeze (set to read-only), even for final renderings. This saves time and often allows you to use a higher Final Gather setting for the smaller image and still get high-quality results. A half-size rendering (more or less) is usually sufficient. I detail these Final Gather techniques in Chapter 5.

The Bottom Line

Strategize rendering scenes, including Batch Render and Backburner network rendering Utilizing all available computer resources not only helps you to render large images and animations but also assists you in the numerous iterations required to fine-tune your scene. Using Batch Render allows you to manage and queue jobs with or without a network.

Master It How do you configure a scene to use the Batch Render utility to render multiple camera views?

Understand the memory management features of mental ray to reduce memory issues, including using mental ray proxy objects Memory issues are one of the biggest complaints users have had over the years. Newer versions of 3ds Max/Design and mental ray have significantly reduced these issues; however, many users find that using 64-bit operating systems and having 8GB or more of DRAM is essential for large projects. The additional resources speeds rendering by eliminating swapping data to disk, along with reducing memory errors.

Master It What are some common causes for memory issues?

Use visual diagnostic modes to configure the Samples Per Pixel and BSP options Visual diagnostics modes help you to see what is going on internal to mental ray to guide you in determining changes to settings.

Master It How do you enable the visual diagnostics tool for the Sampling Rate setting and adjust Samples Per Pixel?

Chapter 5

Indirect Illumination and Final Gather

Indirect illumination is the bounced light within an environment. In the real world, it accounts for as much of the illumination you see, and simulating its effect is essential to creating realistic and compelling renderings. Producing indirect illumination in your renderings is a straightforward task with mental ray using the first indirect illumination tool that I cover, Final Gather. Final Gather was originally created as a cleanup tool for another indirect illumination effect, Global Illumination, and helped to reduce noise and smooth the illumination. However, over time, Final Gather has become a fast and useful stand-alone tool that is well suited for most scenes.

In this chapter, you will learn to

◆ Adjust the settings of Final Gather

◆ Use visual diagnostics for Final Gather

◆ Cache Final Gather data for still images and animations

Defining Direct and Indirect Illumination

Direct illumination, as its name implies, is the light rays that shine directly on surfaces from a light source and then directly into the camera; it does not account for bounce, or indirect, illumination effects .

Figure 5.1 shows the classic Cornell Box with only direct illumination. The Cornell Box was originally constructed at Cornell University to assist in validating computer simulations of indirect illumination.

Like the Utah Teapot (included as a geometry primitive with 3ds Max/Design), the Cornell Box could be represented as parameters that included the dimensions of the geometry, material reflectance values, and light properties and shared via the Internet. The Cornell Box could then be used to validate early indirect illumination simulations in a consistent manner. The version of the Cornell Box used in this chapter is in your Chapter 5 project folder, located on the DVD in \ProjectFolders\Ch05_Indirect_Illumination_FG\scenes\Cornell Box\. For best results, copy this folder to a local drive when you work on these projects.

Indirect illumination is the light in your scene that is reflected off and refracted through objects and is light that propagates from surface to surface. In the real world, nearly all objects reflect light and become sources of indirect illumination. The light reflecting from their surfaces propagates, or "bleeds", from that surface to other surfaces, affecting the illumination and color of those other surfaces. For instance, if you wear a bright red shirt and stand next to a white wall, the wall near your shirt will turn pink because of the light bouncing from your shirt. Your shirt and all objects you can see are indirect illumination sources.

FIGURE 5.1
The Cornell Box that shows only the effects of direct illumination. Notice the dark shadows, ceiling, and box sides.

Figure 5.2 shows the Cornell Box scene again, and this time it includes indirect illumination. The strong influence of the red and green walls can be seen on the sides of the small boxes, which were not illuminated in the direct illumination example in Figure 5.1.

FIGURE 5.2
The Cornell Box rendered with indirect illumination and showing the strong influence of light reflected from adjacent surfaces

This scene is available as `.\scenes\Cornell_Box\CB_IndIllum.max` in your Chapter 5 project folder.

The indirect lighting tools in mental ray consider only the aftereffect of direct lighting, which is the reflection and refraction of light between and through surfaces. Irradiance particles are the only exception to this rule and do transport direct illumination; they are the subject of Chapter 7, "Importons and Irradiance Particles," and are introduced later in this chapter. A rendered image that includes indirect illumination contains the combined effect of direct and indirect lighting. As you'll examine in this chapter and the next two chapters, mental ray has several methods of producing indirect illumination, each with their own strengths and inherent limitations.

THE IMPORTANCE OF INDIRECT ILLUMINATION

Perhaps 80 percent of the illumination in an environment is contributed by indirect illumination, and simulating its effect is critical to creating realistic renderings. mental ray includes a variety of techniques for simulating bounced lighting, and in 3ds Max Design 2010 and newer, the Final Gather technique is enabled by default on all new scenes.

Without using methods of calculating indirect light like Final Gather, you must produce brighter and more realistic renderings by adding lights to your scene to simulate that missing "bounced" indirect illumination. This is called *fakiosity*, a fake form of radiosity, which is a legacy method of producing indirect illumination primarily with the scanline renderer. Although fakiosity is an art form in and of itself, it is not the focus of this book. You might find, however, that investigating these methods for lighting your scene can help with overall lighting and assist in smoothing rendered results.

Understanding Indirect Illumination in mental ray

Indirect Illumination in mental ray is produced by a variety of technologies:

◆ Global Illumination

◆ Caustics

◆ Final Gather

◆ Ambient Occlusion

◆ Importons (combined with GI or Irradiance Particles)

◆ Irradiance Particles

Although the focus of this chapter is Final Gather, here are short descriptions of the technologies that comprise indirect illumination in mental ray and 3ds Max/Design:

Global Illumination   Global Illumination (GI) is often used as a generic term for indirect illumination; however, in mental ray it is a type of indirect illumination. With GI, mental ray shoots photons (light energy) into the scene from light sources. The photons then bounce from surface to surface picking up color from the surfaces and leaving behind the light and energy collected at that point. In a way, it is "painting with light" because the photon bounces, leaving a little paint behind, picking up a little of the color and light from the surface it hits, and continues to bounce around until all the paint is depleted. This method closely matches how light works in the real world and follows the inverse-square law of decay over distance.

Figure 5.3 shows the Cornell Box set to show each location where a photon had left behind color and light energy.

FIGURE 5.3
The Cornell Box that shows the location and color of GI photons on the surfaces of the geometry

Albeit this scene has exceptionally low settings for the purposes of this demonstration, you can see how the photons from the red, green, and white surfaces have bounced seemingly randomly in the scene, depositing light and color as they propagate. This scene shows only 20,000 photons, whereas a typical scene might contain many millions of photons from all light sources to produce the smooth illumination shown in Figure 5.2.

GI stores color and light photon data in 3D space everywhere in your scene, even areas not seen during a render, and can consume considerable memory. GI is typically combined with Final Gather, and the combination of the two often produces the best result. This technique is covered in Chapter 6, "Global Illumination and Caustics." This scene is available as `.\scenes\Cornell_Box\CB_GI.max` in your Chapter 5 project folder. GI can also be combined with Importons to significantly reduce memory use and still produce excellent results. GI and Importons are covered in Chapter 7, "Importons and Irradiance Particles."

Final Gather   This process works by looking from a rendered surface out into the scene to collect indirect illumination from other surfaces. Originally used as a cleanup process for GI, it is enabled by default in 3ds Max Design 2010 and newer and produces excellent results for most scenes, both interior and exterior. Final Gather (FG) is a critical part of the Lighting Analysis tools, which rely on the accurate simulation of light in an environment. The Lighting Analysis tools can assist with analyzing lighting levels in your scene for LEED 8.1 certification. LEED stands for Leadership in Energy Efficient Design, and you can find more information on the website for the U.S. Green

Building Council, www.usgbc.org. Figure 5.4 shows a very low setting for Final Gather to high-light specific points where indirect illumination data was stored.

FIGURE 5.4
The Cornell Box that shows the indirect illumination sampling from Final Gather points, shown as color blotches on the surfaces of the scene

At each smudge on the surface, mental ray shot a random ray out into the scene to sample the illumination. That color and light was stored and added to the direct illumination at render time. As you will see in this chapter, Final Gather typically stores millions of points of data rather than the few thousand shown in Figure 5.4, with each point comprising hundreds of samples (rays) rather than the one sample shown in Figure 5.4. This scene is available as .\scenes\Cornell_Box\CB_FG.max in your Chapter 5 project folder.

Caustics Caustic effects are the result of the concentration of photon energy passing through or reflecting off a surface, such as a magnifying glass or the surface of water. Figure 5.5 shows the Cornell Box scene with some additional caustic generators, including a water plane. The light was changed to a point source to sharpen the caustic effects in this image.

Caustics, because they use photons and are related to Global Illumination, are covered with Global Illumination in Chapter 6. This scene is available as .\scenes\Cornell_Box\CB_Caustics.max in your Chapter 5 project folder.

Ambient Occlusion This indirect illumination technology is a short-range detail enhancement option for materials and is covered in Chapter 2, "Maps and Materials." Ambient Occlusion (AO) samples the area around a rendered sample with random rays to see how much of the sample is occluded (blocked) from receiving ambient light, and the sample is darkened based on how much occlusion occurs. Arch & Design and ProMaterials both include the Ambient Occlusion option.

Importons   Importons, by themselves, are not an indirect illumination technology; however, they work to improve the quality of Global Illumination and are used to control the placement of Irradiance Particles (described next). *Importons* (importance photons) are an importance-driven sampling technique and an extra render pass that analyzes the rendered scene before GI or Irradiance Particles are computed. With Global Illumination they are used to merge photons together based on the photons' contribution to the final rendering. The use of Importons with GI allows you to use more photons than you could normally as extra photons that do not add to the quality of the image are eliminated and their energy is merged with adjacent photons. High quantities of photons in large environments can cause memory issues; however, with Importons, only the photons that are most important to the rendered image are actually stored and used in the rendering greatly reducing memory requirements, while helping to add detail to the rendered image. When caching Global Illumination data to disk or performing distributed rendering, using the Importons technology also reduces network traffic because only a fraction of the original Global Illumination photons are stored and used in the scene.

Figure 5.6 shows the Cornell Box scene with the same Global Illumination settings as the Global Illumination sample scene in Figure 5.3 but processed with Importons. There are far fewer visible Global Illumination points, and in nonvisible areas (behind the boxes) *all* Global Illumination samples are removed because they are not important to the rendering.

This scene in Figure 5.6 is available as .\scenes\Cornell_Box\CB_Importons.max in your project folder; however, it requires the installation of the plug-in described in Chapter 7. Importons are required for use with the next indirect illumination technology, Irradiance Particles (covered in Chapter 7).

FIGURE 5.6
The Cornell Global Illumination scene processed with Importons. When properly averaged, far fewer Global Illumination samples are used to produce the same image as Figure 5.3.

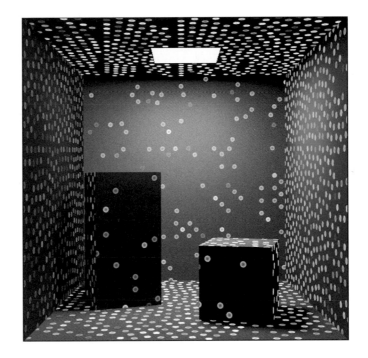

Irradiance Particles   Irradiance Particles (IP) is another new technology that works by shooting Importons into the scene from the camera view to determine where to store irradiance particles, and then both direct and indirect illumination at those points are calculated and stored within the irradiance particle. In some ways, it is an importance-driven version of Final Gather, and many of the controls are similar to Final Gather. Unlike the other indirect illumination techniques, it does store direct illumination. Figure 5.7 shows the Cornell Box rendered using Importons and Irradiance Particles.

The combination of Importons and Irradiance Particles can be a substitute for Global Illumination and Final Gather in many scenes. It does not handle glossy surfaces as well as Final Gather and Global Illumination; however, it can produce image-based lighting effects from a simple high dynamic range environment and works well with difficult scenes. Importons are required for use with Irradiance Particles, and both features are covered in Chapter 7. This scene is available as `.\scenes\Cornell_Box\CB_IP.max` in your Chapter 5 project folder; however, it requires the installation of the plug-in described in Chapter 7.

IMPORTONS AND IRRADIANCE PARTICLES

Importons and Irradiance Particles are not currently part of the mental ray user interface in 3ds Max/Design 2010 or 2011 and are only exposed for your use through an additional plug-in, ctrl.ghost, included in the `\Plugins` folder of your book's DVD or available at www.mastering-mentalray.com. These technologies are examined in Chapter 7.

FIGURE 5.7
Cornell Box rendered with Impor-tons and Irradiance Particles, which results in a smooth and natural feeling rendering

I start the detailed examination of indirect illumination tools by covering Final Gather. Final Gather is quick and easy to set up for most scenes, it adds greatly to the realism of your scenes, and it is enabled by default for new scenes in 3ds Max/Design 2010 and newer.

Understanding Final Gather

Final Gather gives you near-zero-effort way to add indirect illumination to your scenes. Final Gather is used alone for outdoor scenes or can be combined with GI for the highest-quality results on interior scenes. Final Gather is enabled by default in 3ds Max/Design 2010 and newer and must be manually turned on in standard 3ds Max and legacy versions. Final Gather does require your scene to be properly illuminated with some form of direct lighting for it to produce good results. For a pleasing and accurate simulation, you will need perhaps a minimum one-third to one-half of the scene lit with direct light.

Perform the following steps to enable and adjust Final Gather in your own scenes:

1. Open the Render Setup dialog box by pressing F10.

2. Choose the Indirect Illumination tab, and ensure the Final Gather settings are visible, as shown in Figure 5.8.

3. Turn on the Enable Final Gather check box.

4. Choose an FG precision preset, such as Draft or Low.

5. Optionally, increase the number of the Diffuse Bounces setting to 2.

FIGURE 5.8
Final Gather's
Basic settings

Final Gather	☆
Basic	
☑ Enable Final Gather	Multiplier: 1.0 ⬍ ☐
FG Precision Presets:	
━━━━●━━━━	Low
Project FG Points From Camera Position (Best for Stills) ▼	
Divide Camera Path by Num. Segments:	9
Initial FG Point Density:	0.4 ⬍
Rays per FG Point:	150 ⬍
Interpolate Over Num. FG Points:	30 ⬍
Diffuse Bounces 2 ⬍ Weight:	1.0 ⬍

CHOOSING FINAL GATHER PRESETS

For many scenes, using the Draft or Low preset and one or two diffuse bounces is a great starting point. Most images we produce use the Medium preset and two bounces, and some settings may be tweaked beyond that, as you'll see in this chapter. Final Gather, when higher settings are used, can oftentimes take much longer than the rendering itself. Just because a setting goes to Very High does not mean that this setting is practical, or necessary, for your scene.

How Final Gather Works

Final Gather calculation is seen as a three pass, low-resolution, pixilated "rendering" that occurs prior to the actual rendering pass. The indirect illumination collected by the low-resolution Final Gather passes is added to the direct illumination and surface properties at render time to produce the final pixel values and rendered image.

In 3ds Max 2009 and older, the Final Gather data is calculated in a single pass rather than three. If you have used Final Gather in the past, you might find that you can use lower Final Gather settings with 3ds Max/Design 2010 and newer than you needed in previous versions and still get excellent results.

Figure 5.9 shows the Sponza Palace atrium by Marko Dabrovic at approximately 80 percent completion of its Final Gather pass. The right side of the image shows pass 2, while the left side shows primarily pass 3 and additional detail in the image.

FIGURE 5.9
The Sponza atrium
Final Gather pass at
80 percent completion

This visible Final Gather pass allows you to quickly evaluate the lighting of your scene prior to committing to the actual render pass, which allows you to cancel the Final Gather calculation to adjust your scene.

THE SPONZA PALACE ATRIUM MODEL

The Sponza Palace atrium was originally produced by Marko Dabrovic in Lightwave and was donated to the 3D community as part of a Global Illumination competition. This model of a portion of the Sponza Palace in Dubrovnik, Croatia, is notoriously challenging for producing good indirect illumination results and has become a standard in the industry for testing indirect illumination. It is used with permission in this book.

I have converted the materials to Arch & Design and use this scene as an example in all three indirect illumination chapters. The models for this chapter are included in your Chapter 5 project folder on the DVD, in the .\scenes\Sponza folder.

---

mental ray starts the Final Gather process by projecting points from your viewpoint into the scene and onto the surfaces of your geometry. In Figure 5.10, the green line from the camera to the checker box represents the *eye ray*, which is a vector from the camera out into the scene used to place Final Gather points. The number of Final Gather points projected into a scene depends on the Final Gather Density setting.

FIGURE 5.10
A Final Gather eye ray and Final Gather point shown in green, with yellow primary Final Gather rays and magenta diffuse bounces

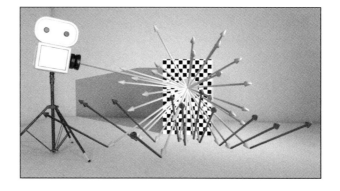

Along the eye ray, mental ray places a Final Gather point on a surface, shown as a green circle on the checker box. From the Final Gather point, mental ray shoots rays (shown in yellow) randomly into the scene to sample indirect illumination. If additional diffuse bounces are enabled, Final Gather rays are reflected from the surface (shown in magenta) and propagated through the scene.

As Final Gather rays travel through your scene, some of the illumination decays over distance, some light is absorbed by the surfaces it strikes, and some of it is recolored at a new intensity and may continue to propagate through your scene. The Final Gather rays follow the inverse-square law for light to produce a natural decay over distance. As enough bounces are made, the cumulative indirect light color and intensity are stored in the Final Gather point.

During the render pass, the illumination from Final Gather points in a radius around a rendered sample are averaged together and then added to direct illumination and the surface color of your geometry to produce the final brightness and color for a sample. The default is to average 30 Final Gather points to produce the indirect illumination value for a particular sample. The higher the Final Gather density and the more rays mental ray shoots from each point, the more accurate and refined the indirect lighting solution will be.

Final Gather data exists in 3D space as a point cloud of data, attached to the surfaces of your scene, and the best way to visualize what is happening with Final Gather is to use the visual diagnostic modes of mental ray, found in the Processing tab or the Render Setup dialog box.

Using a Visual Diagnostics Tool and Final Gather

The visual diagnostics tool of mental ray allows you to see a color representation of data that is internal to the renderer and not directly visible in a rendered image or your scene viewport. Figure 5.11 shows the same scene as Figure 5.9 but with small green dots that represent the position of Final Gather points placed in the scene during the Final Gather preprocessing phase. This is the visual diagnostics tool for Final Gather.

FIGURE 5.11
The Sponza Atrium visual diagnostics rendering that shows the position of Final Gather data points

Each green point is a location where mental ray determined there was a change in contrast and a need for additional Final Gather data. Each Final Gather precision preset, shown in Figure 5.8, produces progressively denser Final Gather results, as I'll show you later in this chapter. Figure 5.11 shows the Medium Final Gather preset and took approximately six minutes to create on a single midrange quad-core machine.

Perform the following steps to enable visual diagnostics for Final Gather within your own mental ray scenes:

1. Open the Render Settings dialog box from Rendering Render Setup, or press F10.

2. Select the Processing tab.

3. Roll down the Diagnostics section.

4. Enable the Visual mode.

5. Select the Final Gather option.

In the next section, I start by going through the Final Gather settings from a technical standpoint, with short examples to illustrate points as needed, before I get into more involved examples near the end of the chapter.

Introducing Final Gather Settings

The settings for Final Gather are located in the Render Setup dialog box on the Indirect Illumination tab, and you can find additional controls in the Rendered Frame Window dialog box under Final Gather Precision.

Using Final Gather Basic Settings

Figure 5.12 again shows the Basic section of the Final Gather settings on the Indirect Illumination tab of the Render Setup dialog box.

FIGURE 5.12
FG Basic settings

The use of the Enable check box is obvious; however, in the Rendered Frame Window dialog box, you can slide the Final Gather Precision slider all the way to the left to disable Final Gather. Many of the Rendered Frame Window sliders work in this way. Figure 5.13 shows the Final Gather settings in the Rendered Frame Window dialog box.

FIGURE 5.13
Final Gather
Precision, Trace/
Bounces Limits,
and Reuse options
in the Rendered
Frame Window
dialog box

The FG Bounces setting is the same setting as Diffuse Bounces, described shortly. The Reuse options are also described later in this chapter.

The remaining settings in the FG Basic section of the Render Setup dialog box (shown earlier in Figure 5.12) are as follows:

Multiplier and color swatch The Multiplier option, shown in Figure 5.12, scales the overall contribution of Final Gather in your rendered image, and the associated color swatch allows you to tint the color of the Final Gather illumination. Slight adjustments might improve the artistic feel of your images; however, the default settings of 1.0 and pure white produces physically accurate results, and normally these settings do not need to be changed. Figure 5.14 shows the Light Lab scene with a Multiplier setting of 2.0 tinted with a red color. These settings also allow you to adjust Final Gather data that has been cached with the Reuse options, discussed later in the chapter.

FIGURE 5.14
The Light Lab scene rendered with a Multiplier setting of 2.0 and a red FG tint

FG Precision Presets   This slider, shown in Figure 5.12, provides some common settings for Final Gather, with each setting from Draft through Very High progressively increasing values for Initial FG Point Density and Rays Per FG Point, and, when on Very High, increasing the Interpolate Over Num. FG Points settings. Figure 5.15 shows a visual diagnostic rendering of the Light Lab scene with the Draft preset and displays a sparse and regular pattern of green FG points across the surface of the image.

FIGURE 5.15
The Light Lab scene rendered with the Final Gather preset Draft and the visual diagnostic mode

The Draft setting has an Initial FG Point Density setting of 0.1, a Rays Per FG Point value of 50, and an Interpolate Over Num. FG Points setting of 30.

Figure 5.16 shows a visual diagnostic rendering of the Light Lab scene using the Medium preset.

Going from Draft to Medium increased render time for this image by 50 percent. The higher setting means better detail in the crevices of your scene, particularly within areas where there are fast changes in contrast and in areas that contain shadows.

FIGURE 5.16
The Light Lab scene rendered with the FG preset Medium and the visual diagnostic mode

Figure 5.17 shows the visual diagnostics result of the Very High preset. This took a single 2.4GHz quad-core machine 19 hours 34 minutes to calculate, or 35 times longer than the Medium preset.

FIGURE 5.17
The Light Lab scene rendered with the FG preset Very High and the visual diagnostic mode

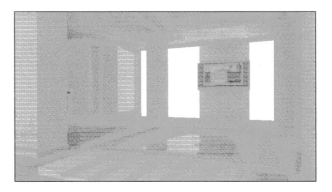

The extreme time for the FG calculation and the dense coverage of green FG points shows pretty clearly that this setting is not something that is useful for the average scene. The only time I would consider using the Very High setting would be if I were going to calculate FG at a very small image resolution and still needed high-quality results for a much larger render.

As a more practical example of how the presets affect the quality of your scene, Figure 5.18 shows an area of the Light Lab scene rendered with the Draft preset.

In this scene, most of the illumination comes from the large windows in the scene open to daylight illumination, and much of the illumination in this view is from indirect lighting. The Draft preset, although not intended for production use, does an OK job providing a soft and diffuse-looking indirect illumination result.

Figure 5.19 is the same view as Figure 5.18 but this time with the Medium preset. You will notice more illumination on the walls and under the cabinet, more defined shadows (particularly under the cabinet), and a much darker gap at the right side of the cabinet.

In Figure 5.20 you can see the same view with the High FG preset. Again, you see further refinement of the shadows under the cabinet, and in general the results are smoother across large surfaces.

FIGURE 5.18
The Light Lab scene
rendered with the
FG preset Draft

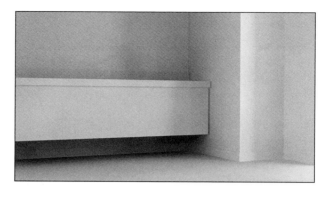

FIGURE 5.19
The Light Lab
scene rendered
with the FG preset
Medium

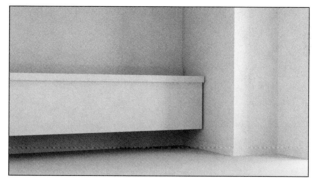

FIGURE 5.20
The Light Lab scene
rendered with the
FG preset High

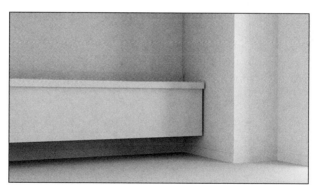

You obviously get superior results with the High settings compared to Draft; however, the High settings took seven times longer to produce than the Draft preset, and they took three times longer than Medium. Much of the detail missing in the scene with the lower FG precision presets can be brought back by enabling the Ambient Occlusion option in Arch & Design materials. Figure 5.21 uses the Medium FG precision preset and the Ambient Occlusion option in an Arch & Design material.

This image with Medium FG precision with Ambient Occlusion has much better detail than even the High FG setting, and it rendered with only 4 percent additional time compared to Medium FG without Ambient Occlusion.

FIGURE 5.21
The Light Lab scene
rendered with the
FG preset Medium
and Ambient
Occlusion tool

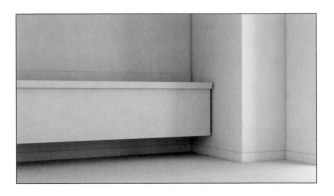

WHEN TO START USING GLOBAL ILLUMINATION

If you find that you need to turn up Final Gather beyond Medium and are using other settings to try to achieve smooth indirect light results, then it might be time to consider adding Global Illumination.

Although it is a bit more to set up and comes with its own challenges, you can achieve superior results in much less time by using Global Illumination combined with low Final Gather settings. The use of combined Global Illumination and Final Gather is covered in Chapter 6.

Although not usually necessary, you can modify the FG Precision Presets settings by changing the `mentalray_fg_presets.ini` file located in the `\plugcfg` folder of your 3ds Max/Design installation, typically `C:\Program Files\Autodesk\3ds Max Design 2011\`.

Using the Project Points and Divide Camera Path by Num. Segments Option

The next settings in the Final Gather tool's Basic settings is actually a drop-down selector with two options: Project FG Points From Camera Position (Best For Stills) and Project Points From Positions Along Camera Path. The first option, the default, calculates FG on a full rendered frame, as I have demonstrated so far. The second method, Project Points From Positions Along Camera Path, is an option that can help reduce rendering artifacts when producing animations.

You should use the default setting, Project FG Points From Camera Position, any time you are producing still images and any time you are producing final-quality animations as each frame of your rendered animation will calculate and use a full frame of Final Gather data. However, because of the random nature of the placement of Final Gather points and the randomness of the Final Gather Rays from each Final Gather point, you will likely see some variation from frame to frame in animations that do not use the *Reuse (FG and GI Disk Caching)* options, described later in this chapter. This randomness might appear as scintillation, as shimmering, or as a subtle crawling of indirect illumination across surfaces during the animation. An animation demonstrating this effect is provided on the DVD as `\ProjectFolders\05_Indirect_Illumination_FG\renderoutput\FG_Crawl.avi`.

The other option, Project Points From Positions Along Camera Path, causes mental ray to split your Final Gather pass view into multiple segments, with each segment rendering a small thumbnail Final Gather pass of your scene, as seen from camera positions along your animation and as shown in Figure 5.22.

FIGURE 5.22

The Final Gather pass when you use the Project Points From Positions Along Camera Path option

Figure 5.22 shows the Final Gather pass results when creating nine segments, prior to rendering this animation segment. The number of segments is determined by the drop-down menu Divide Camera Path By Num. Segments, shown in Figure 5.23.

FIGURE 5.23

The drop-down options for Divide Camera Path By Num. Segments

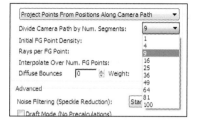

The Final Gather pass image shown in Figure 5.22 was produced with the Calculate FG/GI And Skip Final Rendering option in the Reuse (FG And GI Disk Caching) drop-down menu to disable the render pass. The Divide Camera Path By Num Segments option should be combined with the read/write features for the Final Gather map to save the Final Gather data for reuse during the rendering of the entire animation path.

You can think of each thumbnail in Figure 5.22 as a snapshot where Final Gather data has been sprayed onto the surfaces of your scene, contributing to a single overall three-dimensional point cloud of Final Gather data. Because Final Gather is view dependent, this option needs to see enough of your scene to "paint" all surfaces through your animation path with enough data to give continuous Final Gather data. You must avoid gaps in the Final Gather data, so fast or inconsistent camera motion does not always work well with this option.

After this thumbnail Final Gather pass is done, the Final Gather data on all "painted" surfaces is used in a read-only manner to produce indirect illumination for your animation. Further Final Gather calculation is not produced for the actual rendered images of the animation.

The disadvantage to this method is that the Final Gather data is less dense than Final Gather calculated on a full frame. This means that you need to turn up your Final Gather settings to get reasonable results. The more segments you choose (up to 100 segments can be created), the smaller the Final Gather thumbnail view, and the fewer Final Gather points are created in each thumbnail. Because each thumbnail will place Final Gather points semirandomly, each thumbnail contributes additional detail to a complete three-dimensional Final Gather point cloud. Figure 5.24 shows a visual diagnostic mode rendering that displays the Final Gather points from frame 50 of the animation.

FIGURE 5.24
Frame 50 of an animation produced with a nine-segment "Project Points From positions Along Camera Path" option

Figure 5.25 shows the same scene using the default project option and saving FG data every 10 frames using the Reuse options. As you can see, the Final Gather data is more refined, is less random, and is concentrated in areas with rapid change in brightness, as with corners.

FIGURE 5.25
The same frame rendered with the default Final Gather Project FG Points From Camera Position option and the reusing of cached Final Gather data

USING THE PROJECT POINTS FROM POSITIONS ALONG CAMERA PATH FEATURE

The Project Points From Positions Along Camera Path feature is good for short test-renders, but anything beyond a short animated segment should use the mode Project FG Points From Camera Position along with the *Reuse (FG and GI Disk Caching)* options described later in this chapter. You must cache (reuse) Final Gather data calculated with the Project Points From Positions Along Camera Path option. The advantage to the Project Points From Positions Along Camera Path method is that it does much less work computing Final Gather for your animation and can produce test animations relatively fast with minimal Final Gather overhead. The disadvantage is a lack of Final Gather detail and accuracy.

In your own mental ray 3ds Max/Design scenes, perform the following steps to use the Project Points From Positions Along Camera Path option:

1. Enable Final Gather, and choose an FG precision preset.

2. Choose the Project Points From Positions Along Camera Path option.

3. Select the number of segments from the Divide Camera Path By Num. Segments drop-down menu, ensuring that enough view-dependent FG points will be created to cover the areas visible in your animation.

4. In the Reuse (FG And GI Disk Caching) drop-down menu, shown in Figure 5.26, set the Final Gather Map option to the Incrementally Add FG Points to Map Files option.

FIGURE 5.26

The Reuse (FG And GI Disk Caching) roll-down menu

5. Optionally delete any existing Final Gather map file, or change the FG filename from `temp.fgm` to `ProjPoints.fgm`, as shown in the dialog box in Figure 5.26.

6. With your Camera view as the active view, click the Generate Final Gather Map File Now button in the Reuse menu area, shown in Figure 5.26. The Final Gather map file is created after the FG pass completes.

7. Set the Final Gather Map option to Read FG Points Only From Existing Map Files.

8. Render your animation. The Final Gather pass will be skipped, greatly speeding your render pass.

The remainder of the settings from the Final Gather Basic settings (as shown in Figure 5.12) include Initial FG Point Density, Rays Per FG Point, Interpolate Over Num. FG Points, Diffuse Bounces, and Weight:

Initial FG Point Density   This setting controls how many FG points are generated for your scene — the density of the green dots shown in the visual diagnostics images. The FG Precision Presets settings include Draft = 0.1, Low = 0.4, Medium = 0.8, High = 1.5, and Very High = 4.0. The total number of FG points placed in the scene is not only tied to the Initial FG Point Density setting but also to the size of your rendered image; larger renders will store more FG points. This means that you might be able to render a large image with a Low setting and get the same results as a smaller image at the Medium preset settings. In a recent test, an 800-pixel-wide rendering generated an 8mb FG file with Medium FG preset. The same scene at 1280 wide generated an 18mb FG file.

Rays Per FG Point   This is the number of samples (rays) each FG point will shoot out into your scene to collect indirect illumination. The more samples, the more accurate the estimation of indirect illumination will be. Because some rays may hit very bright areas of your scene, mental ray provides a Noise Filtering option in the Advanced settings to remove any rays that are exceptionally bright and to help smooth your overall rendering. The number of rays range from a 50 at the Draft preset to 250 rays at the Medium preset all the way to 10,000 at Very High. More than 500 rays are not practical for most scenes.

Interpolate Over Num. FG Points   As shown in Figure 5.27, Final Gather points by themselves produce a very mottled appearance in your rendering.

FIGURE 5.27
The Cornell box with very low settings for Final Gather

Each point contains light and color information different from its neighbor. The interpolate Final Gather points option averages a specific quantity of Final Gather points around a sample that is being rendered. By default this number is 30 Final Gather points for all presets, but it changes to 50 at the Very High FG Precision Preset setting. As you can see from the various visual diagnostic images, 30 Final Gather points might represent a very large area on geometry like a wall and a very small area on high-detail geometry or areas where there is a sharp change in contrast. If you're having difficulty getting a smooth Final Gather appearance, increasing the Interpolate Final Gather Points value will not impact render time but will make the indirect illumination solution more diffuse. Adding ambient occlusion to selected materials often improves the detail in the rendering in this instance.

Diffuse Bounces and Weight   As Figure 5.28 shows, the Final Gather point shoots rays out into the scene to collect indirect illumination, shown as yellow arrows. This is effectively one bounce of indirect illumination because a direct light source must first illuminate the location where the ray (yellow arrow) strikes a surface for it to bounce to our FG point. A brighter and a more accurate Final Gather solution is produced by allowing the Final Gather ray to propagate to other surfaces in the scene, shown as purple arrows in Figure 5.28. These are the additional diffuse bounces.

FIGURE 5.28
The FG ray path shown as yellow arrows, with one diffuse bounce per ray shown as magenta arrows

Each additional diffuse bounce level increases your FG calculation time, and you can basically multiply your FG calculation time by the number of diffuse bounces. I find having two or more diffuse bounces essential for my renderings, and they are too dark without the additional calculation. The Weight value adjusts the contribution of diffuse bounces to the FG points. You might find that adding diffuse bounces to the renderings helps smooth out the FG result but brightens the scene more than you would like, and the Weight value allows you to adjust the additional brightness gained by diffuse bounces. I typically leave this at 1.0.

A Diffuse Bounces setting of 2 works well for most scenes; however, settings of up to 5 might be needed for scenes that are having moderate difficulty in producing smooth FG results, and as many as 20 diffuse bounces might be needed for exceptionally difficult scenes. A Diffuse Bounces setting of 4 is used with the Lighting Analysis tools rendering preset, covered in Chapter 9, "mental ray for Architecture."

Increasing the number of diffuse bounces is tempting as a quick way to improve the brightness of an interior scene; however, adding mr Sky Portals where appropriate will allow you to use lower Final Gather settings and produce brighter and smoother renderings.

Adjusting Final Gather Advanced Settings

This section of the Final Gather settings includes options that do not need to be adjusted for most scenes. Figure 5.29 shows the Advanced options for Final Gather.

FIGURE 5.29
The Advanced section of the Final Gather settings

| Advanced |
| Noise Filtering (Speckle Reduction): Standard |
| ☐ Draft Mode (No Precalculations) |
| Trace Depth |
| Max. Depth: 5   Max. Reflections: 2 |
| Max. Refractions: 5 |
| ☐ Use Falloff (Limits Ray Distance) |
| Start: 0.0   Stop: 0.0 |
| FG Point Interpolation |
| ☐ Use Radius Interpolation Method (Instead of Num. FG Points) |
| ☐ Radius: 5.0 |
| ☑ Radii in Pixels   ☐ Min. Radius: 0.5 |

Noise Filtering (Speckle Reduction)   The name for this setting is a little misleading, because I think of speckles as small dots, but this setting typically helps reduce blotchy Final Gather results. This setting filters out any Final Gather rays that are very bright compared to other rays in a particular Final Gather point. You will typically see these speckles (blotches) in indoor scenes that include very bright outdoor daylight illumination. The issue is that the random nature of Final Gather rays means that some Final Gather points will naturally hit some of the extremely bright surfaces illuminated by the daylight system more than other Final Gather points, resulting in bright spots and uneven indirect lighting. Increasing noise filtering can greatly increase your Final Gather calculation time, particularly if you are using high ray settings; however it will darken the rendering. Using an mr Sky Portal and the Standard filter settings with indoor day-lit scenes will typically produce superior results compared to simply increasing the Noise Filtering level.

Figure 5.30 shows the Light Lab scene using Standard level for Noise Filtering and without the use of mr Sky Portal lights across the large windows.

FIGURE 5.30
Light Lab scene rendered without mr Sky Portals and using the Standard setting for Noise Filtering. The Medium FG preset was used.

As this figure shows, the indirect illumination results have a mottled appearance, despite the presence of interior direct lighting. Figure 5.31 shows the same scene, without mr Sky Portals and with the High setting for Noise Filtering.

FIGURE 5.31
Light Lab scene rendered without mr Sky Portals and with the High setting for Noise Filtering

Changing from the Standard to High setting increased render time by only 7 percent and still did not produce acceptable results. The image actually got darker as more bright FG rays were filtered and removed. More prominent direct lighting would help. With the Noise Filtering preset set to Very High, it shows an overall increase in rendering time of 13 percent over the Standard settings for Noise Filtering, with the results shown in Figure 5.32.

FIGURE 5.32
Light Lab scene rendered without mr Sky Portals and with the Very High setting for Noise Filtering

Again, you see more of the light rays being filtered from the solution and a darker and more mottled appearance to the image. At the upper left you can also see some of the incandescent direct light from the wall fixtures, because now the FG illumination is reduced below the intensity of the direct lighting. Obviously, for this interior scene, the Noise Filtering setting is not improving the image.

Figure 5.33 shows the Light Lab scene with the addition of mr Sky Portals across the exterior windows and using the Standard setting for Noise Filtering. The addition of mr Sky Portals increased render time 42 percent compared to the same scene without mr Sky Portals but produced a brighter image with fairly smooth results and was easy to configure.

FIGURE 5.33
Light Lab scene rendered with mr Sky Portals and the Standard setting for Noise Filtering

Draft Mode (No Precalculations)   As its name implies, this is not intended for final renderings; however, it does begin rendering your images right away without the low-resolution FG Pass. You still get very little indirect illumination and it may not be smooth.

Trace Depth Settings   Similar to mental ray's main ray-trace settings, these settings limit how often a Final Gather ray can reflect or refract in your scene. These limits are automatically increased if you set your diffuse bounces higher than the levels in this group.

Use Falloff (Limits Ray Distance)   The Use Falloff settings allow you to limit how far an FG ray will travel in your scene and can speed the FG process. You have settings for Start distance which determines when additional falloff occurs, and Stop which is where the environment color is returned to the Final Gather point. It is particularly useful for outdoor scenes where the FG ray would otherwise go off into space and take mental ray additional time to make that determination; with this option, when an FG ray hits its End value distance it returns the environment color, and computation goes on to the next ray, speeding calculation. Figure 5.34 shows an outdoor scene without the Use Falloff option on the left, and it shows the scene with the Falloff option on the right with a Start value of 12′ and an End value of 24′, rather low values. The image with Use Falloff enabled rendered 15 percent faster than without the option.

FIGURE 5.34
Use Falloff is enabled on the right of this image and disabled on the left.

Although it's subtle, you can see the image split best on one of the support posts in the center bottom, where the image is darker on the left without Use Falloff than on the right with Use Falloff. The overall image on the right has less contrast, the relatively low Start and End values mean that the FG ray returns the Environment color too soon, and FG contribution from surrounding geometry is not present in much of the image. Because the environment is a bright sky in this case, shadows are lost. For an exterior scene, better values for Start and End would be in the range of 100 to 150 feet and provide the same visible results as no falloff with slightly faster speed.

FG Point Interpolation   The following settings for FG Point Interpolation control a legacy method in which FG points can be interpolated (averaged) at render time, the Radius method. This legacy Radius method has been replaced by the Interpolate Over Num. Points method, detailed earlier, and is not a feature I utilize. The fixed size of the Radius setting makes it more difficult to get smooth results and good detail in your indirect illumination, compared to the Interpolate Over Num. Points method. With the Interpolate Over Num. Points method, the radius size is dynamic, and changes based on the density of Final Gather points and the fixed Radius method cannot adapt.

Use Radius Interpolation Method (Instead of Num. FG Points)   Using this option will disable the newer Interpolate Over Num. Points method for averaging Final Gather points.

Radius   Without a Radius value specified, mental ray picks a value based on the scale of your scene, which is 10 percent of the overall scene extents. Set this to 10 percent of overall scene scale or to 10 percent of the area of interest (a room or building floor) as a starting point.

Min. Radius   Set this to 10 percent of the Radius value as a starting point.

The next section of this chapter covers the Reuse options for indirect illumination, which can save considerable time both for still images and animations.

Reusing Final Gather and Global Illumination Data

Computing indirect illumination in a scene can take more computing effort than rendering the image; however it is one of the few commodities in mental ray that can be saved (cached) and reused as often as needed, greatly speeding render time, particularly for animations. Reusing indirect illumination is particularly important when working with machines with limited resources and large images must be produced; you can pre-calculate Final Gather using an image at a lower resolution and reuse that Final Gather data for the high-resolution still image. This reduces render time and memory requirements. The basic process to achieve this savings is to set the cache to incrementally add data to a cache file, set mental ray to pre-compute Final Gather and/or Global Illumination to store the indirect illumination, and then set the cache file to a read-only state (frozen) for use when rendering the larger image. mental ray will then read the cache file at render time and completely skip the Final Gather and Global Illumination calculation. Utilizing the Reuse options can drop render times to a fraction of their previous time, particularly for animations and large high-resolution still images.

Caching data also reduces flicker when creating animations with FG. Without caching, every frame gets a completely new set of FG points with their own set of random FG rays, and each frame will invariably be slightly different from the next frame. By precomputing the FG data and setting it to Read Only, every frame will get the same FG points and indirect illumination data.

When set to Read Only, if the cache file exists, mental ray skips the FG and/or Global Illumination calculation completely; it reads the data from disk and uses that to render the images. If the file does not exist then a file will be created. Figure 5.35 shows the Reuse (FG And GI Disk Caching) options for mental ray. These are found in the Render Settings dialog box on the Indirect Illumination tab.

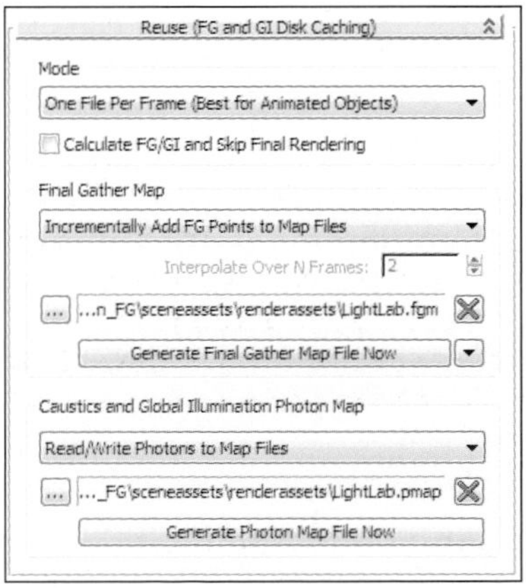

FIGURE 5.35
The Reuse options of the Indirect Illumination tab of the Render Settings dialog box

These are typical uses for the Reuse feature:

◆ Compute Final Gather at a small image resolution, and then render final renderings at a larger size with the read-only cached Final Gather data. You save considerable Final Gather calculation time and you can calculate the smaller image, the *FG pass*, at a higher FG setting than you might practically use for the larger image.

◆ Compute Final Gather and Global Illumination on one computer, and then network render to strips on multiple machines using the read-only cached data.

◆ Compute Final Gather data at intervals along a camera path to "spray" the scene with Final Gather data, and then use the read-only Final Gather data to reduce animation render time. Because Final Gather data is not created per-frame, significant render time is saved.

Final Gather data is stored in files with the `.fgm` extension, and Global Illumination data is stored in files with the extension `.pmap`. By default, both file types are stored in the `.\sceneassets\renderassets` folder of your project.

Understanding the Final Gather Reuse Modes

The Mode setting in the Reuse (FG And GI Disk Caching) settings, shown in Figure 5.35, controls whether a single FGM file is created for your renderings, whether Final Gather files are created for every frame of an animation, and whether the rendering pass is performed at all. The first two Mode settings are a drop-down selector that controls how Final Gather data is cached: Single File (Best For Walkthrough And Stills) or One File Per Frame (Best For Animated Objects). The third option within the Mode settings, Calculate FG/GI And Skip Final Rendering, is a check box that controls whether the render pass is performed or whether only Final Gather is calculated.

SINGLE FILE (BEST FOR WALKTHROUGH AND STILLS)

This is the default mode and the only option for versions of 3ds Max/Design prior to 3ds Max/Design 2010. When selected, one large Final Gather map file is created for all your Final Gather data. For animations that follow a camera path, you typically calculate Final Gather on enough frames to ensure that all your geometry is covered in view-dependent Final Gather data. This mode does not work well in scenes with moving geometry or when there are changing lighting conditions; use the One File Per Frame mode in that instance.

When you choose Single File and set the Final Gather Map drop-down list to Incrementally Add FG Points To Map Files, each time you render an image, any Final Gather points existing in the cache file are reused, and additional points are created and added to the file where needed. Because the data is reused as it goes, the first frame is typically much longer to generate than subsequent frames, depending on how much new Final Gather data needs to be created in each new view.

> **WHEN TO MAKE A NEW FGM FILE**
>
> It is important to note that the Incrementally Add FG Points To Map Files option never removes data from the Final Gather Map file; it only adds. If you significantly change materials or lighting or if you change, move, delete, or add geometry in your scene, then you need to delete and re-create the Final Gather map file. If you start to see unexplained dark or light areas in your renderings that use cached Final Gather data, deleting and re-creating the Final Gather map file (or moving it to another location if you are not sure that is the problem) often fixes the issue.

ONE FILE PER FRAME (BEST FOR ANIMATED OBJECTS)

This FG reuse (caching) mode, accessible from the drop-down Mode selector shown in Figure 5.35, was introduced in 3ds Max/Design 2010 and allows you to produce animations with Final Gather and moving objects. Previously, with the single FG map file, all objects, lights and materials needed to be static and unchanging. Cached Final Gather is a snapshot of a moment in time, stored as a point cloud in 3D. Now with the One File Per Frame option you can create a Final Gather map file for each frame, or you can skip frames and mental ray interpolates the missing data at render time. (See the Interpolate Over N Frames option in the "Understanding the Final Gather Map Options" section later in this chapter.) Because each Final Gather map file for your animation is a stand-alone Final Gather snapshot of your scene, using multiple computers and a network job to calculate individual Final Gather map files works well. This option takes longer than the Single File option because each individual Final Gather map file cannot take advantage of previously calculated Final Gather data and each frame of Final Gather is calculated from scratch.

CALCULATE FG/GI AND SKIP FINAL RENDERING

This check box option, accessible from the drop-down Mode selector shown in Figure 5.35, is almost always used with the Reuse options to save the FGM data to a file for later rendering because, as the name implies, no actual rendering is performed. Calculating Final Gather without rendering can be useful without disk caching if you need a quick, low-resolution image preview. Turning this option on and clicking Render is the same as using the Generate Final Gather Map File Now or Generate Final Gather Map File Now button; however, clicking the Generate Final Gather Map File Now button deletes the existing file and creates a new one. If you just need to add Final Gather data to an existing Final Gather Map, then enable this option, change your view to the area you want to add Final Gather points, and click Render.

FINAL GATHER DATA IS VIEW DEPENDENT

As you know, Final Gather data is projected from the viewpoint of a camera or perspective view and onto the geometry of your scene. From their individual position on the surface, the Final Gather points cast rays into the scene to collect indirect illumination from other surfaces, which can then be stored in an .fgm file and reused. The data is stored in a 3d "point cloud" of data.

Because only the area within the current view is "sprayed" with Final Gather points, any change in viewpoint would require you to add the FG data for the new surfaces in that view to any saved Final Gather data. The following image shows a visual diagnostic render of the Sponza Atrium, showing the Final Gather data created and cached from a different view and then reused (in read-only mode) for this view.

The green dots were placed within the view of a different camera in this scene, located at the right of this camera, and you can see the clean delineation where the FG data stops within the field of view of that other camera. The FG data appears transparent and flat, because the visual diagnostic mode places all points as an overlay of the rendered image; however, each point is stored in 3D space aligned with the surfaces of the scene.

As you will see in the section "Producing Animations with Final Gather," to create animations with Final Gather, you need to "spray" enough of your animated path with Final Gather points to ensure smooth and consistent coverage of points for the final rendering.

Understanding the Final Gather Map Options

The Final Gather Map options, found in the Reuse (FG And GI Disk Caching) menu area of the Render Setup dialog box, allow you to specify and control how the Final Gather map cache file is created and where it is saved.

The three options for using and controlling Final Gather map files are Off, Incrementally Add FG Points To Map Files, and Read FG Points Only From Existing Map Files. The default Off option disables both the reading and writing of FG data to the cache file, and each rendered frame creates new FG data.

Incrementally Add FG Points To Map Files With this option, any Final Gather data stored in the Final Gather Map file is reused, and any additional data created is saved to the Final Gather map file. Final Gather points are always added and never removed, so outdated and erroneous Final Gather data can cause rendering artifacts in your renderings, usually in the form of overly dark or overly bright areas of the image or incorrect colors. At that point, you need to delete the Final Gather file and start again caching Final Gather data.

Read FG Points Only From Existing Map Files Final Gather map data is locked, and no new data is added. If the Final Gather map file does not exist, however, Final Gather data is created and saved for the first frame only.

Interpolate Over N Frames This option is used for the One File Per Frame FG cache mode and when using the Read Only file option. It blends the FG data stored in several individual Final Gather map files for use in the current frame, and the value is the number of frames to use before and after the current frame. This not only helps to smooth the data but also allows you to skip frames when computing FG data.

After you have chosen the options, you can click the Generate Final Gather Map File Now button to create your FG file and skip the rendering of the image. This button deletes the existing FG map file before it creates a new one.

Perform the following steps within your own scenes to generate FG data for an animation:

1. Specify the active time segment you want to render on the Common tab of the Render Setup dialog box.

2. Specify an Every Nth Frame option to skip frames along the animated path. You only need to render often enough to ensure your scene is covered in FG points throughout the path.

3. Click the Generate Final Gather Map Now button.

To the right of the Generate Final Gather Map Now button is a drop-down list that shows the current time segment length (0 to 100 in a default scene) and some common values for Nth frames: 1 (every frame), every 3rd frame, 5th frame, 10th frame, and every 20th frame. This drop-down list saves you from having to change the Common tab's Nth frame settings and having to remember to set it back for a final animation. If you need an interval other than 1, 3, 5, 10, or 20, then setting the Common tab's Nth Frame parameter and clicking Generate Final Gather Map File Now is your only option. Remember that clicking a "Generate…" button deletes the existing file.

USING MULTIPLE COMPUTERS TO PRECOMPUTE FGM FILES

When you are using the Single File Only mode for your Final Gather map file, only one computer should be adding data to that file at a time. In other words, you cannot use multiple computers and a network render job to compute Final Gather map data for an animation and have those multiple machines all adding to that one Final Gather map file. Each machine will be holding a different version of the Final Gather map data in its memory and therefore will be overwriting data saved by other machines. However, you can use distributed bucket rendering and a single computer to update the single Final Gather map file, which allows you to utilize whatever horsepower is available to calculate Final Gather, while also maintaining the integrity of the Final Gather map file.

However, when the Reuse mode is set to One File Per Frame, using multiple computers and a network job to compute Final Gather data works very well. The Final Gather data is unique on each frame, it is interpolated between multiple frames at render time, and any frame-to-frame difference is not noticeable and somewhat expected.

Caching the Caustics and Global Illumination Photon Map

The Caustics And Global Illumination Photon Map options allow you to specify and control the generation of the photon map (PMAP) file. Because photon data is created for an entire scene and not just what is visible to the camera, the section does not have options or limitations found with the FG data files that take into account the view-dependent nature of FG points. As with FG, you have an option to turn off caching of photon data, which causes it to be re-created on every frame when rendering an animation. Caching of photon data is not generally useful for animations with moving or changing objects.

Read/Write Photons To Map Files   If the PMAP does not exist, one is created. If the file exists, it is loaded and reused. You must specify a filename for using this feature, and you must manually delete the file if you want to create a new version.

Read Photons Only From Existing Map Files   This option locks the PMAP file, and existing photon data is read from the file. New photon data is not created.

Generate Photon Map File Now   Clicking this button causes mental ray to process Global Illumination and create the PMAP file, skipping the render process.

In addition to the FG settings within the Render Settings dialog box, each object in your scene has additional settings specific to just that object.

Adjusting an Object's Final Gather Options

Scene geometry includes properties to control how the object interacts with mental ray. To access the object's properties, select an object, right-click to open the quad menu, and select the Object Properties option. For small objects that do not contribute much to the indirect illumination of a scene, you might want to consider setting those objects to Pass Through with this radio button to help speed FG calculation, as shown in Figure 5.36.

FIGURE 5.36
Object properties and Final Gather options

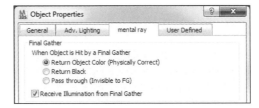

High-density Final Gather points on knickknacks on a storeroom shelf may not be useful, for example; the color of objects around the high-detail pieces might have a higher impact on indirect illumination, and you can save render time by ignoring the small, detailed objects. You can also use this option to have Final Gather pass through an object with a highly saturated color and pass through to a less saturated colored object. For instance, if you're getting too much green reflected from an exterior grass object, you can set the grass object to pass through and have a different object actually produce a lighter green Final Gather effect. In Chapter 6, I also cover the use of the new Color Override/Ray Type Switcher shader to control Final Gather and Global Illumination color bleeding.

Now that I have gone over the nuts and bolts of Final Gather settings, I cover these settings and their use in scenes.

USING THE ARCH & DESIGN FG/GI MULTIPLIER

You can also use the FG/GI Multiplier setting in Arch & Design materials to control the amount of influence a surface has on indirect illumination. Adjusting the Arch & Design material's FG Quality parameter allows you to optimize the Final Gather calculation overhead an object will incur.

Producing High-Resolution Images with FG

Producing a high-resolution still image using Final Gather can often be a challenge because of potential memory issues and the amount of time it takes to calculate Final Gather. If the dimensions of a rendered image double, the area that is rendered quadruples because you double in both the width and height; the Final Gather data and computation time will also quadruple. The amount of Final Gather data generated for an image is not only dependent on the Final Gather settings but also depends on the size of the rendered image. The larger the image, the more data is generated. The Final Gather file is quadrupled in this case, as is the size of the Final Gather map file, the memory required to hold that data, and the amount of time it takes to create the Final Gather data.

You can easily remedy these issues by utilizing the reuse options for Final Gather — you can precompute the Final Gather map file and a relatively small resolution, freeze the Final Gather map file, and then use that precomputed data to render your high-resolution still. Typically you would use a higher Final Gather precision preset when rendering the low-resolution pass, because a smaller image needs more Final Gather points. Overall, you can save considerable time and still achieve excellent results with this two-step process. I describe the process of creating the low-resolution prepass in the next section.

Creating the Low-Resolution Final Gather Precalculation Pass

For the following example, you can use a scene file from the Chapter 5 project folder, located on your DVD in \ProjectFolders\05_Indirect_Illumination_FG. For the best results, copy the contents of the Chapter 5 project folder to a local drive for editing. All files work with 3ds Max/ Design 2010 and newer.

The scenes are from the Karina Bay Resort project, produced by my company, 4D Artists, Inc. The design is by renowned Florida Keys architectural designer David deHaas, and an animation of the final project is provided on the web site www.mastering-mentalray.com. This project is memory and computation intensive, and if you are using computers with limited resources, you can follow these directions with your own scenes or choose the scene included in the .\scenes\ Sponza folder. This project consists of a series of XRef files that includes island terrain and site files, along with numerous buildings. The high-polygon buildings are provided as mental ray Proxy objects to greatly reduce your memory requirements. Polygon versions of the high-resolution buildings are provided in a separate folder and are not required to render the scenes. The camera view should be set to CamMidway; however, you can choose another view if desired. Be aware that other views that include water will take significantly longer to render.

Perform the following steps to create the low-resolution FGM pass:

1. Set your project folder to the location of the \05_Indirect_Illumination_FG folder on your computer. The default MXP file is for 3ds Max Design 2011; edit it or use the other MXP provided for 3ds Max Design 2010.

2. Open the file .\scenes\Karina\Landscaping_2010_Start.max.

   The Sampling Quality settings are irrelevant at this point, because the render process is skipped when the FGM file is created.

3. Open the Render Setup dialog box by pressing F10.

4. Switch to the Indirect Illumination tab.

5. Change the FG Precision preset to Medium. (If you have any issues with creating the Final Gather map file, try lower settings at step 5 and step 6.)

6. Set Diffuse Bounces to 2.

7. Scroll down to the Reuse (FG And GI Disk Caching) section, and open it if necessary.

8. Ensure that Mode is set to Single File Only.

9. Under Final Gather Map, change the option from Off to Incrementally Add FG Points To Map Files.

10. Click the Browse (...) button next to the FGM filename to open the Save As dialog box.

11. Ensure that you are in the .\sceneassets\renderassets folder of your project, and change the filename to Karina. Click Save.

12. Click the Generate Final Gather Map File Now button.

13. Wait as mental ray processes the scene and generates FG data, placing it into the FGM file. A precomputed FGM file is provided as `Karina_Midway.fgm` if you have difficulty creating your own file.

14. From the Render Setup dialog box or Rendered Frame Window dialog box, save your current render settings into a preset file called `FGMpass.rps`.

15. Save your scene as `Karina_Part1.max`.

FINAL GATHER PROCESSING TIME

If you find the Final Gather pass is taking too long, try the following:

◆ Reduce the FG precision preset to Low or Draft.

◆ Reduce the number of diffuse bounces.

◆ Reduce the image resolution.

◆ Switch to the Sponza scene, located in the `.\scenes\Sponza` folder of your Chapter 5 project folder.

The settings shown in the previous example are what you might use to produce HD-resolution stills when there is a need to preprocess Final Gather at a lower resolution because of time or memory constraints.

If you find that the Final Gather pass went rather fast, feel free to increase the FG precision settings to High. Be sure to delete the existing Final Gather map file before you create new data. A precomputed Final Gather map file is provided for you as `.\sceneassets\renderassets\Karina_FGHigh.fgm` in the project folder.

Creating the High-Resolution FG-Freeze Render Pass

Now that you have the FG data saved for this scene, you can produce a high-resolution still image and skip the entire FG process.

Perform the following steps to reuse FG data to produce a high-resolution still image:

1. Open your last file or continue from the previous steps. Alternately, you can open the file `.\scenes\Karina\Landscaping_2010_PartOne.max`.

2. Open the Render Setup dialog box, and switch to the Indirect Illumination tab.

3. In the Reuse section, change the Final Gather Map option to Read FG Points Only From Existing Map Files.

4. Ensure that the file specified for the Final Gather map is correct. Use the `Karina_Midway.fgm` file if needed.

5. Switch to the Renderer tab.

6. Change the Samples Per Pixel option's Minimum value to 1 and Maximum value to 16.

7. Change the filter type to Mitchell.

8. Change the Spatial Contrast values to RGBA 0.03, 0.045, 0.06, and 0.03. (These values are weighted based on how human vision perceives color, and they render faster than using the same values across the board.)

9. Switch to the Common tab.

10. Change the output size to 1920×1080 (or leave at a smaller size such as 960×540 if you have limited memory or time).

11. Change the render output filename to .\renderoutput\Karina\Midway.png.

12. Render your image. A completed image is provided in your project's .\renderoutput folder as Karina_HD.png and is shown in Figure 5.37.

FIGURE 5.37
Karina Bay Resort and the Cam Midway view

13. Save a new render preset called FGfreeze.rps.

14. Save your file as Karina_Part2.max. A completed file is provided as Landscape_2010_PartTwo.max.

Increasing the Samples Per Pixel option's *Maximum* value to 64 helps resolve some of the fine details such as the roof standing-seam geometry and the spindles along the elevated walkways, and it improves the quality of the image. Using ambient Occlusion in selected materials will also help resolve details. This scene includes numerous cameras for specific views, and you can change the Final Gather Map setting back to Incrementally Add FG Points To Map Files, switch your render resolution back to a lower size, and add more points to the Final Gather map file for reuse in a high-resolution render from those alternate views.

 Real World Scenario

DETERMINING RENDER SIZE

Occasionally I have a client who needs a rendered image printed for a billboard to go out in front of their new building, which is currently under construction. They want high quality and think that a 4' by 8' image at 300 dots per inch (dpi) will suffice. After performing some quick calculations, we find that this image would need to be 28,800 by 12,400 pixels, a rather high resolution. 3ds Max/Design allows you to enter these values — you can enter values up to 32,767 — but they are not practical or necessary for something seen at a distance. Even if you could render the image, given enough memory and time, you probably could not get it to the service bureau and have it be usable.

Another client recently needed a 30′ banner at 100dpi, which is 36,000 pixels long and beyond the capabilities of 3ds Max/Design (and certainly beyond reason). Unless you were standing next to the banner, you would never see the detail, and because this banner was going to hang on the side of a large building, it's certainly not necessary. They insisted, though, and Photoshop is great at rescaling images.

The mistake the client made, and the mistake that I see many 3D artists make, is assuming that you need to represent every pixel that will be printed on a sheet of paper, poster, or billboard. This is rarely the case with any print medium larger than a letter-sized sheet of paper. The process of printing naturally blend pixels together on the print medium, and it is unlikely that you will see individual pixels from an image unless you significantly under-size the rendering and blow it up in the print. Many ink-jet printers can print resolutions up to 5760 dpi and beyond, and that resolution is not necessarily there so that you can print a 5760 dpi image; instead, it's there so that the print engine can dither the dots to produce crisp images. It is always a good idea, if possible, to print a sample of your rendering on your final print device at the resolution you can reasonably render. It is a mistake to use your computer display to preview what will eventually be printed, not only because the colors will be different on the printer vs. the screen but because the natural blending of pixels during a print process will make some apparent issues that are visible on your computer monitor disappear. For proper color reproduction, I find that using Epson paper with Epson printers and using HP paper with HP printers helps ensure that the print engine will properly compensate not only for the surface qualities of the paper but also for the underlying color of the paper and produce accurate images.

For the 4′ by 8′ billboard, 72 dpi is sufficient and gives a print resolution of 6912×3456. For a B-sized sheet of paper, I typically render at 200 dpi, which is also close to the same resolution as an A-sized sheet at 300 dpi and a resolution of 3300×2250. For a 30′ banner, 100 dpi is *always* the best choice if the client insists and the resulting 1GB TIFF file works for them, however 20 to 50 dpi is more reasonable.

The Print Size Assistant, located in the Rendering pull-down menu, can assist you in determining print resolution. The Print Size Wizard (Assistant) dialog box is shown here.

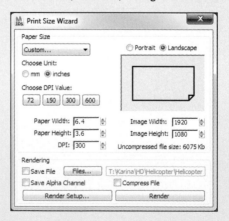

The Print Size Wizard (Assistant) can help you quickly determine a render resolution to use for a specific print size and will copy those settings into the Render Setup dialog box for immediate use when you click the Render Setup button. If you specify a filename within this dialog box, it defaults to the TIFF file format that has the ability to store the dpi of an image for use by print service bureaus, which is often their preferred file format. With other image file formats such as JPEG and PNG, 3ds Max/Design sets the file dpi to 72, and you must change the specification in photo-editing software.

As covered in Chapter 4, "Rendering," for large images you can use the network rendering option Split Scan Lines to render large images in small horizontal strips, which reduces memory requirements and allows you to utilize multiple machines.

Using Batch Render to Create Final Gather Map and High-Resolution Render Passes

Because you saved render presets for your Final Gather and render passes, you can use the Batch Render utility to help automate the creation and use of the FGM files.

Perform the following steps to create and use the Batch Render settings for this project:

1. Open your last scene or continue from the previous example. Alternately, open the file .\scenes\Karina\Landscaping_2010_PartTwo.max.

2. Select Rendering ➢ Batch Render to open the Batch Render dialog box, as shown in Figure 5.38.

3. Click the Add button to add a default batch render job to the list. It uses the filename specified in the Render Setup dialog box and adds _View01 to the filename.

4. In the Selected Batch Render Parameters section of the dialog box, enable the Override Preset option.

5. Set the Width value to 960 and the Height value to 540 (quarter-sized full-HD).

FIGURE 5.38
The Batch Render dialog box that shows the completed example

6. Change the Output Path filename if desired.

7. Change the Camera setting to CamMidway.

8. Change the Preset setting to the FGMpass.rps file created earlier.

9. Click Add to create another batch job.

10. Turn on Override Preset, set the width to 1920, and set the height to 1080. This is the same value as the preset you will choose, and technically you don't need to use Override Preset unless these values are different. If no preset is used and Override Preset is off, then the current render resolution is used by default.

11. Change the Output Path setting to a filename such as `.\renderoutput\Karina\Midway.png`.

12. Set the Camera setting to CamMidway.

13. Choose the `FGfreeze.rps` file in the Preset drop-down list.

14. Save your scene.

15. Click Render in the Batch Render dialog box to create both the FGM pass and the final image. A completed scene is provided on the DVD as `Landscape_2010_PartThree.max`.

Backburner has the capability to set up dependencies between jobs. If you submit the batch renderings as network jobs and have multiple machines on your render farm, you need to set dependencies when the job is submitted via the Network Job Assignment dialog box, or via Backburner's Monitor program. Obviously the FG pass needs to complete before any other machines start rendering the final image strips. In the Monitor application right-click a job name and choose the Dependencies option to define jobs that must finish before this one is allowed to start.

You might need to manually delete an existing FGM file prior to running the Batch Render queue; otherwise, mental ray will only add missing FG points to the FGM file.

In the next section, I detail some of the settings and techniques necessary for exterior daylight scenes.

RENDERING AN IMAGE DURING THE FINAL GATHER MAP PASS

When you use the Batch Render tool to render the two passes, with the preset files you have at this point, an image will be rendered during the Final Gather map pass, which does not happen if you use the earlier manual method of clicking the Generate Final Gather Map File Now button. I usually like having this small rendered image because it allows me to check my rendering before the high-resolution pass is created. If you do not want this low-resolution image to render, perform the following steps:

1. Open the Render Setup dialog box.

2. Load the `FGMpass.rps` preset file.

3. Switch to the Indirect Illumination tab.

4. In the Reuse section, turn on the Calculate FG/GI And Skip Final Rendering check box.

5. Save the preset to the `FGMpass.rps` file.

Your Final Gather Map pass in the batch render will now skip the render process and complete faster.

Using Daylight and Final Gather

Using Final Gather in an exterior daylight scene requires minimal setup to achieve excellent results. Because the light from the mr Sky portion of a daylight system, along with reflections from the mr Physical Sky, contribute to the appearance of illumination on your surfaces, you can use presets such as Low or Medium, at most, with one or two diffuse bounces to achieve excellent results. Remember that diffuse bounces are in addition to the one bounce you get already with indirect illumination and that they can brighten your render when rays are allowed to propagate to brighter areas of your scene. There are some special cases that might require additional techniques to brighten them up or extreme settings to get nice results in dark areas of an exterior scene. Most exterior scenes, however, simply need a daylight system, Final Gather set to the Medium preset, and one or two diffuse bounces and that is all.

I start the examination of exterior daylight scenes by covering a common issue when using Final Gather with an exterior, and that is dark entryways and interiors seen from outside.

Improving Dark Interiors and Entryways

One specific issue you will find when rendering an exterior scene is that interior spaces and deep-set entrances will render unnaturally dark. Adding an mr Sky Portal to openings in these scenes brings in outdoor illumination and gives a more realistic appearance to the rendering. Figure 5.39 shows a split rendering without an mr Sky Portal on the left of the image and with an mr Sky Portal on the right.

Adding the mr Sky Portal across the entrance added 18 percent to the render time yet significantly brightened the interior of the entry. The intensity of the light is proportional to the size of the mr Portal object, and no adjustment is generally needed to the Multiplier value. In this application, you might want to turn off shadow casting for the mr Sky Portal to speed rendering; however you may need to ensure that the light does not spill into unintended areas that are visible from the outside. The relatively low intensity of the mr Sky Portal compared to sunlight makes this an issue only in areas that are in shadow.

FIGURE 5.39
A split rendering that shows the entry to an industrial facility without an mr Sky Portal on left and with an mr Sky Portal on the right

As an alternative to the mr Sky Portal, you can also add photometric lights to fill the dark areas. Exterior daylight is about 90,000 candelas, and any fill lights you add are competing with that intensity and need to be scaled accordingly. A 100-watt bulb will have little influence in your rendering compared to strong sunlight. As you are evaluating the effect of your fill lights, remember to work with the lights in isolation and in keeping with the exposure value (EV) of your final image, typically an EV of 14.75 to 15.0 for an exterior day-lit scene.

Rendering the Sponza Palace Atrium

The Sponza Palace atrium scene has become a classic demonstration model for indirect illumination techniques in a wide variety of applications. Not only is the Sponza Palace atrium an interesting architectural model, but it poses a few challenges for rendering because the natural illumination of the space all comes from a single opening at the top of the courtyard and because almost all of the lighting is from indirect illumination. It is not quite an outdoor scene and not quite an indoor scene, yet many of the techniques for both kinds of scenes apply. Figure 5.40 is a reference picture taken by Marko Dabrovic, architect and partner at 3LHD (www.3lhd.com) and the creator of the original 3D model. A full-size reference picture is provided as .\scenes\Sponza\SponzaReference.jpg in the Chapter 5 project folder.

For the following steps, ensure your 3ds Max/Design project is set to the Chapter 5 project folder as described in previous examples. The Sponza model is provided with all materials; however, the demonstration scene is set by default to use a white Material Override for the testing of FG properties. Disable this setting in the Processing tab of the Render Setup dialog box if you want the original materials, although they will take longer to render. This scene contains a daylight system set to match the coordinates of the location and orientation of the original building and the date and time the image was photographed.

All scenes referenced in this example are stored in the .\scenes\Sponza folder of your Chapter 5 project folder, and all images are in the .\renderoutput\Sponza folder. Copy the \ProjectFolders\05_Indirect_Illumination_FG project folder from the DVD to a local drive for best results.

FIGURE 5.40
The Sponza Palace atrium in Dubrovnik, Croatia

Image courtesy of Marko Dabrovic

Perform the following steps to use Final Gather with this scene:

1. Open the file .\scenes\Sponza\Sponza_FG_2010_Start.max.

2. Press 8 to open the Environment And Effects dialog box. Set the mr Photographic exposure control's settings to match the original camera settings: Shutter Speed 1/100, Aperture f/4.0, and Film Speed ISO 100. Close the dialog box.

3. Render the Camera02 view, and note the render time; a rendered image is provided as `.\renderoutput\Sponza\Step-3.jpg`. Save the rendered image to Channel A in the RAM Player. The render resolution is set to the same size as a small Sponza reference image saved in the scene folder, and you can compare the two in the RAM Player as desired. The image will be quite dark, and FG is set to Draft, so the image has a spotty appearance.

4. Open the Render Setup dialog box, and switch to the Indirect Illumination tab.

5. Change the FG Precision Preset setting to Low, and set Diffuse Bounces to 2. Render the scene, and save to Channel B of the RAM Player. A completed image is provided as `.\renderoutput\Sponza\Step-5.jpg`. The image will be a little brighter but will not have a natural appearance; there is just not enough light coming through from the sky. The areas to the side and back of the scene are also quite dark.

6. Set Diffuse Bounces to 5, and render the scene. Save to Channel A of the RAM Player and compare. A completed image is provided as `.\renderoutput\Sponza\Step-6.jpg`.

7. Set Diffuse Bounces to 10, and render the scene; the render time may be twice that of step 6. Figure 5.41 shows the scene with the Low preset and two diffuse bounces on the left and ten bounces on the right. A completed image is provided as `.\renderoutput\ Sponza\Step-7.jpg`.

FIGURE 5.41
Sponza model with two diffuse bounces on the left and ten diffuse bounces on the right

8. To further brighten the scene and eliminate the uneven Final Gather solution, set Diffuse Bounces to 20 and change Rays Per FG Point to 500. Note that machines with limited resources will have issues at this setting. A precomputed FGM file is available as `Sponza_DB20_NoPortal.fgm`, along with the scene `.\scenes\Sponza\FG_2010_Step-8.max`.

9. Render the scene, and save to Channel B of the RAM Player. A completed image is provided as `.\renderoutput\Sponza\Step-8.jpg`. The image is further brightened, and the additional FG rays have smoothed out the FG on the sides and back of the model.

DIFFUSE BOUNCES AND BRIGHTNESS

The Diffuse Bounces setting improves the accuracy of your Final Gather solution and will increase the brightness of this scene as the Final Gather rays are propagated onto many more surfaces and collecting brighter indirect illumination. Different scenes that propagate rays into more dark areas instead would not see an increase in brightness, so it is best not to think of the Diffuse Bounces setting as a brightness control. It depends on the scene.

At this point in this example, the image is brighter within the courtyard with additional bounces; however, it is still dark and uneven along the sides. The Final Gather solution in the side areas is spotted because of inconsistencies in Final Gather sampling and the randomness of FG rays; some FG rays hit a higher number of brighter areas of the model than others, and this becomes visible as splotchy artifacts.

---

10. Add an mr Sky Portal across the top of the scene. Use the AutoGrid option for placement, and ensure the flux arrow points downward.

11. Set Diffuse Bounces to 5 and the FG Precision Preset to Medium.

12. Optionally disable the Material Override option; then render the Camera02 view, and save to Channel A of the RAM Player to compare. Figure 5.42 shows the results.

A completed image is provided as `.\renderoutput\Sponza\Step-12.jpg`. A precomputed FGM file is provided as `Sponza_DB5_Portal.fgm`, along with the scene at this point as `.\scenes\Sponza\FG_2010_Step-12.max`.

13. Change to the Camera05 view. Render the image, and save to Channel A of the RAM Player. A completed image is provided as `.\renderoutput\Sponza\Step-13.jpg`. Notice the overly bright area along the opening to the sky as shown in the sidebar on the next page.

14. Adjust the size of the mr Sky Portal to Length = 2m and Width = 15m.

15. Change the Multiplier setting of the mr Sky Portal to 3.0 to compensate for the smaller size.

16. Open the Environment And Effects dialog box, and set the Highlights (Burn) setting to 0.05.

17. Render Camera05, and save the results into B of the RAM Player. A completed image is available as `.\renderoutput\Sponza\Step-17.jpg`. The area along the top of the opening is bright but similar to the reference image, and the remainder of the scene should be a good brightness as compared to the reference image. When you used the FG Precision Preset setting in step 11, it changed the number of FG rays, and therefore some splotchiness will now be evident.

FIGURE 5.42
Camera02 with the
addition of an mr
Sky Portal across
the upper opening

USING THE MR SKY PORTAL IN THE SPONZA SCENE

Adding the mr Sky Portal across the top of the scene will send more illumination into the courtyard and both brighten the scene and smooth the FG solution without resorting to exceptionally high values for the Diffuse Bounces setting or a high number of FG rays. Because the intensity of a mr Sky Portal is related to its size and this is quite large, the amount of light produced is quite bright and appears too bright near the position of the opening, as seen in another view, the Camera05 view. The following image shows that view with an mr Sky Portal across the opening before making other adjustments to mental ray. At the edges of the opening, the illumination is pushed into the Highlights (Burn) region of the mr Photographic exposure control's settings.

You can do several things to help remedy the situation and still bring additional diffuse light into the scene:

◆ Set the Highlights (Burn) setting down to perhaps 0.05 to 0.0.

◆ Move the mr Sky Portal away from the opening, or reduce its size to bring it away from the edges.

◆ Reduce the Multiplier setting of the mr Sky Portal.

Reducing the physical size reduces the intensity of the portal light, and to maintain brightness, you need to turn up the Multiplier setting. Because the portal is a hemispherical light, you need to reduce the size significantly to reduce the excess lighting along the edge. Ultimately, you might need a combination of these techniques to help tame the brightness.

18. Set the Rays value to 500, disable the Material Override check box on the Processing tab if you have not already, and render Camera02. The completed image is available as `.\renderoutput\Step-18.jpg`. A completed scene is with a precomputed FGM is available as `.\scenes\Sponza\FG_2010_Finish.max`. You might also want to increase the Diffuse Bounces setting to 10, as shown in Figure 5.43.

FIGURE 5.43
The final image with the Medium preset, FG Rays at 500, and Diffuse Bounces at 10

19. Save your file.

The images so far were generated with exposure values that matched the original camera settings and were a good place to start; however, adjusting the exposure value of the mr Photographic exposure control will help match the original. The Sponza Palace atrium certainly presents some challenges, particularly if you are trying to use only Final Gather. I continue the examination of this scene in Chapter 6.

The next Final Gather example scene is a traditional interior environment, one that you will also look at with Global Illumination in Chapter 6.

Rendering a Bathroom Scene

In this section, you'll work with the bathroom for one of the models in the Karina Bay Resort project. It combines interior photometric lights with daylight illumination from two windows. As with any scene, it is always best to work with lights in isolation as you add and adjust them. The beauty of photometric lights is that they are relatively straightforward to set up because you can choose real-world properties to set the illumination value, and they work in a realistic manner. For this scene, because the accurate representation of the colors was critical to the client, the photometric lights all use the D65 Illuminant reference color rather than an Incandescent Filament Lamp color. As you saw in Chapter 3, "Lights, Shadow, and Exposure Control," you can optionally compensate for an incandescent light color with the Whitepoint setting of the mr Photographic exposure Control; however, this scene includes a strong daylight component, and a Whitepoint setting of 6500 Kelvin works well.

The bath scene has many reflective surfaces and area lights and can take considerable time to render on some machines. To speed the process of testing, the scene comes with Material Override enabled with a Multi/Sub-Object material, soft shadows disabled, and draft-quality Samples Per Pixel and Filter settings. Using the material override also allows you to see some of the issues with the Final Gather solution that may be hidden by surface materials, as evident in the final images of the Sponza scene; the stone textures blended with much of any remaining Final Gather unevenness. The original materials are available to you by disabling the Material Override option in the Render Setup dialog box's Processing tab. Turning down the number of reflections allowed per material would speed rendering when Material Override is not used, which is left to you to choose to adjust if desired. You can also set the Max Reflections in the Rendered Frame Window to 1 or 2 to speed rendering when using the original materials.

This scene starts with an Exposure Value setting of 7.0, which is much lower than the preset for an interior day-lit scene, 10.0. I chose this value through some experimentation with the scene and evaluating the brightness of the surfaces with only the photometric lights. In any scene, you have to make a choice about what you will focus on, and for an interior day-lit scene, you can set the exposure for the extremely bright portions where the sun strikes the interior, or you can set it for the other lighting; you cannot have it both ways. Either some area is going to be extremely bright or some area is going to be dark. Rendering to an HDRI format and adjusting the image in an external application may resolve this issue.

Because I already covered the specifics of the Final Gather settings, I will quickly cover the process of setting up and adjusting the interior for rendering using Final Gather. This scene is also an animation, and producing a Final Gather–based animation is covered later in this chapter.

All scenes referenced in this example are stored in the .\scenes\Bath folder of your Chapter 5 project folder, and all images are in the .\renderoutput\Bath folder. Copy the \ProjectFolders\05_Indirect_Illumination_FG project folder from the DVD to a local drive for best results.

Perform the following steps to adjust the Final Gather settings for this scene and adjust the lighting:

1. Open the file FG_2010_Start.max in the .\scenes\Bath folder.

2. Render the Camera01 view, note the time, and save the image to Channel A of the RAM Player. The image will be relatively dark with very bright streaks of light from the sunlight and a spotty FG result, as shown in Figure 5.44. The image is also available as .\renderoutput\Bath\Start.jpg and is shown without Material Override.

FIGURE 5.44
The bath scene with photometric lights and daylight system. The exposure value is set low for an interior day-lit scene at 7.0.

3. Open the Light Lister by selecting Tools ➤ Light Lister.

4. Disable the two lights listed in the Photometric category. These are the ones above the mirror and at the ceiling. You need to work on the daylight in isolation first, and because it is a bright light source, you need to even out its effect on your rendering.

5. Open the Render Setup dialog box, and switch to the Indirect Illumination tab.

6. Set the FG Precision Preset slider to Medium. This is the practical top end for most scenes.

7. Set Diffuse Bounces to 2.

8. Render the image, note the render time, and load the results into Channel B of the RAM Player. The scene is brighter from the additional bounces; however, the surfaces are exceptionally uneven in appearance, as shown in Figure 5.45. The scene is available as .\renderoutput\Bath\Step-6.jpg, and a scene with a precomputed FGM is available as .\scenes\Bath\FG_2010_Step-6.max. The Medium preset and additional diffuse bounces result in a much longer render time.

9. Switch the Camera02 view to show the windows for the bathroom.

10. Using the Autogrid option, add an mr Sky Portal across each window of the bathroom only. The other windows do not need mr Sky Portals.

11. Render the Camera01 view, note the render time, and save the image to Channel A of the RAM Player. A completed image is available as .\renderoutput\Bath\Step-10.jpg, and a scene with precomputed FGM file is available as .\scenes\Bath\FG_2010_Step10.max. Set FG Precision Preset to Low.

FIGURE 5.45
The bath scene with the Medium FG preset and two diffuse bounces. This mottled appearance is typical in interior scenes that have an exterior daylight component.

INTERIOR DAYLIGHT WITH mr SKY PORTALS

Simply adding a mr Sky Portal to an interior day-lit scene vastly improves the quality of the FG solution and brightens the scene, and mr Sky Portals should always be used in these instances. Despite the lower FG preset in the scene at this step, the results are much improved over the previous image, and you should have about the same render time. The image, though, is still not acceptable, and switching to Medium preset (which sets the Initial Point Density setting to 0.8) and setting Rays to 500 yields about the same results with more than double the render time. This result is shown here.

The lack of direct lighting inside the scene and standard FG filtering is contributing to the uneven results. The image is available as `.\renderoutput\Bath\Step10B.jpg`.

12. Change the Noise Filtering (Speckle Reduction) setting from Standard to High.

13. Render the view, note the render time, and save the image to Channel B of the RAM Player for comparison. The image is available as `.\renderoutput\Bath\Step12.jpg` and is shown as Figure 5.46. A scene with a precomputed FGM file is available as `.\scenes\Bath\FG_2010_Step12.max`. As the image shows, the result will be a bit darker but smoother even with a Low FG preset.

FIGURE 5.46
The bath scene with
the Noise Filtering
(Speckle Reduction)
setting at High

14. Set the FG Multiplier value to 1.5 to increase the brightness lost from the filtering.

15. Change the Noise Filtering setting to Very High.

16. Open the Light Lister, and enable the two lights in the Photometric section of the dialog box.

17. Open the Environment And Effects dialog box by pressing 8, and click the Render Preview button. Adjust the exposure value if necessary. This is a much faster way of previewing your rendering and ensuring the exposure is correct without committing to a full-frame render.

18. With these settings, calculating the FG solution takes a lot of time. Open the final scene file .\scenes\Bath\Bath_2010_Finish.max, which includes a precalculated FGM file, Bath_Medium.fgm, or set your scene to use that FGM file in a read-only mode.

19. Render the view, note the render time, and save to Channel A of the RAM Player for comparison. This image is available as .\renderoutput\Bath\Finish.jpg. Figure 5.47 shows the final image without the Material Override setting and with soft shadows.

FIGURE 5.47
The final bath
scene with the
Medium FG pre-
set, four diffuse
bounces, and the
Noise Filtering set-
ting set to High

This scene takes time to render, no doubt about it. Anyone can show you how to render a teapot in a box, and the purpose of going through the settings and rendering iterations was to highlight typical pitfalls in a production scene to work toward a workable solution and a production render. As mentioned in the text, a Final Gather map file calculated at the Medium preset

for this final scene is precomputed for you and is available as `.\sceneassets\renderassets\`
`Bath_Medium.fgm` in the Chapter 5 project folder.

IMPROVING THE BATH SCENE

As you can see in the bath examples, using only FG for a scene that relies heavily on the illumination from a daylight system can be problematic, and the bath scene was set to be purposely difficult. The extreme brightness of the daylight system tends to skew some FG points to be overly bright, and you will have uneven results at the onset. Ensuring that your scene has adequate direct illumination and adding mr Sky Portals is a good start. If the scene is still problematic, consider repositioning the angle of the daylight system or turning off the mr Sun light and replacing it with a bright spotlight or a Standard light with a directional distribution style. As you have seen in this chapter, high FG Precision Preset settings add detail to your renderings, but low FG settings and a diffuse-looking FG solution will render faster and the diffuse results can be improved by using ambient occlusion in select materials.

An animation of a version of the bath scene is available as `.\renderoutput\Bath\Bath.avi`. This scene has the daylight system replaced with a standard directional light scaled to half daylight intensity, and it relies more on bright direct illumination from interior lights. It was produced using the FG Reuse options, which are detailed in the next section.

Although Final Gather can do a good job, you will often find that Global Illumination combined with medium or low Final Gather settings produce the best renderings in the shortest amount of time. This can be a bit trickier to set up, however, and is covered in Chapter 6.

In the next section, I cover effective ways to produce animations using Final Gather and the caching tools of mental ray.

Producing Animations with Final Gather

Caching Final Gather data is the best way to eliminate flicker from indirect illumination in an animation. An example of the Sponza Palace scene that was produced without using FG caching is provided on your DVD as `FG_Flicker.avi` in the Chapter 5 project folder, `.\renderoutput\`
`Sponza`. While playing the animation you will notice variation in the indirect lighting from frame to frame and it seems to crawl across the surface. A version with visual diagnostics enabled is available as `FG_Flicker_Diag.avi` in the same folder; with that video, you can see a little clearer how the location of FG points changes from frame to frame. Because of the random nature of FG point placement and the randomness of FG rays, this will always be an issue unless you precompute and cache FG data used in animations.

Different Final Gather caching options are required for scenes that have static objects, as with a building or product render, than for scenes that have animated objects. The first example in this section covers a static scene — the Sponza Palace atrium — using a camera animated along a path. Caching Final Gather points serves two purposes in a scene such as this. First, it allows you to skip frames along the animation and only precalculate Final Gather points at enough positions along the path to "spray" the scene with indirect illumination. Second, the first frame you render takes the longest for Final Gather to calculate, and then each subsequent frame is able to use the Final Gather data already cached and only needs to add missing Final Gather data. Each frame of

Final Gather precalculation takes less time than it would if you calculated Final Gather per frame and did not cache, and you can skip 5, 10, or even more frames, depending on the speed of your camera through the environment. Therefore, with caching, you get faster overall Final Gather calculation both by skipping frames and because of the speed benefit gained by reusing Final Gather data previously calculated in the view.

Fast-moving cameras may need Final Gather calculated as much as every other frame, and you can use different Nth Frame settings for different sections of your animation if necessary. If there are areas where you need to add some Final Gather, set your camera or perspective view to that area and render the view and mental ray adds the Final Gather points in that area to your Final Gather map file. Do not use the Generate Final Gather Map File Now button in this instance, because it will delete the existing FGM file. Remember when using FGM files that Final Gather data is always added and never removed; if the Final Gather data is incorrect for your current geometry, lighting, or materials, it needs to be deleted and re-created.

Animation of Static Scenes

Completed examples of all animations are provided in the `.\renderoutput\Sponza` folder of the Chapter 5 project.

Perform the following steps to cache and reuse FG data for a scene with an animated camera path and static scene:

1. Open the file `.\scenes\Sponza\Ani_2010_Start.max`.

2. The scene is set to view Camera06, which is animated along the spline CameraPath. Select the Animation ➢ Make Preview menu option and create a preview of the animation path, or select the Animation ➢ View Preview menu option for a precompiled animation. You will see that a large percentage of the scene is viewable in the animation.

3. Open the Render Settings dialog box, and switch to the Indirect Illumination tab.

4. In the FG settings, ensure that the FG Preset is set to the Low preset with two diffuse bounces, and also select Project FG Points From Camera Position.

5. Open the Reuse (FG And GI Disk Caching) menu area.

6. Ensure that mode is set to Single File Only.

7. Set the Final Gather Map option to Incrementally Add FG Points To Map Files. If you want to use a precalculated file, skip to step 10.

8. Set the Final Gather map filename to `Sponza_Ani_Static.fgm`.

9. Next to the Generate Final Gather Map File Now button, open the drop-down list, and choose the From 0 To 300, Every 5 Frames option. Your final gather file is created frame by frame, and rendering will be skipped.

10. Set the Final Gather Map option to Read FG Points Only From Existing Map Files. If you want to use the precomputed FG map file for this scene, simply choose `Sponza_Animation_Static.fgm` as your filename.

11. On the Common tab of the Render Setup dialog box, set the Render Output filename to `Sponza_FG_Ani.jpg`, and set Time Output to the Active Time Segment option. Render

Camera06. The JPEG format causes 3ds Max/Design to save your animation to individually numbered JPEG images, and you can compile to AVI using Video Post or view the animation in the RAM Player.

12. Play your AVI file in the RAM Player or Windows Media Player, and evaluate the results. Figure 5.48 shows the final frame of the animation.

FIGURE 5.48
The final frame from the Sponza animated camera scene

13. Save your scene. A completed scene is provided as .\scenes\Sponza\Ani_2010_Finish.max, and a completed animation is provided as .\renderoutput\Sponza\FG_Animation.avi.

EVALUATING YOUR ANIMATION

Because of the interpolation of FG points, it might be difficult to determine whether you have enough coverage unless there are definite areas that are particularly dark. Enabling the visual diagnostics mode and rendering some or all of your animation might help to diagnose issues. Set the Final Gather Map option to Incrementally Add FG Points To Map Files, and manually add points in suspect areas by rendering a frame in that spot, adding points to your existing FGM file. You can even move to the location in a perspective view and render that viewpoint to add FG points; however, do not use the Generate Final Gather Map File Now button, because that deletes the existing file.

The completed animation is provided for you in the .\renderoutput\Sponza folder of your Chapter 5 project as Sponza_FG_Animation.avi.

In the next section, I examine settings for caching Final Gather data in this scene with animated objects.

Animations of Dynamic Scenes (Animated Objects)

The previous example for caching FG data relied on a single FGM file to store all points; however, this cache method with all FG points stored statically in one file will not work when objects, lighting, or materials are animated. Instead, you must store a unique FG file per frame.

Perform the following steps to make an animation with animated objects:

1. Open the file .\scenes\Sponza\AniObj_2010_Start.max. The Sponza scene uses the same camera path as the previous example but includes biped objects animated with footsteps and motion-capture files.

2. Open the Render Setup dialog box, and switch to the Indirect Illumination tab.

3. Set the FG precision preset to Medium.

4. Open the Reuse (FG And GI Disk Caching) section, and change Mode to One File Per Frame (Best For Animated Objects).

5. Set the Final Gather Map option to Incrementally Add FG Points To Map Files.

6. Change the name of the Final Gather map file to Sponza_Animated_Objects.fgm.

7. Next to the Generate Final Gather Map File Now button, open the drop-down list, and choose the From 0 To 300, Every 1 Frames option. Your final gather file is created frame by frame, and rendering will be skipped.

   Precalculated Final Gather map files are in the .\sceneassets\renderassets folder of your Chapter 5 project as Sponza_Animated_Objects0000.fgm through Sponza_Animated_Objects0300.fgm, in compressed Zip format.

ADVANTAGES AND DISADVANTAGES OF USING THE ONE FILE PER FRAME MODE

There are two big advantages to using the One File Per Frame mode. First, it lets you have multiple machines creating the individual Final Gather map files all at the same time using a Backburner network render job. Because each file is stand-alone, you will not run into the issues you will have with the single Final Gather map file where different machines have different versions of the Final Gather map in memory and subsequently overwrite each other's data. The second benefit of the One File Per Frame mode is that you can replace Final Gather data in areas of your animation if needed without having to redo the entire animated sequence. For instance, if you change some things in a particular room of a building, you only need to recompute the Final Gather map file sequence that affects that specific room.

The disadvantage, as you will see when you calculate your own One File Per Frame Final Gather Map files, is that it does not take advantage of previous Final Gather points that have been calculated, and each entire frame of Final Gather must be computed. That makes sense, because you expect each frame to be different from the previous one, but do be aware that it will take much more time than using the single-file Final Gather map method.

8. Set the Final Gather Map option to Read FG Points Only From Existing Map Files.

9. The Interpolation Over N Frames option is currently set to two frames before and after the current frame.

10. Switch to the Common tab.

SETTING SINGLE-FILE FGM INTERPOLATION

Because of the lack of direct illumination in this scene, this animation will be noisy without additional interpolation, so set the Interpolation Over N Frames value to 4. This might be high for your characters, and adjusting the scene for more direct light and adding ambient occlusion would help reduce the need for more interpolation.

---

11. Set the render output filename to Sponza_AniObj.jpg, and render the Camera06 view. Compile to an AVI using Video Post, or view in RAM Player. A completed animation is provided as .\renderoutput\Sponza\Sponza_AniObjects.avi in your project folder, and Figure 5.49 shows a frame from the completed animation.

FIGURE 5.49
A frame from the Sponza animated objects scene that shows several animated biped objects

12. Save your 3ds Max/Design scene.

A completed file is provided as .\scenes\Sponza\AniObj_2010_Finish.max in your project folder.

The final animation of this scene with visual diagnostics is available in the Chapter 5 project folder as .\renderoutput\Sponza\AniObj_Diagnostic.avi.

SELF-ILLUMINATION WITH FG

mental ray materials that use self-illumination can produce indirect illumination only when used with Final Gather. Because this effect is created within Final Gather it is not direct illumination and will not create discernable shadows, but it can use physical units and produce realistic glow and self-illuminated effects. It is perfect for neon and other soft lighting effects.

The Bottom Line

Adjust the settings of Final Gather   Final Gather is the simplest method of providing indirect illumination in your scene and is enabled by default in 3ds Max Design 2010 and newer. Understanding key settings allows you to improve your rendering quality and brightness while also keeping render time to a minimum.

> **Master It**   Your rendering lacks details in indirect illumination. How would you adjust the Final Gather settings to improve the quality of your rendered image?

Use visual diagnostics for Final Gather   The visual diagnostics mode allows you to see the underlying data points that make up Final Gather.

> **Master It**   How do you enable visual diagnostics mode to see Final Gather density?

Cache Final Gather data for still images and animations   Caching Final Gather data for reuse provides many benefits, including the ability to create Final Gather points at a low resolution to save time in a high-resolution rendering, and it allows you to skip frames in lengthy animations and helps prevent flickering during animations.

> **Master It**   Your animation is suffering from long render time and flickering indirect illumination. How do you enable the reuse of Final Gather data and precalculate Final Gather points for your animation?

Chapter 6

Global Illumination and Caustics

In this chapter, I cover indirect illumination using Global Illumination and Caustics. *Global Illumination* is a diffuse transfer of illumination between surfaces and a large-scale effect that creates an indirect illumination effect often times larger than 1 meter. *Caustics* are the concentration of light energy into focused patterns, as with a magnifying glass in the sun or patterns of light reflected from water. Both indirect illumination effects are accomplished through the transfer of illumination between surfaces using points of light energy and color called *photons*, which are emitted from light sources. Photons more closely mimic the way that indirect illumination works in the real world, and when combined with Final Gather, they produce the highest-quality images in the least amount of time.

In this chapter, you will learn to

◆ Cache photons for reuse

◆ Utilize Global Illumination in a scene

◆ Utilize Caustics in a scene

Understanding Global Illumination

Global Illumination works from light sources that emit photons into the scene, bouncing them around to deposit indirect illumination on the surfaces they strike. This illumination is typically cleaned up using Final Gather and then combined with direct illumination and surface finishes to produce a final render. I find that Global Illumination is essential for most interior scenes and is not generally as useful for exterior scenes. Exterior scenes that use Final Gather with a daylight system often produce great results without adding Global Illumination. That said, Global Illumination can be effective for specific outdoor scenes and can greatly boost illumination, as I cover later in this chapter. Final Gather was first used as a cleanup mode for Global Illumination, eliminating the need for exceptionally high settings for photons and removing noise from the Global Illumination solution. Although Final Gather has improved greatly over the years, the combination of Global Illumination with Final Gather often produces the best results with the least amount of render time. As I cover in Chapter 7, "Importons and Irradiance Particles," Global Illumination also works with Importons to reduce memory consumption and improve Global Illumination results.

Figure 6.1 shows a comparison of a scene from Chapter 5, "Indirect Illumination and Final Gather," with Final Gather only on the left and with both Global Illumination and Final Gather on the right.

There are two primary differences between the sides: the right side of the image has more color and contrast and took about one-third the time to render. With Final Gather, I needed a high Diffuse Bounce setting to get a good level of illumination, which in comparison appears to have reduced the color contrast. The Global Illumination solution kept more of the color of the surface and appears just as bright without excessive computation time.

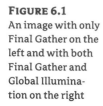

FIGURE 6.1
An image with only
Final Gather on the
left and with both
Final Gather and
Global Illumina-
tion on the right

As I cover later in this chapter with the combination of Global Illumination and Final Gather, you can reduce render time considerably by eliminating high Final Gather settings, while more accurately transporting indirect illumination between surfaces.

Defining Photons

The photons for Global Illumination and Caustics are two-dimensional points in 3D space and are bundles of red, green, and blue (RGB) light energy emitted from a light source. Each photon carries only a portion of the energy from a light source; the total RGB color energy of each light is divided by the number of photons emitted by that light. Brighter lights in a scene emit more photons than dimmer lights to help even out the Global Illumination solution. This way each photon has a more similar weight and a more even distribution. Photons are reflected off diffuse surfaces in your scene, transporting color energy from surface to surface. The photon method of producing indirect illumination is closer to what occurs in nature, and photons can trace through reflections, can bend through refractions, and are absorbed and reflected by surfaces in a scene. A diffuse surface, however, is required for a photon to have an effect on that surface, because mirrored and transparent surfaces will reflect or refract a photon and not store the photon's energy.

Figure 6.2 illustrates the path a photon might take in a scene. In this scene, a photon is emitted from a white spotlight source, shown as a white vector striking the green right wall of a Cornell Box.

No photons are stored at the first contact with a surface because that is direct illumination; however, the effect of the photon reflecting from that surface is taken into account, and the photon will have a new color energy level based on the first surface but will not leave any energy behind. This new color energy is reflected into the scene by the surface and continues along a new vector, shown as green. Because diffuse surfaces are not perfect reflectors, the actual direction of the new photon will vary. When the photon strikes the next surface, the floor in this case, the photon is stored on the surface and is represented by the green circle. mental ray spawns a new photon with the color energy reflected from the floor and the new photon continues along to the next surface. The color energy of the new photon is dependent on the properties of the reflective diffuse surface and the color energy of the incoming photon.

That new photon continues to the red wall along the light green vector. The process repeats, and the current photon is stored in the red wall; mental ray spawns a new photon with a color energy level that is the result of the incoming photon's color energy and the properties of the reflecting surface. The new photon is projected along the pumpkin-colored vector to be stored on the ceiling surface, and the process continues. At render time, mental ray averages together photons that are within a certain range of a render sample to get a final indirect illumination value for that sample.

In the scene in Figure 6.2, the one photon from the light resulted in three photons being stored on the surfaces, each one a different color energy level that is blended with the surface finish at render time. This photon trace example shows one possible path for a photon and does not describe the direction taken by all photons; the diffuse surfaces of the scene scatter photons in many directions, and you can see that effect in the real Global Illumination photons shown distributed through the scene. The varied colors means that many different paths were taken to deposit those photons.

Another effect to point out in Figure 6.2 is that the influence of a photon did not appear to go from the edge of one wall and up the other wall. A photon might not have influence on adjacent surfaces with a low inside angle, such as these 90-degree walls; the wall would need to be well beyond 120 degrees for photons to continue across the surface. The outside angle also affects whether photons will influence adjacent surfaces, and a five-sided cylinder at 72 degrees per side will not show the effect of photons from side to side; however, a six-sided cylinder at 60 degrees per side will. Of course, having a lot of overlapping photons and using Final Gather will not make this an issue. Brief animations that demonstrate photons moving within the Cornell Box are in the \renderoutput\CornellBox\ folder of your Chapter 6 project folder: `GI_Surfaces.avi` and `GI_Surfaces_LightRotate.avi`. By watching the animations in the RAM Player, you can single-step and see how the angle between surfaces and the proximity of the photon to the edge both influence whether a photon affects the adjacent surface(s). Some of that apparent influence at acute angles on the Cornell Box walls will actually show mismatched size and colors in photons on each surface, which is likely the result of two photons near that edge, not one. Ensuring adequate over-lapping photon coverage in production scenes and using Final Gather avoids this issue.

WORKING WITH LIGHT AND SURFACE COLORS

For an object to reflect a color, the light source and surface material must both contain that color. For example, a pure red light falling onto a pure blue surface would not reflect any light from that surface; it would appear black because a pure blue surface absorbs red and green and reflects only blue. You need blue in the light to reflect blue from any surface. This is true in the real world and the artificial world.

To help illustrate this point, the following image shows pure RGB spheres with pure RGB lights above.

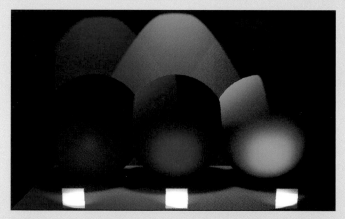

This scene is the Cornell Box with a red wall on the left and a green wall on the right. In addition to the colored lights above, three small white lights are shining onto the front of each sphere to help identify the colors of the spheres. As the image shows, the red sphere and wall on the left is not illuminated from above at all. The blue and green spheres get some illumination from the light above and left of each but not from directly above or above and right. The back wall and floor are white and reflect all light colors. As the image demonstrates, a surface must contain a color to reflect that color, and a light must contain a color that the surface will reflect in order for the surface to be illuminated by the light. Pure black surfaces also do not reflect light or photon color energy.

This light and surface color issue affects photons, too. Both the photons and surfaces must contain the same colors to some degree in order for the photons to have the color energy to affect the surface and have the energy to reflect and transmit through the scene. Just as with the direct lights in the previous image, if a photon is carrying the light color contained in the surface it is interacting with, then energy gets bounced back into the scene, and indirect illumination will be visible on the surface. If there is a mismatch in light and surface color, the bounced energy of the photon is diminished.

Because 100 percent saturated colors do not exist in nature, you should generally keep a color's Saturation setting to 0.9 or less, and closer to 0.5 is more realistic. Lower saturation values ensure that each RGB color exists to some degree in the surface or light.

Unlike Final Gather where Final Gather points are projected only into the area seen by the camera, Global Illumination is not view-dependent. mental ray computes the Global Illumination solution for the entire scene all at once, for all geometry and lights. You can save the Global Illumination solution using the mental ray Reuse (Final Gather And Global Illumination Disk Caching) features, provided the scene is static and does not have animated geometry or lights. Global Illumination calculation, like the single-file mode for Final Gather caching, is a snapshot of a moment in time. If your scene lights or objects change during the animation, the Global Illumination must be computed on every frame.

With Global Illumination, you need photon generators (lights) and objects enabled to produce and use Global Illumination. By default all objects are set to receive and generate Global Illumination photons. To enable or disable Global Illumination on a specific object, select and then right-click that object, go to the Quad menu's Object Properties option, and then go to the mental ray tab in the dialog box. Figure 6.3 shows the Caustics And Global Illumination (GI) options.

FIGURE 6.3
Object Properties
dialog box settings
for Caustics And
Global Illumination (GI)

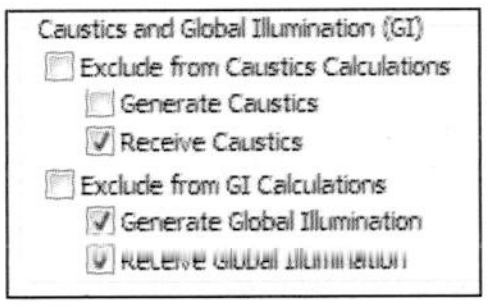

Caustics are not enabled by default on objects. You can enable Global Illumination and Caustics globally from the Render Setup dialog box by turning on the Enable setting for Global Illumination from within the Indirect Illumination tab's GI group and then selecting the All Objects Generate & Receive GI And Caustics option.

For efficiency, enabling Caustics on only the objects that will generate Caustics can save you a lot of calculation time. In 3ds Max/Design 2011, the All Objects Generate & Receive GI And Caustics setting does not apply to lights, and you must enable caustic generation on a light-by-light basis.

Next I cover some of the settings for Global Illumination before I move on to some example scenes.

Understanding Global Illumination Settings

You can find the Global Illumination settings in the Render Setup dialog box on the Indirect Illumination tab, as shown in Figure 6.4.

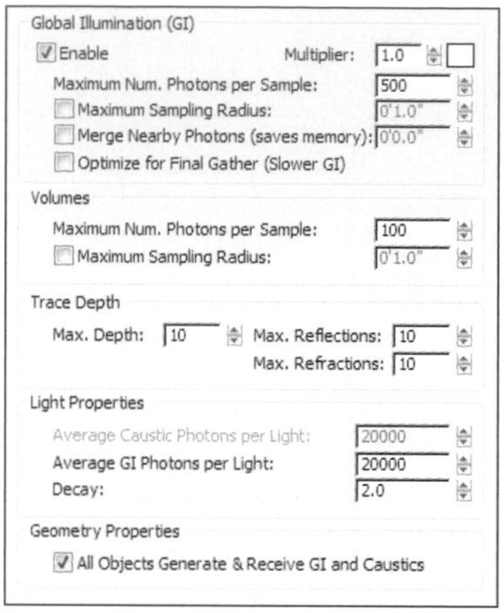

FIGURE 6.4

The Global Illu-
mination (GI) set-
tings in the Render
Setup dialog box

I cover the following settings from a technical standpoint before I cover how to use them in typical scenes:

Multiplier and the color swatch The Multiplier setting allows you to control the brightness of the photons stored in the Global Illumination calculation phase. The color swatch allows you to tint the color of the photons. The default white color produces accurate results. Cached photons are also affected by these settings, because this is a render-time adjustment.

Maximum Num. Photons Per Sample This setting controls the number of photons collected at render time around a particular rendered sample. The photons collected are averaged to give a final Global Illumination value to the rendered sample, and the final illumination is dependent on the averaged photon's interaction with the surface finish and the direct illumination at that point. The Maximum Num. Photons Per Sample default value is 500 photons, and you can set it to a low value of 10 to 50 for fast draft-mode Global Illumination previews.

At render time, there are two limits that control how many photons are actually collected and averaged for a render sample: this Maximum Num. Photons Per Sample limit and the Maximum Sampling Radius setting described next. In regions of dense photon coverage, mental ray will gather photons in an ever-increasing radius around the current sample until the maximum number is reached. The area of influence, then, for a photon will vary depending on the number of photons in a particular region. In regions of your scene with low photon density, mental ray will stop collecting photons when the Maximum Sampling Radius value is reached (described next) and the area of influence is limited.

Large values for the Maximum Num. Photons Per Sample setting can significantly increase render time, and for most scenes the default of 500 photons is sufficient. Large values, combined with a large Maximum Sampling Radius, can make for a very flat-looking rendering because the large influence of an individual photon washes out the contrast in the surfaces of your scene. The correct value to use takes trial and error and is affected by the density of photons stored on the surfaces of your scene. Higher-density scenes might need larger Maximum Num. Photons Per Sample values so that a large enough area is averaged to achieve a smooth Global Illumination result.

Maximum Sampling Radius The Maximum Sampling Radius setting allows you to set a limit on the averaging and influence of a Global Illumination photon. With this setting disabled, mental ray calculates a Maximum Sampling Radius setting that is $^1/_{10}$ th the overall radius of your scene, or $^1/_{20}$ th the diameter. For relatively small interior scenes within a larger scene (a conference room in a large office building, for instance), this setting allows you to force a reasonable maximum size. The actual radius used to average Global Illumination photons is determined by the Maximum Num. Photons Per Sample value, and for areas of high density the radius will be significantly smaller.

The Maximum Sampling Radius value sets the effective size of each photon. Although a photon represents a two-dimensional point in 3D space, with too few photons they will appear the size of the radius value because that is its area of influence. The Global Illumination path trace example in Figure 6.2 had a Maximum Num. Photons Per Sample of 1 and a Maximum Sampling Radius of 1′ and displayed a 1′ radius circle around each photon's location; each pixel sample within 1′ of the photon was able to add that photon to its indirect illumination.

For an outdoor scene, a sampling radius of 20 feet or more might be appropriate. For a large indoor scene, 3 to 9 feet might be a good Maximum Sampling Radius value.

When you disable this setting and mental ray calculates its own radius value, you can see what value it used by examining the dialog box that opens when you select Rendering ➢ Render Message Window.

Merge Nearby Photons (Saves Memory) The amount of memory used for storing photons can become quite large when you are calculating many millions of photons. You can significantly reduce the number of photons stored by using this setting to merge photons that are within a small distance of one another. Merging photons can smooth the Global Illumination results and reduce the number of photons in a given area, resulting in a larger effective photon radius because mental ray will then average photons a larger area to reach its (default) 500 photon quota. The photon energy in the merged photon is the sum of the photons merged. Because of this, bright spots can occur if the Merge Photon Radius value is too large.

REDUCING PHOTON MEMORY IMPACT

Because mental ray computes photons for all lights everywhere in your scene, the large number of photons needed to generate a smooth result might take a lot of memory. You can reduce your photon memory footprint by doing the following:

◆ Using the Merge Nearby Photons option with a relatively small radius value.

◆ Disabling photon generation in lights that do not contribute significantly to indirect illumination. See the mental ray Indirect Illumination setting for each light, and decrease the Global Illumination photons Multiplier value.

◆ Disabling Global Illumination on objects that are not visible or do not contribute significantly to Global Illumination. See each object's Object Properties dialog box (in the Quad menu) and the mental ray tab.

◆ Disabling lights in areas of your scene that are not visible.

◆ Using Importons, discussed in Chapter 7.

An added benefit of disabling Global Illumination on objects outside your area of interest is that it forces mental ray to store its photons only on the areas important to your image and might allow you to use fewer photons overall.

Optimize For Final Gather (Slower GI) With the Optimize For Final Gather (Slower GI) option enabled, additional processing is performed to store brightness information about neighboring photons for fast lookup by Final Gather. This optimization process might cause Global Illumination to take noticeably longer, but this additional time is usually offset since the option speeds up Final Gather processing because it can quickly look up the information it needs on photons. This optimization process increases the size of your photon map (PMAP) file because more data is stored with each photon.

Trace Depth This setting limits how many times photons are reflected and refracted in your scene. With a well-configured scene, shooting and bouncing photons is very fast, and millions of photons can be shot and stored without having to be concerned with limiting the number of reflections or refractions. Reducing the values might result in insufficient distribution of photon color energy.

Average GI Photons Per Light This setting is an average for all lights and not necessarily a total number of photons shot per individual light. This means that lights which produce more energy, and subsequently have more influence over the illumination of your scene, will shoot more photons and divide that energy into a greater number of smaller energy photons. This keeps the illumination per photon in a reasonable range. Without this weighing of photon quantities, you would have few very bright photons from a daylight sun object, for instance, and the same quantity of photons from a small photometric light source, resulting in a very uneven rendering.

The Average GI Photons Per Light value is also not the number of photons to be emitted by lights but is the number of photons to be *stored* on the geometry. mental ray will continue to shoot photons from a light until the correct number of photons is stored from each light or it generates an error that it can't store photons.

You can see how many photons are emitted and stored in a scene by opening the Render Message Window (Rendering ➤ Render Message Window). You must also enable the Show/Log options in the Preference Settings dialog box's Rendering tab, as shown in Figure 6.5.

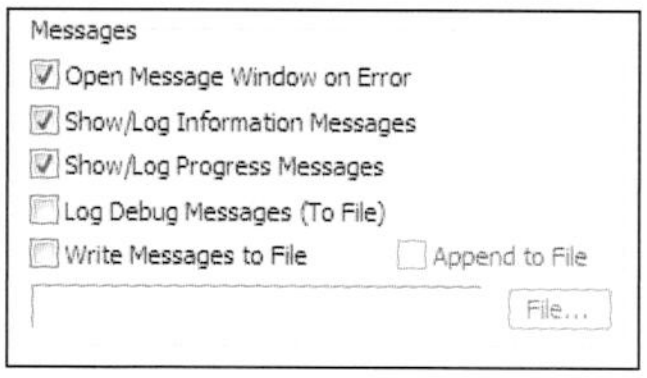

FIGURE 6.5
The Show/Log options to enable render-time statistics in 3ds Max/Design 2011

```
Messages
☑ Open Message Window on Error
☑ Show/Log Information Messages
☑ Show/Log Progress Messages
☐ Log Debug Messages (To File)
☐ Write Messages to File        ☐ Append to File
_____
                                  [ File... ]
```

You can also change the Render Message options by right-clicking on the dialog box. Figure 6.6 shows the Render Message dialog box for 3ds Max/Design 2011, showing the photons shot for the Bath example file detailed later in this chapter.

In 3ds Max/Design 2010 and earlier, the mental ray message Window shows a slightly different statistics format.

FIGURE 6.6
The Render Message
dialog box in 3ds
Max/Design 2011

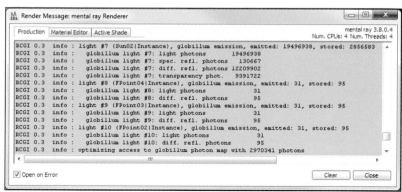

PHOTONS ARE GENERATED UNTIL THE AVERAGE GI PHOTONS LEVEL IS ACHIEVED...

...or mental ray decides to give up. If mental ray takes a very long time to calculate GI or you get an error for "No photons stored...," then you might need to make geometry, lighting, or mental ray adjustments to allow photons to be stored efficiently on your scene geometry. I cover some of these issues in the later example scenes.

For an outdoor scene or a scene that uses a daylight system through a window, the fact that photons keep emitting until enough are stored can mean having to add geometry off-camera to catch photons that bounce into space and would not have contributed to the illumination in your scene, as well as ensuring that lights are directional and not omnidirectional or are enclosed by geometry. In the scene used to generate the messages in Figure 6.6, adding simple geometry to catch most stray photons dropped the number of sun photons emitted by mental ray from 19.5 million to 2.6 million to get 2.8 million stored photons and significantly decreased the Global Illumination calculation time. Sun objects in a daylight system should have the Use Photon Target option enabled, and the radius value set as described later in this chapter.

Reusing Global Illumination Data

As with Final Gather, Global Illumination photons can be cached to a file for immediate reuse without the need for recalculation. This is only practical for static scenes, because the stored Global Illumination data is a snapshot of a moment of time and does not take into account object movement or lighting changes. Changing the Average GI Photons Per Light value also requires replacing the cache file. Figure 6.7 shows the Reuse options for Caustics and Global Illumination photons for creating a PMAP (*.pmap) file.

FIGURE 6.7
The Reuse caching
options for Caus-
tics and Global
Illumination pho-
ton maps

If the Reuse option is set to Read Only and a PMAP file does not exist, one is created. The menu area also includes a Generate Photon Map File Now button that deletes any existing PMAP file, creates a new PMAP file, and skips the rendering phase.

After Global Illumination is stored, you may change the Global Illumination settings Multiplier, Maximum Num. Photons Per Sample, and Maximum Sampling Radius without having to reshoot the Global Illumination photons, because these settings are used only at render time. This means that as long as you have enough photons shot in your scene, you can fine-tune these settings without having to reshoot photons.

Next I look at the two visual diagnostic modes available for Global Illumination.

Using Visual Diagnostic Modes with Global Illumination

There are two diagnostics modes for Global Illumination: Photon Density and Irradiance. They each produce color images with blue, cyan, green, yellow, and red, and each color represents a different quantity of photons or value for irradiance. On the blue end of the spectrum, the value is always zero photons or irradiance. The value of each color is determined by mental ray and is shown in the Render Message window. Prior to rendering a scene, you must first enable messages by selecting Customize ➤ Preferences, going to the Rendering tab, and selecting the Show/Log options. Then open the Render Message window.

Photon Density   Photon Density is a representation of your scene with colors ranging from dark blue at the lowest photon density to cyan, green, yellow, and red, with each progressively "hotter" color representing a relatively higher density. The Photon Density diagnostics mode is useful for identifying the overall coverage of photons in your scene and helps determine whether adjustments need to be made to photon quantity to ensure all surfaces have an even coverage in photons. The left side of Figure 6.8 shows Photon Density, and in this case Blue is 0 photons, Cyan is 591 photons, Green is 1183 photons, Yellow is 1775 photons, and Red represents 2367 photons, which is the maximum density in this rendering of half the Sponza image.

Irradiance   Irradiance is defined as the "area density of flux" and is measured in watts per meter squared (W/m^2). This diagnostics mode shows the relative brightness of the stored photons in the same color scheme as Photon Density. On the right side of Figure 6.9, Blue is 0 irradiance, Cyan is 4949 W/m^2, Green is 9918 W/m^2, Yellow is 14878 W/m^2, and Red is 19837 W/m^2, as read from the Render Message dialog box. It only displays the irradiance of the photons and not direct illumination or Final Gather.

The color chart values display within the Render Message dialog box. Rendering a smaller area of the same view or a different view generates a different color scale for the values, because a different region might have a different maximum range.

In the next section, I begin to cover some Global Illumination solutions to the scenes highlighted in Chapter 5, as well as the workflow for using Global Illumination combined with Final Gather.

Using Global Illumination

All scenes and files related to the example scenes are located on your DVD in the \ProjectFolders\ 06_GI_Caustics. For best results, copy this folder to a local drive for editing, and set your copy of 3ds Max/Design to use this as its project folder.

FIGURE 6.8
Visual diagnostic modes for Global Illumination that show Density on left and Irradiance on right

In this section, I'm using the Bath scene from Chapter 5 and using Global Illumination to improve the illumination and reduce the need for high Final Gather settings. All scene files are in the DVD's \ProjectFolders\06_GI_Caustics\Scenes\Bath folder. All rendered images for this section of the chapter are stored in the .\renderoutput\Bath folder. Images may be suffixed with render times in the MinuteSecond format (Filename_1m30s.jpg for example) and have _diag in the name to indicate a visual diagnostics version of an image. The scene initially has a Material Override setting that you can disable.

TESTING YOUR GLOBAL ILLUMINATION SOLUTION WITHOUT FG

When you adjust and test your initial Global Illumination settings, it's important that you disable Final Gather until you have a reasonable distribution of photons in your scene. Final Gather is a cleanup process for Global Illumination and can mask irregularities in the Global Illumination distribution. This is a good thing and means that your Global Illumination does not have to be perfect to get great results. Start with good direct lighting, enable Global Illumination and adjust, and then turn on Final Gather in the final stages for final rendering.

Preparing the Initial Render Settings

I start this section by using the Bath scene where I left off in Chapter 5. You need to strip out the unneeded settings and turn down a few others so that you can work quickly as you test-render the scene.

Perform the following steps to adjust the initial scene settings:

1. Open the file .\scenes\Bath\Bath_GI_2010_Start.max.

2. Open the Rendered Frame Window dialog box, and change the Image Precision setting to Medium, with Min 1/4 and Max 4.

3. Change Glossy Reflections Precision to Draft.

4. Change Glossy Refractions Precision to Draft.

5. Change Trace/Bounce Limits to Max. Reflections 4, Max. Refractions 4, and FG Bounces 0.

6. Deselect the check box next to the Final Gather portion of the Reuse dialog box.

7. Set the Final Gather Precision setting all the way to the left to disable Final Gather. Your settings should look like Figure 6.9.

FIGURE 6.9
The initial settings in the Rendered Frame Window

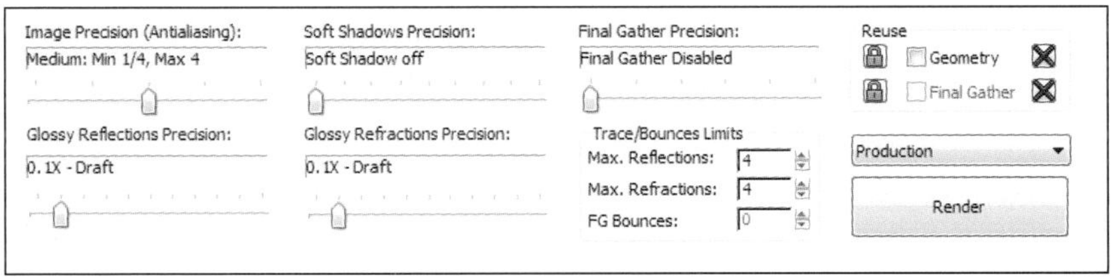

8. Select Tools ➤ Light Lister, and disable the two lights listed in the Photometric Lights section together with the two mr Sky Portals. You'll first work with Daylight in isolation. Close Light Lister.

9. Open the Render Setup dialog box.

10. Switch to the Processing tab.

11. Enable Material Override.

12. Render the scene, and note the render time as a baseline for this scene without indirect illumination. Save to the RAM Player Channel A for later comparison.

    A rendered image is available in your project folder as .\renderoutput\Bath\GI-01.jpg.

13. Save your scene.

USE ENERGY-ACCURATE MATERIALS IN YOUR SCENES

In your own scenes, ensuring that all your materials are either Arch & Design, Autodesk, or ProMaterials is essential to ensure that surfaces work in a realistic manner. Using Standard and Architectural materials and also materials that contain other materials such as Composite can skew results and also cause the surface to reflect more illumination than it receives.

The rendered image will be very dark with only the bright sunlight area illuminated because there is no indirect illumination. Before you enable Global Illumination, you need to adjust the position and settings of the Daylight and Compass Rose objects.

ADJUSTING THE DAYLIGHT SYSTEM FOR INTERIOR GLOBAL ILLUMINATION

Without some adjustment to the daylight system, the daylight system will shoot photons in all directions, which is inefficient and takes a considerable amount of time. If a photon simply goes off into space or it bounces once and does not hit anything else, then mental ray keeps emitting photons until the Average GI Photons Per Light number is achieved, and the Global Illumination calculation can take a long time. You'll get a warning in the mental ray Message window if mental ray cannot store any photons in your scenes, and you'll just experience a long delay if photons are going nowhere fast.

Perform the following steps to adjust the daylight system for an interior Global Illumination scene:

1. Continue with the previous scene, or open `Bath_GI_2010-01.max`.

2. Switch to CamExt, and position the daylight system's Compass Rose between the two windows for the bathroom, near the bottom edge of the windows, as shown in Figure 6.10.

FIGURE 6.10
The approximate final position of the Compass Rose object near the bath windows

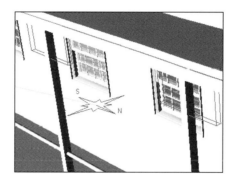

3. Select the Daylight01 object.

4. Enable the Use Photon Target option in the mr Sun Photons roll-down menu.

5. Change the view to a Perspective view, and adjust the view so you can see the cylinder-shaped gizmo surrounding the line from the Daylight object to the Compass Rose.

6. Adjust the Radius value for mr Sun photons until the radius is slightly larger than the two windows, about 7' to 8'. Because it is a cylinder area, you want to make sure that the photon target encompasses the entire set of windows from corner to corner, as shown in Figure 6.11.

7. Save your scene.

Some photons will still go off into space, and some photons will be deposited on the outside of the scene if they happen to bounce off the porch or wall and then hit another exterior object. Overall the GI calculation time will be fast and most photons will be stored inside the bathroom.

Next you'll enable Global Illumination and examine your scene with the basic Global Illumination settings.

FIGURE 6.11
A top view that shows the position of the Daylight System and the new photon target radius in magenta

ENABLING GLOBAL ILLUMINATION

Depending on your scene, the default settings for Global Illumination combined with Low Final Gather settings is enough to get good results with Global Illumination in a scene, provided you have well-adjusted direct lighting to start. The example daylight system, as you saw with Final Gather, tends to skew the results with Global Illumination and might not produce ideal results.

Perform the following steps to enable Global Illumination:

1. Continue with the previous scene, or open `Bath_GI_2010-02.max`.

2. Go to the Caustics And Global Illumination (GI) roll-down menu on the Indirect Illumination tab of the Render Setup dialog box.

3. Select the Enable check box for Global Illumination.

4. Ensure that the three other Global Illumination–related check boxes are disabled.

5. Render the Camera01 view, note the time, and save the image in Channel B of the RAM Player to compare. Figure 6.12 shows the Bath scene with the default settings for Global Illumination.

FIGURE 6.12
Rendering of the Bath scene with the initial Global Illumination settings and Material Override

This image is available as GI-02.jpg in the .\renderoutput\Bath folder of your project. You will notice in Figure 6.12 that there is very soft illumination; however, the shower area on the left is dark despite the clear glass, and that area shows large Global Illumination light circles within the enclosure. The circles are the size of the Global Illumination radius as determined by mental ray, and they represent the area of influence a single photon might have on a surface. The circles are from the few stray photons that made it over the glass and onto the surface of the shower.

The light from the sun is bouncing off the floor and depositing a lot of Global Illumination energy on the front left of the cabinets. The scene illumination seems too soft to me and needs some adjustment to help bring out details, as I explain in the next section.

Adjusting Global Illumination Settings

The first thing you need to do to improve the Global Illumination solution is to correct the area in the shower stall and change the object properties for the glass.

Perform the following steps to adjust the glass properties:

1. Continue with the previous scene, or open Bath_GI_2010-03.max.

2. Select the object ShowerDoorGlass in your scene.

3. Right-click the object to bring up the Quad menu.

4. Select the Object Properties option.

5. Switch to the mental ray tab.

6. Enable the Exclude From GI Calculations check box.

7. Render the scene, and save it to the RAM Player Channel A for comparison. The rendered image is available as file .\renderoutput\Bath\GI_Exlude.jpg.

8. Save your scene.

Your own side-by-side comparison will now show the shower area properly illuminated and a subtle change in the lighting in other areas. Because more light energy was deposited in the shower, less was available for other areas of the scene. The energy a light object produces is divided among all photons; they all carry about the same "weight" of illumination, and if more are deposited in an area, then the illumination in that area will be brighter. Figure 6.13 shows the current scene using visual diagnostics and the Density parameter.

FIGURE 6.13
Visual diagnostics
Photon Density
image of current
scene. Cyan equals
a density of 1.1.

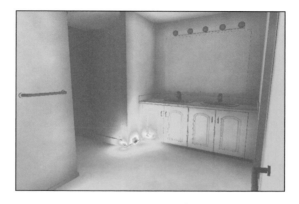

The Render Message dialog box reports that the Cyan color represents a density of 1.1, Green 2.2, Yellow 3.3, and Red 4.4, as you might have guessed. This is a very low density, so you need to significantly raise the Average GI Photons Per Light value to get a much higher density. Looking further into the Render Message dialog box shows that the computed "globil.radius" value is 42.9 units, which is perhaps a little large for this small scene. Because this is a small room in a much bigger scene, you can sharpen your Global Illumination results by specifying a radius that makes sense for the space you are working with and not necessarily the entire scene space. You need more photons first, though.

Increasing the photon density so that mental ray sees more than 500 photons within that range will automatically reduce the area of influence of your photon and increase contrast. Because the overall illumination from just the sun object seems OK, you need to see what your settings look like when you enable the illumination from the light fixtures inside the room.

Using Visual Diagnostics Mode for Global Illumination

To assist with analyzing your current Global Illumination settings, perform the following steps to visually diagnose the Bath scene with all light sources enabled:

1. Continue with the previous scene, or open `Bath_GI_2010-04.max`.

2. Open the Rendered Frame Window dialog box, and set Image Precision to Low or Draft.

3. Select Tools ➢ Light Lister.

4. Enable check boxes for the two photometric lights at the top of the list. Close the dialog box.

5. Open the Render Setup dialog box, and switch to the Processing tab.

6. Enable Diagnostics, set the mode to Photon, and set the drop-down menu to Density.

7. If you have not previously enabled messages, in 3ds Max/Design 2011 select Customize ➢ Preferences, go to the Rendering tab, and enable the two Show/Log options for Messages. You can also right-click the Render Message window to change log options.

8. Open the Render Message dialog box (Rendering ➢ Render Message). In 3ds Max/Design 2010, open the mental ray Message Window (Rendering ➢ mental ray Message Window), enable the Information option, and minimize the mental ray Message window.

9. Render Camera01, and view the "diagnostic: false color" information from the Render Message window. This image is available as `.\renderoutput\Bath\GI_100k.jpg`.

For my scene, the visual diagnostics image showed Cyan at a density of 35.26. Increasing the Average GI Photon Number beyond 250,000 on a 32-bit machine will most likely cause it to run out of memory, and if you experience issues you should reduce the photon count accordingly.

Correcting the Bright Areas around Lights

One issue you will see in both Final Gather and Final Gather/Global Illumination scenes is that the areas around light fixtures can become very bright and "blown-out" in intensity. With Global

Illumination, much of the problem is because of photons being bounced back into the area that is also receiving direct illumination from the light, pushing the illumination to the extreme. The following are a few solutions that work for many light fixtures:

◆ Move the photometric light outside the fixture. Using self-illuminated globes on lights with Final Gather can give you the soft glow you expect around the fixture, and moving the light eliminates the photon reflection back to the wall.

◆ Change the light to a diffuse or spot to direct photons away from the fixture.

◆ Change the object properties of the interior of the light fixture to not interact with photons.

You might need to do a combination of these things for a particular fixture, or even exclude the influence of the light for certain objects, such as the outside of a fixture. In this Bath scene, the globes are self-illuminated, so the lights do not need to be inside the fixture. In your current Bath scene, move the lights in the ceiling fixtures down in the Z direction, a few inches outside the light fixture. For the light objects above the sink and mirror, move them a few inches outside the fixture globes toward Camera01.

Perform the following steps to render the final image with the current Global Illumination settings:

1. Continue with the previous scene, or open Bath_GI_2010-05.max.

2. Open the rendered Frame Window dialog box, and set the Image Precision setting to High.

3. Set the Glossy Reflection Precision and Glossy Refraction Precision settings to the middle 1.0X - Default setting.

4. Open the Render Setup dialog box, and switch to the Processing tab.

5. Disable Diagnostics.

6. Disable Material Override.

7. Switch to the Indirect Illumination tab.

8. Enable Final Gather with the Medium setting.

9. In the Reuse (FG And GI Disk Caching) menu area, set the Final Gather Map mode to Read FG Points Only From Existing Map Files, and set the filename to .\sceneassets\ renderassets\Bath_Medium.fgm.

10. Set the Caustics And Global Illumination Photon Map option to Read Photons Only From Existing Map Files, and change the filename to .\sceneassets\renderassets\Bath.pmap.

11. Render Camera01, and save your image file. A completed rendering is available as .\renderoutput\Bath\Bath_GI_Finish.jpg and is shown in Figure 6.14.

A final scene is available as .\scenes\Bath\Bath_GI_2010-Finish.max.

Next I cover the Light Lab scene with only photometric lighting so that I can show you two methods for controlling color bleed in a Global Illumination rendering: the Photon Basic shader and the Color Override/Ray Type Switcher.

FIGURE 6.14
The final Bath scene with 100,000 average photons per light and Medium FG preset

CONTROLLING GLOBAL ILLUMINATION COLOR BLEED WITH THE PHOTON BASIC SHADER

Often when you use Global Illumination, the amount of color energy bounced from a surface exceeds what is desirable in your rendering. A brilliant red floor will turn a room pink, as you will see with the Light Lab scene where the floor has been set to a deep red color to help illustrate how to control color bleed in a Global Illumination scene. All scene files are in the .\scenes\LightLab folder. This scene is configured with default settings for Global Illumination and a mr Photographic exposure control's EV setting at 7.0.

Perform the following steps to render the Light Lab scene, and control the color bleed with the Photon Basic shader:

1. Open the scene .\scenes\LightLab\LightLab_GI_2010_Start.max.

2. Render Camera02, and open it in the RAM Player for later comparison. The results are in image file .\renderoutput\LightLab\Initial_GI.jpg and shown in Figure 6.15.

FIGURE 6.15
The Light Lab scene with a saturated red floor and significant color bleed to other surfaces

As Figure 6.15 shows, the otherwise white walls and ceiling are tinted red because of the color bleeding from the floor and pool materials. Anywhere that direct light falls on the walls is slightly whiter, but anywhere with primarily indirect illumination includes a red cast.

Perform the following steps to correct the red cast from the flooring:

1. Continue with the previous scene, and open the SME by selecting the Rendering ➤ Material Editors ➤ Schematic Material Editor menu option.

2. Drag the Floor Tile material into View1, and make it an instance.

3. Double-click the Floor Tile material to bring it into the Parameter Editor.

4. Scroll the parameters to the mental ray Connection parameters, and click the lock symbol next to the Caustics And Global Illumination Photon shader. This disconnects it from the default photon shader and allows you to use your own shader instead.

5. In View1, expand the bottom of the Floor Tile Arch & Design material to expose the mr Connection parameters.

6. Add to View1 a Photon Basic mental ray shader.

7. Connect the output of the Photon Basic shader to the photon input of the Floor Tile material.

8. Double-click the Photon Basic shader to open its parameters.

9. Set the Diffuse color swatch to HSV 1.0, 0.2, and 0.5, a dim reddish gray.

10. Render your scene, and load it into Channel B of the RAM Player for comparison. Because the floor was the main source of the red splash, a majority of the red is removed from the scene.

THE PHOTON BASIC SHADER

Placing the Photon Basic shader into the photon input replaced the physically accurate photon shader used by default in the material and allowed you to choose what color (hue and saturation) and brightness (value) the photons saw when they hit that surface. The Photon Basic shader can also replace the specular color seen by photons, can change the transparency of the surface, and can change the index of refraction that the photon experiences.

Next you'll use a new map for 3ds Max/Design 2011, the Color Override/Ray Type Switcher shader, which not only allows you to control the color the photon sees at the surface but also allows you to change *any* map component a material returns to mental ray.

CONTROLLING GLOBAL ILLUMINATION COLOR BLEED WITH THE COLOR OVERRIDE/RAY TYPE SWITCHER

Autodesk created this shader to allow access to a new hidden mental ray shader, the mip_rayswitcher shader, which is not supported in 3ds Max/Design 2010 and older.

As Figure 6.16 shows, this shader allows you to replace a variety of rays returned from the material surface, including colors for Global Illumination photons and Final Gather. Final Gather experiences the same issues as Global Illumination when it comes to color bleeding.

The Color Override (Color Override/Ray Type Switcher) shader typically replaces the diffuse map in an Arch & Design material. The Default ray type slot allows you to essentially assign a map/shader to any undefined ray type slots, shown as "None" in the shader. As shown in Figure 6.16, placing a Color Correction shader in the Final Gather and Photons ray type slots replaces the "glazed ceramic tiles (tiles)" shader in the Default ray type slot. The Color Correction shader in this case allows you to modify the color of a map before Final Gather and Global Illumination use it to produce indirect illumination.

FIGURE 6.16
Color Override (Color Override/Ray Type Switcher) shader as shown in the SME

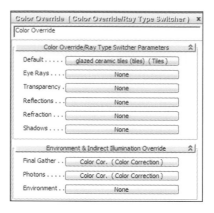

If you are using 3ds Max/Design 2010 or older, skip this example and go to the next example. Perform the following steps to use the Color Override/Ray Type Switcher map in 3ds Max/Design 2011 to control color bleed from the pool:

1. Continue from the previous steps, or open LightLab_GI_2011-01.max (or use the 2010-01 version).

2. In the SME, drag the Pool Tile material from the Material/Map Browser into View1, and double-click to open its parameters.

3. From the Material/Map Browser, drag a Color Override/Ray Switcher shader (map) into the view.

4. Connect the output of the new shader to the Diffuse Color Map input of the Pool Tile Arch & Design material.

5. Double-click the Color Override/Ray Type Switcher to open its parameters.

6. Connect the output of the "glazed ceramic tiles (tiles)" Tiles shader to the Default input of the Color Override/Ray Switcher shader.

7. Add a Color Correction map to View1.

8. Connect the output of the "glazed ceramic tiles (tiles)" Tiles shader to the input of the Color Correction shader.

9. Click the + next to Additional Parameters in the Color Correction shader to open its parameters.

10. Adjust the Saturation value to −65, press Enter, and then press the − symbol next to Additional Parameters to collapse the parameters.

11. Connect the output of the Color Correction shader to the Photon and Final Gather inputs of the Color Override/Ray Switcher shader. These two features will now return the color of the Color Correction map and not what is connected to the Color Override/Ray Switcher's Default input.

12. Render Camera02, and save your rendering into Channel A of the RAM Player. Figure 6.17 shows the final node configuration in the SME for the Pool Tile material.

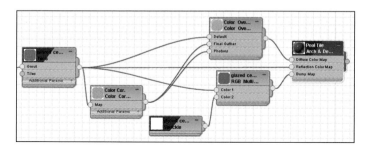

A version of this scene is available as LightLab_GI_2011-02.max. Your rendering should now have virtually no red splash. The Global Illumination solution, however, is not very smooth. The next section is memory intensive, so adjust the parameters downward as needed if you have limited resources, and save often so you can recall your current settings.

Perform the following steps to adjust Global Illumination and add Final Gather:

1. Continue from the previous scene, or open LightLab_GI_2011-02.max.

2. Open the Render Setup dialog box, and switch to the Indirect Illumination tab.

3. Enable Final Gather, and set the FG Precision Preset slider to Low or Draft.

4. In the Caustics And Global Illumination (GI) rollout settings and the Light Properties group, set the Average GI Photons Per Light value to 100,000 (or less if you are resource limited).

5. Render Camera02, and save it in the RAM Player Channel B for comparison. A completed scene is provided as LightLab_GI_2011-03.max.

Changing these settings caused red to appear again on the white surfaces in your rendering, although they are only a fraction of the original color bleed. The Floor Tile material is changing the color of the photons, but the problem is that Final Gather still sees the original red flooring.

Perform the following steps in 3ds Max/Design 2011 to eliminate color bleed in Final Gather:

1. Continue with your scene from the previous steps, or open LightLab_GI_2011-03.max.

2. Delete the input connection for Diffuse Color map on the Floor Tile Arch & Design material.

3. Delete the Photon Basic map.

4. Double-click the Floor Tile material to open its settings in the Parameter Editor.

5. In the mental ray Connection, relock the photon map previously unlocked.

6. Add a Color Override/Ray Switcher and Color Correction map to View1.

7. Connect the output of the "glazed ceramic tiles (tiles)" Tiles shader to the Default input of the Color Override/Ray Switcher and to the Map input of the Color Correction map.

8. Connect the output of the Color Correction map to the Final Gather and Photons input of the Color Override/Ray Switcher.

9. Connect the output of the Color Override/Ray Switcher to the Diffuse Color Map input of the Floor Tile material.

10. Right-click the Floor Time material's header in View,1 and select the Hide Unused Nodeslots option. The size of the material in the view is reduced. Figure 6.18 shows the final SME configuration for the Floor Tile material.

FIGURE 6.18
Final SME layout for the floor material

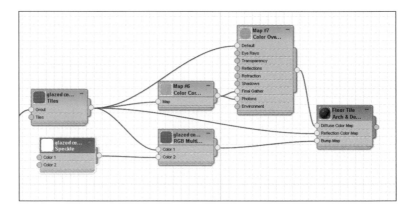

Because the Color Override/Ray Switcher map takes only maps as parameters, not color swatches, in your own scenes that require only a color swatch, you can use the Gamma & Gain map (Utility Gamma & Gain in 3ds Max/Design 2010 and earlier) to give you a simple color swatch to use as an input to the Color Override/Ray Type Switcher shader. You need to set the Gamma & Gain map's Gamma parameter to 1.0 and disable Reverse Gamma when used for a color. Alternately you can use the the Object Color shader

Figure 6.19 shows the final image with very little red bounce in the scene.

FIGURE 6.19
Final rendered image with minimal red color bleed

A complete scene is available as `.\scenes\LightLab\LightLab_GI_2011_Finish.max`. Next I cover how to set up the Sponza model for use with Global Illumination and Final Gather.

> **THE NEED TO CONTROL BLEEDING**
>
> As odd as it sounds, often when you use Final Gather and Global Illumination, you will find that you will get a lot of color splash from highly saturated surfaces, and when the red flooring turns the ceiling pink, the client is usually not happy and wants that effect reduced. Having worked in an office for several years that had a bright red floor, I can tell you firsthand that it will turn the ceiling a nice shade of pink and give everyone a healthy glow. For a rendering, however, it comes down to giving the client what they expect in the image even if it does not represent reality. Although this might be the image your client desires, helping them to understand that their choice of colors will have consequences can also help increase the value of your services.

Using Global Illumination with the Sponza Model

The Sponza scene has all materials enabled; if you need faster performance, you can enable the Material Override option. This is a large scene with a lot of nooks and crannies for the photons to find, and it will take a lot of photons to evenly illuminate the scene. Be sure to save your scene along the way in case of memory issues. At any point you can enable Final Gather and evaluate whether you need higher settings.

Perform the following steps to configure the Sponza scene for initial use of Global Illumination and Final Gather:

1. Open the scene `.\scenes\Sponza\Sponza_GI_2010_Start.max`. This is the final Sponza scene from Chapter 5.

2. Switch to a Perspective view.

3. Select the Compass01 object, and position it centered at the top of opening to the courtyard.

4. Select the Daylight01 object.

5. In the Modify tab, roll down the mr Sun Photons menu section, and enable the Use Photon Target option.

6. Set the Radius value to 3.5m. The sun is at a glancing angle to the opening, so a large radius is not necessary unless you modify the sun's position or date and time.

7. Move the Compass01 object again to center the sun's photon radius in the opening, adjusting your view to look along the sun's direction helps.

8. Open the Render Setup dialog box, and switch to the Indirect Illumination tab.

9. In the Reuse (FG And GI Disk Caching) menu roll-down section, set the Final Gather Map mode to Off (Do Not Cache Map To Disk).

10. In the Final Gather rollout, set FG Diffuse Bounces to 0.

11. Set the FG Precision Preset to Low.

12. Disable Final Gather; you will use the new settings after enabling and checking GI.

13. Enable Global Illumination in the Caustics And Global Illumination roll-down menu.

14. Enable the All Objects Generate & Receive GI And Caustics option in the Geometry Properties section of the Caustics And Global Illumination roll-out menu. This step is necessary because the object properties for objects in this scene have Global Illumination disabled.

15. Render Camera02, note the render time, and save the image to Channel A of the RAM Player.

This image is available as `.\renderoutput\Sponza\Part01.jpg` together with a visual diagnostics image that shows photon density; Red in this image is only 70 photons, as I read from the Render Message window. Your results will show large photon circles on some geometry, indicating a low number of photons in the scene and also showing you the Maximum Sampling Radius value that mental ray determined for this scene. Examining the Render Message dialog box will show that more photons were generated by the mr Sky Portal than the sun object, which indicates that the large size of the mr Sky Portal is producing a lot of illumination in the scene.

Perform the following steps to adjust Global Illumination for adequate photons:

1. Continue with the previous scene, or open the file `Sponza_GI_2010-01.max`.

2. Open the Render Setup dialog box, and switch to the Indirect Illumination tab.

3. Change the Average GI Photons Per Light setting to 500,000 from the default 20,000 (use a lower setting if you are resource limited).

4. Render Camera02, note the render time, and save the image to Channel B of the RAM Player.

This image, available as `.\renderoutput\Sponza\Part02.jpg`, still shows a Global Illumination circle on the floor of the scene. Adding Final Gather at this point, even in draft mode, will actually fix these few issues. First, though, you will pump more photons into the scene to get a decent Global Illumination solution before you enable Final Gather. Because the sun in this scene provides only glancing illumination, you first add photons to the mr Sky Portal.

Perform the following steps to add more photons to your mr Sky Portal and the entire scene:

1. Continue with the previous scene, or open `Sponza_GI_2010-02.max`.

2. Select the mr Sky Portal object, and switch to the Modify tab.

3. Roll-down the mental ray Indirect Illumination menu area, and change the GI Photons setting to 2.0. This doubles the photons allocated previously to this light.

4. In the GI settings of the Render Settings dialog box, change the Average GI Photons Per Light value to 2,000,000 (2 million). Because there are only two photon-generating lights, this is a reasonable number if you have the memory resources.

5. In the Reuse (FG And GI Disk Caching) roll-down menu, set the Caustics And Global Illumination Photon Map mode to Read/Write Photons To Map Files, and set the filename to `.\sceneassets\renderassets\Sponza.pmap`. A precomputed PMAP file is provided as `Sponza_2mP.pmap`. (Due to DVD space considerations this has been optimized with Importons however works identically).

6. Render Camera02, note the time, and save the image to Channel A of the RAM Player for comparison to the previous rendering. The image is provided as `.\renderoutput\Sponza\Part03_2mP.jpg`.

You'll notice that the circles are getting smaller and there are more of them. This means that mental ray is finding 500 photons in a smaller and smaller area. Figure 6.20 shows the current diagnostics image, and the photon values are from the Render Message window. Setting the PMAP option to Read/Write means you are done adding photons for the moment with this scene. If you change any settings affecting light intensity, position, or Global Illumination settings for the quantity of photons, delete and re-create this PMAP file.

Figure 6.20 shows a Photon Density image of your current scene with Cyan at approximately 3,300 photons, Green at 6,600, and Yellow at 9,900 photons. If you are using the pre-computed PMAP file included on the DVD, it has been processed with Importons due to DVD space requirements. The DVD's PMAP file is a small fraction of the original PMAP without Importon processing (4.5MB compared to 160MB), and your diagnostic density values with this smaller PMAP file will be in the range of 85 to 350 photons. I cover Importons in Chapter 7, "Importons and Irradiance Particles." There is no difference in the final renderings.

FIGURE 6.20
Sponza diagnostics
image at 2 million
photons

The Photon Density diagnostic image shows photons stored consistently at 3.3k and higher, although it is still a bit unevenly distributed on the bottom floor level in particular. Because the bright circles in the rendered image are relatively small, it shows that mental ray is finding 500 photons to average within that small area. Based on that, you can increase the Maximum Num. Photons Per Sample setting to see whether you need to keep adding photons or to switch on Final Gather.

Perform the following steps to adjust the Maximum Num. Photons Per Sample value:

1. Continue with the previous file, or open `Sponza_GI_2010-03.max`.

2. Open the Render Setup dialog box, and switch to the Indirect Illumination tab.

3. In the Reuse section, change the Caustics And Global Illumination Photon Map option to Read Photons Only From Existing Map Files.

4. In the Caustics and Global Illumination settings, change the Maximum Num. Photons Per Sample option to 1500.

5. Render Camera02, note the time, and load the rendering into Channel B of the RAM Player to compare it to the previous rendering.

The rendered image is available at `.\renderoutput\Sponza\Part04_1500samples.jpg`. This rendering should take an average quad-core computer four to five minutes to complete. This image still has some unevenness to the illumination; however, I will leave that as an exercise for you to increase the Maximum Num. Photons Per Sample setting to 2500 or more and to also try a higher Average GI Photons Per Light setting. For now, the image will look good after Final Gather is added to filter some of the unevenness of the Global Illumination.

Perform the following steps to enable Final Gather for this scene:

1. Continue with the previous scene, or open `Sponza_GI_2010-04.max`.

2. Open the Render setup dialog box, and switch to the Indirect Illumination tab.

3. Roll down the Final Gather section.

4. Enable Final Gather.

5. Ensure the FG Precision slider is at Low and that Diffuse Bounces is set to 0.

6. Render Camera02. The Global Illumination phase is skipped, and Final Gather begins immediately. Note the final render time, and load the image into Channel A of the RAM Player for comparison to the previous rendering.

Figure 6.21 shows the final image with Global Illumination and the Low preset for Final Gather. This image completed in less than seven minutes on a mid-range quad-core machine.

The final image is available as `.\renderoutput\Sponza\Part05_Final_Image.jpg`, and the completed scene is provided as `.\scenes\Sponza\Sponza_GI_2010_Finish.max`. Because the combination of Global Illumination and Final Gather works so well with this scene, you *can* get away with an average of 500,000 photons per light and the Draft Final Gather setting. A version of this scene using these low Final Gather/Global Illumination settings with an animated daylight system is provided as `.\scenes\Sponza\Sponza_GI_2010_Animation.max`, and the animation file is provided as `.\renderoutput\Sponza\Sponza_GI.avi`. Despite the low 500,000 average photons and Draft Final Gather mode, the rendering is very even throughout the change in daylight on through dusk. The average render time on my render farm over the 300 frames was only 3 minutes 46 seconds each. Overall, the combination of Global Illumination and Final Gather gives you better image results with significantly shorter render times. The animation was also produced with Global Illumination and Final Gather calculated on every frame and produced good results. This would not have been possible with calculating Final Gather alone per frame.

FIGURE 6.21
The final Sponza Global Illumination scene with 2,000,000 average photons per light and 1,500 photons per sample

Next I cover using Global Illumination with the Karina Bay Resort project in addition to Final Gather.

Using Global Illumination with the Karina Bay Resort Scene

The Karina Bay Resort exterior scene is a model I covered in Chapter 5. With a large outdoor scene, you need a considerably high number of photons to get a reasonably low Global Illumination size (more photons means smaller radius) and achieve an even distribution of energy. Because this is not a closed environment (like the Bath or Sponza Palace scene), a lot of photons will be bouncing off into space, and it will take longer for mental ray to calculate Global Illumination. All scene files are in the .\scenes\Karina folder of the Chapter 6 project. The scene has Material Override disabled that you can enable if required for faster rendering.

Perform the following steps to add Global Illumination to the Karina Bay Resort scene:

1. Open the .\scenes\Karina\Landscaping_GI_2010_Start.max file.

2. Open the Render Setup dialog box, and switch to the Indirect Illumination tab.

3. Disable Final Gather.

4. Enable Global Illumination.

5. Set Average GI Photons Per Light to 2,000,000 (2 million); use a lower setting on resource-limited systems.

6. Switch to the Top view.

7. Select the Compass01 object, and move it to the center of the island.

8. Select the Daylight01 object, and switch to the Modify tab in the Command panel.

9. Enable the Use Photon Target setting, and change the Radius value to 600′ to encompass the island. This option not only focuses the photons but prevents them from being emitted in all directions from the daylight system.

10. Render the CamMidway view, and load the image into the RAM Player Channel A. A completed image is provided as `.\renderoutput\Karina\Karina_GI.jpg`.

11. In RAM Player Channel B, open the image file `.\renderoutput\Karina\Karina_FG.jpg`; this is the final result from Chapter 5.

You can now compare a Final Gather version of the scene with your current rendering. The completed image is available as `.\renderoutput\Karina\Karina_GI_2mP.jpg` and is shown as Figure 6.22.

FIGURE 6.22
The Karina Bay Resort scene with a 2,000,000 Average GI Photons Per Light setting and 500 photons per sample

At this point, the Global Illumination solution, from this view, does not look good. The restaurant is in shadow and unusually dark on the left in contrast to the otherwise bright and low-contrast scene. Two million photons spread across the entire island scene doesn't mean a lot of photons are in any specific area, and with the angle of the sun and wide gap between buildings, there are even fewer photons reaching the in-shadow restaurant wall at left. Figure 6.23 shows a visual diagnostics for the scene at this point.

FIGURE 6.23
The Karina Bay Resort scene Photon Density diagnostics image

From this image, it looks like photons are getting to all surfaces; however, a look at the Render Message dialog box shows that each color represents only a fraction of a photon per pixel. Looking further into the log shows that the computed Maximum Sampling Radius (shown as "globil. radius") for this scene is more than 800 feet, which means that the Global Illumination effect is basically a blur across the entire scene. You lose contrast and definition in your scenes, but it does brighten things up, including the inside of buildings, and you might find on your own that you regain some definition if you add FG.

For the previous procedure, I enabled the GI Reuse option, and the size of the PMAP file is one-third the size of the final Bath scene's PMAP file—not many photons compared to the small Bath scene. Render times on my test system are around 4 minutes with High Image Precision settings, so I have some room to grow the photon count. You need to greatly increase the number of photons for this scene, which can lead to memory issues in 32-bit computers and computers with less than 4GB of memory. To assist with this issue, the PMAP file in the next procedure has been precomputed on a 64-bit system. Average GI Photons for this map is set to 25 million.

Perform the following steps to use the precomputed PMAP file:

1. Continue with the previous scene, or open the file `Landscaping_GI_2010-01.max`.

2. Open the Render Setup dialog box, and switch to the Indirect Illumination tab.

3. In the Reuse (FG And GI Disk Caching) dialog box, set the Caustics And Global Illumination Photon Map option to Read Photons Only From Existing Map Files.

4. Select the PMAP file `.\sceneassets\renderassets\Karina_25m.pmap`.

5. Render CamMidway, and open it in Channel B of the RAM Player to compare with the previous rendering.

A completed image is available at `.\renderoutput\Karina\Karina_GI_25m.jpg` together with a Photon Density diagnostics image with Cyan = 0.016 that shows few photons in any given area.

At 50 million photons, the size of the PMAP file is more than 500MB and took 30 minutes to generate, and its size now exceeds that of the bathroom scene. Because of the large area of the Karina Bay Resort scene, however, you still have relatively few photons in a given area. Again, the large computed Maximum Sampling Radius value combined with Final Gather produces reasonable results, particularly if you also add ambient occlusion to materials that need more detail. The last step in the examination of Global Illumination with the island scene is to add Final Gather and evaluate the results.

Perform the following steps to add Final Gather to the Karina Bay Resort scene:

1. Continue with the previous scene, or open `Landscaping_GI_2010-02.max`.

2. Open the Render Setup dialog box, and switch to the Indirect Illumination tab.

3. Enable Final Gather, and set the FG Precision slider to the Medium preset. The FGM file has been precomputed for this view.

4. In the Reuse (FG And GI Disk Caching) dialog box, set the Final Gather Map mode to Read FG Points Only.

5. Set the FGM filename to `.\sceneassets\renderassets\Karina_Medium.fgm`.

6. Render the CamMidway view, and open it in RAM Player Channel A to compare it to the previous image. A rendered image is available as `.\renderoutput\Karina\Karina_GI_FG.jpg` and is shown as Figure 6.24.

FIGURE 6.24
The Karina Bay Resort scene with 25,000,000 average photons per light and FG

If this were the only camera view of the island that you were producing, then setting the daylight system to concentrate its photons only in the visible area would greatly increase the photon density and reduce the Maximum Sampling Radius setting, thus improving the contrast of the image and allowing you to use fewer average GI photons in your Global Illumination settings. This scene, however, was originally used for both still images and as an animation, so I examined settings to achieve results for multiple views. Global Illumination has a great advantage in that it calculates Global Illumination for the entire scene; however, this can create exceptionally large Global Illumination PMAP files of 500MB or more. Given more DVD space, I'd calculate a larger PMAP for you; instead, I'll set the daylight system to focus photons into the general area of CamMidway, adjust the settings for fewer photons, and configure mental ray for this one shot. This scene is available as `.\scenes\Karina\Landscape_GI_2010_Finish.max`, and a rendering is available as `.\renderoutput\Karina\CamMidway_GI_FG.jpg`.

In the next section, I cover the settings and use of the Caustics Indirect Illumination effect.

Defining Caustics

Caustics are an indirect illumination effect that uses photons to simulate the concentration of light through transparent objects (refraction) and the scattering of light off reflective surfaces. Examples of Caustics would be magnifying glasses, light through the wavy surface of water that is projected onto the ocean floor, and the reflection of light off the water onto objects above.

Understanding Caustics Settings

The values for Caustics are similar to that of Global Illumination and use the parameter Average Caustic Photons Per Light to determine the number of emitted photons. Caustics photons are separate from Global Illumination photons and are intended for selective use on specific transparent and/or reflective objects, and not all objects as with Global Illumination. Caustics is also a focused indirect lighting effect with the goal of placing many small photons in a given area rather than large photons across all areas as with Global Illumination.

For many scenes, the default values give good results provided you have enough Caustics photons. As with Global Illumination, the radius automatically shrinks and gives better definition to the Caustics effect as more Caustics photons are shot into the scene.

The following settings are for Caustics, and you can find them on the Indirect Illumination tab in the Caustics And Global Illumination roll-down section.

Multiplier and the color swatch   The Multiplier setting allows you to control the brightness of the Caustics photons, and the color swatch allows you to tint the Caustics photons. You can vary these settings on both cached and uncached caustics data.

Maximum Num. Photons Per Sample   This setting affects the sharpness of your Caustics. Larger values produce blurrier caustics. Higher Average Caustics Photons Per Light counts generate sharper results, and you can adjust this value to control the area of influence.

Maximum Sampling Radius   This setting is automatically calculated by mental ray as 1/100th the scene radius. For some scenes, setting a smaller radius value can help focus the Caustics; however, adding more Caustics photons will also sharpen the effect.

Filter   The default Box filter is fast and general purpose. The Cone is a sharpening filter, and Gauss gives a slightly blurred result.

Opaque Shadows When Caustics Are Enabled   Disabling this check box allows shadows to be partially transparent. Opaque shadows render faster.

Individual objects contain properties that control both receiving and generating Caustics effects; these object-specific settings are accessible from the right-click Quad Menu and the Object Properties option, and found in the mental ray tab of the Object Properties dialog box. All new objects are set to receive Caustics by default, and all new objects have the generation of Caustics effects disabled by default. The ability to create Caustics for geometry can be enabled globally for all objects by setting the check box All Objects Generate & Receive GI And Caustics, found in the GI and Caustics settings in the Render Setup dialog box. Enabling Caustics generation per object rather than globally, however, can make for a faster rendering scene. The Sponza scene has GI and Caustics disabled on objects, and requires the global option enabled.

ENABLING CAUSTICS LIGHTS

New for 3ds Max/Design 2011 is the requirement that you must enable the Generate Caustics option in a light's Object Properties dialog box that is found on the mental ray tab. The Render Setup dialog box option All Objects Generate & Receive GI And Caustics does not apply to lights in 3ds Max/Design 2011.

Next I cover some common Caustics scenes and some of the settings that you can use to create them.

Using Caustics

In a practical sense, Caustics are not something that are added to many of my scenes because it does take time to set up properly, it is often a small-area effect, and it is rare that the realism of a large scene is improved. For instance, producing Caustics for a dining room full of tables with wine glasses is probably not practical as the number of photons need to produce a sharp result will be excessively high. In contrast a close-up still-image render of one table would be enhanced with Caustics. For interior scenes that include pools of water, such as a bathroom or the Light Lab scenes, adding Caustics as described later in this chapter greatly improves the feel and realism of the scene. Small scenes with focused Caustics, used selectively, can add a nice finishing touch. Like lens flares in Photoshop, though, too much of a good thing can detract from a rendering. One thing to consider before using Caustics on large water objects is that this effect can often be faked by the use of projection lights with Cellular map projection shaders; it is often difficult to tell that there is a mismatch between what should be there and what is projected by the light.

In the next two sections, I present two common Caustics scenes: a pool of water and a small glass object on a table.

CREATING CAUSTIC WATER

In this section, I show the large pool of water in the Light Lab scene.

Perform the following steps to add Caustics effects to the pool:

1. Open the scene `.\scenes\LightLab\LLCaustics_2010_Start.max`.

2. In the Camera03 view, select the Water object.

3. Right-click, and select Object Properties from the Quad menu.

4. Switch to the mental ray tab, and in the Caustics And Global Illumination (GI) group, enable the Generate Caustics function.

5. Open the Render Setup dialog box, and switch to the Indirect Illumination tab.

6. Enable Caustics.

7. Render Camera03, and save the results in Channel A of the RAM Player. A rendered image is available at `.\renderoutput\Caustics\Pool_20k.jpg`.

One issue with the scene at this point is that the Caustics are not well defined. The large photometric light above the pool will work to place 20,000 Caustics photons in the scene, and that is certainly not enough for the large pool area.

Perform the following steps to increase the number of photons in this scene:

1. Continue with the previous scene, or open `LLCaustics_2010-01.max`.

2. Open the Render Setup dialog box, and switch to the Indirect Illumination tab.

3. In the Light Properties section of the Caustics And Global Illumination (GI) settings, change the Average Caustic Photons Per Light setting to 500,000.

4. Render Camera03, and save the results in Channel B of the RAM Player. A rendered image is available at `.\renderoutput\Caustics\Pool_500k.jpg`.

5. Save your scene as `LLCaustics_2010-02.max`.

The definition of the Caustics effect is much better but is still not sharp. As you increase your Average Caustics Photons Per Light count, the photons become more focused in the pool because mental ray will only look up at most 100 photons with the current settings, and 100 photons represent a smaller and smaller area. You'll find that shooting 500,000 or even 1 million photons takes only one or two minutes. You can significantly decrease your render time and improve the Caustics brightness and detail by using a separate, focused, light source to generate only Caustics photons, eliminating the diffuse spray of photons from the current light source.

Perform the following steps to configure a separate light for Caustics generation:

1. Continue with your previous scene, or open `LLCaustics_2010-02.max`.

2. Switch to the Left viewport.

3. Select the object PhotometricLight01 in your scene.

4. Hold the Shift key, and move the light downward about 12 inches; then choose the Copy option for cloning the light.

5. Select the PhotometricLight01 object again, and switch to the Modify tab.

6. In the mental ray Indirect Illumination settings, set the Caustic Photons setting to 0.0.

7. Select your new PhotometricLight02 object.

8. On the Modify tab, change the Light Distribution to Spotlight.

9. Set Hotspot/Beam to 90.

10. In the Advanced Effects rollout, deselect the check boxes for Diffuse and Specular. This light will no longer produce illumination for surfaces.

11. In the mental ray Indirect Illumination menu area, set the GI Photons value to 0.0. This light will now only affect Caustics in the pool area.

12. Render Camera03, and save the results in Channel A of the RAM Player for comparison. A rendered image is available at `.\renderoutput\Caustics\Pool_Final.jpg` and is shown in Figure 6.25. The finished scene is available as `.\scenes\LightLab\Caustics_2010_Finish.max`.

FIGURE 6.25
The final caustics effect for the Light Lab pool with 500,000 caustic photons

Caustics is not only a refractive effect, as shown here, but also a reflective effect. Switching to Camera02 and rendering the scene, however, does not produce much reflected energy in the ceiling because the energy reflected to the ceiling will naturally be more diffuse and less focused. Because this viewpoint sees into the pool, you cannot change many options to help improve the brightness of the photons at the ceiling without making the pool seem radioactive. To help define the ceiling Caustics without adversely affecting the pool, set the Maximum Num. Photons Per Sample option in the Caustics settings to between 10 and 50; I leave that to you for experimentation. As mentioned earlier, faking Caustics with a projector light for some Caustic effects can produce nice results.

In the last example for this chapter, I show a focused Caustics effect through a transparent object.

CREATING CAUSTIC STILL LIFE

To demonstrate Caustics on objects with complex transparent shape, I have provided a scene with a torus knot with a rainbow gradient material across its surface. The torus knot is in a bright environment, and one of its rendered effects includes ray-traced colors projected through the material in addition to the focused Caustics effect. The overlapping surfaces of the torus knot make for interesting patterns for a Caustics effect but also require higher settings for Trace Depth both for mental ray general settings and for Caustics. As with the final version of the Light Lab scene, this scene has one light set to generate Caustics and one to only provide diffuse illumination. The Caustics-generating light in this scene, however, does produce general illumination and shadows to project the color of the torus knot onto the floor of the scene.

As with lighting any scene, working with lights in isolation, even Caustics generators, can help speed the process of completing your scene.

Perform the following steps to configure the next scene for Caustics:

1. Open the file `.\scenes\Caustics\Torus_2010_Start.max`.

2. Open the Render Setup dialog box, and switch to the Indirect Illumination tab.

3. Disable Final Gather.

4. Disable Global Illumination.

5. Close the Render Setup dialog box.

6. Open the Light Lister, and disable the Plight02 light object. Close the dialog box.

7. Render the Camera01 view, and save it to Channel A of the RAM Player. The image will be a little dim with diffuse Caustics projected onto the ground. The low reflection and refraction settings also cause black areas in the torus, which you will correct next.

8. In the Render Setup dialog box, switch to the Renderer tab.

9. In the Rendering Algorithms roll-down, set the Max. Trace Depth, Max. Reflections, and Max. Refractions settings each to 12.

10. Render Camera01, and open the rendering in Channel B of the RAM Player. You should see some additional refinement along the refractive edges in particular. The floor shows a blurry Caustics effect and a projected image of the torus knot.

11. On the Render Setup dialog box's Indirect Illumination tab, set the Average Caustic Photons Per Light value to 500,000.

12. Render Camera01, and open it in Channel A of the RAM Player for comparison. You should have much sharper definition in your caustic effect, but it can still improve.

13. Increase the Average Caustic Photons Per Light setting to 1,500,000, and render the scene. The effect is much sharper, and increasing this value further will add only minimal detail to the effect.

14. Enable Global Illumination.

15. Enable Final Gather.

16. Set Average GI Photons Per Light to 200,000.

17. Open the Light Lister, and enable PLight02.

18. Render Camera01, and open the image in Channel B of the RAM Player. The additional direct and indirect light will wash out the Caustics effect, so there is one more setting to adjust to compensate for the lack of intensity.

19. On the Indirect Illumination tab of the Render Setup dialog box, set the Multiplier value for Caustics to 6.0.

20. Render the scene.

The final image is shown as Figure 6.26 and is available as `.\renderoutput\Caustics\Torus_Finish.jpg`. The finished scene is available as `.\scenes\Caustics\Torus_2010_Finish.max`. This version includes a connection to a precomputed PMAP file called `Torus.pmap`, along with a `Torus.fgm` file for FG.

FIGURE 6.26
The final Caustics effect for the torus knot with 3,000,000 Caustics photons

The Bottom Line

Cache photons for reuse   mental ray provides the Reuse functionality to store and retrieve (cache) Global Illumination and Caustics photons for later reuse.

Master It   You are producing a walk-through animation of an interior space. How would you generate, cache, and reuse Global Illumination photons to render the scene?

Utilize Global Illumination in a scene   Global Illumination, combined with Final Gather, gives the highest-quality renderings in the least amount of time. For interior scenes, the default Global Illumination settings are often useful as is with only the adjustment of the Average GI Photons Per Light setting. For exterior and interior scenes that use a daylight system, Global Illumination photons typically need to be focused around the area of interest to give the best results in a minimum amount of time.

Master It   You are producing an interior rendering with Final Gather and Global Illumination. What are the basic steps to enable and adjust Global Illumination settings in the Render Setup dialog box?

Utilize Caustics in a scene   Caustics add a great deal of realism to a scene; however, it might take additional setup and a high number of photons to produce a satisfactory Caustics solution.

Master It   You are producing still images of a restaurant dining room table scene including clear glass objects. How do you enable Caustics and adjust settings to ensure a sharp result?

Chapter 7

Importons and Irradiance Particles

Importons and Irradiance Particles are two relatively new indirect illumination technologies in mental ray. The term *Importons* is short for "importance photons" and is a technology that minimizes Global Illumination data based on how important a rendered area is to the illumination of the final image. Importons allow you to emit more photons into your scene; they keep just the photons you need for your image to reduce the memory requirements that high photon numbers might require.

Importons also work with the next technology, Irradiance Particles. Unlike the other indirect illumination technologies, irradiance particles calculate direct *and* indirect illumination for every particle. Importons determine the placement of irradiance particles on surfaces in your scene, ensuring that irradiance particles are placed along the most important regions of your image. Irradiance particles can replace Final Gather and Global Illumination for use in scenes, and they produce faster and higher-quality renders in many cases. Irradiance particles have a set of parameters similar to Final Gather, and they can produce image-based lighting effects that include shadows.

Both importons and irradiance particles are evolving technologies and continue to improve with each release of 3ds Max/Design and mental ray. No technology is ideal for all purposes, and this chapter will help you get your feet wet with these new technologies.

Importons and irradiance particles are available in 3ds Max/Design 2011 via new MAXScript string options and available in 3ds Max/Design 2009 and newer with a special plug-in produced by Maximilian Tarpini and originally provided at www.maxplugins.de. The free plug-in is available on the DVD in the \Plugin folder; you can also find it at www.mastering-mentalray.com.

In this chapter, you will learn to

♦ Install the plug-in to access importons and irradiance particles

♦ Add importons to a scene

♦ Add irradiance particles to a scene

Installing the ctrl.ghost Plug-In

Importons and irradiance particles have been part of mental ray since 3ds Max/Design 2009; however, they are not exposed in the 3ds Max/Design user interface. To access these technologies, you must first install a small plug-in to access the features and their settings. A *plug-in* extends the capabilities of 3ds Max/Design, and a plug-in can include new types of geometry, new materials and effects, and even new rendering engines, among other things.

The ctrl.ghost plug-in is provided on your DVD in the \Plugins folder. For installing to 3ds Max/Design 2010, for instance, there is the \Plugins\ctrl.ghost.settings 2010\ folder with subfolders that you copy directly into your 32- or 64-bit version of 3ds Max/Design. Each subfolder contains the folders \Max2010x32 and \Max2010x64. There are separate folders for 3ds Max/Design 2009, 2010, and 2011 provided in the \Plugins folder.

3DS MAX/DESIGN PLUG-IN ARCHITECTURE

On some level, nearly every visible feature of 3ds Max/Design is a plug-in. Some things, like the Teapot object or photometric lights, are standard plug-ins that are included with the shipping version of 3ds Max/Design. Some plug-ins are provided by third parties such as the developer and 3D artist Maximilian Tarpini, Archvision (its RPC product), and 3DConnexion (for the 3D mouse), to name just a few. An excellent source for 3ds Max/Design plug-ins is www.maxplugins.de, a site by David Baker of Dusseldorf, Germany. Most plug-ins available at this site are maintained and provided free by Baker and other developers, and a few are demo plug-ins and links to commercially available plug-ins from a variety of sources. Baker produced the mr Shader object needed to host the ctrl.ghost shader.

Some plug-ins install themselves, and others can be added to 3ds Max/Design simply by copying files to your 3ds Max/Design installation, usually in the .\plugins folder.

Perform the following steps to install the ctrl.ghost plug-in in 3ds Max/Design 2011:

1. Close 3ds Max/Design if it is running.

2. Insert your book's DVD, and open the \Plugins folder with Windows Explorer.

3. Open the \Plugins\ctrl.ghost.settings.2011 folder.

4. If you are running 3ds Max/Design x32, open the Max2011x32 folder; otherwise, open the Max2011x64 folder.

5. Select both the stdplugs and mentalimages folders, right-click, and choose Copy.

6. Open the 3ds Max/Design installation folder, typically C:\Program Files\Autodesk\3ds Max Design 2011. If you are running the 32-bit version of 3ds Max Design on a 64-bit system, then the installation folder is C:\Program Files (x86)\Autodesk\3ds Max Design 2011.

7. Right-click the \3ds Max Design 2011 folder name, and select Paste. Click Yes when prompted to merge the folders.

8. Run 3ds Max/Design.

PLUG-IN VERSIONS AND NEW MENTAL RAY MAXSCRIPT OPTIONS

Included on the DVD's Plugin folder are folders for 3ds Max/Design 2009 and 2010, which include different plug-ins and a different folder structure from what was described earlier for 3ds Max/Design 2011. Because 3ds Max/Design 2011 was not completed at the time of this writing, there may be updated plug-ins and instructions at www.mastering-mentalray.com. New for 3ds Max/Design 2011 is the ability to access mental ray string commands via MAXScript. A mental ray string option allows direct access to features within mental ray with a command in a script such as '"irradiance particles" true'. This scripting capability gives you new methods to access features such as importons, irradiance particles, and newer features such as progressive rendering. Progressive rendering updates your entire screen as mental ray renders and refines the image in multiple passes and allows you to set time and quality limits. See www.mastering-mentalray.com for scripts and additional information on mental ray string commands and progressive rendering.

Perform the following steps to access the ctrl.ghost settings in your own scenes:

1. Open your scene.

2. In the Command panel, on the Create tab, choose the mental ray object classification from the drop-down menu.

3. Select the mr Shader object, and create one mr Shader object in your scene. This is a nonrendering helper object, so make it large enough to find but not so large that it is in the way.

4. Click None for the shader, and choose the Ctrl.Ghost.Settings (ctrl.studio) option from the Material/Map Browser. The shader is shown in Figure 7.1.

FIGURE 7.1
The Command panel with the mr Shader setting configured with the Ctrl.Ghost .Settings map

5. Open the Compact Material Editor or SME, and drag the new map into a sample sphere or view. Make it an instance.

You now have the settings available within the material editor, as shown in Figure 7.2.

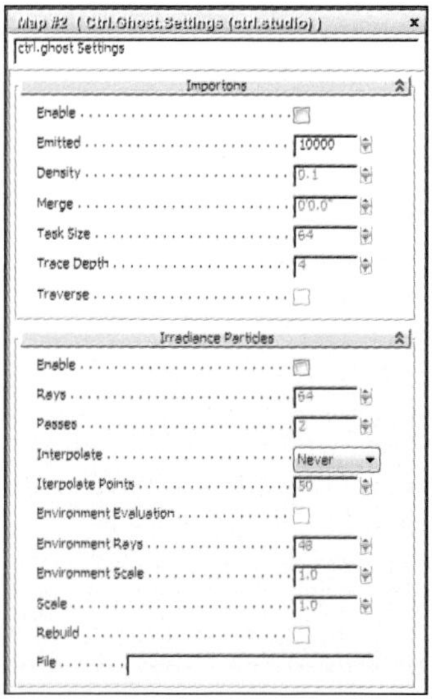

FIGURE 7.2
The SME parameter editor for the Ctrl .Ghost.Settings (ctrl.studio) map

Although I have not experienced any issues with this plug-in, there is always the possibility with any plug-in that it might affect your copy of 3ds Max/Design. This plug-in is unsupported by Autodesk. To uninstall the plug-in, simply delete the `mrGeomShaderObject.dlo`, `ctrl_ghost_settings.dll`, and `ctrl_ghost_settings.mi` files from your 3ds Max/Design installation. If you install the wrong version (x32 instead of x64, for instance), simply copying the correct version into the 3ds Max/Design installation will overwrite the incorrect version and get you working again.

LEARN, DISCOVER, TEACH, REPEAT

To date, the importon and irradiance particle technologies have not been utilized extensively in 3ds Max/Design, and I've gleaned much of the information on the settings and techniques for these two tools from numerous test-renders, from documentation of other mental ray applications such as Maya and Softimage, and from the writings of numerous users and mental ray experts. As anyone who has been in the 3D community for a while knows, half the battle is understanding the tools, and the other half is knowing the techniques; and sometimes you have to pull from a number of resources to learn both sides.

The people who have helped me the most with both information and techniques for mental ray have been, in no particular order, Jeff Patton, Maximilian Tarpini, Zap Andersson, Thorsten Hartmann (aka "hot chip"), and Bart Gawboy. Although they are not the only ones participating extensively online, these particular individuals give a lot of time and effort back to the mental ray community. Patton maintains a blog at www.jeffpatton.net, is active in numerous online forums, and is one of the founders of www.mrmaterials.com, a repository for custom materials for mental ray. Tarpini can be found at http://forums.cgsociety.com. He is active assisting users, in addition to providing custom shaders like ctrl.studio. Hartmann runs the German mental ray forums at www.germanmentalray.de and can be found in CG Society's forums. Andersson is a software engineer at mental images and maintains a personal (unofficial) mental ray blog at http://mentalray-tips.blogspot.com, in addition to helping out on many online forums. Gawboy organizes the Los Angeles mental ray User's Group (www.lamrug.org) and is the moderator at the mental ray forums at mental images (http://forum.mentalimages.com). He is also the director of training at mental images.

The use of importons and irradiance particles is a moving target at this point. This chapter should get you started understanding these tools and learning some techniques. I hope it will intrigue you to not only experiment further with the tools but to also participate and share what you have learned. For you to help advance the state of the art, you only need to follow four simple steps: learn, discover, teach, repeat.

Next I cover how importons work to reduce Global Illumination overhead.

Introducing Importons

Importons are "importance-driven" photons used to clean up and optimize Global Illumination in your scene and to define where mental ray stores irradiance particles. Like Global Illumination photons, importons are distributed throughout your scene by bouncing from surface to surface; however, unlike Global Illumination and Caustic photons, importons do not distribute light energy and are emitted from cameras instead of light sources. Rather than transferring light energy, importons measure how visible a surface is in the final image and how the illumination at a point contributes to the final image. Objects shown in a reflection, for instance, would receive less importance — and less attention at render time — based on its visibility within the reflection. Less important areas have their photons merged in varying amounts depending on their contribution to the image. Merging photons transfers the illumination from the merged photons into the remaining photon, and energy is never lost. This intelligent merging helps improve the quality and smoothness of the Global Illumination solution and greatly reduces the memory requirements because fewer photons are stored. The PMAP file size will be a small percentage of the size it would be without importons, and although the new PMAP size depends a lot on the content of your visible scene, file reductions of 90 percent or more are common.

Disable the Global Illumination setting Merge Nearby Photons when you use importons because importons perform that function.

Rendering with importons adds another preprocessing phase to the rendering of your image, which happens before Global Illumination photons are emitted from light sources or before irradiance particles are generated. There are no visual diagnostics modes for importons because they are discarded right after they are used by Global Illumination or irradiance particles; however, you can see the end result they have on Global Illumination with the Global Illumination visual diagnostics modes. As with Global Illumination calculation, with importons creation, there is no visual feedback to the user beyond what is visible in the Render Message dialog box. 3ds Max/Design displays the "Current Task: xx.x% Rendering" status in the Rendering status dialog box as importons are emitted and importance calculated.

Figure 7.3 shows the Bath scene rendered with Global Illumination and importons.

FIGURE 7.3
Bath image rendered with Global Illumination, Final Gather, and importons

Figure 7.4 shows the Bath scene's diagnostic image for the photon map without using importons and an even gradient of photon density. Cyan for this image shows a density of 9.3 and created a PMAP file of 402MB.

FIGURE 7.4
Bath scene with
Global Illumination
and no importons

Figure 7.5 shows the same scene with Global Illumination computed with 1 million importons. Cyan for this image shows a density of 3.1, and the PMAP file is 5.2MB. You can clearly see how importons have removed the photons in many areas of the scene. The rendered results, however, are identical between the image with and without importons.

FIGURE 7.5
Bath scene diag-
nostics image with
Global Illumination
and importons

You can see from the rendered image in Figure 7.3 that despite the small PMAP size, the rendered results look very good. Importons effectively stripped photons from all areas outside the bath area and optimized the photons within the current view, leaving the PMAP file 1.2 percent the size of the original (a 98.8 percent reduction). The small PMAP size means that 32-bit machines with limited memory can be used to render images, although you might need a 64-bit machine to compute the original PMAP with importons just as you would without importons.

Next I cover the parameters that control importons.

Setting Importon Parameters

To access the settings for importons, you must create an mr Shader object, assign it the ctrl.ghost shader, and then drag and drop the ctrl.ghost shader from the Modify tab into one of the material editors. In the SME, drop the shader into a view, and double-click to open the Parameter Editor or press the plus (+) sign next to Additional Parameters to access the settings. Figure 7.6 shows the ctrl.ghost settings for importons.

FIGURE 7.6
Importon settings

Enable   This controls whether importons are generated, obviously; however, it is temporarily enabled if this option is off and irradiance particles are used.

Emitted   This setting is the total number of importons emitted from the camera view. The Emitted value can be a small fraction of the total image pixels up to the number of pixels in an image and well beyond. As a reference, a 1920×1080 image is 2,073,600 pixels, and you might start with 200,000 importons in that case and work up to 2 million importons, as the quality of your Global Illumination solution requires. Importons can either use the Emitted number or use the Density setting described next; the Emitted number must be 0 for the Density value to be used.

Unlike Global Illumination photons, the Emitted amount is not necessarily the number of importons stored. For example, 10,000 emitted importons with a Trace Depth setting of 4 may generate more than 20,000 importons in one scene and as many as 40,000 stored importons in another scene. Because the number of importons stored might be much higher than the number emitted, high Emitted numbers combined with a high Trace Depth setting might result in a significant number of importons being stored, and memory issues might occur. Irradiance particles are calculated at each importon location, and high importon numbers can greatly increase the irradiance particle calculation time. You can see the number of importons used within the Render Message dialog box.

Density   This setting is the approximate number of importons emitted per rendered pixel; the Emitted setting must be 0 for this setting to have an effect. The default setting of 0.1 gives you one importon for every 10 pixels and is effectively a draft setting. The recommended setting is 1.0. Think of this setting in a similar way to the Final Gather Point Density setting with the Draft setting at 0.1, Low at 0.4, Medium at 0.8, High at 1.5, and Very High at 4.0.

For scenes that need many importons bounced through the scene, settings several times the number of pixels might be required to ensure adequate distribution, and settings of 2.0 to 4.0 are common in my scenes; however, I have seen some example scenes set as high as 300.0.

Merge   This setting is a distance to combine importons to optimize the temporary importon map. This setting reduces memory requirements prior to the cleanup of Global Illumination data and will reduce the quantity and density of irradiance particles. I generally use this if I have memory issues while generating importons or irradiance particles, and I keep this to a small value of no more than a few centimeters to keep detail in the rendering. The value for a particular scene varies based on the scale of the scene.

Task Size   This setting controls the rays per importon used for sampling your scene to determine importance. Larger numbers increase the accuracy of the importance sampling. This is functionally similar to the Rays setting for Final Gather; however, you can generally use half as many rays as you might for Final Gather. Sixty-four is the default, 128 is a good middle-of-the-road setting, and 256 to 512 is a high-end setting.

Trace Depth   This setting is similar to the Global Illumination Trace Depth setting and controls additional bounces of importons and subsequent storage of importons on additional surfaces throughout your scene. Four traces is the default, and zero means importons are view-dependent, similar to Final Gather points. Higher Trace Depth settings lead to a better distribution of importons, lead to larger Global Illumination PMAP files, and might be required both for image quality and if you are producing animations.

Generally, this setting should be greater than zero when importons and Global Illumination are combined with Final Gather. This option is typically not used with the Traverse option.

Traverse   With the Traverse option's check box selected, importons act like X rays and continue through opaque objects without stopping at surfaces; however, mental ray will store importons at each surface encountered. The Traverse option allows importons to be emitted throughout the 3D environment in the directional view of the camera and might improve images produced with Global Illumination. Importons, like all photons, bounce around your scene from surface to surface; the Traverse option helps ensure that more surfaces have the opportunity to have their importance sampled. The Traverse option takes additional computation time and is for use only with Global Illumination, not irradiance particles.

IMPORTONS AND VIEW DEPENDENCE

Because importons are shot from the current camera view, the main concentration of importons is primarily within that view, similar to Global Illumination photons that are emitted from a single light source.

Unlike Final Gather points that exist only within your view, however, importons bounce off surfaces just like Global Illumination photons and are stored in areas outside your view. The importon density outside your initial view, however, might be insufficient for scenes that have an animated camera or are rendering multiple views, and like Global Illumination photons, you might need to emit millions of importons to ensure sufficient coverage outside the field of view.

Think of the view dependency issue like the Global Illumination produced by the single daylight system in Chapter 6, "Global Illumination and Caustics"; you need to emit a lot of photons from that single photon source to ensure photons are dense enough on all surfaces to produce a smooth rendering. With importons, you always have a single emitter, the camera, and you need to emit enough importons to ensure coverage everywhere they are needed.

Because of this semi-view dependence, stored Global Illumination PMAP files that used importons will have much of the off-camera surfaces of the scene stripped of Global Illumination, and a change in camera view might not produce a good rendering. The image shown here is a rendering produced with a cached Global Illumination solution that shows a Global Illumination density diagnostic view looking away from the direction where importons were shot.

In this image, some importons were stored on the surfaces outside the camera view, which preserved some Global Illumination photons, although you can clearly see on the left wall and floor where the camera view ended and there was a sharp drop-off in density. Shooting more importons with a higher Trace Depth setting would assist in getting importons, and thus Global Illumination photons, into this back area of the scene; however, you will always have more photons stored within the camera view.

Cached Global Illumination PMAP files that use importons might not be ideal for producing images from multiple viewpoints or for animations, because Global Illumination might be missing or sparse in areas not visible when Global Illumination and importons were computed.

As mentioned earlier, without importons, mental ray generated a PMAP file of 402MB for the Bath scene; photons are stored on all surfaces, regardless of whether they influence or are seen the rendering. With importons and without the Traverse option, the PMAP file was only 5.2MB. The Traverse option generated a PMAP file of 24MB. Images generated with each technique are available for you in the Chapter 7 project folder and the .\renderoutout\Bath folder as Bath_GI_21m22s.png, Bath_GI_Importons_NoTraverse_20m06s.png, and Bath_GI_Importons_Traverse_20m17s.png. Comparing each version shows that the versions for Bath_GI_21m22s.png and Bath_GI_Importons_NoTraverse_20m06s.png to be identical and shows Bath_GI_Importons_Traverse_20m17s.png to have slight darkening on some surfaces. The images were created with a value of 100,000 for the Average GI Photons Per Light setting and 1,000,000 importons with a task size of 128 and a trace depth of 6. These settings were determined through multiple test renders to evaluate and compare results. These settings for this small room also work well for creating an animation of that space because an adequate number of importons were reflected into the other areas of the Bath scene. Additional images are available in the `.\renderoutput\Bath` folder of the Chapter 7 project folder of your DVD.

Next I cover the use of Importons to reduce the PMAP size when rendering the Sponza Palace scene.

Using Importons in the Sponza Scene

In Chapter 6, the Sponza scene required a lot of Global Illumination photons to be emitted into the scene to produce acceptable results. This resulted in a PMAP file size of approximately 160MB. Although this is not unusually large, 32-bit machines with only 1GB or 2GB of DRAM will most likely experience issues when producing indirect illumination with any technology. For best results with demo scenes, copy the contents of the `\ProjectFolders\07_Importons_IP` folder on your DVD to a local hard or USB drive. Drag and drop the appropriate MXP file into 3ds Max/Design to set your copy of 3ds Max/Design to use this folder for its project folder. For machines with limited resources, reduce settings as needed.

Perform the following steps to use importons in the Sponza scene:

1. Open the file `.\scenes\Sponza\Sponza_Importons_2010_Start.max` from the Chapter 7 project folder.

2. In the Render Setup dialog box, enable Final Gather, and choose the Low preset.

3. Enable Global Illumination, and set the Average GI Photons Per Light setting to 2000000. This was the final setting used in Chapter 6.

4. In the Reuse (FG And GI Disk Caching) settings, enable the Reuse options for both Global Illumination and Final Gather, setting them to Incrementally Add FG Points To Map Files and Read/Write Photons To Map Files, respectively. Precomputed Final Gather maps and PMAP files are provided in the `.\sceneassets\renderassets` folder.

5. Create an mr Shader object in the viewport.

6. Click None for the Shader, and choose the Ctrl.Ghost.Settings (ctrl.studio) option from the Material/Map Browser.

7. Open the Compact Material Editor or SME, and drag the new map into a sample sphere or view. Make it an instance.

8. Double-click the map to open the Parameter Editor.

9. Select the Enable check box for Importons, and then set the Emitted value to 0.

10. Set the Density value to 2.0.

11. Set the Trace Depth value to 4.

12. Render Camera05. A rendered image is provided as `.\renderoutput\Sponza\Sponza_Importons.jpg`, and a completed scene is available as `.\scenes\Sponza\Sponza_Importons_2010_Finish.max`.

You can adjust the overall brightness of the scene in the mr Photographic exposure control. After you compute Global Illumination and cache the data to a file, you will discover that the

PMAP file is just over 3MB rather than the 160MB without importons. The importons settings in this example were arrived at through repeated trials and seemed to generate good results. The results are view-dependent and both Global Illumination and importons need to be calculated on every frame of an animation; animations using a PMAP generated only on frame one are available in the `.\renderoutput\Sponza` folder, `Sponza_Importons.avi`, along with an animation with Photon Density visual diagnostics mode, `Sponza_Importons_Density.avi`. When you watch the animations and compare to the Sponza animation from Chapter 6, you get a better sense of what importons do to the Global Illumination data.

Next I cover the new Irradiance Particles technology, which combines features of both Final Gather and Global Illumination.

Introducing Irradiance Particles

Irradiance Particles is a technology for calculating direct and indirect illumination based on importance sampling. Irradiance particles use importons shot prior to rendering; if importons are disabled, then mental ray temporarily enables them in order to place irradiance particles in the scene. After importons are placed, irradiance is calculated at each importon location. *Irradiance* is defined as the amount of electromagnetic radiation at a surface, typically measured in watts per square centimeter or watts per square meter. During the rendering pass, mental ray uses stored irradiance particles to estimate the amount or irradiance at a particular rendered sample (a sample may be a pixel, a group of pixels, or subpixels). Irradiance particles can be cached to disk for reuse.

Irradiance particles do not handle glossy surfaces as well as Final Gather and Global Illumination, and for scenes with many reflective surfaces, using Final Gather and Global Illumination might be a better choice. The current irradiance particle technology is best when used on scenes with many diffuse surfaces.

You can use irradiance particles to create *image-based lighting effects* — light produced solely from an environment map that is high quality and contains defined shadows and lighting detail.

Setting Irradiance Particle Parameters

To access the settings for irradiance particles, you must create an mr Shader object, assign it the ctrl.ghost shader, and then drag and drop the ctrl.ghost shader from the Modify tab into one of the material editors. In the SME, drop the shader into a view, and double-click to open the Parameter Editor or press the + next to Additional Params. Figure 7.7 shows the settings for irradiance particles.

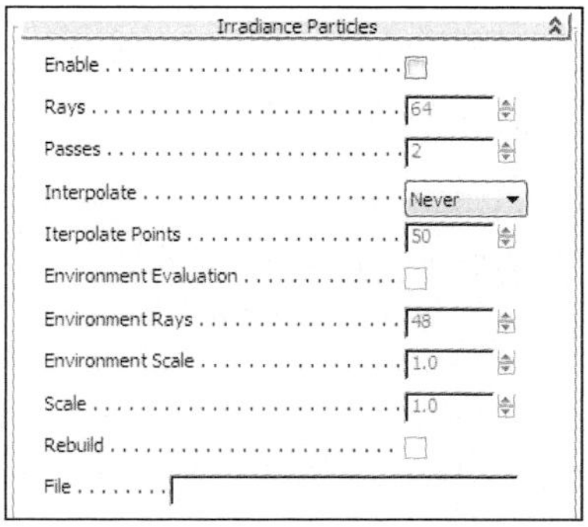

FIGURE 7.7
Irradiance particle settings within the ctrl.ghost shader

Enable   This enables irradiance particles. You should also enable and adjust importons and ensure that both Final Gather and Global Illumination are disabled; otherwise, irradiance particles will not function.

Rays   The Rays setting is the number of random rays per irradiance particle to shoot into the scene to estimate irradiance for that point. The default is 64 and is essentially a draft quality setting. This is similar to the Rays setting for Final Gather; however, you can generally use fewer rays and get better results with irradiance particles. A medium setting is 128 or higher. Lower settings can lead to spotty results. Try increasing the setting in steps of 64. A high setting is perhaps 512.

Passes   This setting is the number of indirect illumination passes. When greater than 1, irradiance particles include indirect illumination from diffuse bounces. When 0, irradiance particles contain only direct illumination. This setting is similar to Diffuse Bounces in Final Gather.

Interpolate   At render time, this setting determines whether points are interpolated for eye rays (from the camera to objects), and/or whether points for secondary rays (reflections, refractions, and so forth) are interpolated. The options are Never, Always, and Secondary. The Never option forces irradiance particle calculation at each sample and no interpolation. The Secondary option interpolates only secondary rays and not primary rays.

Interpolate Points   This setting is the number of nearby irradiance particles points to interpolate and is similar to the Interpolate Num. Of Points setting in Final Gather. Low settings result in spotty renderings (you may see the individual irradiance particles), and high settings can lead to a loss of detail in your renderings.

Environment Evaluation   This check box setting enables irradiance particles to do image-based lighting based on an environment map. It causes a second particle map to be created just for the environment.

Environment Rays   This setting is the number of rays used to compute the irradiance coming from the environment map. This setting determines the granularity of your lighting solution and can be much higher than normal irradiance particles rays. Settings from 64 to 512 are common.

Environment Scale   This setting is the scale factor for the environment irradiance particles map and controls the brightness of environment (image-based) illumination. This is typically left at 1.0, and other values would vary based on your preferences.

Scale   This setting is the irradiance particle brightness scale. It is similar to the Final Gather Multiplier setting and is generally left at 1.0.

Rebuild   This check box forces mental ray to ignore an irradiance particle map file if it exists and re-creates importons and irradiance particles. If a file is specified (in the next setting), then it is replaced.

File   This setting specifies a file location to save the irradiance particle map file. The data saved is a single scene snapshot from the current viewpoint and does not accumulate irradiance particles data like Final Gather.

Next I cover some general guidelines for using irradiance particles in your scenes.

Using Irradiance Particles

To use irradiance particles, you must disable Final Gather; otherwise, mental ray uses Final Gather instead of irradiance particles. Global Illumination, however, is automatically disabled when you enable irradiance particles. Always use importons with irradiance particles; importons are enabled temporarily if they were disabled at the start of render.

A low number of importons, a low irradiance particle rays setting, or inadequate interpolation can result in spotty and uneven rendered results. In addition to speeding up the testing of scenes, the diffuse white material in the Material Override feature of mental ray makes it easier to see rendering artifacts, particularly with irradiance particles.

The default importon and irradiance particle settings are generally minimum settings; a large scene that might have benefited from 2 million Global Illumination photons could use that many total importons. For irradiance particles, however, it is important to remember that each importon and subsequent irradiance particles have much more overhead than a Global Illumination photon, because each importon must take the time to evaluate its importance, and at each importon an irradiance particle must then take the time to calculate its direct and indirect illumination values, including multiple indirect passes, which can quickly cause render times to skyrocket.

Generally, I adjust importons first to get a good distribution, and then I tweak irradiance particles settings. I use a small Merge distance to keep the number of importons and irradiance particles down and to avoid a high concentration of irradiance particles that will unnecessarily increase render time. The Render Message window displays the number of irradiance particles actually used in your scene, which is typically more than the number emitted. The number used appears to depend on the Emitted or Density value, the Trace Depth setting, the scene geometry, and the surface materials.

As you increase importon levels, you might find a point where increasing the Emitted setting for importons or the Trace Depth setting does not significantly add to the number of importons (and irradiance particles) used in your rendering; that means you have hit a saturation point. Additional importons might not add to your rendering, so you need to start looking at irradiance particles settings to improve your rendering.

USING THE RENDER MESSAGE DIALOG BOX

To keep the Render Message list to a minimum and focus on important feedback during rendering, right-click the Render Message window and set it to show Information but not Progress.

Evaluating the irradiance particles at each importon takes time, and each irradiance particles *Passes* setting multiplies the irradiance particle's calculation time. Every scene is different, and it is up to you to find the balance between the number of importons and the settings for irradiance particles Rays and Passes.

After irradiance particles are distributed and their values determined, the Render Message window displays "wallclock 0:00:xx:xx for computing irradiance particles." Along with your total render time, you can use these values to determine how much of your render time is spent calculating irradiance particles and how much is spent rendering your image. Understanding irradiance particles takes experimentation, watching, and many test renderings.

When using the Interpolation setting of irradiance particles to help smooth the rendered results, you might need to add ambient occlusion (AO) to your materials if you lose detail in your rendering. Adding AO with irradiance particles is no different than you might need to do with Global Illumination and Final Gather; however, I find that irradiance particle renderings tend to have better contrast between surfaces, contain contact shadows, and AO-like effects at corners that would be washed-out if done in a Final Gather/Global Illumination rendering.

Irradiance particles are better suited to scenes with more diffuse surfaces, rather than scenes with significant glossy and mirrored surfaces. Figure 7.8 shows the Bath scene using irradiance particles as its only source of indirect illumination.

FIGURE 7.8
The Bath scene rendered with irradiance particles

This scene is highly reflective, and despite relatively long render times of nearly three hours for an image of 720×480, the results are not optimal. The shower area, in particular, is very dark, and there is no way to brighten that area without hiding the glass doors. The rendered image is available in the Chapter 7 project folder on the DVD as `.\renderoutput\Bath\Bath_IP_3h56m.png`. Close examination shows a somewhat speckled surface, which may be helped with significantly more importons. For a scene like the bathroom scene, using Final Gather, Global Illumination, and importons seems to produce the best results in the least amount of time. Figure 7.8 was created with the following settings:

◆ Density: 2.0

◆ Merge: 0.25″

◆ Task Size: 128

◆ Trace Depth: 4

◆ Rays: 256

◆ Passes: 2

◆ Interpolate: Always

◆ Interpolate Points: 100

Figure 7.9 shows the interior for a restaurant designed by the team at Knauer Inc. and consists of more diffuse surfaces rather than highly reflective surfaces.

FIGURE 7.9
A restaurant din-
ing room rendered
with importons
and irradiance
particles

This large environment with numerous lights and a moderate level of reflective and refractive surfaces rendered faster with irradiance particles than the small Bath scene and also rendered faster than the same scene using Final Gather and Global Illumination photons. Figure 7.9
was created with the following settings:

◆ Emitted: 20000

◆ Merge: 1″

◆ Task Size: 200

◆ Trace Depth: 4

◆ Rays: 250

◆ Passes: 3

◆ Interpolate: Always

◆ Interpolate Points: 75

Full-size images of this scene rendered with irradiance particles and these settings are provided in the \07_Importons_IP\renderoutput\Knauer folder of your project folder.

Irradiance particles are useful for producing animations; however, importons and irradiance
particles need to be computed for each frame. The irradiance particles' File feature does not add
irradiance particles data in a cumulative fashion like Final Gather, and it does not consider the
entire scene like Global Illumination photons. It is only a snapshot of the irradiance particles at
the location of importons essentially from the viewpoint of the camera at a specific frame. Given
a smooth irradiance particle solution, per-frame computing of irradiance particles does not generate the noise artifacts you might find with per-frame Final Gather calculation I cover in Chapter
5. However, the inability to cache the irradiance particles calculated along a camera path will lead
to higher render times for animations compared to cached Final Gather and Global Illumination,
and Final Gather/Global Illumination is likely a better choice in these instances.

Next I cover the process of adding irradiance particles to the Light Lab scene.

Working with Irradiance Particles

As you begin to experiment with irradiance particles, I highly recommend starting with simple scenes using Material Override in order to be able to see how various settings affect the rendered results. For more complicated production scenes, testing lighting and render settings as early as possible in the design process allows you to work through possible setting options before committing to final settings.

For the irradiance particles sample scene, I use the Light Lab from previous chapters. As with the importons example earlier in this chapter, I arrived at the settings described in the procedure through experimentation after numerous tests. Because space for images within this book is limited, the .\renderoutput folder of your Chapter 7 project and the www.mastering-mentalray.com web site have rendered images achieved with irradiance particles, both for the Light Lab and using many of the other scenes shown throughout this book.

USING IRRADIANCE PARTICLES FOR AN INTERIOR SCENE

Perform the following steps to use irradiance particles in the Light Lab scene:

1. Set your project folder to the \07_Importons_IP folder of your local drive or DVD.

2. Open the .\scenes\LightLab\LightLab_2010_IP_Start.max file.

3. Open the Render Setup dialog box, and disable both Final Gather and Global Illumination.

4. Add an mr Shader object to the scene.

5. Click None for the shader, and choose the Ctrl.Ghost.Settings (ctrl.studio) option from the Material/Map Browser.

6. Open the Compact Material Editor or SME, and drag the new map into a sample sphere or view. Make it an instance.

7. Double-click the map to open the Parameter Editor.

8. In the Importons rollout, select the Enable check box, and then set Emitted to 0.

9. Set Density to 3.0.

10. Set Task Size to 128.

11. Set Trace Depth to 4.11.

12. In the Irradiance Particles rollout, select Enable.

13. Set Rays to 128.

14. Set Passes to 1.

15. Set Interpolate to Always.

16. Set Interpolate Points to 128.

17. Save your file, and render Camera04.

While processing importons and irradiance particles, your rendering will be black; there is no visual feedback in the rendered window during processing. It is common for some scenes to produce apparently harmless "Attempt to unpin null tag" messages in the Render Message dialog box.

Figure 7.10 shows the results of these steps.

FIGURE 7.10
The Light Lab scene rendered with irradiance particles

To save the time of computing irradiance particles, you can set the File parameter to point to the `LightLab.ipf` file located in a Zip file in the root folder of your DVD; copy to a local drive and unzip to access the files. Because the dialog box does not allow browsing for files, place the files where they can be easily found. The file `.\scenes\LightLab\LightLab_2010_IP_Finish.max` is preconfigured to use the file `D:\LightLab.ipf`. You might need to change the drive path for your particular machine.

The settings can certainly go higher, and I chose these settings to give smooth results on most surfaces when Material Override is disabled.

Next I cover irradiance particles' unique ability to sample your scene's environment to produce illumination.

CREATING IMAGE-BASED LIGHTING WITH IRRADIANCE PARTICLES

In this example, I show a simple scene that uses a number of diffuse and reflective 3D primitives within a high dynamic range (HDR) environment. The HDR environments included in the book's DVD are provided by Spheron-VR AG (`www.spheron.com`), the leader in full spherical and HDR imaging. Additional high dynamic range image (HDRI) files from Dosch Design for your own experimentation are in the `\Bonus\Dosch` folder of your DVD and in the `.\maps\HDRs` folder of your 3ds Max/Design installation..

Figure 7.11 shows the final scene with image-based lighting from an HDRI environment.

Perform the following steps to configure the scene for irradiance particles and image-based lighting:

1. Open the file `.\scenes\Teapots_IBL_2010_Start.max` from the `\07_Importons_IP` project folder.

2. Open the Environment And Effects dialog box (press 8).

3. Set the environment map to the file `.\sceneassets\images\SpheronVR_hdri_01.hdr`. In the Select Image Bitmap File dialog box, ensure that Gamma is set to the Override option at a value of 1.0. Do not close the dialog box.

4. In the Select Image Bitmap File dialog box, click the Setup button.

FIGURE 7.11
Scene lit only from
an HDR image and
irradiance particles

5. In the HDRI Load Settings dialog box, turn on the Real Pixels (32bpp) and Def. Exposure options for the bitmap, and then click OK.

6. Click Open in the Select Image Bitmap File dialog box.

7. Change the exposure control to the mr Photographic exposure control.

8. Set the Exposure Value (EV) option to –2.0, and close the dialog box.

9. Open the SME.

10. From the Scene Materials group in the Material/Map Browser at the left, drag the bitmap that contains the HDR image into the view, and make it an instance.

11. Double-click the bitmap to open the bitmap parameters in the Parameter Editor.

12. Change the map name to Enviro.

13. Set the Coordinates Mapping option to the Spherical mapping style. Close the SME.

Rendering the scene now will show diffuse objects with bright illumination from the default lighting that 3ds Max/Design adds to every scene, and there are no shadows under the objects. For the image-based lighting to work, you need to disable the default lights, and for shadows you need to add a Plane object and create a material to catch only shadows.

Perform the following steps to add a shadow-catching Plane object to the scene:

1. Create a photometric Free Light, and turn off the light object. Adding any light objects disables the default lights.

2. Create a Plane object approximately 2′ by 2′, and set Scale to 10.

3. Open the SME.

   4. From the Material/Map Browser, drag a new Matte/Shadow/Reflection material into the view.

   5. Double-click the material to open its parameters.

   6. Rename the material to MatteShadow.

   7. Connect the output of the Enviro bitmap to the Camera Mapped Background input of the MatteShadow material.

   8. Drag the output node of the MatteShadow material onto the Plane object. You are now able to see through the plane to your environment, and shadows will be produced on the plane from the other geometry.

   9. Create an mr Shader object in your scene.

   10. Assign the Ctrl.Ghost.Settings (ctrl.studio) map to the mr Shader's Shader map.

   11. Drag the Ctrl.Ghost.Settings map from the Control Panel into the view of the SME, and choose the Instance option.

   12. Double-click the map to open its parameters for editing.

   13. Rename the map CtrlGhost.

   14. Enable importons, and set Emitted to 0, Density to 0.5, and Trace Depth to 1.

   15. Enable irradiance particles, and set Rays to 128, Passes to 1, Interpolate to Always, and Interpolate Points to 30.

   16. To enable image-based lighting, enable the Environment Evaluation option.

   17. Set Environment Rays to 256.

   18. Save your scene, and render the Camera01 view.

The number of importons determines the quantity of irradiance particles, and that combined with the Environment Rays setting determines the refinement of the shadow and light produced by the environment map. High-resolution HDR like the Spheron maps are required for best results both for lighting and reflections with this example. To better see the shadows produced by image-based lighting, you can replace the Matte/Shadow/Reflection material with a flat white paint material or use Material Override.

The Bottom Line

Install the plug-in to access importons and irradiance particles   Using importons and irradiance particles requires the installation of the ctrl.ghost plug-in.

   Master It   How do you install the ctrl.ghost shader and add the shader to a scene to make it possible to edit the parameters?

Add importons to a scene   Importons are used to intelligently merge Global Illumination photons to reduce PMAP size and memory requirements and also to position irradiance particles.

> **Master It**   Your rendering with Global Illumination is creating PMAP files too large for your 32-bit machines to render. How do you add importons to a scene to minimize the PMAP file?

Add irradiance particles to a scene   Irradiance particles can replace both Final Gather and Global Illumination, along with creating image-based lighting effects.

> **Master It**   You need to create image-based lighting for an outdoor scene. How do you use irradiance particles to accomplish this goal?

Chapter 8

Effects

In mental ray, camera effects can be any one of a variety of things, including lens shaders that distort or change the rays coming into the camera, output shaders that process the image after it is rendered, and volume shaders that simulate suspended particles in an environment. Effects produced with camera shaders have the advantage that they often process the rendered image or work with other rendered data, rather than work in true 3D, and can therefore produce effects much faster than a true 3D effect. One disadvantage to using effects in 3ds Max/Design rather than an application like 3ds Max Composite is that the effect is burned into the rendered image, so you can only change it by rerendering the scene.

In this chapter, you will learn to

◆ Use camera lens shaders

◆ Use camera output shaders

◆ Use camera volume shaders

Introducing mental ray Lens Shaders

The Rendering tab of the Render Setup dialog box includes a roll-down section entitled Camera Effects, which includes Motion Blur, Camera Shaders, and Depth Of Field settings. This chapter focuses on camera shaders for mental ray, and Figure 8.1 shows the Render Setup dialog box settings for the Camera Shaders settings.

FIGURE 8.1
The Camera Shaders settings in the Render Setup dialog box

Figure 8.1 shows the shaders assigned to each of the lens, output, and volume shaders. The DefaultOutputShader (Glare) setting shown is always present in new scenes; however, it is disabled by default. To assign a shader, click a button on the right to open the Material/Map Browser, and choose a shader. The Material/Map Browser's list contains only the shaders that apply to the kind of shader you are attempting to change. To edit a shader, drag the shader from the Render Setup dialog box to the Slate Material Editor (SME) or Compact Material Editor (CME).

A lens shader operates on the rays coming into the virtual lens of the active camera object and performs a function on the rendered samples before returning the samples to mental ray. The shader function may distort the rays to mimic specific lens effects such as depth of field, barrel distortion, and wraparound, or it may change the color or intensity of the samples, as with the Night and Gamma & Gain shaders.

In this section of this chapter, I cover eight lens shaders: the new Depth Of Field/Bokeh effect, Distortion, mr Physical Sky, Night, Render Subset, Shader List, Gamma & Gain, and the WrapAround shader.

Depth Of Field/Bokeh Parameters

Depth of field is a blurring of your image before and after a focus plane distance, which is a region of your scene that is in sharp focus. Bokeh — a rough approximation of the Japanese word for *blurry* — is a shape-based filtering used in the depth of field. The Depth Of Field/Bokeh shader is new in 3ds Max/Design 2011 and available in earlier versions by editing a specific file, described later in this section. Figure 8.2 shows the Depth Of Field/Bokeh shader settings.

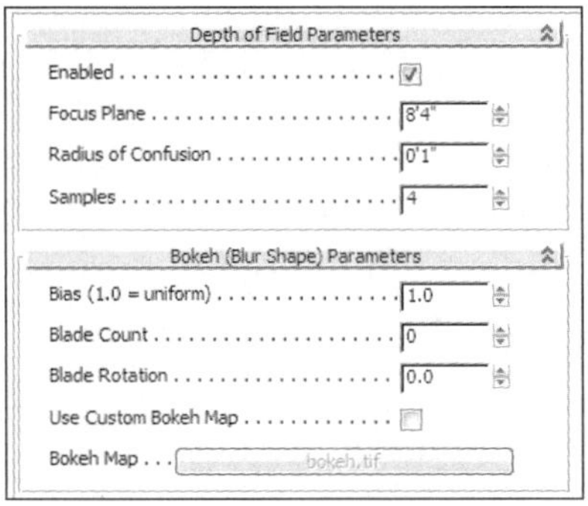

FIGURE 8.2
The Depth Of Field/Bokeh shader settings

The settings are split into two groups, one for the Depth Of Field Parameters and another for Bokeh (Blur Shape) Parameters. The Depth Of Field/Bokeh shader uses a circular shape for the Bokeh effect by default. You can modify the shape and its effect by adjusting the Bias, Blade Count, and Blade Rotation settings, or you can use a custom bitmap to control the shape and color of the Bokeh effect. You can use custom Bokeh maps to produce special depth-of-field effects including chromatic aberrations often seen in low-cost and wide-angle lenses. Chromatic aberrations are caused by the light of different wavelengths being shifted in direction as they travel through camera lenses.

Focus Plane   This setting sets the distance where objects are seen in focus. For accurate results, use the Tape Measure object, and measure the distance between your camera and the desired focus plane. You can also temporarily turn on the Clipping Plane option of the camera and adjust the plane until it intersects your geometry to determine the distance. Disable the Clipping Plane setting before rendering.

Radius Of Confusion   This setting is the approximate size of the aperture of the iris of your virtual camera. The default value is one scene unit, and for a metric scene it may be 1mm or 1m and would need to be adjusted to perhaps 25mm or 50mm, which are more realistic values. Larger values increase the blurriness of the out-of-focus regions of your rendering. This value should be kept in a realistic range for a camera, and if you are comparing this to real-world camera settings, the value is Radius Of Confusion = (Focal Length ÷ f-stop) ÷ 2. A lens with a 135mm focal length and an f-stop setting of f/8 will have a diameter of 16.875mm and a Radius Of Confusion setting of 8.4375mm, or 0.332″. Be certain that you enter radius values in the proper units; 3ds Max will let you enter your value in millimeters even if your display units are inches. Just add **mm** to the end of your value entry. Figure 8.3 shows Radius Of Confusion settings of 25mm, 50mm, and 100mm in the Sponza Palace atrium scene.

FIGURE 8.3
Radius Of Confusion settings of 0.25mm, 50mm, and 100mm

Each different Radius Of Confusion setting had some impact on render times, with the Radius Of Confusion setting of 100mm at 9 minutes, 50mm at 7 minutes, and 25mm at 5.5 minutes.

The Radius Of Confusion setting is the value at the camera, and the actual Radius Of Confusion setting experienced at your geometry will vary based on the distance from the camera and the distance to the Focus Plane and beyond. The Radius Of Confusion setting goes from 100 percent of the radius value at the camera, diminishes to zero at the focus plane, and then increases to 100 percent at double the focus plane distance as you move away from the camera. For example, if your focus plane is at 10m and your Radius Of Confusion setting is 100mm, then you will have a radius of 100mm at the camera, 50mm at 5m, 0mm at 10m, 50mm at 15m, and a Radius Of Confusion setting of 100mm at 20m.

Additional sample images with various Radius Of Confusion and other Depth Of Field settings are available in the `.\sceneassets\DOF_Bokeh\` folder of your Chapter 8 project.

Samples   This setting determines the smoothness of the Depth Of Field effect. The default setting of 4 results in a fairly grainy effect, and the values of 8 to 16 are reasonable. This setting, more than any other, will greatly affect render time. Figure 8.4 shows three regions rendered with samples settings of 2 on the left, 4 in the center, and 16 on the right.

FIGURE 8.4
Samples of 2 (left), 4 (center), and 16 (right)

The render time for each third of the image was 4 minutes, 7 minutes, and 17 minutes, respectively. The primary difference you will see with higher settings is less random scattering of pixels in the DOF area, better rendering of bright areas, and the Bokeh effect seen in highlights and visible lights.

A full-sized sample of this image is available as .\renderoutput\DOF_Bokeh\Samples_Compare.png. You'll also find additional samples that show the DOF/Bokeh effect within that folder.

Bias   The Bias value controls how the circle of confusion is sampled in the image, and the default of 1.0 gives uniform sampling across the circle. A low Bias value forces sampling toward the center and creates a softer Depth Of Field effect. A higher Bias value forces sampling to the outside of the circle of confusion. If you use a custom Bokeh bitmap, described later in this section, then setting Bias to 2.0 will improve the ability to see the image shape. Figure 8.5 shows the effect of adjusting the Bias setting.

FIGURE 8.5
Bias of 0.25 on the left, 1.0 in the center, and 2.0 on the right

Blade Count   The iris of a real-world camera contains multiple blades that move to control the aperture size. The default Blade Count setting of 0 gives a perfect circle for the circle of confusion sampling. A Blade Count setting of 4 is a square, 5 is a pentagon, 8 sides is an octagon, and so on. Figure 8.5 was produced with a Blade Count setting of 5.

Blade Rotation   This setting is a percentage of 1 to 360 degrees, with 0 being 0 degrees and 1.0 being 360 degrees. A value of .25 gives the same effect as four blades. This setting is an alternative to the automatic calculation of the Blade Count parameter.

Use Custom Bokeh Map and Bokeh Map   You can use a custom bitmap defining a shape rather than the internal shape of a circle (or an *n*-sided polygon when using Blade Count or Blade Rotation). This shape is defined as a small bitmap, and I have provided a few sample bitmaps in the .\sceneassets\images folder of your Chapter 8 project, along with scenes that utilize these maps. Enabling the custom map disables the Blade Count and Blade Rotation parameters.

You can simulate the chromatic aberration effect by using a Bokeh bitmap with red, green, and blue circles. A chromatic aberration is the separation of red, green, and blue (RGB) light as the light travels through the lens of the camera and appears as blurry RGB lines along the edges of objects, primarily along the periphery of images and in the burred depth of field in images taken with less expensive and wide-angle lenses. With the Use Custom Bokeh Map option, the arrangement of the RGB circles can produce varying chromatic aberrations. Higher Bias values produce more profound results. A scene that demonstrates this effect is available as .\scenes\Sponza\Chromatic_2010.max and .\scenes\Sponza\Chromatic2011.max, and renderings are available in the .\renderoutput\DOF_Bokeh\ folder.

DEPTH OF FIELD AND ENVIRONMENT MAPS

The Depth Of Field shader will see the pixels of an environment map as being at an extreme distance and will blur the entire map. A sample image that shows this distortion is provided as .\renderoutput\DOF_Bokeh\DOF_with_HDRI.jpg, and a sample scene is provided as .\scenes\DOF_HDRI_2010.max. If you are rendering an image in a spherical environment and need DOF, then consider rendering each in separate passes and compositing in Photoshop or a similar application.

USING THE DEPTH OF FIELD/BOKEH SHADER

The Depth Of Field/Bokeh shader is available in the user interface for 3ds Max Design 2011, but you need to unhide it before you can use it in 3ds Max/Design 2010 and earlier. The user interface between the two versions of 3ds Max will vary slightly; however, the steps to produce the effect are the same.

To unhide the Depth Of Field/Bokeh effect in 3ds Max/Design 2010, you need to edit the file architectural_max.mi using Notepad. The file is located in the .\mentalray\shaders_standard\include\ folder of your 3ds Max/Design 2010 installation. Put a hash mark (#) before the word "hidden" in the section for gui_mia_lens_bokeh, as shown here:

```
gui "gui_mia_lens_bokeh" {
  control "Global" "Global" (
    "uiName"    "Arch: DOF / Bokeh",
    # "hidden"
```

While you are in the file, you can also unhide the gui_mia_envblur shader, which you will use later in this chapter. Preedited mental ray include files are provided on the book's DVD in the \3ds Max Design 2010\mentalray\shaders_standard\include folder. Be sure to save your files and then open 3ds Max/Design for the changes to take effect.

As always, for the best results, copy the contents of the DVD's \ProjectFolders\08_Effects folder to a local drive for use with the examples.

Perform the following steps to add the Depth Of Field/Bokeh effect to a scene:

1. Set your project folder to the Chapter 8 project folder, which is \08_Effects\.

2. Open the file .\scenes\Sponza\DOF_2010_Start.max.

3. Open the Render Setup dialog box (press F10), and switch to the Renderer tab.

4. In the Camera Effects rollout, on the Camera Shaders group, click the empty shader slot labeled None for the lens shader, and select the Depth Of Field/Bokeh shader (3ds Max/Design 2011) or Arch: DOF/Bokeh (3ds Max/Design 2010 and earlier with an edited architectural_max.mi file).

5. Open the Compact Material Editor, and drag the new lens shader into a sample slot. Choose Instance when prompted, and click OK.

6. Set Focus Plane to 6.0m.

7. Set Radius Of Confusion to 0.1m.

8. Set Samples to 6.

9. Set Bias to 2.0.

10. Enable the Use Custom Bokeh Map option.

11. Click the filename in the Bokeh map slot to open the Open Texture File dialog box, and choose `bokeh.tif` in the `.\renderassets\sceneassets\` folder of your Chapter 8 project. This image is a simple plus (+) sign.

12. Render the Camera02 view. Figure 8.6 shows a completed render that is provided as `.\renderoutput\DOF_Bokeh\DOF_2010_Finish.jpg`. A completed scene is available as `.\scenes\Sponza\DOF_2010_Finish.max`.

FIGURE 8.6
Extreme Depth Of Field effect with a custom Bokeh map

The relatively large teapots aside, you might find the extreme Depth Of Field effect can often make the image appear as if it is a miniature set rather than a full-scale model.

PRACTICAL DEPTH OF FIELD

The Depth Of Field effect, when produced in the renderer and effectively burned into the image, has two drawbacks. The first drawback is that it is time-consuming to render and is time-consuming when testing to find the settings to use for that particular scene and a final render. What may be a five-minute render without DOF may be 50 minutes when DOF is enabled with sufficient samples to produce a nice image.

The second drawback beyond time is that the image has to be completely rerendered if you need to change the effect. The best solution to get around both of these drawbacks is to create the DOF (along with motion blur and other image effects) in a product like 3ds Max Composite. In addition to the non-DOF rendered image, you render the z-depth channel in Render Elements and use those two images to interactively adjust the DOF within 3ds Max Composite. The initial render will be much faster, the results will be smooth, and you can change the DOF at any time without rerendering. For more on how to use 3ds Max Composite for depth of field, see Chapter 10, "mental ray for Design."

Next I cover the Distortion lens shader for bowing the edges of rendered images.

Distortion Parameters

As shown in Figure 8.7, this shader has two options: Pin Cushion and Barrel.

FIGURE 8.7
The Distortion
shader settings

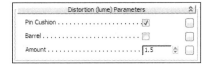

Pin cushion distortion causes the left and right edges of your image to bow inward toward the center. Barrel distortion has the opposite effect and causes pixels to be shifted outward. Images taken with a camera typically have barrel distortion, which would need to be corrected in photo-editing software; this option can assist in matching a rendered image to an uncorrected background image or in producing special effects.

Images that show the Distortion effect are available in the .\renderoutput\Distortion folder, and scenes are available in the .\scenes\Distortion folder of the Chapter 8 project.

The next shader, mr Physical Sky, can be used for an environment map, a lens shader, and a volumetric shader.

mr Physical Sky Setting

When the mr Physical Sky shader is used as a lens shader, the Aerial Perspective atmospheric effect is applied to the primary rays, generating the appearance of mist. Disable the Inherit from mr Sky option within the mr Physical Sky settings if you want to adjust the Visibility Distance settings independent of the daylight system; Figure 8.8 shows the Aerial Perspective setting. Adding a haze or mist atmospheric effect can make a big difference in the realism of your renderings. Too small of a distance, however, can result in a rendering that is completely white.

FIGURE 8.8
The Aerial Per-
spective setting
of the mr Physical
Sky shader

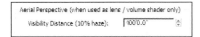

A scene by Emil McCauley of TGWB that demonstrates this effect is provided in the .\scenes\Hospital folder as mrPS_2010.max, and a rendered image is available as .\renderoutput\mrPS.jpg.

Night Parameters

The Night shader desaturates your rendered image and boosts the brightness of your scene, simulating the way that the human eye operates in low-light situations where very few color receptors function. This shader's settings, as shown in Figure 8.9, include a Multiplier setting to adjust the brightness of the low-light image and a Cutoff value to determine where the multiplier begins to have an effect.

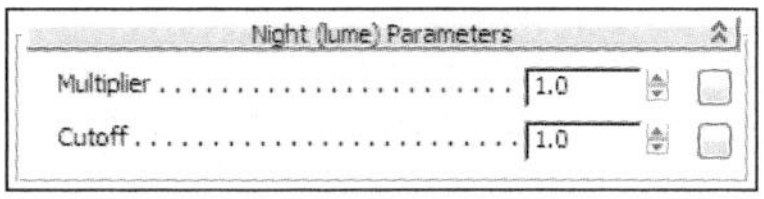

FIGURE 8.9
The Night shader
parameters

Because the Night shader affects the brightness of your scene, it is best to make final adjustments of your lighting after you enable the Night shader.

Render Subset Of Scene/Masking Parameters

This lens shader works in a similar way to the Render Subset option in the Rendered Frame Window dialog box, covered in Chapter 4, "Rendering." As shown in Figure 8.10, this shader includes additional options that help when compositing the subset image into the original to help reduce edge artifacts on the rerendered objects, and you have the option with this shader to either rerender specific objects in a list or rerender all objects with a specific material.

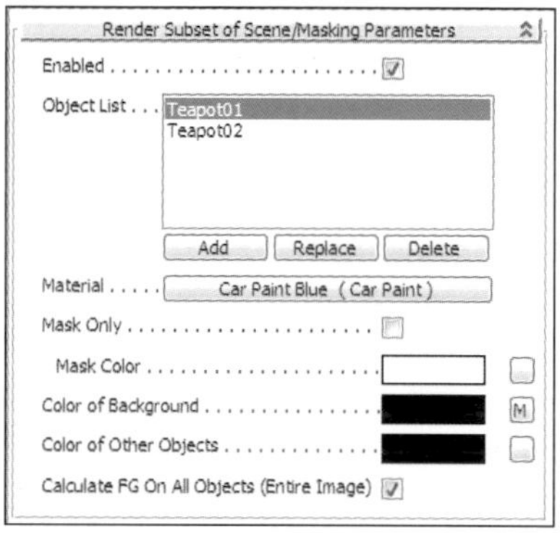

FIGURE 8.10

The Render Subset Of Scene/Masking lens shader

This is a terrific option for scenes that need either a few select objects rerendered or a minor adjustment in a material in the scene. It does suffer from some of the same problems as the Render Subset rendering option shown in Chapter 4; extreme changes in materials may show edge artifacts on objects when composited with the original image, and since this shader operates only on *primary rays*, or rays from the camera to the objects, anything reflected or refracted will not be correct.

Figure 8.11 shows a teapot in the Light Lab scene originally rendered with a red car paint material and then rerendered with the Render Subset Of Scene/Masking shader and composited in Photoshop.

FIGURE 8.11

Teapot original render (left) and composited Render Subset (right)

A close inspection of Figure 8.11 reveals some reddish pixels along the outer edges of the teapot; however, this is minimal compared to Figure 4.24 in Chapter 4. In Figure 8.11 the refracted area below the waterline did not render correctly because these are not primary rays. In this instance, using the Region option in the Rendered Frame Window dialog box would produce better results.

This lens shader renders only the objects and materials selected and does not preserve the Rendered Frame Window, therefore the resulting image must be saved with a transparency channel and composited in another application. The lens shader can also produce a separate mask file for use in compositing. You can create multiple copies of the lens shader with different object lists or materials to quickly render options for scenes.

The settings for the Render Subset Of Scene/Masking shader are as follows:

Object List Click the Add button to include specific objects in the lens shader's processing. The objects are rendered within the full context of your scene. Use the Calculate FG On All Objects option (described later in this list) to ensure that the objects are properly illuminated and better aliased to the surrounding objects.

Material If no objects are selected in the Object List and a material is in this slot, all objects containing this material will be rerendered. If there are objects in the Object List, then only those objects with this material will be rerendered. The Multi/SubObject material is not supported in this option.

Mask Only This will quickly render a black image that contains only an alpha channel. This image, when saved to a format such as PNG that supports alpha, can be used in your compositing application to mask the rerendered areas. An example is provided as `.\renderoutput\Subset\Mask.png` in your Chapter 8 project folder.

Mask Color This is the color returned from the shader for all objects and/or materials specified when the Mask Only option is enabled.

Color Of Background This is the color returned for the background when the Mask Only option is enabled.

Color Of Other Objects This is the color returned for nonselected objects when this shader is used with Mask Only.

Calculate FG On All Objects (Entire Image) Disabling this option speeds calculation but might affect the accuracy of your results and might increase the blending errors along the edges of objects when composited. Leave this option off when you use cached Final Gather maps.

This shader does not work correctly with the Fast Rasterizer rendering algorithm. Example scenes for this shader are provided in the `.\scenes\Subset\` folder of your Chapter 8 project folder, and rendered samples are available in the `.\renderoutput\Subset` folder.

Shader List (Lens, Output, Volume) Parameters

The Shader List allows you to combine multiple effects into the one Lens shader slot in the Render Setup dialog box. The Shader List shows up as an option for all three camera shader categories: lens, camera, and volume. As shown in the Selection section in Figure 8.12, the Shader List allows you to enable and disable shaders as required.

You can click a shader in the Selection area or drag it into the Slate Material Editor or the Compact Material Editor to edit their parameters.

FIGURE 8.12
The Shader List
shader

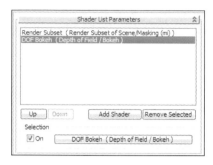

Gamma & Gain Parameters

Formerly named the Utility Gamma & Gain map, this shader allows you to make overall corrections to the image as seen by the lens. The settings include Input (for inputting a color swatch or bitmap), Gamma, Gain (Multiplier), and Reverse Gamma Correction (De-Gamma), as shown in Figure 8.13.

FIGURE 8.13
The Gamma &
Gain Parameters
section

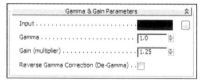

The Input color swatch/bitmap setting is not used when Gamma & Gain is used as a lens shader; instead, the primary ray is returned to the input of the Gamma & Gain shader. The Reverse Gamma Correction option should be disabled unless you are canceling out the global file output gamma in 3ds Max/Design's preference settings. Use this shader when you want to control the brightness of gamma correction of your image independent of the global gamma settings or exposure settings. For example, you can use the lens shader when region-rendering a window that's facing a bright sunlit area to bring down its brightness. As a lens shader, typically you would not use the De-Gamma option. Also, remember to avoid gamma-correcting your image twice by setting Gamma to 1.0 in this dialog box if you are using gamma in your output file.

WrapAround Parameters

This lens shader produces a spherical projection of your scene, centered on the position of your camera. You can then use these images as a spherical environment or as reflection maps, for instance. This shader has no parameters to adjust. Figure 8.14 shows the output of this shader in the file .\scenes\LightLab\WrapAround_2010.max and as seen in the file .\renderoutput\WrapAround.jpg.

I have tried this shader for precomputing Final Gather FGM files; however, examining the FG visual diagnostics shows there is very little in the plane where the camera sits. An image showing the visual diagnostics for this scene is available as .\renderoutput\WrapAround_Diag.jpg, and a precalculated FGM file is available as .\sceneassets\renderassets\LightLabWrap.fgm.

In the next section, I cover the camera output shaders, which operate on the image as a post-rendering process.

FIGURE 8.14
The WrapAround
lens shader in the
Light Lab scene

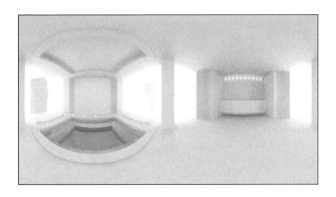

FIGURE 8.14
The WrapAround
lens shader in the
Light Lab scene

Understanding Camera Output Shaders

A camera shader performs additional processing on your images before they are saved to a file or displayed in the Rendered Frame Window dialog box. The default shader is the Glare shader, which is disabled in new scenes but is present in the Render Setup dialog box and which may cause a missing bitmap error if your project file does not point to the `.\maps\glare` folder of your 3ds Max/Design installation. The output shaders covered include both a lens-flare-like Glare shader and the HDR Image Motion Blur shader, which is a fast approximated motion blur.

Glare

The Glare shader creates a glow around bright pixels in a rendered image. Figure 8.15 shows the settings for Glare.

FIGURE 8.15
The Glare shader's
parameters

The Glare shader produces an effect similar to the Highlights (Burn) option in the mr Photographic exposure control (see Chapter 3, "Light, Shadow, and Exposure Control"), and for straightforward Glare effects, I prefer the Highlights (Burn) feature. The Glare shader, however, gives you an option to use a bitmap to produce streaks from the glare area. If you have a lot of reflective materials, this will produce an overabundance of streaks.

Although the Glare shader is disabled by default in new scenes, oftentimes you will get a warning about a missing `glare_streaks_star_camera_filter.tif` bitmap when opening a scene that contains this disabled shader. This file is located in the `.\maps\glare` folder of your 3ds Max installation. The error occurs even when Glare and the Streaks bitmap are disabled. To fix this, either add the correct path to your project MXP file for the map or right-click the Glare shader in the Render Setup dialog box and then choose the Clear option to remove the shader.

The settings for the Glare shader are as follows:

Quality   Higher *Quality* numbers provide more detail in the glared area but will take additional time to produce.

Spread   This controls the pixel size of the Glare effect. If this setting is too large, then it tends to produce glare in lower-light areas. If too small, then the Glare effect may not be produced in the areas you expect, as with reflections from large light sources.

Streaks   Streaks is an optional parameter, which produces streaks through a rendering similar to those produced by a camera lens.

Streak Image   The Streak Image setting controls how the effect is applied to the image. The default image is the `glare_streaks_star_camera_filter.tif` file, and Autodesk also provides the `glare_streaks_eye.tif` file to use.

Streaks Weight   Set to a value between 0 and 1.0, this setting controls the opacity of the streak effect.

Resolution For Glare Processing   This setting is the size of the Glare effect, and the default is 500 pixels. This is the processing size for the entire rendered image, and high-resolution still images will need correspondingly larger settings to ensure adequate detail in the Glare effect.

Replace Rendered Image With Glare Only   If you are compositing the Glare effect in a post-processing application, then use this option to generate a glare-only image. Be sure to use a file format that supports transparency (an alpha channel). A sample is included as `.\renderoutput\GlareOnly.png`.

A scene that demonstrates the Glare shader is available as `.\scenes\Sponza\Glare_2010.max`, and a complete rendering is available as `.\renderoutput\Glare.jpg` in your Chapter 8 project folder.

HDR Image Motion Blur Parameters

This output shader produces fast and simple motion blur and is ideal for scenes without a lot of rotating objects or objects that move quickly in an arc, because the blur effect always goes in a straight line from one frame to another. The blur also affects only primary rays, and not reflected or refracted rays, so objects visible in mirrors are not blurred. The shader uses motion data produced during the rendering phase to produce the blur and is very fast compared to other methods within 3ds Max. If you want more control over the motion blur and interactive adjustments, consider using 3ds Max Composite.

Figure 8.16 shows the settings for the HDR Image Motion Blur shader.

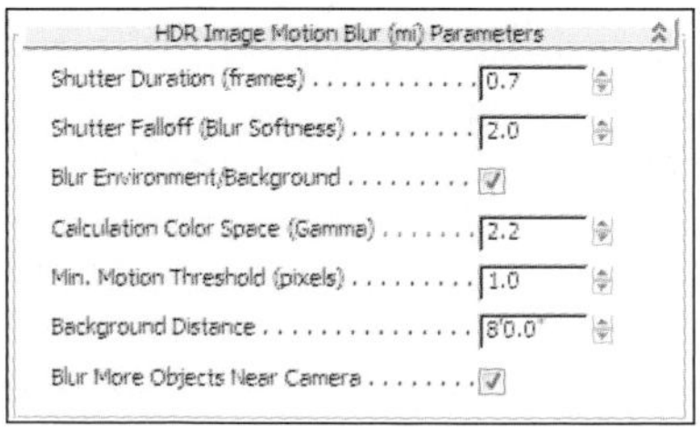

FIGURE 8.16
HDR Image Motion
Blur settings

HDR Image Motion Blur (mi) Parameters	
Shutter Duration (frames)	0.7
Shutter Falloff (Blur Softness)	2.0
Blur Environment/Background	✓
Calculation Color Space (Gamma)	2.2
Min. Motion Threshold (pixels)	1.0
Background Distance	8'0.0"
Blur More Objects Near Camera	✓

The parameters for this shader are as follows:

Shutter Duration (Frames) This setting is the total duration that the virtual shutter is opened. Half that time is before, and half is after the current frame. The default is 0.5 (one-half frame) and is usually sufficient for many scenes to add a subtle blur and eliminate some of the CG feeling to a rendering.

Shutter Falloff (Blur Softness) This setting controls how quickly the blur effect dissipates as it reaches the ends of the shutter duration. If you use high softness values, then you may need to increase the Shutter Duration setting to compensate.

Blur Environment/Background Use this option to blur objects that are determined to be in the distance, including the environment bitmap. For this option to work, you need to disable the scanline rendering algorithm in the Render Setup dialog box; it's in the Rendering Algorithm rollout on the Renderer tab.

Calculation Color Space (Gamma) Set this to match your system output gamma setting, if used. Typically this is 2.2, as set in your Preference settings.

Min. Motion Threshold (pixels) This setting allows you to limit which pixels will be blurred. Setting this to 0.0 will blur everything. 1.0 is the default.

Background Distance This value helps the shader determine the depth of the scene and should be set to the farthest visible object. Anything beyond this distance is considered background geometry. This setting varies based on the extent of your scene.

Blur More Objects Near Camera If you select this box, anything close to the camera receives additional blurring.

A scene that demonstrates this effect is available as `.\scenes\LightLab\HDRI_Blur.max`, a rendered image is available as `.\renderoutput\HDRI_MotionBlur.jpg`, and an animation is available as `.\renderoutput\HDRI_MotionBlur.avi` in your Chapter 8 project. Good motion blur shouldn't be too obvious, so you may need to look at the still images provided to evaluate the blur effect.

In the next section, I cover camera volume shaders, which provide atmospheric effects tied to a light or the volume of your scene.

Understanding Camera Volume Shaders

A camera volume shader creates a mist, glow, or other effect that appears to exist within an area or the entire volume of your scene.

Beam Parameters

The Beam shader produces an atmospheric effect around all lights, or specific lights, along with an overall haze through the rendering. I find this effect to be best used in an outdoor scene for dusk or night renderings or reserved for more artistic renderings for interiors because it makes the indoor air seem smoke-filled. Figure 8.17 shows the parameters of the Beam shader.

The Beam effect works best with directional standard lights such as the Spot light. You can use a solid color value for a smooth volumetric effect centered on the light, or for an added effect, you can use a shader such as Smoke to give variety to the effect. The value to use for Density depends on the scale and depth of your scene; the default of 5 is a good place to start.

You do not need to add lights to the light list if you are going to use the effect on all lights in the scene. A scene that demonstrates this effect is available in `.\scenes\Cornell Box\`, and images are available in the `.\renderoutput\Parti_Volume\` folder of your Chapter 8 project.

FIGURE 8.17
Beam Parameters
section

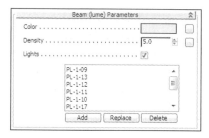

Mist Parameters

This shader produces a haze or fog effect that gets thicker as you get farther away from the camera, or the effect can be layered as a ground-fog effect. Figure 8.18 shows the Mist parameters.

FIGURE 8.18
The Mist volume
shader parameters

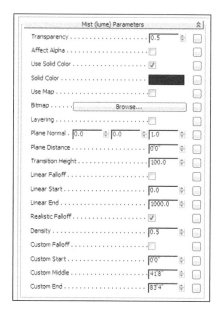

Transparency This setting controls the maximum transparency of the fog, with 0.0 being completely opaque at a maximum distance and 1.0 being completely transparent.

Affect Alpha This setting controls whether the alpha (transparency) channel is affected by the Mist shader.

Use Solid Color/Solid Color/Use Map/Bitmap The Mist shader can use either a solid color or a bitmap, and you should enable one or the other.

Layering, Plane Normal, Plane Distance, and Transition Height The rendered mist effect can affect your entire rendered scene or can exist as a low "layered" mist. When Layering is enabled, set Plane Normal to define which direction is "up"; the default is the Z direction. Then set Plane Distance to the point where the effect has the least transparency, and set the Transition Height setting to the distance it takes for the effect to transition to transparent.

Linear Falloff/Linear Start/Linear End When you enable the Linear Falloff setting, you can define the distance from the camera where the effect begins to get opaque (Linear Start) and where it is opaque (Linear End). The values are determined by the scale of your scene.

Realistic Falloff check box and Density Setting With the Realistic Falloff option, the fog falls off exponentially from the camera. Your only adjustable option is the Density value, and its value depends on how far you need to see through the mist.

Custom Falloff/Custom Start/Custom Middle/Custom End With these options, you control the Custom Start, Custom Middle, and Custom End values to accurately specify where the effect transitions. The values you use are determined by the scale of your scene.

A sample scene with each falloff style saved in the Compact Material Editor is available as `.\scenes\Cornell Box\CB_Mist.max`, along with rendered images in the `.\renderoutput\Mist` folder of your Chapter 8 project. Simply drag the desired map from the CME into the Render Setup dialog box and the volume shader to assign the map.

mr Physical Sky as a Volume Shader

Similar to the effect produced when the mr Physical Sky is used as a lens shader, the primary difference between its use as a volume shader vs. a lens shader is that the haze produced when used as a volume shader applies to both the primary rays from the camera to the scene and also through reflections and refractions. Using the mr Physical Sky shader in the camera effect's Volume slot takes additional computation time compared to using mr Physical Sky as a lens shader.

Parti Volume Parameters

Air and water tend to scatter light as the light hits particles within the atmosphere. The Parti Volume shader is an effect that works within a specific participating (parti) media, in this case light objects, and that simulates the scattering of light in water vapor, smoke, or mist, illuminating the particles inside the volume. You're probably familiar with the volumetric effect of street lights on a foggy night.

The Parti Volume shader needs to have geometry behind the lights specified in the shader in order for the effect to operate. For an outdoor scene that may not have geometry around a light, placing a large sphere around the scene will ensure that all the camera angles and light positions are covered. Apply an Arch & Design material to the sphere with Transparency set to 1.0 and an Index Of Refraction (IOR) setting of 1.0. Place the object on a layer with the Visible To Reflection/Refraction, Receive Shadows, and Cast Shadows options disabled, or set the Object Properties settings directly, provided the Object Properties dialog box (right-click the sphere and choose the Object Properties option to open it) has the Rendering Control option set to By Object. Although not required, this effect is usually used with lights set to the "Spotlight" *Light Distribution* type option, which will speed rendering because the effect is concentrated within the cone of light. When used with an area spotlight, the effect appears as a point-light source and a diffuse shadow within the volume. For the most defined shadow effect, use a point light source.

Figure 8.19 shows the parameters for the Parti Volume (physics) shader.

FIGURE 8.19

The Parti Volume (Physics) Parameters section

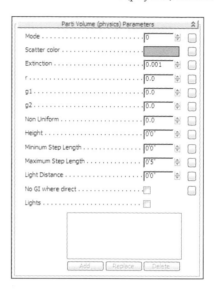

The settings of the Parti Volume shader are as follows:

Mode This setting has two options, 0 or 1. Mode 0 causes the volumetric effect to occur throughout the participating light object, as if the entire space contained fog. Mode 1 causes a layered effect to the fog, and then the Height value determines where the fog layer ends above the ground plane.

Scatter Color The Scatter Color option is the color of the fog, in other words, the color of the suspended particles that are scattering the light. The default color is 50 percent gray; however, the final color of the effect is tinted by the color of your light source.

Extinction This setting controls how much of the light is absorbed and scattered in the participating medium. The higher the setting, the denser the effect you achieve, and because more light is blocked by the volume effect, your rendering will be darker. Smaller numbers produce less light scattering and a brighter volumetric effect. The setting range is 0.0 to 1.0, and a setting of 0 disables the volumetric effect. The settings, as with most things in 3ds Max, can be animated to vary the effects over time. A higher density typically requires brighter light sources to illuminate your scene away from the light source. Figure 8.20 shows Extinction values of 0.005, 0.01, and 0.025.

r, g1, and g2 These three settings control the scattering within the volume, and the default values of 0 provide an overall diffuse effect. The *r* parameter is a value between 0 and 1, *g1* and *g2* are values between −1 and 1.0. According to mental images, settings of r = 0.50, g1 = −0.46, and g2 = 0.46 generate what is called the *Raleigh scattering effect*, which is like dust or smoke in an environment. Settings of r = 0.12, g1 = −0.50, and g2 = 0.70 generate the Hazy Mie effect, which is moderately hazy. Settings in the range of r = 0.19, g1 = −0.65, and g2 = 0.91 produce the Murky Mie effect, which is a dense effect. Figure 8.21 shows the effect of each of these settings, with Raleigh on left, Hazy Mei in center, and Murky Mei on right.

FIGURE 8.20
This image shows Extinction values of 0.005, 0.01, and 0.025.

FIGURE 8.21
The Raleigh, Hazy Mei, and Murky Mei suggested settings

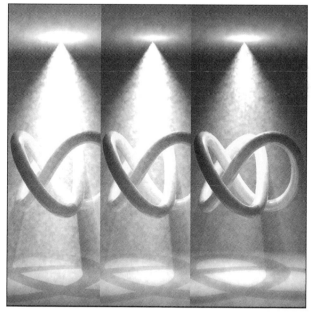

Non Uniform The setting adds noise to the volumetric effect, and the setting ranges from 0 to 1.0. At 0, the effect is uniform through the volume, and the Extinction setting controls the falloff, and at 1.0, the effect is wispier and cloud-like.

Height   When the Mode parameter is set to 1.0, the Height setting controls the distance above ground where Extinction becomes 0.0 and the atmosphere is without the water vapor effect.

Minimum and Maximum Step Length   The Parti Volume effect uses a technique called *ray marching* where rays are projected into the participating media in small steps instead of the traditional way, from camera to surface and from surface to surface. The step size is randomized between the minimum and maximum values, and it affects volumes when the Non Uniform parameter is greater than 0. Smaller values produce more accurate shadow effects within the volume but will take more render time. The Minimum size should be no more than 10 percent the value of the Maximum Step Length setting.

Light Distance   This parameter is used to optimize the sampling of light sources and determines the distance where additional sampling of the light is necessary.

No GI Where Direct   This option tells mental ray to not use global illumination within the volumetric area and to only use direct illumination.

Lights   This is an optional list of lights; if left empty, then all lights get this volumetric effect. You can use the Shader List and multiple Parti Volume shaders to produce different effects for different groups of lights.

A scene that demonstrates various settings for the Parti Volume shader is available as `.\scenes\Cornell Box\CB_PartiVolume.max`, and renderings of this effect are in the `.\renderoutput\Parti_Volume\` folder of your Chapter 8 project.

Submerge Parameters

This shader causes objects to appear wet — as if submerged below the waterline of a surface — when used as a texture shader. However, when used as a camera effect volume shader, it makes it appear as if everything below a specific height is below water. Figure 8.22 shows the parameters of the Submerge shader.

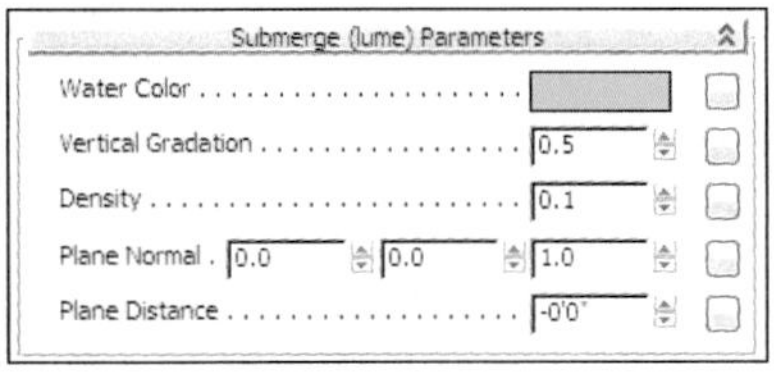

FIGURE 8.22
Submerge Parameters shader

If your camera is above water, then objects below the waterline appear wet, and a volumetric effect gets denser as the water gets deeper. When the camera is below the water plane, then your rendering includes the volumetric scattering effect of water and is tinted the color of the Water Color parameter. The other parameters for Submerge include the following:

Vertical Gradation   This setting determines how quickly light falls off in the water. Murkier water needs a higher setting.

Density   The Density setting determines how quickly the underwater region becomes opaque and underwater objects are no longer visible.

Plane Normal   The Plane Normal settings are XYZ parameters, and a 1.0 in the Z is correct for a flat plane of water in 3ds Max.

Plane Distance   This is the point at which the volumetric effects begin to tint geometry and produce the volumetric effect. This setting should be slightly below any actual geometry representing the water plane so the effect is rendered correctly.

A scene that demonstrates this effect is available as .\scenes\Submerge_2010.max, and renderings with various Density and Vertical Gradation settings are available in the .\renderoutput\ Submerge folder of your Chapter 8 project.

Using Special Effects

My experience with the effects discussed in this chapter is that less is more, and a subtle effect is better than something dramatic. Sometimes you want to take some artistic license and push an effect to the extreme; however, that style of render is usually not ideal as a production render for a client. A subtle DOF effect can add a lot to the realism; it can improve the feel of a rendering, can help to focus attention on the focal point of the scene, mask the flatness of grass in the foreground of images, and add a professional edge to your work. But an extreme effect is often distracting and will have the undesired effect of detracting from the area of interest. In the early days of Photoshop, I saw many renders by others that were edited to add lens flares to an extreme degree; the flares were distracting, and they obscured details in the rendered model.

On the practical side, performing some effects will always be easier and faster when using a post-processing application such as 3ds Max Composite.

The Bottom Line

Use camera lens shaders   Camera lens shaders affect how rays are brought in and processed from a camera and include the Depth Of Field/Bokeh, Distortion, mr Physical Sky, Night, Gamma & Gain, and WrapAround shaders. Applying a camera effect is an identical process for each class of effect (lens, output, and volumetric), although each shader has different parameters.

> **Master It**   How do you add the Depth Of Field/Bokeh shader to a scene and make it possible to adjust its parameters?

Use camera output shaders   A camera output shader is a post-rendering process applied to an image and includes the Glare and HDR Image Motion Blur effects.

> **Master It**   How do you add the HDR Image Motion Blur shader to a scene and make it possible to adjust its parameters?

Use camera volume shaders   Camera volume shaders allow you to produce fog and distance-dependent effects and includes the shaders Beam, Mist, mr Physical Sky, Parti Volume, and Submerge.

> **Master It**   How do you add the Mist volume shader to a scene and make it possible to adjust its parameters?

Chapter 9

mental ray for Architecture

In this chapter, I focus on a number of tools and techniques related to producing renderings for the architecture, engineering, and construction (AEC) industry. I cover the Autodesk Revit application and how geometry and materials come into 3ds Max Design, I provide an overview of the lighting analysis tools that can assist with LEED 8.1 certification for designs, and I cover a few techniques for nonphotorealistic renderings.

In this chapter, you will learn to

- ◆ Use a Revit FBX file within 3ds Max/Design
- ◆ Create light meters and a lighting analysis image overlay
- ◆ Create nonphotorealistic renderings

Using Revit Architecture Models in 3ds Max/Design

Of course, the first thing you need to do before being able to use a Revit model in 3ds Max/Design is to export the model from Revit. Revit and 3ds Max/Design 2011 both support three common CAD file formats: SAT, DWG, and FBX. To export a file with Revit 2010 and newer you must be in a 3D view then click the Application button, select Export, and then select either the CAD Formats or FBX menu option. The CAD Formats option allows you to export as a SAT or DWG file, among other CAD file formats. The FBX file format stands for FiLMBOX, which is a generic 3d scene file that can carry complex data such as mental ray materials, cameras, photometric lights, and object animation.

Using the SAT Format

The SAT format is a 3D solid model format, and the resulting data imported into 3ds Max/Design is a series of *body* objects. A body object is a boundary representation (*brep*) of a solid object, and not an actual mesh, and like a NURBS object is converted to a mesh only for display in the viewport and for rendering. NURBS (Non-Uniform Rational Basis Splines) are defined by curves and surfaces and are used primarily for curved models. The body object's resulting 3D mesh surface is parametric, and you can adjust the mesh detail independently for viewport display and rendering allowing you to have a fast low-detail representation in the viewport while rendering a high-resolution model. Although Revit has its roots as a solid modeling program, the SAT format is usually reserved for transferring data from programs such as Inventor or Solid Works, where the accurate representation of curved surfaces is more important. The ability to tune the resolution of the mesh is not generally needed with architectural models unless you have curved surfaces that are otherwise not represented well as mesh objects. Because the body object provides separate controls for both viewport and render mesh quality, it can provide improved performance in the viewport when lower geometry display settings are used. Translation time into 3ds Max/Design with large SAT files can take a considerably longer time compared to other import formats from Revit. The imported models also lack any useable materials, and have simple Standard material stand-ins on surfaces rather than mental ray ProMaterials as you would have with the FBX format. If you need to import your design as a body object due to tessellation issues, then isolating only the object(s) in Revit that actually *need* to be imported as SAT and exporting just those objects as SAT will reduce the amount of material rework you will need to do in of 3ds Max/Design.

THE FUTURE OF SAT

SAT is a format that is seeing rapid development from Autodesk because it allows lossless bi-directional transfer of CAD data between programs. For instance, if you import a Revit or Inventor file into 3ds Max/Design in the SAT format, you can add modifiers to bend, twist, scale, and deform the geometry, and then export the file as SAT to bring it back into Revit or Inventor in an editable state. Despite the long import times I have experienced, for select objects it can allow you to combine the power and flexibility of 3ds Max/Design, Revit, and Inventor for creating and editing objects.

Next I look at cover the advantages and disadvantages of using the DWG format to transfer Revit designs.

Using DWG Exports from Revit

The next translation format is DWG, the AutoCAD drawing format. The advantages to using DWG over other formats such as FBX are as follows:

Works well with large designs   The DWG format handles large designs better than the current implementation of FBX, which I cover in the next section of this chapter.

File linking in 3ds Max/Design 2010 and older   DWG files can be linked to your scene to allow changes in AutoCAD or Revit to be reflected in your scene geometry throughout the design process and subsequent revisions. 3ds Max/Design 2011 now supports file linking with FBX files.

Smaller file size   The file sizes are significantly smaller with DWG, and the import process is relatively fast. The small size and faster import speed, coupled with the DWG file linking capability, has made DWG my choice for using Revit models in 3ds Max/Design 2010 and older.

The disadvantage to DWG is that the materials come in as either Architectural or Standard materials, which should not be used for lighting analysis in mental ray, and might produce inaccurate renderings. The *mr Arch & Design Tools* script covered in Chapter 2, "Materials and Maps," should be used to convert the materials to Arch & Design before use.

As mentioned, when working with 3ds Max/Design 2010 and older, you can utilize the file linking capabilities of 3ds Max/Design only with the DWG format. File linking creates a one-way connection between the DWG file on the disk and the scene geometry in 3ds Max/Design. The linked scene geometry, whether it is splines or mesh objects, can be modified in the original DWG file (via Revit export or directly in AutoCAD), and the changes will appear when you refresh your file link in 3ds Max/Design. The unique identifier used for each DWG drawing element is used to coordinate the connection from the DWG elements to 3ds Max/Design scene geometry, so edits to elements in AutoCAD, or changes to elements in Revit, will be evident in your scene. If an object is deleted, any replacement object would receive a new unique identifier and therefore any transforms, modifiers, or materials applied to the original in 3ds Max/Design would need to be applied to the replacement object. Therefore, it is best to edit an element in AutoCAD or Revit when possible, rather than deleting and replacing that element.

INTRODUCING THE LINKORIGINPTHELPER OBJECT

New for 3ds Max/Design 2011 is the "LinkOriginPtHelper" object that is included with each file-linked model. All geometry in a linked model is linked to the LinkOriginPtHelper object in a parent-child hierarchy. To move your entire linked model to a new position or orientation, you transform this helper instead of the individual elements. Any new or updated geometry in your linked file will be positioned relative to the LinkOriginPtHelper object.

In 3ds Max 2009 and older you open the File Link Manager, shown in Figure 9.1, by selecting File ➤ File Link Manager. In 3ds Max/Design 2010 and newer open the File Link Manager by clicking the Application button, select References, and select File Link Manager. New for 3ds Max/Design 2011 is the ability to use the File Link Manager for FBX files; however, in earlier versions, you must use the DWG format when you use file linking.

FIGURE 9.1
The File Link Manager for DWG files

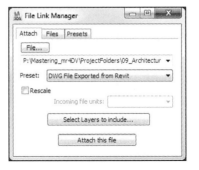

In 3ds Max/Design 2011, you now have three preset options for importing a DWG file: DWG File Saved From AutoCAD, DWG File Exported From Revit, and DWG File Saved From AutoCAD Architecture. Switching the File Link Manager dialog box's tab to the Preset tab and editing a preset shows you how that preset is set to import the geometry and allows you to edit the preset.

To import a DWG file into 3ds Max/Design, open the File Link Manager, select your DWG file, choose the appropriate preset, and click Attach This File. If your DWG file changes during your 3ds Max/Design session, open the File Link Manager and switch to the Files tab. Any DWG or FBX files that have changed will show a red flag next to their filenames. Select the file in the list, and click the Reload button. If the Show Reload Options check box is enabled, you get a File Link Settings dialog box that is similar to one found when editing presets in the Presets tab of the File Link Manager. One particular option to be aware of is on the Advanced tab of the File Link Settings dialog box, as shown in Figure 9.2.

FIGURE 9.2
The Advanced tab
of the File Link Set-
tings dialog box

FIGURE 9.2
The Advanced tab
of the File Link Set-
tings dialog box

Figure 9.2 shows the Use Scene Material Definitions and Use Scene Material Assignments On Reload options. The Use Scene Material Definitions option checks your current scene for a material that matches the name of a material on the imported geometry and uses the scene material instead. If you are importing multiple DWGs or have previously edited an imported material, you might want this option enabled to automatically use materials existing in your scene. The Use Scene Material Assignments On Reload option preserves any materials you might have replaced on the scene geometry rather than using the material on the incoming DWG. I typically turn both of these options on to ensure that materials are not overwritten when updating the linked drawing.

In the next section, I cover the FBX file format and new file linking feature.

Introducing FBX File Import and Linking

An FBX file is a universal 3D data translation format originally developed for character animation and which has evolved to support features from a number of Autodesk and third-party product lines including Revit and 3ds Max/Design. As long as the proper FBX version is installed, you can transfer data between different versions of 3ds Max/Design and to other 3D modeling and animation platforms such as Maya and MotionBuilder. Support for the FBX format in 3ds Max/Design continues to expand with the 2011 release and with the ability to use the File Link Manager to attach FBX models to your scenes. I will now detail the advantages of this format.

ADVANTAGES OF THE FBX FORMAT OVER DWG

As the FBX format evolves, you will no doubt see additional advantages to this format over others, and although there are only three bullet points here, they are significant advantages:

◆ Any materials, any lights, and many render settings come through to 3ds Max/Design as defined within Revit, including daylight systems. Both applications use mental ray, and you can reuse the work already performed in Revit.

◆ All maps used by materials are contained in a folder with the FBX file and are referenced to that location within the FBX file. This reduces the possibility of missing material errors at render time. The folder name matches the name of the FBX file.

◆ The Scene Explorer supports displaying and sorting Revit elements by category, family, level, and type.

The first point, that materials and lights are imported as defined in Revit, can save you a considerable amount of time when working with a Revit model in 3ds Max/Design. Both applications use mental ray, and in many instances very little may need to be modified in order to render the model. The interoperability between these two applications continues to improve with each new release, and 3ds max/Design 2011 now supports file linking with the FBX format, which was previously the big advantage that DWG had over FBX. See "Using the File Link Manager with FBX Files" later in this chapter.

Despite these distinct advantages, the format has both limitations and pitfalls that you should be aware of as you move forward.

LIMITATIONS AND CAVEATS OF THE FBX FORMAT

The FBX format is the newest and most feature-rich format for transferring data from Revit into 3ds Max/Design; however, it has some limitations, and there are a few things to be aware of as you work with the imported FBX data. Many of these issues are minor or affect only large designs. Particularly for 3ds Max/Design 2011, the advantages of the format far outweigh the following limitations:

◆ The FBX export from Revit tends to be many times the size of a comparable export of a DWG file. A 500KB DWG file for a moderately sized building may equate to a 30MB (or larger) FBX file. For very large buildings, this large file size may be an issue because the scene may take a considerable amount of time to import. In that case, turning off objects in Revit that do not contribute to the renderings (such as furniture defined for interior spaces) or exporting the model in several parts may assist with a successful import. If you apply your materials in 3ds Max/Design rather than rely on Revit, then consider the DWG format, and use the Use Scene Material Assignments On Reload option in the File Link Manager.

◆ The FBX format does not bring objects in on individual layers; they are all on one layer based on the name of the imported object. Even though Revit does not use layers internally, the DWG export from Revit has layer names that equate roughly to the class of object, such as 3D-WALL, 3D-DOOR, and so forth.

◆ Revit will export only one camera from your model, the current view. Any cameras you create in Revit will need to be re-created.

◆ 3ds Max/Design does not support Revit camera features such as Film Offset and Optical Center Offsets, and your image framing may look different in 3ds Max/Design compared to renderings in Revit.

◆ Lights in Revit use watts and are converted automatically to lumens. All lights use the Dimmer parameter in 3ds Max/Design.

◆ Photometric lights for the same family and type in Revit are not instanced in 3ds Max/Design. Each light is an independent object, which can make it difficult to manage and adjust within

3ds Max/Design. Using 3ds Max/Design's Clone and Align tool will allow you to replace non-instanced lights with instanced clones, and then you can delete the noninstanced original light objects.

◆ A high number of objects may result in viewport performance issues in 3ds Max/Design. Using NVIDIA Quadro graphics cards and the performance drivers for 3ds Max/Design makes a significant difference in the display performance for high-polygon scenes, and combining objects via an Edit mesh or Edit Poly modifier and the Attach tool can help further reduce overhead. As I cover shortly, the FBX file linking tool offers several ways to combine objects automatically on import.

◆ In versions of 3ds Max/Design 2010 and older, there is no file linking capability to FBX files, only to DWG format models. This means that any time you need to update your FBX imported model, you need to delete and reimport your FBX model with the older versions of 3ds Max/Design. Without the FBX file linking capability, many users will instead import the Revit FBX file into a separate 3ds Max/Design scene and XRef this new `.max` file into their main site `.max` scene along with site models and landscaping and then render the final images. With this method, you can then easily delete the entire Revit imported model and replace it within the XRef scene in the event the model needs to be updated. Saving any material changes to a material library allows you to quickly overwrite any newly imported materials.

◆ Imported Revit FBX models will have nonessential edges visible in the model, which can slow viewport performance and is visually distracting. Selecting all objects and adding a Quadify modifier can significantly reduce the extra edges.

◆ Pivot points for all objects are at 0,0,0, and not at object centers. If you need to animate an object around a different pivot point, select the object, and modify the pivot point from the Control Panel's Hierarchy tab.

Despite the seemingly long list of caveats, the FBX format is quickly evolving to become the format of choice for transferring scene data, particularly now that file linking is supported.

DEALING WITH DESIGN REVISIONS

It is rare for an architectural project to come to us and stay the way that the initial designs detailed. Architects can usually imagine their design in 3D to some degree, but once they can see their designs in the correct proportions and from various camera angles, the designs often change, sometimes subtly and sometimes significantly. The architect's client, city planners, village boards, and so on, typically have a lot of difficulty visualizing designs in 3D from 2D plans, and once the 3D model and renders are available, changes usually occur. That is, after all, one reason why they need our services, so they evaluate their designs and make decisions.

Whether it is changes in the number or sizes of columns to improve an open space or changes in ceiling heights or window sizes, these model changes can take time on your end to complete. Using parametric building modelers like Revit has greatly simplified the process of both building the initial models and making changes without the extensive manual mesh editing of the past. Using the file linking capability of 3ds Max/Design allows you to continually develop the 3D building model throughout the life of the project, independent of other development within 3ds Max/Design, and it has drastically changed the way we build architectural models over the last few years. As I have hinted at throughout the book, "test early and test often." File linking allows you to work with numerous building iterations and test lighting and materials at every step of the design process.

Using the File Link Manager with FBX Files

The File Link Manager in 3ds Max/Design 2011 allows you to import FBX files with five preset options:

Combine By Revit Material   Objects, no matter what their family or category, are combined into a single object with one specific material per object.

Combine By Revit Category   A category is defined as top-level objects such as Walls, Windows, Doors, and so on.

Combine By Family Type   A family type is defined as Basic Wall, Floor, Roof, and so on. Stacked walls are shown by their separate wall types and not as Stacked Wall.

As One Object   As its description implies, this setting means all objects are combined into a single object, and the material for this object will be one large Multi/Sub-Object material.

Do Not Combine Entities   This is my preferred import method for many scenes because I can then sort objects in a Scene Explorer by category, family, or type.

Unlike when you import a DWG file, importing or file-linking an FBX file does not generate separate layers for objects. Depending on how objects are combined using the import options, I can quickly select objects by name or use the Scene Explorer to select by category and then separate into layers to better control the geometry. I prefer the Do Not Combine Entities option so that in a Scene Explorer I get the Revit Categories, Revit Family, Revit Level, and Revit Type column headers to help me with sorting and using the Revit data.

Perform the following steps to link a file to your current scene:

1. Open the File Link Manager using the Application button, References sub-menu, and the File Link Manager option.

2. On the Attach tab, click the File button to select the FBX file.

3. Select the preset to optionally combine imported data or leave it uncombined.

4. Click the Attach This File button.

To update a linked CAD file, you need to go back to the File Link Manager, switch to the Files tab, and click the Reload option. You can also permanently detach or bind the scene to your file, breaking the link to the external CAD file. Figure 9.3 shows the file link manager's FBX reload options.

FIGURE 9.3
The File Link Manager's Reload reload options for FBX files

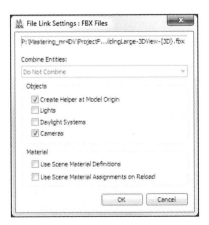

You can open the Reload Options dialog box from the File Link Manager's Files tab, and by clicking the Reload button while the Show Reload Options check box is enabled. The settings in Figure 9.3 are the same settings you would see if editing one of the presets in the File Link Manager for the FBX formats, except that here you cannot change how objects are combined (or not) during import. There are a few settings to be aware of, namely, the list of objects imported and the Use Scene Material Assignments On Reload option. For many scenes, you will want the photometric lights and the daylight system to be included.

Next I cover the differences between mental ray rendering in Revit and 3ds Max/Design.

Comparing Revit Rendering to 3ds Max/Design

Using 3ds Max/Design over Revit has a number of advantages, and for the most part it comes down to increased quality and reduced render time. The following list shows some of the advantages to using mental ray in 3ds Max/Design vs. Revit:

Advanced animation capabilities   With 3ds Max/Design, you can create complex and compelling animations of your designs, and leverage the optimizations available in 3ds Max/Design for caching and reusing indirect illumination data for animations.

Ability to easily modify and override materials   In Revit your materials are tied to the properties of the elements in your 3D model, and it is neither convenient nor desirable to change all the materials to produce a simplified image or even multiple variations of a design. With 3ds Max/Design, you can replace materials at will, you can easily modify materials from those defined for an element, and you can also override all materials to produce renderings without the potential confusion of materials.

The ability to easily change materials also means you can adjust the settings for an improved finish and reduce the settings for reflections and refractions to greatly reduce render time. To preserve material changes, be certain to enable the Use Scene Material Assignments On Reload option in the File Link Manager's reload options, as described earlier in this section.

Advanced settings   The tools for adjusting render settings, materials, and lighting within Revit are greatly simplified to fit a specific purpose. With 3ds Max/Design, you gain access to the wealth of settings discussed throughout this book and beyond. The ProMaterials on imported FBX geometry include settings to tune the quality and render time as found in the material's Performance Tuning Parameters. For custom materials, the new Autodesk materials in 3ds Max/Design 2011 closely mimic the Revit materials reducing the learning curve in using 3ds Max/Design. With the two material editors you can quickly replace the imported materials with Arch & Design materials to access other advanced features.

Advanced effects   For an architectural rendering, adding depth-of-field and atmospheric effects can add a lot to the feel of your rendering.

Faster rendering   My experience has shown that scenes imported from Revit models typically render at least twice as fast within 3ds Max/Design vs. Revit on the same computer. Revit is intended for relatively small images and lacks the features and settings that can optimize and speed your rendering process. With faster rendering comes the ability to produce larger images in less time.

Ability to use distributed bucket rendering and Backburner   With 3ds Max/Design, you have the ability to leverage the power of all your 3ds Max/Design-capable computers to produce your renderings, either through distributed bucket rendering or through the Backburner network rendering tools. With Revit you are limited to your single local computer for rendering images.

Ability to precompute Final Gather   As I covered in Chapter 5, "Indirect Illumination and Final Gather," you can precalculate and reuse Final Gather (FG), potentially saving you considerable time because you can precalculate FG at a smaller resolution and reuse it on a large rendering. This also reduces memory requirements, which helps on machines with limited resources.

Access to Global Illumination, Importons, and Irradiance Particles   Global Illumination (GI) combined with FG often produces better results in less time than using Final Gather alone. With 3ds Max/Design, you also have access to the Importons to optimize GI and Irradiance Particles for next-generation indirect illumination and image-based lighting.

Lighting analysis   3ds Max Design includes the Autodesk Exposure technology that allows you to perform lighting analysis on your designs to assist with LEED 8.1 certification.

This list is simply an overview of the advantages I see in 3ds Max/Design over Revit for rendering in mental ray.

In the next section, I cover how materials are brought into 3ds Max/Design from an FBX Revit file.

Revit Materials vs. 3ds Max/Design

In the current implementation of Revit and 3ds Max/Design the materials from an FBX file come into your scene as ProMaterials. The bitmaps specified in the ProMaterials are not the standard Bitmap map type and are instead the Simple Image Map type. This map cannot be added by you in a material editor and can only be found in imported materials. The Simple Image Map type has the advantage that is reduces the confusion many casual users experienced with the more complex Bitmap map, particularly when most features of the Bitmap shader are rarely used. The disadvantage to the Simple Image Map type is that there is no way to view the bitmap in the viewport, and if you need to see your map, you must render an image or replace the Simple Image Map type with a Bitmap shader. Figure 9.4 shows the settings for the Simple Image Map type.

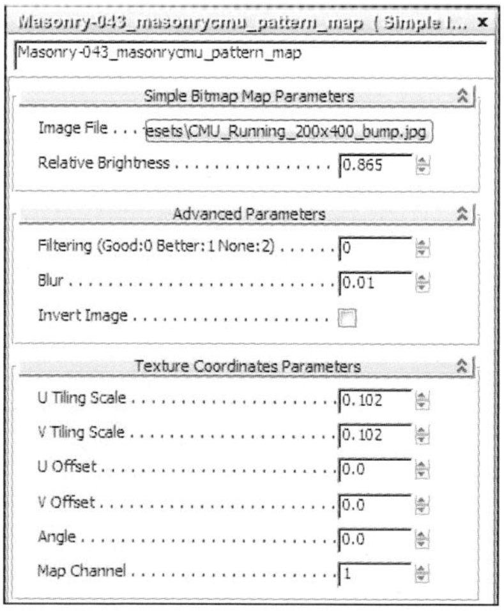

FIGURE 9.4
The Simple Image
Map settings

With 3ds Max 2011 the new Autodesk material type is functionally similar to its predecessors, the ProMaterials; however, the user interface has been simplified further to closely match the controls found in Revit. Rather than a Simple Image Map, you now have the Unified Image Map (adsk) map. Like the Simple Image Map, this cannot be created from within a material editor but appears on imported scene geometry. The new Autodesk material does not contain tuning parameters.

In the next section, I cover the Autodesk Exposure lighting analysis tools in 3ds Max Design. The inclusion of lighting analysis in 3ds Max Design is one of the main differences between the 3ds Max and 3ds Max Design versions.

Introducing the Autodesk Exposure Technology

The 3ds Max Design application includes Autodesk Exposure technology, which is a series of lighting measurement and analysis tools. The results of the Exposure tools have been validated for measurement accuracy by the National Research Council Canada and Harvard University's Graduate School of Design. The Exposure tools can assist designers working toward LEED 8.1 certification of their building designs. LEED stands for Leadership in Energy and Environmental Design and is a rating system developed by the U.S. Green Building Council; you can find more information at www.usgbc.org. Many buildings these days proudly tout their LEED certification, and more and more architects are adding "LEED AP" (Accredited Professional) to their list of accreditations.

The lighting analysis tools come only in 3ds Max Design and not 3ds Max. The lighting analysis tools work with the mental ray renderer using Final Gather and the mr Sun and mr Sky objects provided within a daylight system. Lighting analysis is not intended for use with Global Illumination as the use of GI has not been validated. All validated results are obtained with the Perez All Weather sky model for the daylight system, and you can further enhance their accuracy by using a Weather Data file from www.eere.energy.gov. The analysis tools are not intended to work with the mr Sky Portal lights and instead use high Final Gather settings for accurate lighting simulation. Although the mr Sky Portals are physically correct they will skew results, and are not validated for use in lighting analysis. Autodesk recommends setting the ground color in the daylight system's mr Sky to RGB 0,0,0 to prevent undue ground reflectance and recommends creating accurate surrounding exterior geometry to reflect light into your interior scene.

When I perform lighting analysis I typically hide any non-critical objects that will increase calculation of Final Gather and do not add much to the indirect lighting of a scene. It is also important that your model be "light tight" and not leak any high-intensity illumination from outside, and it's important for your materials to have reasonable and, if possible, accurate reflectance values so that the light reflected from the surfaces and indirectly illuminating the scene are correct for that material and color. Many paint samples have a light reflectance value (LRV) printed on the back, and LRV and reflectance values are available at many manufacturer websites. Reflectance varies by material and surface finish, and materials often have a range of reflectance values (white porcelain, for instance, has a reflectance range of 65 to 75), so it will often take some research to find the proper range for the materials in your scene. See www.mastering-mentalray.com for reflectance resources.

I have already covered much of what you need to know to use the lighting analysis tools, including using daylight systems, photometric lights, and the mr Photographic exposure control. I'll cover two key tools in the following sections: Lighting Analysis Overlay and the Light Meter object. The Lighting Analysis Overlay option is a render effect that is created after your image is rendered, which places light measurements across your image. The Light Meter object allows you to measure lighting directly on surfaces of your scene. In Chapter 3, "Light, Shadow, and Exposure Control," I covered the Pseudo Color exposure control that replaces your rendering with a false-color image that represents the illumination in your scene; that is technically not part of the lighting analysis toolkit.

To assist you in configuring your scene for accurate lighting analysis, 3ds Max Design includes the Lighting Analysis Assistant, which both validates your settings and assists in converting, configuring, and adding lighting analysis objects and energy-accurate materials.

Introducing the Lighting Analysis Assistant

Before you use any of the tools that make up the Exposure lighting analysis technology, the Light Meter object, or the Lighting Analysis Image Overlay, it is important to first open the Lighting Analysis Assistant from the Lighting Analysis menu in the top menus of 3ds Max Design and check the settings, materials, and objects in your scene to ensure that they will produce the most accurate results possible. You can find all the example scenes used in this chapter on your DVD in the \ProjectFolders\Ch09_Architecture folder. For best results, copy the contents of this folder to a local drive to allow editing of the scenes, and set your project folder to this location. To follow along with the descriptions of lighting analysis, open the scene .\scenes\LA\House_2010_Start.max.

Figure 9.5 shows the General tab of the Lighting Analysis Assistant.

FIGURE 9.5

Lighting Analysis Assistant's General tab

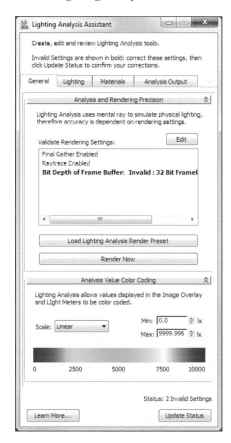

There are four tabs for settings: General, Lighting, Materials, and Analysis Output. Any settings that are missing or incorrect are highlighted in each tab, and Figure 9.5 shows that the renderer frame buffer is not in 32-bit mode. Clicking the Edit button will bring you to the Render Setup dialog box and the Indirect Illumination tab; switch to the Renderer tab to change a 16-bit frame buffer mode to 32-bit. You can optionally click the Load Lighting Analysis Render Preset button to load settings ready for lighting analysis. This render preset has very high settings for both Final Gather and Spatial Contrast and also disables gamma correction for the scene; it is not intended for rendering your image. After correcting the invalid settings, click the Update Status button in the Lighting Analysis Assistant to recheck your scene. If nothing is highlighted in bold in the dialog box, then any further invalid settings may be on other tabs.

The dialog box's Analysis Value Color Coding section affects the color range used for both the light meters and the analysis Image Overlay. Creating a light meter and calculating its values shows in the viewport the current range used, and modifying the values in the Lighting Analysis Assistant immediately changes the color of the Light Meter object.

The Lighting tab includes settings to create and validate a daylight system and also to validate and create photometric lights for your scene. The validation for the daylight system does not ensure that Sky Model is set to Perez All Weather, which is needed for an accurate simulation. Switching the daylight system in the `House_2010_Start.max` file from Haze to Perez All Weather reduces the values of a Light Meter object placed on the floor from a nearly 2500lx peak to less than a 1300lx peak.

The photometric light settings allow you to quickly select invalid lights to delete, but it does not replace them. I typically use the Clone and Align tool to replace invalid lights with photometric equivalents prior to deleting the Standard lights. Adding an XForm modifier to the instanced light and transforming the gizmo allows you to move and rotate all lights for proper placement within light fixtures, if required.

Figure 9.6 shows the Lighting Analysis Assistant's Materials settings.

FIGURE 9.6

The Materials tab of the Lighting Analysis Assistant

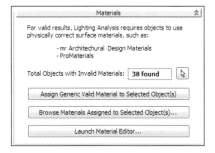

As you can see in Figure 9.6, this scene has objects that have invalid or missing materials; the `House_2010_Start.max` model is a DWG import from a Revit file, and many of the materials are still Architectural or Standard or are not defined. The quickest way to convert the materials without losing the associated colors, maps, or finish settings is to use the mr Arch Design Tools covered in Chapter 2 and click the Convert Materials To mr Arch & Design button. More than likely, your materials will still need some tweaking to ensure they look correct. Clicking the Assign Generic Valid Material To Selected Object button in the Lighting Analysis Assistant instead will eliminate all material settings that may have been useful in the original material. If an object does not have a material assigned, then selecting the invalid objects and clicking

Assign Generic Valid Material To Selected Objects assigns an Arch & Design material named Lighting Analysis Assistant Default Material, which is a 50 percent gray nonreflective flat color. One disadvantage is that you need to go through the entire scene and assign materials, and you will need to hunt for those materials and objects. If your glass does not use Arch & Design, ProMaterials: Glazing, or Autodesk Glazing, then it will be opaque. Using the mr Arch Design Tools is preferred over Assign Generic Valid Materials To Selected Objects.

The Analysis Output tab has two sections: Light Meters and Image Overlay. Figure 9.7 shows the Light Meters portion of the dialog box.

FIGURE 9.7
The Light Meter settings found in the Lighting Analysis Assistant

In this dialog box, you have the ability to select and create light meters, toggle settings, and perform lighting analysis with all meters, as well as export all data to CSV files. These are similar to the individual settings found in the Light Meter object, discussed in the next section, "Using the Light Meter Object."

The Create Image Overlay Render Effect button in the Image Overlay section of the Analysis Output tab automatically creates the analysis overlay. Click this button to open the Environment And Effects dialog box to the Effect tab. Figure 9.8 shows the settings for the Lighting Analysis Image Overlay.

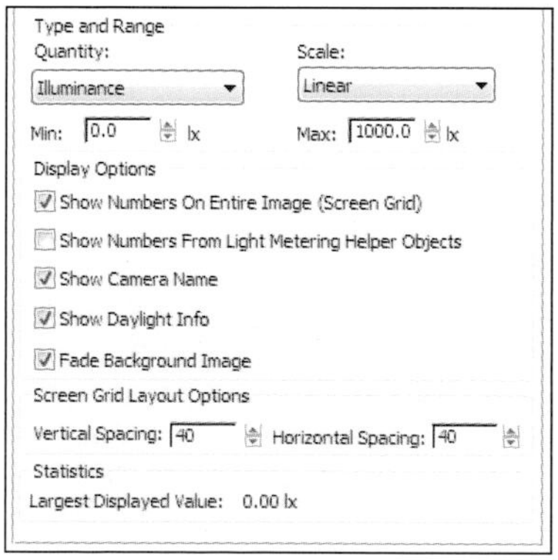

FIGURE 9.8
The Lighting Analysis Image Overlay settings

Values can be represented as illuminance or luminance and scaled as linear or logarithmic. *Illuminance* is the light hitting a surface from all sources over a given area and is measured in lumens per meter squared (lm/m^2), or lux (lx). *Luminance* is the light passing through or emitted from an area in a particular direction and is measured in candelas per meter squared (cd/m^2). The remaining settings are fairly straightforward. Figure 9.9 shows the output of the Image Overlay for the `House_2010_Finish.max` scene.

FIGURE 9.9
A rendered output with Image Analysis overlay

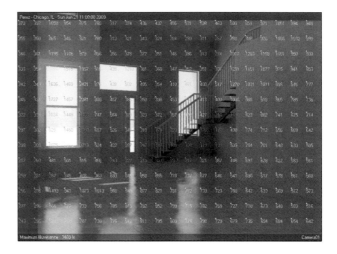

Even if your goal is not lighting analysis, you might find that providing feedback to your clients on light levels will help them evaluate their designs and increase your value as a design visualization partner.

Next I cover using the Light Meter object for measuring and exporting various illuminance values in your viewport.

Using the Light Meter Object

You can find the Light Meter object in the Lighting Analysis menu and also in the Create ➤ Helpers menu. It is a planar object with a series of arrows across the surface. Changing the Length and Width segments for a light meter changes the number of arrows, and at each arrow a measurement is taken of illuminance. Illuminance is measured in lumens per square meter. Once the light meter points are calculated, illuminance is then visible in the viewport as a value and represented as a color gradient across the light meter.

Perform the following steps to use Light Meter objects light meters and the Lighting Analysis Image Overlay in your own scene:

1. Open the Lighting Analysis Assistant from the Lighting Analysis menu.

2. In the Lighting Analysis Assistant, validate the render settings, the lights, and the materials, and make any corrections as required.

3. On the Analysis Output tab, click the Create A Light Meter button, and place a light meter across the surface to be measured.

4. Click the Calculate All Light Meters Now button to measure illumination at the meter points. Adjust the Analysis Value Color Coding range in on the General tab if needed.

5. In the setting for the light meter, click the Export To CSV File button to save the measures data to a file.

6. Click the Create Image Overlay Render Effect button in on the Lighting Analysis Assistant's Analysis Overlay tab.

7. Render your scene.

You can export these measurements to a CSV (comma-separated value) file for further study. Figure 9.10 shows a light meter in the .\scenes\LA\House_2010_Finish.max scene after the light meters have been calculated.

FIGURE 9.10
Light Meter objects shown in the house model

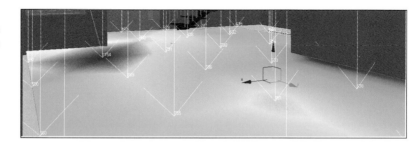

You can adjust the color range of the gradient dynamically on the Lighting Analysis Assistant's General tab by changing the maximum value for the Analysis Value Color Coding setting. Figure 9.11 shows the settings for the Light Meter object.

FIGURE 9.11
Light meter parameters

Clicking Edit opens the Lighting Analysis Assistant and switches to the General tab. The light meter shows illuminance values either for combined direct and indirect light, for indirect or direct in isolation, or for just the daylight illumination. Links to additional detailed coverage of the Autodesk Exposure tools are provided on your DVD in the \WhitePapers folder.

Next I cover nonphotorealistic rendering techniques that reduce or eliminate the confusion of maps and materials and allow your clients to concentrate on the design.

Using Nonphotorealistic Rendering Techniques

Nonphotorealistic rendering (NPR) consists of techniques that simplify or eliminate materials and their bitmaps and replace them with either simple muted colors or a white "chalklike" rendering. I cover three techniques for producing NPR images: using the Material Override setting, Ambient Occlusion, and Contour rendering.

So far, the focus of this book has been on producing realistic renderings, and photorealism is typically the desired end result for a vast majority of my 3D architectural projects. The only drawback to photorealistic images is that it can cause people (clients, governments, and the public) to focus too much on things that are not critical or may be preliminary in nature, and then they lose sight of the design of the building or space, in other words, the "massing" of the overall design. Photorealism can also work against you when the clients gets hung up on the color of a material you temporarily chose on an early rendering, which then becomes a never-ending focus of client critique and subsequent rerenders. Issues like that can, however, work for the designer when the client or government is focused on how the brick looks rather than another design issue they don't want to draw attention to, such as a poorly placed column that cannot be moved. If a little "confuse a cat" helps the client, then we can take the hit.

Too much realism has been an issue on a couple of occasions as I met with prospective clients who were concerned that the local government would insist on everything matching the rendering perfectly. Although seemingly not logical to expect, that particular government body was noted for a lack of reasonableness. NPR was all they needed.

Nonphotorealistic rendering can help your client focus attention on the design of the space rather than the finishes for the surfaces. With NPR, it is easily understood that the white or muted finish is not intended to be representative of the final product, and more artistic license can be used for any surface colors or finishes. Users familiar with Photoshop could render a black-and-white NPR image from 3ds Max Design and then "colorize" it in Photoshop. My focus when producing NPR images is more for in-process renderings rather than final.

Next I cover the NPR techniques on a simple design.

Using Material Override for NPR

The Material Override is a single material which replaces all scene materials at render time with the single material. The Material Override feature is found in the Render Setup dialog box and the Processing tab. The Material Override setting can be a Multi/Sub-Object (MSO) material type that allows you to assign different IDs to objects to control which of the MSO materials appear on each surface. Typically, ID 3 is reserved for glazing, because that is the ID used for glazing in 3ds Max/Design's doors and windows. Material Override combined with a MSO material can be a quick way to apply simple diffuse materials to surfaces that are representative of their individual final colors. This is ideal for quick NPR renderings while still allowing you to switch to final materials by disabling Material Override. The only drawback to the MSO material is that you may need to add a material modifier to most objects to force the use of a specific material ID. Objects imported from Revit might have a variety of material IDs used on the geometry , and a box object has six different material IDs by default, one for each side. Figure 9.12 shows a rendering that uses a Material Override and an MSO material to provide simple colors and bump maps.

FIGURE 9.12
A nonphotorealistic rendering that uses an MSO material as a Material Override

This scene is available as `.\scenes\NPR\MSO_2010.max` in your Chapter 9 project folder. Another related technique is to use the Shell material rather than Material Override to hold two versions of materials, one for NPR and another for production renders. Changing from one to the other is simply a matter of choosing a material to use in the renderer, the original or baked material. Figure 9.13 shows the Shell material settings.

FIGURE 9.13
The Shell material used to switch between production and NPR materials

Although the Shell material is used for controlling "baked" materials from the Render To Texture utility, it can be used to quickly swap any two materials. In the Compact Material Editor, change your Arch & Design material (in this example) to the Shell material, keeping the existing material. Then drag the original material into the Baked Material slot, making a copy. Modify the copy to create your NPR equivalent; I will often use a Color Correction shader on top of a bitmap to reduce the map's saturation for NPR use.

Perform the following steps to create a nonphotorealistic rendering for your own scene:

1. In your scene, open the Render Setup dialog box, and switch to the Processing tab.

2. Enable Material Override, and click None to select an Arch & Design material.

3. Drag the new material into the Compact Material Editor, and make it an instance.

4. Set the diffuse color to a white material with a value of 0.75, and set Reflectivity and Glossiness to 0.

5. In the Special Effects roll-down, enable Ambient Occlusion.

6. For a paper-white effect, add the Ambient/Reflective Occlusion shader to the Self Illumination Filter color swatch, and adjust the self-illumination to brighten the scene.

An example scene using this technique is available as `.\scenes\NPR\Shell_2010.max`. The next technique, using ambient occlusion, also uses Material Override to achieve its effect, but with a specific goal to the appearance of the model.

Using Ambient Occlusion for NPR

Ambient occlusion (AO) is a method of darkening portions of surfaces based on how occluded (blocked) the surface is from ambient light. Random rays are shot from samples along the surface into the scene to a certain distance, and if a ray is blocked by an object, then that sample is darkened slightly as a result. AO is great for adding detail back into a model that may have been washed out by the combined effects of Final Gather (FG) and Global Illumination (GI), and it is a fast and simple method of producing a grayscale rendering of your scene with additional darkening in crevices and inside corners.

For this technique, I used a flat Arch & Design material as a Material Override with the color set to a bright white (a diffuse color Value setting of 0.85 and zero saturation). In the Arch & Design material, I enabled the Ambient Occlusion option and set the distance to a large value, such as 48 inches. This large distance will give more contrast across the surfaces away from the crevices and adds interest to the image in my opinion. An example scene is provided as `.\scenes\NPR\AO_2010.max` in your Chapter 9 project folder.

You might find that your image is very gray with this method, however. To take some of the gray out of the image and make it more like a drawing rather than a grayscale rendering, you can enable the Self Illumination (Glow) feature of the Arch & Design material. Simply enabling self-illumination, however, will take away the darkness you may want in the corners; therefore, you can add into the Self Illumination's Filter color the Ambient/Reflective Occlusion (3dsmax) shader. This shader will return a grayscale color based on how occluded the surface is, returning the desired detail to the model while allowing the self-illumination to bring out some details in areas in shadow, as shown in Figure 9.14.

Scale the self-illumination's Illuminance value based on the brightness of your scene and exposure values. Figure 9.15 shows the settings for the Ambient/Reflective Occlusion shader.

You can also use the Ambient/Reflective Occlusion shader in the diffuse color of the Arch & Design Material, if desired, to further enhance the darkening of the occluded area. An example scene using this shader both for self-illumination and for diffuse shading is provided as `.\scenes\NPR\ARS_SI_2010.max` in the Chapter 9 project folder, along with other examples of NPR techniques.

FIGURE 9.14
An example of ambient occlusion used to produce a nonphotorealistic image

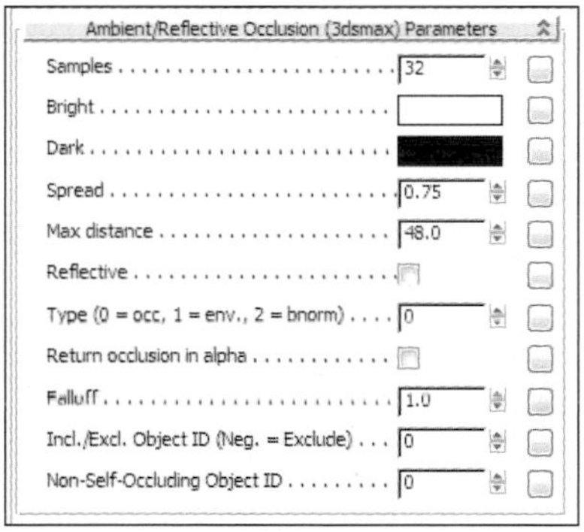

FIGURE 9.15
The Ambient/ Reflective Occlusion shader

Ambient/Reflective Occlusion (3dsmax) Parameters		
Samples	32	
Bright		
Dark		
Spread	0.75	
Max distance	48.0	
Reflective		
Type (0 = occ, 1 = env., 2 = bnorm)	0	
Return occlusion in alpha		
Falloff	1.0	
Incl./Excl. Object ID (Neg. = Exclude) . . .	0	
Non-Self-Occluding Object ID	0	

The next example of NPR is the use of the contour shaders in mental ray. These allow you to do an "edge detect" on your model geometry to place lines along every visible edge.

Using Contour Rendering for NPR

Of all the NPR techniques I have used over the years, contour rendering is a client favorite. Contour rendering produces a line drawing type of effect in your rendering, leaving you with an easy-to-understand image with well-defined edges. Figure 9.16 shows the gazebo scene rendered with contour lines.

There are two steps to using contours in your renderings. First, you must use a material that supports contours, such as the Arch & Design material, and put a contour shader into its Contour map slot, which is located in the mental ray Connection roll-down section of the material's settings. ProMaterials and Autodesk materials do not have the mental ray Connection series of maps. Click the Contour map slot to bring up the Material/Map Browser and the list of contour shaders.

FIGURE 9.16
Contour rendering as
a material override

The second step is to enable contour shaders on the Render Setup dialog box's Renderer tab. Figure 9.17 shows the Render Setup dialog box's Contours settings.

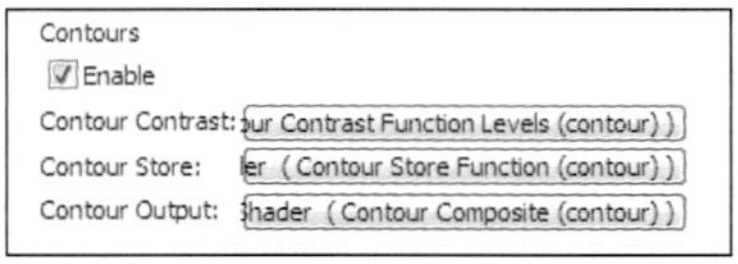

FIGURE 9.17
The Contours set-
tings in the Render
Setup dialog box

Contours
☑ Enable
Contour Contrast: ur Contrast Function Levels (contour))
Contour Store: er (Contour Store Function (contour))
Contour Output: hader (Contour Composite (contour))

After the Contours feature is enabled, the fastest way to produce a contour rendering is to place an Arch & Design material into Material Override, instance it to the Compact Material Editor, and then place a Simple *(contour)* *map* into the Contour slot found in the mental ray Connection roll-down area. Adjust the contour width to adjust the thickness of lines along your object edges. The contours appear in the final stages of rendering after the surfaces are fully rendered.

You can combine contours with NPR techniques covered previously in this chapter and add the Ambient/Reflective Occlusion map to the Diffuse and Self Illumination Filter map slots to add some surface variation and make the rendering more paper-white in appearance. That is how Figure 9.16 was produced. This scene is available as .\scenes\NPR\Contour_Depth_2010.max of your Chapter 9 project folder.

The drawback to using contours in a material override is that some details may be lost because you have only one contour width parameter for all objects, and using a Shell material to apply different contour materials more selectively may be a better approach, albeit time-consuming. To assist with setting all materials to use the Original or Baked option, I have included two small scripts in the DVD's .\Scripts folder: setBakedMtl.ms and setOriginalMtl.ms. To run a script, go to the MAXScript menu, and choose the MAXScript Editor option. In the editor, choose File ➤ Open, and load the desired script, and then press Ctrl-E to evaluate all of the steps. The only difference between the two scripts is the line `s.material.renderMtlIndex` and whether it sets the value to 0 or 1. The 0 value sets all Shell materials to use the Original material, and the 1 value sets it to use the Baked material. As long as you are consistent with which Shell slot gets the original and which gets the NPR/contour materials, this will work very well.

The contour features of mental ray include a number of features that control how the effect is produced on the surface. When you choose a contour shader for your material, you have the following shader options:

Combi   This shader is a combination of the Depth Fade, Layer Thinner, and Width From Light shaders.

Curvature   This shader produces lines that vary in width based on the angle between normals of adjacent faces. There are controls for minimum and maximum width, and the contour lines will vary based on the angle of adjacent normals. Higher angles result in wider lines.

Depth Fade   Contour width gets thinner as lines get farther from the camera. For large architectural scenes, this depth-fade option can give a more pleasant appearance as a Material Override shader than the Simple contour shader because distant details naturally get smaller. Use a Tape helper to measure distances for this shader, or temporarily turn on your camera's Clip Manually option and adjust the ranges to determine the distances for near and far. Remember to set the far color to something other than white; otherwise, your edges will appear white. A sample scene is provided as `.\scenes\NPR\Contours_Depth_2010.max`.

Factor Color   This contour shader allows the surface color to determine the color of the contour. A factor of 0 draws a black line, and between 0 and 1 the contour uses more of the material color. Values greater than 1.0 create a bright contour edge. A sample scene is provided as `.\scenes\NPR\Contours_FactorColor_2010.max`.

Layer Thinner   This shader causes contours seen through transparent surfaces to become thinner. There are two parameters: one for the line thickness in front of the glass and a Depth Factor setting that is the percentage reduction for the line behind each level of transparency. A Depth Factor setting of 0.5 reduces the line by 50 percent for each level of transparency. Set the maximum trace depth in the Contours Contrast Function Levels shader in the Render Setup dialog box.

Simple   All contour lines are drawn the same width. For most architectural and product design projects, this might work well on an object-by-object material but is often too limiting for use in a Material Override on all objects.

Width From Color   The relative brightness of the surface determines the thickness of the contour with brighter colors receiving thinner lines.

Width From Light   This contour shader allows you to specify a specific light, and the illumination from that light determines the width of the contour line. The minimum width is placed in the brightest areas.

Width From Light Direction   This shader doesn't use a real light but instead has XYZ parameters to determine a virtual light location for the purposes of shading. The Width From Light Direction shading option can give an interesting, shadowlike shading to the contours.

In addition to the shader chosen for a particular material, there are shaders in the Render Setup dialog box you should be aware of, in particular the Contours Contrast Function Levels shader.

These shaders are in the Renderer tab and the Contours section in the Camera Effects roll-down menu. The Contours Contrast Function Levels shader has a few settings that you might find useful and important as you play with contours. Drag the shader from the Render Setup dialog box to a material editor to adjust the settings. Figure 9.18 shows the parameters for the Contour Contrast Function Levels (Contour) shader.

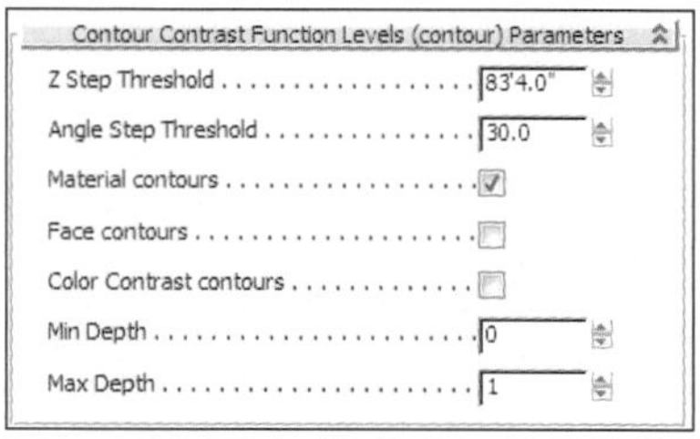

FIGURE 9.18

The Contour Contrast Function Levels (Contour) shader

Contour Contrast Function Levels (contour) Parameters	
Z Step Threshold	83'4.0"
Angle Step Threshold	30.0
Material contours	✓
Face contours	☐
Color Contrast contours	☐
Min Depth	0
Max Depth	1

This shader determines when a new contour is generated for your rendering. The most noticeable effect so far has been the Angle Step Threshold setting where the angular edges of the architectural model each had a contour line as the angle exceeded the default setting of 20 degrees. The following settings are for this shader:

Z-Depth Threshold   This is the minimum depth difference required to generate a contour, in scene units. The Z-Depth Threshold has a very large default setting: 1,000 scene units, or 83′4″ in this case. Significantly smaller values can add detail to your contour rendering, and 10 units for a small scene like the gazebo works well. Product renderings may need smaller values.

Angle Step Threshold   The Angle Step Threshold setting is the minimum angle between adjacent surface normals needed to generate a contour. Lowering this angle will cause additional contours to appear along curved objects. Smoothing groups affect contour generation; if a contour is not appearing where you expect, try adding a Smooth modifier and adjusting the angle.

Material Contours   Enabled by default, this option causes a contour to be generated where materials change, including the same object/faces.

Face Contours   Contours are generated at the edge of each face of the mesh. Using the Quadify or Optimize modifiers may simplify some objects. Both visible and invisible edges are contoured, including individual faces of polygon objects. A sample scene is available as .\scenes\NPR\Contours_Faces_2010.max.

Color Contrast Contours   Areas of contrast change, such as areas in shadow, with highlights, or with surface patterns, will receive contour lines.

Min Depth and Max Depth   The Min Depth and Max Depth settings limit the reflections and refractions for contour generation. Increase these settings if you are working through transparent objects, or decrease them to eliminate contours through glass or in reflections.

Any rendering where contours are used will always use the Box filter for sampling, regardless of the settings in the Render Setup dialog box. Another issue to be aware of is that contour materials seen in the reflection of other objects will get the contour effect passed to the reflection, and you may need to turn off the object parameter Visible To Reflections or adjust the Min and Max settings discussed with the Contours Contrast Function Levels shader. The contour may appear splattered across your rendering if you have glossy materials reflecting the contour material.

I have found the contour shaders to be valuable for projects when materials have not yet been specified at that point. When realism is the ultimate goal, my philosophy is, however, to test scenes early and often with the real materials and lighting to get feedback as the project develops. NPR is useful for presentations your client may have with the building owner when they do not want to focus on materials and lighting.

OTHER NONPHOTOREALISTIC TECHNIQUES

Photoshop is certainly one of the more useful tools you may need outside of 3ds Max/Design because there are a multitude of built-in filters for automatically changing your rendered images into a nonphotorealistic work of art. With Photoshop, you can work on your 3D model in a photorealistic manner while easily producing a less detailed image for early presentations. As such, I highly recommend learning and using Photoshop. Applications such as Piranesi (www.piranesi.co.uk) and Autodesk Impression are built specifically for NPR. You can also use Piranesi to add NPR effects and entourage to a photorealistic rendering. Entourage typically consists of people, plants, animals, and other scanned items added to enhance the realism or feel of the image.

If your goal is a nonphotorealistic approach within 3ds Max/Design, one other useful technique involves the use of the Ink'n'Paint materials. For these to function well in mental ray, you must add them to an Arch & Design material in the Diffuse slot with the Material To Shader shader. See www.mastering-mentalray.com for more NPR information and links.

The Bottom Line

Use a Revit FBX file within 3ds Max Design   The combination of Revit and 3ds Max Design makes for a powerful partnership. The enhanced file linking capabilities of 3ds Max Design 2011 allow the artists to maximize the use of materials and lights defined in the Revit model, reducing the time needed to produce rendering and animations.

Master It   You must connect design data in a Revit FBX file export to a scene in 3ds Max Design 2011. How do you use the File Link Manager to attach the FBX file to your scenes?

Create light meters and lighting analysis image overlay   Using lighting analysis in 3ds Max Design can assist architects and lighting designers in validating and improving their designs and assist them with LEED 8.1 design certification.

Master It   You are assisting an architect in producing lighting documentation for a building interior space. How do you add an image overlay and light meter to your scene?

Master It   You are in the process of developing a 3D model and rendering a proposed building, and your client wants a progress image. How would you produce a nonphotorealistic rendering using the Material Override and Ambient Occlusion settings?

Chapter 10

mental ray for Design

Industrial designers often find themselves in the position of having to produce images for marketing or as virtual prototypes for feedback on their designs. Although the rendering tools in Inventor, SolidWorks, and others may include mental ray as the rendering engine, oftentimes the tools are greatly simplified and leave you without adequate options for a truly photorealistic rendering. In this chapter, I cover how to create a rendering environment for your projects, how to post-process edit your renderings in the new 3ds Max Composite applications, and how to use the new solid-model import options for 3ds Max/Design 2011.

In this chapter, you will learn to

- ◆ Use render studios

- ◆ Create and use render elements

- ◆ Import render-ready solid models

Creating Render Studios

A *render studio* is a premade, render-ready environment to showcase a product. Sometimes a render studio is as simple as a spherical high dynamic range image (HDRI) environment and default lighting, or it can be as elaborate as a scene with a combination of HDRI reflective environments, background plates, and scene geometry to provide entourage and a means of individually controlling the background and foreground.

Reflective objects need something to reflect; for example, chrome logos in space would only reflect the blackness of space, not the beautiful chromic reflections you may be used to from TV and movies. This sounds straightforward, of course, but it is a subject that many artists may struggle with — creating an environment to showcase their work, particularly when the surface is highly reflective.

These are some of the great advantages you have with 3D rendering compared to real-world photography:

- ◆ Cameras can be anywhere, even inside walls and other objects, and still see the environment (in other words, see the camera's clipping plane settings).

- ◆ You can have objects not reflect the environment or reflect something different, like the chrome logos in space.

- ◆ You can have lights that do not cast shadows.

- ◆ You can control where a light illuminates, how far that light is thrown, and which objects are affected by the light, or not affected.

◆ Lights can be invisible in reflections, or they can produce realistic highlights.

◆ You can control and vary the color of a light independent of the lighting technology, and you can dim and fine-tune a light without being concerned about the color temperature shifting.

Real-world photographers would love to have the ability to break the laws of physics to create the images they need or to levitate to get the camera shot they need. Although you have the capability to bend reality, some of the best advice when learning how to compose and light a rendering comes from conventional photography. Reading or taking a class on photography or even theater lighting can greatly enhance your skills. Depending on your goals, consider the following ideas:

Avoiding lights from above   Lights above a model generate strong shadows; this can generate an interesting rendering, certainly, but it is most likely not going to show your product or design in its best light, so to speak. It's "harsh." Using a daylight system to quickly light a scene is terrific for noncritical work or for things that will ultimately be rendered in daylight but is probably not what you want for a product render. You'll get over-bright highlights and deep shadows. If you want an "outdoor" rendering for a vehicle, then consider an early-morning or late-afternoon daylight setting with the sun low in the sky behind the camera, and use fill lights to even out illumination. In cinematography, they have what is called the *golden hour* (or *magic hour*) just after sunrise and just before sunset where the light is low in the sky, the color is warmer, and the shadows are longer. Positioning your subject and camera to minimize harsh shadows and color-correcting for the warm light can produce an excellent rendering. For an outdoor scene, also consider simulating an overcast day by eliminating the sun illumination and instead utilizing a large mr Sky Portal with a Kelvin Temperature Color shader to produce diffuse shadows.

Use large area lights that are close to horizontal or that roughly follow three-point lighting with a main key light slightly above and to the side of your camera, with a fill light slightly below the camera and to the opposite side, and with a rim, or *hair*, light behind the subject and above the camera. For some product renderings, you might also need soft illumination from below your subject, similar to bounce cards used for photography and TV/movies. An mr Sky Portal with the Kelvin Temperature Color shader in the Custom color source works exceptionally well for all lights in a product render where harsh shadows are not desired because it acts like a true area light. See Chapter 3, "Light, Shadow, and Exposure Control," for more information about the mr Sky Portal.

No matter what lighting rig you choose, remember to follow the guidelines in Chapter 3 and adjust the lights in isolation, particularly if you need to do a little troubleshooting on an image that is not turning out the way you like.

Adding lights that do not exist in the environment   Proper lighting often means a lot of light. The goal is often an even distribution of light across your subject with minimal unwanted or confusing shadows. Use photometric area lights (or mr Sky Portals and the Kelvin Temperature Color shader), and use attenuation on photometric lights to control how far the light travels; this way you can light part of your scene without over-lighting adjacent areas.

In movies, television, and professional photo shoots, the photographers add lights galore, along with bounce cards, to help eliminate harsh shadows and improve lighting. For an interior scene, this may mean modeling enough of the exterior to provide the correct bounced light from the ground (even if it is from an adjacent roof or unseen pavement) or adding soft area lights (or mr Sky Portal lights with the Kelvin Temperature Color shader) to help brighten an area and reduce shadows.

Never use the ambient light environment setting to soften shadows or brighten a scene. Ambient light should always be set to a value of 0. No exceptions. Also avoid using lights that do not cast shadows unless you otherwise limit their influence.

Adjusting light and surrounding surface colors   The rendered color of a surface is determined by direct and indirect light interacting with the color and finish of the object's surface. For reflective surfaces, the environment also greatly influences a surface's color because the more reflective a surface is, the less of the underlying color is shown at the surface and the more you see of the environment. As you saw in Chapter 3, the color of a light can greatly impact the resulting color of your objects, and using the presets often drastically changes your light's color together with the intensity. Using a D65 Illuminant color preset for your photometric light along with setting the mr Photographic exposure control's Whitepoint setting to 6500 Kelvin ensures a nice white light and accurate colors from your surfaces. However, if you place this all in a red room, then all your objects will be tinted pink. In Chapter 6, "Global Illumination and Caustics," I covered methods of controlling light color bleeding using the Color Override/Ray Type Switcher shader.

Using different camera angles may require different lighting rigs   If you have different camera angles for different product renderings, either you might need different lighting configurations for different viewpoints or you might need to reposition existing rigs for each new camera position. If you have great lighting for a particular camera angle, you might find that rotating the entire camera and light rig, or rotating the objects like on a turntable, produces better results than simply moving the camera. For a building, you might need to rotate the daylight system's Compass Rose to get a good rendering of the front and back of the building even though this may not be physically correct.

Using the environment/background switcher and Gamma & Gain shaders to control reflective environments   In brief, you can control environment reflection levels with the Gamma & Gain shader. This is an essential technique in product renders because the reflective environment can greatly affect how your surface appears. For the more adventurous, you can refer to the "Using Render Elements" section of this chapter to discover a post-processing way to control reflections. I cover the Environment/Background and Gamma & Gain shaders later in this chapter.

Applying the rule of thirds   Placing your subject in the frame of the camera is often just a matter of centering the object or building in the field of view and rendering the image; for catalog shots and building images, this is typically what the client wants and needs. For larger and more complex scenes, you can create a more comfortable image by placing the focal-point objects offset from the center. Imagine your rendered image cut evenly by two lines horizontally and two vertically, like a tic-tac-toe grid. Placing your focal-point object along one of these grid lines can create a more pleasing composition and a more comfortable picture to view.

Avoiding wide-angle and telephoto lenses   Do this only when possible, of course! A wide-angle lens tends to distort the image considerably but might be the only way to render a scene, particularly interior spaces. I have used wide-angle (28mm or less) lenses for walk-through animations, and although I was concerned that it would be a distorted mess, it came out just fine. For many still shots, the addition of a Camera Correction modifier will remove undesired distortion from the frame.

A telephoto lens (100mm or more) will flatten out your perspective. This can work for you to reduce perspective distortion on a 3D logo or extruded text; however, is often not desirable on something like a building.

In the next section, I cover using various bitmaps as render studio environments.

Using Environment Maps

The quickest way to produce a render studio is to use bitmaps, and in this section I'll show you several methods of using bitmaps for your environment. Utilizing bitmaps can be as simple as a spherical HDRI environment with your product in the middle or a more elaborate scheme with a background plate and a separate image for reflections. All render studios that use exclusively bitmaps for the environment must use some method of producing shadows onto the environment to connect the 3D objects to the 2D images, typically using a Plane object with a Matte/Shadow/Reflection material.

The files for this chapter are located on your DVD in the \ProjectFolders\10_Design folder. For best results, copy this folder to your local hard drive to allow editing and saving of scene data, and be sure to set your copy of 3ds Max/Design to use this folder as its project folder. You might need to edit the project MXP file for your version of 3ds Max/Design and your computer's configuration.

You can find the environment map settings under the Common Parameters roll-down menu in the Environment dialog box (open it by selecting Rendering ➤ Environment or press 8). Clicking the Environment Map button allows you to assign the Bitmap map type from the Material/Map Browser and then an image file from your drive. When rendered, 3ds Max/Design places your entire bitmap across the background of your rendering, scaling it to fit the screen, which might not be what you intended. Environment maps are often spherical or panoramic, and their settings must be adjusted to appear correctly in your rendering.

You must drag and drop a map or shader from the Environment dialog box to a sample sphere in the Compact Material Editor or into a view in the SME in order to configure its settings. Be certain to select the Instance option when prompted. To assign a map from the Compact Material Editor or SME to the Environment map slot, drag the material from a sample slot to the Compact Material Editor, or click and drag from the output of the Bitmap node in the SME onto the map slot in the Environment dialog box.

BACKGROUND IMAGES MIGHT APPEAR BLACK

Background bitmaps might appear black in your renderings when you use the mr Photographic exposure control, particularly low dynamic-range images. The bitmaps are essentially nonilluminated, and you must scale (brighten) them to match the illumination of your scene. You can do this through the Unitless option of the mr Photographic exposure control (see Chapter 3), or you can wrap the environment map with a Gamma & Gain map and set the Gain setting to the brightness of your light sources (be sure to disable the Gamma options in the Gamma & Gain shader). For a daylight environment, the gain setting would be 90,000 to 100,000, and for an interior scene or product render with artificial lighting it might be from 50 to 5000, depending on your exposure value. Always use the "Process Background and Environment Maps" option when using the mr Photographic exposure control.

In the next section, I cover the various options for using bitmaps for your backgrounds and reflective environments, including advanced methods for using combinations of maps for different purposes.

CONTROLLING MAPPING FOR ENVIRONMENTS

Bitmaps have two methods to control their coordinates, either as a texture map to be applied to an object or as an environment map (the *Enviro* option). The texture mode is the default for new bitmaps created in the SME and is appropriate only for use in materials. With an environment map, you can directly control how that image is mapped at render time to a virtual object at the extents of your scene. The *Enviro* option is needed whenever you use a bitmap for an environment unless you apply it to physical geometry in your scene, such as a hemispherical sky dome object. Figure 10.1 shows the four mapping options available.

FIGURE 10.1
Environment
mapping options

The environment Screen option maps your image to each of the six sides of a cube and forces it to the aspect ratio (width divided by height) of your rendering. The Spherical Environment option is used for most HDR environment images, and the image wraps around the equator of an imaginary sphere aligned with the world coordinate system. The Cylindrical Environment option is for panoramic images wrapped around the horizon, and the Shrink-Wrap Environment option is like the spherical mapping except the image is wrapped from above down around the sphere.

If you have an image of an existing site, you can match your scene camera location to the image's camera location (camera match) and use the Screen mapping option for the background environment. Set your rendering resolution to match the aspect ratio of the background image to prevent stretching. The mental ray Matte/Shadow/Reflection material then allows you to mask out parts of the image to render in the foreground of your image instead of behind your geometry and even cast shadows and geometry reflections on the background, as I cover in examples later in this section.

The Screen option for an environment can cause undesired results when you have highly reflective geometry. As shown on the chrome vase object in Figure 10.2, the screen-mapped environment makes the object look oddly transparent despite the opaque and highly curved surface in this scene; a copy of the bitmap is on all sides and reflects from behind the camera, too. The bitmap is also scaled to fit the render size, which causes distortion because it is squashed to fit the rendered image's aspect ratio. The scene file for this example is in the Chapter 10 project folder as `.\scenes\Enviro\Vase_Screen.max`. The background image is from your 3ds Max/Design installation's `.\maps\Backgrounds` folder.

FIGURE 10.2
Reflective objects
appear transparent
when you use the
screen environ-
ment mapping.

As you can see, simply placing an image into the environment with screen mapping does not work well for reflective objects. You can fix the stretching and shrinking of a background environment with the shader covered next, Environment/Background Camera Map.

Using the Environment/Background Camera Map Shader

This special mental ray shader provides a screen-mapped environment background; however, unlike normal screen mapping, it prevents rescaling and distortion when used with its Per-Pixel Matching option; the background is cropped to the lower left of the image and mapped pixel per pixel into your rendered background. This map wrapper can also scale the image brightness and optionally return a solid color for off-screen reflections rather than the environment map. Figure 10.3 shows the settings for the Environment/Background Camera Map shader.

FIGURE 10.3

Settings for the Environment/ Background Camera Map shader

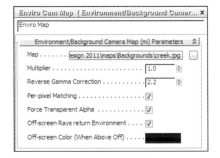

As shown in Figure 10.3, there are two buttons for map parameters: a large one (labeled Browse… when no map is defined and showing the bitmap name when one is defined) and a small unlabeled button at the far right on the Map line. The small one allows you to use any standard 3ds Max/Design shader, and is the same as connecting a map to the input nodeslot of the Environment/Background Camera Map shader in the Schematic Material Editor; the Per-Pixel Matching option might not work properly with this option. The larger button is specific to mental ray and bypasses any settings you might otherwise apply to the incoming image file for gamma, color adjustments, and other Bitmap shader settings; this is the preferred method for using a map if the Per-Pixel Matching option is required. You need to set the Environment/Background Camera Map shader's Reverse Gamma Correction settings when you use the large Map button and low dynamic range images, or your image may be too light; Reverse Gamma is typically set to 2.2 in this instance. If you use a standard Bitmap shader, be sure you do *not* double gamma-correct your image with the Environment/Background Camera Map shader because it might appear very dark; set Reverse Gamma Correction to 1.0 if this occurs.

Perform the following steps to use the Environment/Background Camera Map shader in 3ds Max/Design 1011:

1. From your Chapter 10 project folder, open the file .\scenes\Enviro\Vase_ECM_2010_ Start.max.

2. Open the SME, and add an Environment/Background Camera Map shader (from the Default group's mental ray subgroup) into the view.

3. Double-click the new map to open its settings.

4. Rename the map to Enviro Map.

5. Click the large Map button, and choose the `creek.jpg` image file (or another file of your choice). The file is typically located in the `C:\Program Files\Autodesk\3ds Max Design 2011\maps\Backgrounds\` folder.

6. Set the Reverse Gamma Correction value to 2.2 to match your global gamma settings.

7. Enable the Per-Pixel Matching option to eliminate any stretching or shrinking of the bitmap to fit the render area. The material sample swatch might turn black.

8. Open the Environment And Effect dialog box.

9. Drag the output nodeslot of Enviro Map in the SME to the Environment Map slot in the Environment And Effects dialog box. Select the Instance option to ensure any changes made in the SME also occur in your environment.

10. Save your scene as `Vase_ECM.max`.

Perform the following steps for 3ds Max/Design 2010 and older:

1. Open the Environment And Effects dialog box, and set your environment map to the Environment/Background Camera Map option.

2. Open the Material Editor.

3. Drag the new environment map into an unused sample window, and select the Instance option.

4. Click the Browse button in the map, and select the `creek.jpg` file from the `.\maps\Backgrounds` folder of your 3ds Max Design installation.

5. Set the Reverse Gamma Correction value to 2.2.

6. Enable the Per-Pixel Matching option.

The best solution for environments that include reflections and/or a moving camera is to use a spherical HDRI bitmap.

USING SPHERICAL HDRI BITMAPS

One solution to the screen-map reflection issue is to use a spherical environment map. These are typically created with special camera equipment from companies like Spheron VR (`www.spheron.com`) and are often provided in HDR formats. Commercially available high-quality spherical HDR images are available from resources like Dosch Design (`www.doschdesign.com`); in fact, Dosch has provided HDR images for your use in the DVD's `\Bonus\Dosch` folder.

Spherical HDR images create brilliant reflections and can produce illumination when used with Irradiance Particles in mental ray. The downside to a spherical environment is that the resolution tends to be relatively low, so you might end up with a highly pixelated background; therefore, spherical maps are not always suitable for high-resolution renders. In that instance, rendering to an image format that supports transparency allows you to replace the background in an image-editing application, or you can use the Background/Environment Switcher shader described next. Figure 10.4 was produced with the sample scene `.\scenes\Enviro\Vase_Spherical.max`.

FIGURE 10.4
Chrome vase in
a spherical HDRI
environment

USING THE ENVIRONMENT/BACKGROUND SWITCHER

The Environment/Background Switcher shader allows you to, for instance, have a high-resolution screen-mapped background and a separate spherical map for reflections. In your scenes, drag the current environment map into the Material Editor for editing, change it to the Environment/Background Switcher, and keep the old map. Your current environment is now your background, and you'll have an empty map for your environment for reflections; place a spherical bitmap into the Environment/Reflections slot.

Figure 10.5 was created from the file .\scenes\Enviro\Vase_EBS_2009.max. This scene provides control for the brightness of the two environment maps through the use of a Gamma & Gain shader on the spherical environment map and also via the Multiplier setting of the Environment/Background Camera Map shader used for the background image.

FIGURE 10.5
Scene that uses the
Environment/Background Switcher
and Environment/
Background Camera Match with a
screen-mapped
background and
HDRI spherical
environment

Perform the following steps to use an Environment/Background Switcher in 3ds Max/ Design 2011:

1. From your Chapter 10 project folder, open the file `.\scenes\Enviro\Vase_EBS_2010_ Start.max`.

2. Open the SME.

3. Type **Environment** into the Search box to filter the list, and then drag the Environment/ Background Switcher into the SME view. Searching is not required, but it helps you find what you need.

4. Double-click the new map to open its parameters, and change its name to EBS.

5. Type **Bitmap** into the search box, and drag two Bitmap 2D maps into the view.

6. Connect the output of one map to the Background input of the Environment/Background Switcher, and connect the other bitmap's output to the Environment/Reflections input.

7. Double-click the bitmap for the background, and change its name to Bkgnd.

8. Change its coordinates to Environ, and ensure that the mapping is set to Screen.

9. Click the large None button in Bitmap Parameters, and choose the `creek.jpg` image file from the `C:\Program Files\Autodesk\3ds Max Design 2011\maps\Backgrounds\` folder.

10. Double-click the other bitmap, and rename it to Enviro.

11. Change its Coordinates setting to Environ, and set its Mapping drop-down to Spherical Environment, as shown in Figure 10.6.

FIGURE 10.6
The Environment/Background Switcher configured in the SME

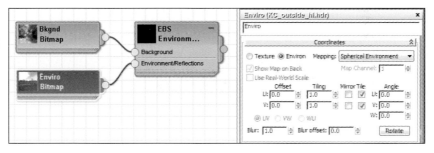

12. Select the `KC_outside_hi.hdr` bitmap from the `C:\Program Files\Autodesk\3ds Max Design 2011\maps\HDRs\` folder. Use the Real Pixels (32 bpp) setting and the Def. Exposure option.

13. Open the Environment And Effects dialog box.

14. Drag the output of the Environment/Background Switcher to the Environment Map slot in the Environment And Effects dialog box, and choose the Instance option.

You can also use the Environment/Background Camera Map in place of the bitmap that connects to the Background input of the Environment/Background Switcher map.

Perform the following steps to use the Environment/Switcher Map shader in 3ds Max/Design 2010 and older:

1. Open the Environment And Effects dialog box, and set your environment map to the Environment/Background Switcher option.

2. Open the Material Editor.

3. Drag the new environment map into an unused sample window, and select the Instance option.

4. Change the name to EBS.

5. Select the button for the Background map, choose the Bitmap option, and then choose the `creek.jpg` file from the `.\maps\Backgrounds` folder of your 3ds Max/Design installation.

6. Click the Up To Parent button in the horizontal toolbar to return to the EBS map level.

7. Select the button for the Environment/Reflection map, choose the Bitmap option, and select the `KC_outside_hi.hdr` bitmap from the `.\maps\HDRs\` folder of your 3ds Max Design installation. Use the Real Pixels (32 bpp) setting and the Def. Exposure option.

8. Change the Mapping drop-down menu to Spherical Environment, and click Up To Parent to return to the EBS map.

9. Render your scene.

CREATING YOUR OWN ENVIRONMENTS

There are a few good ways to create your own HDRI spherical environments: you can create a 3D scene and render to a spherical HDR or OpenEXR map using the WrapAround lens shader, you can buy or rent a camera from a company like Spheron (www.spheron.com), or you can create artificial environments by using one of the emerging products, such as HDR Light Studio (www.hdrlightstudio.com).

To create your own nonspherical low and high dynamic range images, you can use your own camera. For HDRI, you must take a series of images with specific f-stop settings and combine them into an HDR image using software such as Paul Debevec's HDRShop (http://projects.ict.usc .edu/graphics/HDRShop/). For a reflective environment, a high-quality digital SLR camera combined with a spherical chrome ball will allow you to create both HDR and LDR images that you can place in the Environment Probe/Chrome Ball shader, combined with a background plate in the Environment/Background Camera Map shader.

Several high-quality HDRI environments for your use are provided on your book's DVD in the \Bonus\Dosch folder. Dosch Design (www.doschdesign.com) is my primary source for HDRI environments and 3D entourage, and Dosch has generously made this demo content available exclusively for my readers. Many of the examples in this chapter are made with the Dosch products. My friend Pete Taylor of Spheron VR generously provided a HDR image he created with the Spheron VR technology, and this is provided in the \Bonus\Spheron folder and in the Chapter 10 scene assets.

In the next section, I cover using environments that are a single color, a favorite of many product renders.

Using Solid-Colored Environments

One request I get quite often from artists is how to create those brilliant white environments for product renders that you see in ads — a solid white environment with a floor that catches shadows and reflections and that goes off into infinity behind the product. I have created a number of product renderings over the years where it seemed like I spent more time tweaking the background or "floor" color than anything else on the model; therefore, I'll show how to create a general-purpose environment that is fairly easy to modify. Creating a simple one-color environment is not difficult. You just press 8 to open the environment settings and choose a color, after all. That does not provide an interesting environment or provide reflections on your objects that improve the realism and create interesting surfaces.

Perform the following steps to set up a white product environment in 3ds Max/Design 2011:

1. Open the file WhiteEnv_2010_Start.max from the Chapter 10 project folder.

2. Open the Environment And Effects dialog box by pressing 8 on the keyboard.

3. Click None for the Environment Map setting, and choose the new Environment/Background Switcher shader from the Material/Map Browser.

4. Open the SME.

5. Drag the new environment map into the SME's View1, and choose the Instance option. Close the Environment And Effects dialog box.

6. From the SME's Material/Map Browser, drag a new Color Corrector map into View1.

7. Connect the output of the Color Corrector to the Background input of the Environment/ Background Switcher.

8. Double-click the Color Correction map to open its parameters in the SME.

9. Change the Map color swatch in Basic Parameters to use a value of 0.75.

10. Drag a Bitmap shader into View1 from the Material/Map Brower. Choose a spherical HDR bitmap from your 3ds Max/Design .\maps\HDRs folder or from the samples provided in the .\renderassets\images folder of your Chapter 10 project, or \Bonus folder of the DVD. Use the Real Pixels And Default Exposure option in the settings for the HDR file.

11. Double-click the Bitmap shader to open its settings.

12. Change the mapping style to *Environ* and the Mapping setting to Spherical Environment.

13. Drag a Gamma & Gain shader into View1 from the Material/Map Browser. Connect the output of the HDR bitmap to the input of the Gamma & Gain shader and the output of the Gamma & Gain shader to the Environment/Reflections input of the Environment/Background Switcher.

14. Double-click the Gamma & Gain map to open its parameters. Change the Gamma value to 1.0, set the Gain value to 0.75, and turn off the Reverse Gamma Correction check box. Your schematic should look like Figure 10.7.

FIGURE 10.7
Your SME schematic at step 14

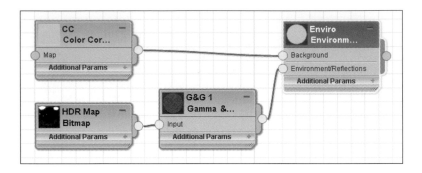

15. Drag a Matte/Shadow/Reflection material into View1 from the Material/Map Browser.

16. Connect the output of the Color Correction map to the Camera Mapped Background input of the Matte/Shadow/Reflection map.

17. Double-click the Matte/Shadow/Reflection map to open its parameters.

18. In the Reflections roll-out, enable the Receive Reflections check box.

19. Drag the output of the Matte/Shadow/Reflection map onto the Plane01 object in your scene.

20. Render the Camera01 view.

A completed scene is available as `WhiteEnv_2011_Finish.max`, and a completed image is available as `.\renderoutput\WhiteEnv_Finish.jpg`.

The last example for render studios is the use of geometric environments for your scenes.

Using Geometry for Your Environment

It is hard to beat a photo of a real environment for, well, realism. Combining a product or building into a background photo is an art form in itself. The downside is that a photo may be difficult or impossible to change if the client wants something different in the background or different reflections. Using geometry to surround your environment holds many advantages over HDRI or other simulated spaces in that the resolution of the background does not degrade when you render a high-resolution image, and you can change the environment in whatever way you need to produce the required shot.

I often reuse models from architectural projects I've done for use in product renders because they give me the ultimate flexibility for lighting and provide an interesting environment for reflections. A geometry-based render studio does not need to be complex, and in your Chapter 10 `.\scenes` folder are the scenes `Product_Environment_Daylight.max` and `Product_EnvironmentPMetric.max`. Each has a different simple geometric environment and lighting scheme. For a majority of in-process projects, I will drop in these simple sets of objects as an XRef to provide quick lighting and backgrounds as I develop the scene. Be sure to enable the XRef option Overlay to prevent the XRef'd environment from propagating to additional scenes.

In the next section, I cover some techniques for importing and cleaning up solid-model geometry.

Using Render Elements

One essential skill when you work with complex renderings is the art of compositing. 3ds Max/Design and mental ray allow you to produce *render elements*, which are components of a complete rendering that you can then composite into a complete "beauty" image that contains all the render elements. The advantage to this process is that you can make adjustments to elements after they are rendered and produce effects much faster than they can be produced in 3D. It takes some knowledge and forethought, but it can save you when a client wants a color adjusted or when you need to adjust the depth of field or motion blur.

You can find the Render Elements settings on the Render Elements tab of the Render Setup dialog box, as shown in Figure 10.8.

FIGURE 10.8

The Render Elements settings

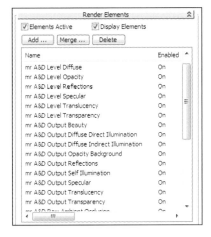

Clicking the Add button opens the list of available render elements. If a specific render element, such as Z-Depth, has parameters associated with it, then those parameters appear in a roll-down menu at the bottom of the Render Setup dialog box.

Several of the critical standard (non–mental ray) render elements that are available with 3ds Max/Design are as follows:

Alpha   This element is the transparency channel of your rendering and is critical for compositing renderings.

Atmosphere   This render element contains the atmospheric component of a rendering, typically containing any haze generated by mr Physical Sky.

Matte   This element allows you to select objects or surfaces by material ID, object ID, or by specific scene objects to create an image that you can use to mask out those specific elements. The mask will be a black image with white where the matte object or materials exists. The edges of the mask will be antialiased for clean compositing.

Object and Material IDs   Object IDs are numbers manually assigned to objects from their object properties in the viewport's right-click Quad menu. Material IDs are set per material in the SME or CME. The result is a render element with specific colors corresponding to the ID that you can extract for compositing. For use with the 3ds Max Composite application, you might get better results using the Matte render element.

Z-Depth   This element is a grayscale representation of the relative depth of the scene. You must set the distances that determine the brightest (Z Min) and darkest (Z Max) distances. The settings also include an Update check box to set the values to the extents of your scene. Z-Depth can be used for Depth Of Field and atmospheric effects.

In addition to these render elements, mental ray adds a wealth of render elements that include the final render output of various channels together with the raw rendered data for manual multiplication and compositing. These require Arch & Design, ProMaterial, or Autodesk materials to function and are described in the next section.

Introducing 3ds Max Composite

Included with 3ds Max/Design 2011 is the new 3ds Max Composite application, formally known as Toxik. 3ds Max Composite is the successor in many ways to Autodesk's Combustion compositing product and is designed to work with compositing and adjusting HDR images. Although it is beyond the scope of this book to cover the basic use of 3ds Max Composite, I do cover the 3ds Max and mental ray render elements and some typical uses of 3ds Max Composite for compositing, adjusting, and producing effects with your rendered scenes. If you have not done so already, take some time to view the *Essential Skills* movies that are provided with 3ds Max Composite. Compositing and post-production are used in the following critical areas:

◆ Adjusting reflections and shadows

◆ Tone mapping (exposure control)

◆ Color adjustment

◆ Depth of field (DOF)

◆ Motion blur

◆ Atmospheric fog

It is much faster to do many effects in post-processing than in 3D, and in many cases you can avoid rerendering an image when you need to make color adjustments. When rendering for compositing, I recommend that you render to the highest bit depth possible, a 32-bit or 16-bit floating-point (not integer) file format that supports transparency such as OpenEXR (EXR). The low dynamic range integer-based PNG format works well for noncritical work because it supports transparency and is a lossless format. For LDR work, I recommend using the 16-bit per channel (48-bit) mode with an alpha channel.

Avoid any format such as JPEG that performs lossy compression and does not support transparency. For the best results, use a high dynamic range format that is a lossless format, and remember to disable output gamma correction when you use HDR formats; gamma correction should be done in post-processing if the image is eventually converted to an LDR image. Figure 10.9 shows the top portion of the OpenEXR settings dialog box; I suggest using the Half Float format, RGBA type, and Zip Compression Per Scanline option.

FIGURE 10.9
The OpenEXR output and global options in 3ds Max 2011

The default Full Float format is not generally necessary, and the Half Float setting still gives you a high dynamic range image with plenty of colors to work with, with some file-size savings. With earlier versions of 3ds Max/Design, you get a different OpenEXR settings dialog box, and for that I suggest using the Zip (16 Scanline blocks) compression, the Half Float – 16 Bits Per Channel format, and the Use RealPixel RGB Data option. One other quick option to set in the new OpenEXR dialog box is the Automatically Add/Remove Render Elements From Render Dialog option, as shown in Figure 10.10.

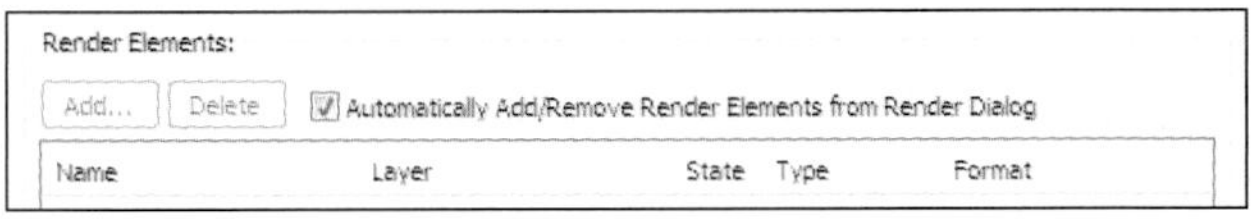

FIGURE 10.10

The Automatically Add/Remove Render Elements From Render Dialog option in the new OpenEXR settings

Enabling this option brings in all render elements defined in the Render Setup dialog box and includes them within the single OpenEXR file. With the OpenEXR image format and this check box enabled, the individual render element files are not saved.

Unlike Combustion, 3ds Max Composite does not support the Render Print Format (RPF) image file format, so you should consider outputting to PNG for LDRI or to EXR for HDRI formats. 3ds Max Composite is designed around support for high dynamic range images and OpenEXR, but it also works with LDR images.

Introducing the mr A&D Render Elements

In addition to the basic render elements that 3ds Max/Design provides (Alpha, Background, Matte, Z-Depth, and so on), mental ray provides a series of render elements that allow you to separate the components that make up the rendered surface of an Arch & Design material; they are the mr A&D series of render elements. For these render elements to work, your scene must consist of Arch & Design, ProMaterial, or Autodesk materials.

The three general classes of mental ray render elements are mr A&D Level, mr A&D Output, and mr A&D Raw. Each of these classes consists of several different render output subtypes, as listed here:

mr A&D Level   The mr A&D *Level* render elements act as multipliers to the mr A&D *Raw* render elements to give you a final image result for that element item. For instance, you can take the mr A&D Raw: Reflections element and multiply it in a compositing program with mr A&D Level: Reflections element to produce a final reflection for further compositing.

The mr A&D Level render elements consist of the following: Diffuse, Opacity, Reflections, Specular, Translucency, and Transparency.

mr A&D Output   The mr A&D *Output* render elements are the final output of each of the rendered elements. The Output group includes elements for the following: Beauty, Diffuse Direct Illumination, Diffuse Indirect Illumination, Opacity Background, Reflections, Self Illumination, Specular, Translucency, and Transparency. Output elements are typically added together to create the beauty image.

mr A&D Raw   The mr A&D *Raw* series of render elements are the unclamped and unmodified values of each render component, including Ambient Occlusion, Diffuse Direct Illumination, Diffuse Indirect Illumination, Opacity Background, Reflections, Specular, Translucency, and Transparency.

The Raw element is multiplied by the corresponding Level element to produce the final composition.

When using the mr A&D Raw outputs, you need to use floating-point output formats such as EXR to prevent clipping of the data; however, the Level element does not require floating point. In addition to the three general classes of render elements are three mental ray specific render elements: mr A&D Extra: Diffuse Indirect Illumination with AO, the mr Labeled Element, and the mr Shader Element.

mr A&D Xtra: Diffuse Indirect Illumination with AO   This render element is the monochrome AO multiplied by the color raw diffuse indirect illumination information. It is the indirect illumination affected by ambient occlusion but without also being multiplied by the diffuse color.

mr Labeled Element   The mr labeled Element allows you to isolate any branch in a material (maps and shaders) and render the branch to a separate render element image or OpenEXR channel; this render element works with an mr Labeled Element shader added to a material or map. For instance, you can take the bitmap in the diffuse channel of an A&D material and wrap it in the mr Labeled Element shader and give it a specific name, or in the SME you can create a separate branch for the diffuse map that goes into the A&D material and also the mr Labeled Element. After adding the mr Labeled Element shader, you then create an mr Labeled Element render element and use the same specific name assigned to the shader. Your A&D material's bitmap or shader will then appear in the render element image or OpenEXR channel after rendering. The mr Labeled Element can output a material when the material feeds into a Material To Shader shader and then into the mr Labeled Element shader.

mr Shader Element   The mr Shader Element allows you to choose a specific shader from your scene materials and render that to a separate element. It is more direct than using the mr Labeled Element as you do not have to first place an mr Labeled Element into your material and match labels. The downside is that it does not show in the SME and can only be controlled in the Render Elements dialog box, and will not work from a Material To Shader to capture the output of a material; that is not the intended function of this element.

MR A&D RENDER ELEMENTS AND MR PHOTOGRAPHIC EXPOSURE CONTROL

The mr A&D render elements bypass the mr Photographic exposure control. If you render to an LDRI file format, you might not be able to recover the color information because bright renders will be clipped to white. Always use an HDR file format with the mr A&D render elements. An HDR workflow will give you the most flexibility in adjusting and controlling your renderings.

In the next section, I cover how to set up render elements and the OpenEXR file output and also how to create a basic composite in 3ds Max Composite.

Creating a Basic Composite

When you create a composition for use in 3ds Max Composite (formerly known as Toxik), the first thing you want to do within 3ds Max/Design is define the render elements needed. For a basic composition, the four basic render elements you need are as follows:

- ◆   mr A&D Output: Diffuse Direct
- ◆   mr A&D Output: Diffuse Indirect

- mr A&D Output: Reflections

- mr A&D Output: Specular

When exported to the OpenEXR format, the render elements appear as separate image channels available within the single EXR image file.

The general formula, from mental images, for combining the A&D Output render elements for a basic composition is this:

Beauty Image = Output Diffuse Direct Illumination + Output Diffuse Indirect Illumination + Output Specular + Output Transparency + Output Translucency

Other render elements, such as Atmosphere, Background, and Z-Depth, are often used in a basic composition. However, for this example, I will add only Atmosphere and Background. The Z-Depth channel can be used as a modulation image with a Blur node in 3ds Max Composite to give you an adjustable DOF effect; you may want to invert the brightness of the image with an Invert node before using it for Blur modulation.

A more complicated composition with maximum flexibility will use the mr A&D Level and Raw render elements instead of the mr A&D Output elements. The Raw element must be multiplied by its corresponding Level element before being combined with other elements. The formula for a Raw and Level composition is as follows:

Beauty Image = Level Diffuse $\times$

(Raw Diffuse Direct Illumination + (Raw Diffuse Indirect Illumination $\times$ Raw Ambient Occlusion))

+ (Level Specular $\times$ Raw Specular)

+ (Level Reflections $\times$ Raw Reflections)

+ (Level Transparency $\times$ Raw Transparency)

+ (Level Translucency $\times$ Raw Translucency)

+ Self Illumination

3ds Max Composite projects that use this formula are provided in the `.\renderoutput\Elements` folder of your Chapter 10 project.

Perform the following steps to configure render elements for a basic composite:

1. Open 3ds Max/Design, and set your project folder to the Chapter 10 project folder `\10_Design`.

2. Open the file `.\scenes\Karina\Landscaping_2010_Start.max` file.

3. Press 8 to open the Environment And Effects dialog box.

4. Because you are saving to an HDR image, click and turn off the exposure control's Active check box to disable the exposure control. Close the dialog box.

5. Open the Render Setup dialog box.

6. On the Common tab, change the render output to `Karina.exr` and to the OpenEXR format. Click Save.

7. In the OpenEXR Configuration dialog box, change the Format setting to Half Float, and ensure that the Automatically Add/Remove Render Elements From Render Dialog check box is enabled. Click OK.

8. Switch to the Render Elements tab.

9. Click the Add button, and hold the Ctrl button to choose Atmosphere, mr A&D Output: Diffuse Direct Illumination, mr A&D Output: Diffuse Indirect Illumination, mr A&D Output: Reflections, and mr A&D Output: Specular. Click OK.

10. A prerendered OpenEXR image is provided in the .\Composite\Footage folder of your Chapter 10 project. If desired, render the CamMidway camera to create your own EXR file. A scene file with preconfigured render elements is available as .\scenes\Karina\ Landscaping_Toxik.max.

USING FILE PATHS IN 3DS MAX COMPOSITE

3ds Max Composite will look for and create files in the C:/Users/<UserName>/Documents/toxik folder by default. You can change this default "home" location and create bookmarks to other content by clicking the Bookmarks button at the bottom of the File Browser dialog box. Whenever you open compositions produced on another user's machine, you might need to reassign the file paths for imported footage.

Perform the following steps to composite the elements into a final image using 3ds Max Composite:

1. In 3ds Max Composite, select File ➢ New.

2. Select the file location, define a filename in the Create Composition dialog box, and click Create. An Output node appears in the schematic view.

3. Click the Output node, change the Image Format setting to 1280 wide by 720 high, and change the duration to 1, as shown in Figure 10.11.

FIGURE 10.11
The Output node settings

4. From the File menu, select Import.

5. In the File Browser, select the Karina.exr file from the Chapter 10 project's .\ Composite\Footage folder. Close the dialog box.

6. With the image node selected, switch to the Options tab in the detail area at the bottom portion of the screen, and then change Channel Views from None to the mr A&D Output Diffuse Direct option, as shown in Figure 10.12. At the lower-right of the program, change the node name to Out Diff Direct.

FIGURE 10.12

The Image Import node's Option settings

7. With the Image Import node selected, press Ctrl+C to copy the node, and then press Ctrl+V to paste the node. Move the node out of the way, and change its Channel View setting to mr A&D Output Diffuse Indirect. At the lower right of the program, change the node name to Out Diff Indirect.

8. Press Ctrl+V to create another Image Import node (it will be placed at your mouse location), and change its Channel View setting to mr A&D Output Reflections. Change the node name to Out Reflections.

9. Press Ctrl+V to create another Image Import node, and change its Channel View setting to mr A&D Output Specular. Change its name to Out Specular.

10. Press Ctrl+V to create an Image Import node, and change its Channel View setting to Atmosphere. Change the node name to Atmosphere, and set its output to RGB.

11. Press Ctrl+V to create an Image Import node, change its Channel View setting to Background, and change its name to Background. It will appear completely white because of its high dynamic range and brightness. Set its Output to RGB.

12. Near the Out Diff Direct node, press the center mouse button/wheel, and sweep to the right gate to open the Tools menu, or use the Pick List in the lower quadrant of the display, and then select and drag a CC Basics node from the Color Correction group into the view. Rename the node to CC Basics ODD.

13. Connect the output of the Out Diff Direct node to the input of the CC Basics ODD node.

14. Add a CC Basics node to the schematic view, rename it CC Basics ODI, and connect the output of the Out Diff Indirect node to the input of the CC Basics ODI node. Repeat this with the Out Reflections and Out Specular Image Import nodes. You should now have four CC Basics nodes connected to the four "Out…" nodes.

15. From the Pick List tab or via the Tools gate, select the Composition category, and then drag three Blend & Comp nodes into the view. Set each node to use the Add blend method.

16. As shown in Figure 10.13, connect the output of the CC Basics nodes to the Front and Back inputs of Blend & Comp nodes, and then connect the output of the first two Blend & Comp nodes to the Front and Back inputs of the third Blend & Comp node.

17. Add a Photo Lab node to the schematic view from the Pick List and Color Correction group. Connect the output of the third Blend & Comp to the input of the new Photo Lab node. Name the node Photo Lab Main.

18. In the Photo Lab settings, change the L parameter for the Exposure – F-Stops setting to –5.5. The RGB values should all be –5.5, as shown in Figure 10.14.

FIGURE 10.13
The nodes after
step 16

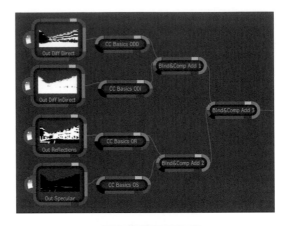

FIGURE 10.14
Photo Lab's Exposure –
F-Stops setting

19. Using Figure 10.15 as a guide for the remaining steps in this example, add the Photo Lab nodes to the Atmosphere and Background Image Import nodes. Name the nodes as appropriate.

FIGURE 10.15
The schematic lay-
out of the final steps

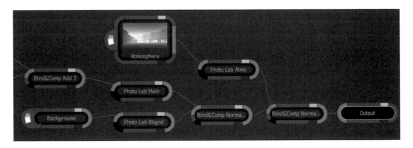

20. Add a Blend & Comp node, and connect the output of the Photo Lab Main and Photo Lab for the Background layer, making the Photo Shop Main the Front image. Rename the node, and leave it set to Normal compositing.

21. Connect the output of the Photo Lab for the atmospheric layer to the Front input of the final Blend & Comp, and connect the Blend & Comp in step 20 to the Back input. Rename the node, and leave it at Normal compositing.

22. Connect the output of the last Blend & Comp node to the Output node.

You can now adjust a variety of layers via the CC Basic, Photo Lab, and Blend & Comp nodes. The first thing to change when you make adjustments is to right-click the Player View image display and choose the Display ≻ Composition Output option; this keeps the Player View image on the final result and not the currently selected tool as you edit parameters. You'll see that the atmospheric effect is completely opaque and that none of the other components of the image are visible. Select the final Blend & Comp node (before the Output node), and set the Front Gain's Opacity setting to 0.25 or less.

The Blend & Comp nodes have a setting group called Method that controls how the compositing and blending occurs. At this stage, you might see a black edge around the buildings as the layers are combined. Change the Correlation setting for all the Blend & Comp nodes to the Superimposed method to tell the node that the outlines are the same between the Front and Back. The dark edge should disappear.

Try increasing the CC Basic ODD master gain to increase the brightness of surfaces hit with direct illumination. Turn the master gain down to 0.5 for the CC Basics ODI node to darken the indirect illumination, and do the same for the CC Basics OR and CC Basics OS nodes. For the Photo Lab Bkgnd node, change the Exposure – F-Stop setting to –2.5.

You can define the resolution and image format of your composition by clicking the Output node and selecting the Output tab. The Output node's Render tab allows you to define the output path and also the specific file format. To output (render) your composition, press Alt+R to open the Render dialog box. A completed rendering is available as `.\Composite\Renders\Karina.jpg` in the Chapter 10 project folder.

WHY USE CC BASICS AND BLEND & COMP TOGETHER?

I could have eliminated the CC Basics nodes on the output of the Image Import nodes if controlling gain was my only need, because there is a Gain control for each of the inputs in the Blend & Comp node. The CC Basics node, however, allows you to make a number of fine-tuned adjustments to the image layer such as Hue, Saturation, and Contrast adjustments, along with controls for Gamma, Gain, and Offset. It is handy to place the CC Basics nodes wherever they might be needed in the schematic so they are readily available. They could be eliminated.

Another simpler option is to use the Math Ops composition node instead of the Blend & Comp composition node. You then only have to choose the Add or Mult option and adjust an optional Blend value if needed.

To color-correct a single material or object, render out a Matte render element and use that as the Mask input of the CC Basics node to modify only that object or material. More examples are at `www.mastering-mentalray.com`.

To ensure that I am using the full dynamic range of the output, I typically add a CC Histo (histogram) or the Remap Color node before the Output node to make final adjustments to the range of the output. With the Remap Color node, try the EXRDisplay mode; it does a good job of compressing the high dynamic range of the floating-point format into a range for display, and you can set it to reveal detail in the low or high range of the image. The Remap Color node can be useful for an EXR image that includes an indoor and outdoor component of the rendering.

Use the Remap node with its Linear mode option instead of the Photo Lab node in your project if you do not need to color correct and would prefer a histogram graph for adjustment with adjustment curves similar to the Photoshop Curves tool.

The final 3ds Max Composite project is available as `Karina_Basic.txcomposition` in the `.\Composite\` folder of the Chapter 10 project together with a more complex example `Karina Advanced.txcomposition` that utilizes the mr A&D Raw and mr A&D Level render elements together with other options to allow for color correction. For these files, you need to select the Image Import nodes and ensure that the file path is correct for your system.

 Real World Scenario

COMPOSITING SAVES THE DAY

On more than one occasion using render elements and compositing has saved me considerable rework and helped me meet my deadline. One client in particular was fixated on the color of the wall used in an animation of a kitchen. Because this rendering used Final Gather, Global Illumination, and photometric lights combined with mr Sky Portals and a daylight system, the renders were time-consuming to say the least. Using a material ID and providing a Matte render element allowed me to sit down with the client and color-correct the wall separately from the other objects in post-production. I could tweak the color to the client's satisfaction with immediate feedback and without days of rerendering and guesswork.

For even relatively simple renders, setting up some basic render elements and rendering to an EXR file helps to give you both a high dynamic range for making exposure and color adjustments and the ability to modify images and animations with prerendered masks, material IDs, and object IDs.

In the final section of the book, I cover some of the new features of 3ds Max/Design 2011 that can help you when working with solid models and can significantly help produce artifact-free renderings in mental ray.

Working with Solid Models

With 3ds Max/Design 2011, Autodesk has added an option for importing and working with 3D solid model data that includes the SAT file format along with enhancements in importing native Inventor parts and assemblies.

When you work with a solid-modeling program, the SAT format or native Inventor import is preferred; SAT is covered in the "Introducing SAT and the Body Object" section, and Inventor is covered in "Understanding Native Inventor File Import" later in this chapter. An installation of Inventor is no longer required to import Inventor models, and additional Inventor import options such as the new Body objects are supported. The Body object allows you to work with fluid, organic shapes similar to Non-Uniform Rational Basis Splines (NURBS) and can accurately represent the curves and surfaces of a solid model. The Body object first became available in the Connection Extension for 3ds Max/Design 2010, which was a subscription benefit.

Although people do not always think of Revit as a solid-modeling product, it has its roots as a solid-modeling program adapted for architecture, and Revit supports the export and import of SAT files. With the addition of the SAT file format in 3ds Max/Design, you can now transfer data to and from 3ds Max/Design, Inventor, and Revit without a loss of surface detail. This allows for the editing of 3D data model in any SAT-compatible program.

Introducing SAT and the Body Object

When using 3ds Max/Design 2011, you get a new import/output format called SAT and a new object type called the Body object. A Body object is a *brep* (for "boundary representation") of your geometry and does not contain renderable triangles like a mesh object. Instead, it consists of a mathematical description of the curves and surfaces, similar to a NURBS surface, and the renderable surface triangles are created when needed. Figure 10.16 shows the dialog box that displays when you import a SAT model.

FIGURE 10.16

The SAT Import dialog box

The SAT Import options are as follows:

Standard – No Welding   The imported curves are not combined into a single object, and the objects will not be welded together. You will have separate objects for each component of an assembly, for instance. The Body object gives you editing options for welding surfaces if needed.

Single Body – No Welding   All parts of an assembly will be in a single Body object. If you are animating or manipulating objects separately, then try the Standard or Each option. Individual parts of an assembly will still be selectable as element subobjects.

Single Body – Weld Trimmed Surfaces   Weld trimmed surfaces can help eliminate gaps in your imported object if the incoming object consists of separate surfaces. Individual parts of an assembly will still be selectable as subobjects, and elements can be detached if necessary.

Each Trimmed Surface In Separate Body   With this option, you might find that some imported objects that logically should be combined are split into multiple Body objects. It depends on how the model was created, of course.

Viewport Body Mesh Quality   This option is the viewport resolution and not the render resolution. Typically I set this low to keep the viewport operating quickly. You can change this at any time from the Modify tab in the Command panel while the object is selected, as shown in Figure 10.17.

3D Trimming Tolerance   I find that Normal works well for a wide variety of models. If you see anomalies in your surfaces, try a tighter tolerance, or try another Import Option.

Automatic Face Flipping   For imports from Inventor, I have not found this to be required.

Convert SAT Y Axis to Z Axis   This option is always required for SAT files imported from Inventor, or your model will be on its side and will need to be reoriented.

Select Additional SAT Files For Import   This option gives you the ability to import multiple files as a single batch. Each imported file will be a separate object or objects as determined by the SAT Import options.

Imported Body objects contain editable subobjects for edges, faces (surfaces), and elements. The final tessellation of the surfaces of a Body object for render or display can be changed at any time and can be different for viewport and renderer. Figure 10.17 shows the Modify tab settings for much of the Body object.

FIGURE 10.17

The basic Body object's Modify panel

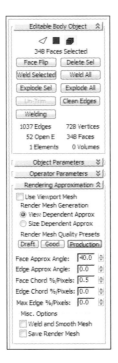

The key settings related to render quality are in the Rendering Approximation roll-down menu. The object is stored as a mathematical representation of the surface, and it must be converted to triangles for display in the viewport and for rendering. Separate controls are provided for display and render mesh approximation, or you can optionally have them be the same with the use of the Use Viewport Mesh option shown in Figure 10.17. For rendering, the resulting mesh can be View Dependent Approx or Size Dependent Approx and allows for a lower-polygon surface for objects that are not prominent in the view.

The resulting Body objects, compared to using the old AutoCAD DWG file format or mesh Inventor import methods, solve a host of geometry problems such as gaps, seams, and flipped faces that make the upgrade to 3ds Max/Design 2011 or the purchase of the nPower Software's PowerTranslator for earlier versions of 3ds Max/Design well worth the money. My experience is that the resulting Body objects render with no discernible artifacts.

To convert primitive and mesh objects in 3ds Max/Design to Body objects, select the object to be converted and then create a Body object. You create Body objects from the Create tab in the Command panel, within the Geometry class of objects, and while the Body Objects subclass is selected in the drop-down list, click the Body Object button. The current object will then have edges and polygons that can curve and are not limited to straight edges. This way an object like a box can have smooth, curved edges and an organic shape, as shown in Figure 10.18.

FIGURE 10.18
A box primitive converted to a Body object, with Bend, Taper, and Twist modifiers added

Note the slight distortion in the mapping of the checkerboard. With the SAT file's two-way data transfer capability and the ability to change standard 3ds Max/Design objects into Body objects, you can easily model organic building components, bring them into Revit, or modify Inventor or Rhino objects with smooth, curved results.

I have provided example SAT files on the book's DVD in the Chapter 10 project folder .\import. In the next section of the book, I cover the new options for importing Inventor part and assembly files.

Understanding Native Inventor File Import

You can directly import Inventor part and assembly files from the File Import dialog box (click the Application button, and select Import), and you simply need to select the assembly or part file you want to bring into your current scene. 3ds Max/Design prior to 2011 cannot open an Inventor file by itself; it needs Inventor installed on the local machine. Although you can select an Inventor file to import from *any* copy of 3ds Max/Design, if you do not have Inventor series 8 or newer installed on your machine, then this function *will not work*, and you'll get an error message when you try to use this feature. With 3ds Max/Design 2011 you do not need Inventor installed; the new Inventor import functionality is installed with 3ds Max/Design 2011.

NEW OPTIONS FOR IMPORTING INVENTOR MODELS IN 3DS MAX/DESIGN 2011

You no longer need an installation of Inventor on your machine in order to import part and assembly files in 3ds Max/Design 2011; your installation now automatically includes Inventor import functionality for model import. You also have a new option to import geometry as static mesh objects or as Body objects.

For legacy versions of 3ds Max/Design, you can download a trial version of Inventor from www.autodesk.com, and you do *not* need a registered version of Inventor to use the Inventor import feature of 3ds Max/Design.

Sample Inventor files are provided in the .\import\PipeVise folder of your Chapter 10 project folder. You can import parts or assemblies. Figure 10.19 shows the Autodesk Inventor File Import dialog box.

FIGURE 10.19
The native Autodesk
Inventor File Import
dialog box

The important option categories for importing are as follows:

Import As The incoming geometry is imported either as the new Body object (the same as with SAT models described earlier in this chapter) or as standard editable mesh objects. For most instances, using the Body object type produces the best results and gives you more options after the objects have been imported. If you import the object as a mesh, then you can control the overall mesh tessellation with the Mesh Resolution slider shown in Figure 10.19. Once imported as a mesh, the resolution of the object is fixed.

Assembly Options 3ds Max/Design gives you options to create duplicates of imported objects as *references* rather than unique objects to reduce memory use and to allow the editing of one object to affect all similar objects. You also have options to create layers based on material name and to rename materials based on the object name. The default for these options is to create references, to create layers, and to not rename materials.

Material Options You can optionally import the materials defined in the Inventor model and assign material IDs for use with Multi/Sub-Object materials.

Mesh Resolution This slider only functions when you import Inventor files as meshes. Knowing what settings to use depends greatly on how visible the object will be, depends on if you need to limit the polygon count, and depends on how acceptable it is to have artifacts. You can't easily add detail to an imported mesh file; however, using the ProOptimizer modifier on geometry can intelligently reduce polygon count and minimize artifacts.

Inventor File Vertical Direction This determines which direction the Inventor model uses for the Up direction. The default of Y is correct for most models.

After you choose your import options and click OK, 3ds Max/Design opens Inventor or the new Inventor Server as a background process and then translates the data and brings it directly into 3ds Max/Design as meshes or Body objects.

The Bottom Line

Use render studios Render studios can provide quick, high-quality environments for rendering everything from cell phones to vehicles to buildings.

> **Master It** You are a design visualization specialist who must create a series of small product renderings for a catalog. The products must have consistent lighting and a solid-colored environment that might vary based on the final catalog page color. How do you create a general-purpose environment for all products?

Create and use render elements Render elements allow you to separate different components of a rendering into separate images that can be layered, edited, and combined into a final "beauty" rendering.

> **Master It** You are a design visualization specialist and must create a rendering where the reflective qualities of the objects might need to be changed while sitting with the client. How do you allow adjustment to the reflectivity in post-processing?

Import render-ready solid models Using 3ds Max Design 2011's new SAT and Inventor import options, the resulting Body objects provide models with little or no artifacts that are ready to render.

> **Master It** You are an industrial designer who must produce a high-quality rendering of your product. How do you import your SAT model and use a render studio of your CAD model?

Appendix A

The Bottom Line

Each of The Bottom Line sections in the chapters suggest exercises to deepen skills and understanding. Sometimes there is only one possible solution, but often you are encouraged to use your skills and creativity to create something that builds on what you know and lets you explore one of many possible solutions.

Chapter 1: mental ray Essentials

Set up mental ray There are relatively few global mental ray preferences for mental ray, and they primarily affect the visibility of render buckets and the functionality of the mental ray Messages window.

Master It Change the mental ray preferences to allow logging of render-time information.

Solution Select Customize ➤ Preferences and then the Rendering tab. Select the Show/Log Information Messages check box.

Master It Enable mental ray for your current scene.

Solution Select Rendering ➤ Render Setup, and on the Common tab of the dialog box that opens, open the Assign Renderer drop-down menu. Change the default scanline renderer to mental ray by clicking the Choose Renderer button next to the Production renderer definition. Then select mental ray in the Choose Renderer dialog box, and click OK.

Configure 3ds Max/Design 3ds Max Design 2011 is preconfigured with mental ray as the preferred rendering engine for all new scenes and has other internal presets to assist artists and designers specifically manage imported CAD data, among other things. Proper configuration ensures that sample files and imported data operates correctly.

Master It Configure Max to use the DesignVIZ.mentalray preset template and ame-light user interface.

Solution Select Customize ➤ Custom UI And Defaults Switcher, and select the DesignVIZ .mentalray initial setting and the ame-light UI scheme. Click Set; then exit and restart 3ds Max.

Master It Set your project folder to the Chapter 1 location.

Solution From the Quick Access Toolbar (or the File menu in 3ds Max/Design 2009 and older), choose the Project Folder option. Browse to the \01_Essentials folder, and click OK.

Master It Configure your system units to use millimeters for all scenes.

Solution Select Customize ➤ Units Setup, and click the System Unit Setup button in the dialog box that opens. Change System Unit Scale to 1 Unit = 1.0 Millimeters, and click OK. In the Units Setup dialog box, change Display Units Scale to the Metric radio button, and choose the Millimeters option from the drop-down menu. Close the dialog box.

Configure gamma settings   Gamma is an intensity adjustment made to an image to compensate for nonlinearity in display and print devices and is necessary for low dynamic range images.

Master It   Enable gamma correction, and adjust its preferences.

Solution   Select Customize ➢ Preferences, and go to the Gamma and LUT tab in the dialog box that opens. Select the Enable Gamma/LUT check box. Choose the Gamma radio button for Display, and adjust the value so the inner and outer squares are approximately the same brightness. Select Materials and Colors, and set your Input Gamma and Output Gamma values to 2.2.

Configure essential quality settings   mental ray adaptively samples your scene as it renders, subdividing portions of the image into smaller and smaller parts, to produce the final image. Controlling the sampling has a great impact not only on the quality of your rendered image but on the amount of time it will take to render.

Master It   Choose settings for a fast draft-quality rendering and save as a render preset.

Solution   Select the Rendering ➢ Render Setup menu option, and go to the Renderer tab in the dialog box that opens. Change the global tuning parameters to 0.25 for each. Change the Samples Per Pixel settings: set Minimum to 1/16 and Maximum to 1. Choose the Box filter, and change the Spatial Contrast values to 0.9 for each of RGBA. On the Indirect Illumination tab, choose the Draft preset for Final Gather, and set Diffuse Bounces to 0. In the Preset drop-down, choose the Save Preset option, and save it to your \renderpresets folder as DraftQuality.rps.

Adjust Final Gather presets   Final Gather is one of several methods of calculating indirect, or bounced, illumination in your rendering. It is enabled by default in 3ds Max Design as a draft preset and must be enabled manually in legacy scenes and other flavors of 3ds Max.

Master It   Enable Final Gather, and choose medium-quality settings.

Solution   Select the Rendering ➢ Render Setup menu option. In the dialog box that opens, choose the Indirect Illumination tab. Select the Enable Final Gather check box, choose the Medium preset from the slider, and change Diffuse Bounces to 2.

Chapter 2: Materials and Maps

Use the new Slate Material Editor mode   The SME is a powerful new node-based visual tool for creating, managing, and editing materials and maps.

Master It   How do you create an Arch & Design material for use on a wood kitchen island using the SME?

Solution   Here are the steps:

1. In 3ds Max/Design 2011, open scene .\scenes\MasterIt\Materials_2010.max.

2. Open the SME.

3. From the Material/Map Browser, drag from the mental ray Materials group a new Arch & Design material into the view.

4. Double-click its header to open the material's Parameter Editor window at the right. The label of the Parameter Editor changes to the current material or map's name.

5. Rename the material to **Wood Horizontal**, and click from the material's output nodeslot then drag onto a leg of the island and release, replacing the existing material in the scene.

6. Choose the Glossy Varnished Wood template.

7. Double-click the wood bitmap in the view to open the parameters.

8. Replace the wood bitmap with a map from the `.\sceneassets\images` folder, and set the real-world scale to an appropriate size.

9. Right-click the Arch & Design header in the view, and choose the Show Hardware Map In Viewport option.

Control performance options for bitmaps   3ds Max/Design and mental ray have a variety of options for storing and using bitmaps, including holding maps in memory, caching and resizing to disk, and managing map paths.

Master It   How do you enable the rescaling of large bitmaps, disable the Bitmap Pager option, and enable the mental ray map Manager?

Solution   Here are the steps:

1. From the Common tab of the Render Setup dialog box, choose the Setup button for Bitmap Performance And Memory Options.

2. Select the Enable Proxy System check box.

3. Change the Render Mode drop-down menu to the Render With Proxies option.

4. Click the OK, Generate Proxies Now button. The proxy files now exist in your project's `.\proxies` folder.

5. On the Processing tab, enable the Use mental ray Map Manager option.

Adjust material and map settings that affect render quality and speed   The default settings for bitmaps and materials are not always the best choice for your scene, and it is important to understand the options and how they affect both image quality and render time.

Master It   How do you adjust the Ambient Occlusion, Round Corners, Glossy Samples, and Reflection Trace Depth settings to add detail, eliminate surface speckles, and trim render time?

Solution   Here are the steps:

1. Open the scene `.\scenes\MasterIt\Materials_2010.max` (or `Materials_2011.max`, which includes materials in the SME).

2. Render a cropped area around one corner of the Island, and save it to RAM Player Channels A.

3. Adjust Reflection Glossy Samples to 64, and set Reflection Max Trace Depth to 1.

4. Enable Ambient Occlusion and Round Corners. Set the Round Corners Radius value to 0.125″.

5. Render the cropped image, save it in RAM Player Channel B, and compare.

Chapter 3: Light, Shadow, and Exposure Control

Configure exposure control settings for varying conditions An exposure control maps the high dynamic range of the frame buffer into a low dynamic range for viewing and printing.

Master It How do you assign a mr Photographic exposure control and adjust it for different times of the day for an interior scene?

Solution Follow these steps:

1. Open the scene `.\scenes\MasterIt\Exposure_Start_2010.max`.

2. Press 8 to open the exposure settings, and choose mr Photographic Exposure Control. Choose the Physically Based Lighting, Indoor Daylight preset.

3. Click the exposure Render Preview, and adjust the EV to suit.

4. Select (by name) the Daylight System.

5. Adjust your time slider to frame 300, and turn on the Auto Key button.

6. In the Motion panel, set the time to 20:00:00.

7. In the exposure settings, click Render Preview, and adjust the EV or Shutter Speed setting to suit the new brightness levels. The time of day and corresponding exposure values are animated to give you a transition from daylight to dusk, including a change in exposure. Adjust the animation in the Curve Editor to fine-tune the transition.

8. Turn off Auto Key, and render frames 0 and 300. With Auto Key turned on, adjust the EV values if necessary.

Optimize and control photometric lights and shadow quality There are key light parameters that can have a great impact on rendered image quality and render time.

Master It How do you adjust shadow samples for high-quality results and adjust light parameters to minimize render time and control light distribution?

Solution Follow these steps:

1. Open the file `.\scenes\MasterIt\Lighting_Start_2010.max`, and render Camera02.

2. Use the Light Lister to turn off all lights except for PLight_Key. Click the far-left button next to PLight_Key to select that light in the scene.

3. Adjust Shadow Samples to 64. Render the view, and adjust the light settings as necessary.

4. In the Light Lister, disable the PLight_Key, and enable PLight_Fill. Select PLight_Fill. On the Modify tab, set Distribution Pattern to Spotlight, and adjust the hotspot and light/target position to encompass the biped. Select Far Attenuation, and set the Start value to intersect the biped and the End value just past the feet. Use Hardware Viewport Rendering to preview the results and render the view if necessary. Do not adjust exposure; instead, adjust the light's intensity to brighten the biped.

5. Repeat this process with PLight_Rim at the back-right of the biped, working in isolation. Set it to Spotlight distribution, and adjust the light/target position and intensity values for highlights to the biped.

6. Enable all three lights, and render Camera02 to evaluate the results. Disable the Material Override option for a final rendering.

A suggested final scene is available at `.\scenes\MasterIt\Lighting_Finish_2010.max`.

Chapter 4: Rendering

Strategize rendering scenes, including Batch Render and Backburner network rendering Utilizing all available computer resources not only helps you to render large images and animations but also assists you in the numerous iterations required to fine-tune your scene. Using Batch Render allows you to manage and queue jobs with or without a network.

Master It How do you configure a scene to use the Batch Render utility to render multiple camera views?

Solution Here are the steps:

1. Ensure that the Backburner Manager and Server applications are each running and connected to one another.

2. Open the file `.\scenes\MasterIt\BatchRender 2010_Start.max` in the Chapter 4 project folder.

3. Select the Rendering ➢ Batch Render menu item.

4. Click the Add button.

5. Enable the Override Preset check box, and set Frame Start to 0 and Frame End to 50.

6. Set the Output Path filename to `Dance.jpg` in the `.\renderoutput` folder.

7. Change the Camera drop-down to Camera02.

8. Change the Scene State drop-down to Dance Floor.

9. In the Preset drop-down, select the Load Preset option, and choose the `Animation.prs` file from the `.\renderpresets` project folder.

10. Click the Add button, and enable the Override Preset check box.

11. Set Frame Start to 51, and set Frame End to 125.

12. Set the Camera option to Camera03, Scene State to Dance Floor, and Preset to Animation.

13. Set Output Path to `Dance.jpg` in the `.\renderoutput` folder.

14. Click the Add button, and enable the Override Preset check box.

15. Set Frame Start to 126, and set Frame End to 200.

16. Set the Camera option to Camera04, Scene State to Dance Floor, and Preset to Animation.

17. Enable the Net Render check box, and click Render.

18. In the Network Job Assignment dialog box, click Connect. If machines are not listed in All Servers, ensure that Server is able to connect to Manager. If you are unable to connect, turn off Automatic Search, and enter the name of the computer running Manager.

19. Ensure the Use All Servers radio button is selected in Server Usage, and click Submit. Note: Some versions of 3ds Max and Backburner might require you to submit each Batch Render job one at a time and not all at once to ensure proper file output.

20. When the three render jobs are completed (one per batch render line), open the RAM Player in 3ds Max, and load the sequence of DanceXXXX.jpg files in the .\renderoutput folder.

Completed images are provided in the .\renderoutput\MasterIt folder of your Chapter 4 project folder; a completed scene is provided as .\scenes\MasterIt\BatchRender_2010_ Finish.max.

Understand the memory management features of mental ray to reduce memory issues, including using mental ray proxy objects Memory issues are one of the biggest complaints users have had over the years. Newer versions of 3ds Max/Design and mental ray have significantly reduced these issues; however, many users find that using 64-bit operating systems and having 8GB or more of DRAM is essential for large projects. The additional resources speeds rendering by eliminating swapping data to disk, along with reducing memory errors.

Master It What are some common causes for memory issues?

Solution Memory issues can be caused by a number of factors, including but not limited to the following:

♦ Bitmaps that are exceptionally large

♦ Exceptionally high global illumination photon values

♦ Exceptionally high polygon-count objects

♦ A high quantity of noninstanced objects

♦ Inadequate computer memory and/or 32-bit operating systems

To help reduce memory issues due to polygon count, you can do the following:

♦ You can convert high polygon objects to mental ray proxy objects.

♦ You can instance all identical objects when cloning (duplicating) objects, rather than using the Copy option.

Use visual diagnostic modes to configure the Samples Per Pixel and BSP options Visual diagnostics modes help you to see what is going on internal to mental ray to guide you in determining changes to settings.

Master It How do you enable visual diagnostics tool for the Sampling Rate setting and adjust Samples Per Pixel?

Solution   Perform the following steps to use visual diagnostics for the Sampling Rate setting:

1.   Open the `.\scenes\MasterIt\VisualDiag_2010_Start.max` scene from the Chapter 4 project folder.

2.   On the Render Setup dialog box's Processing tab, enable Visual Diagnostics, and choose Sampling Rate.

3.   Render the camera view. Save the results in Channel A of the RAM Player, and note the render time. The image is available in the `.\scenes\MasterIt` folder as `SampleRate_Low.jpg`. Notice the high amount of white, which indicates that mental ray used the Maximum sampling setting most often.

4.   Adjust the Samples Per Pixel setting to 1 and 16. Render the diagnostics image, save it in Channel B of the RAM Player, and note the render time. The image is available as `SampleRate_Med.jpg`. This image is much grayer, it shows a better balance between light and dark areas, and areas with fine details and a fast change in contrast have more white and therefore more sampling occurring.

5.   Adjust the Spatial Contrast setting to RGBA 0.02, 0.03, 0.05, and 0.05. Render the image, save it to Channel A of the RAM Player, and note the render time. This image is available as `SampleRate_High.jpg`.

6.   You will notice much more area in a brighter gray and white, with only a slight increase in render time, about 7 percent on my test machine. Performing the same series of tests without visual diagnostics will give you additional feedback on how the settings affect your renderings.

Chapter 5: Indirect Illumination and Final Gather

Adjust the settings of Final Gather   Final Gather is the simplest method of providing indirect illumination in your scene and is enabled by default in 3ds Max Design 2010 and newer. Understanding key settings allows you to improve your rendering quality and brightness while also keeping render time to a minimum.

Master It   Your rendering lacks details in indirect illumination. How would you adjust the Final Gather settings to improve the quality of your rendered image?

Solution   Here are the steps:

1.   Adjust the Final Gather precision slider to the Medium setting.

2.   Set the Diffuse Bounces value to 5 to brighten the scene and improve FG accuracy.

3.   Increase the number of rays to 500 to improve the accuracy of the Final Gather solution and reduce visual artifacts.

Use visual diagnostics for Final Gather   The visual diagnostics mode allows you to see the underlying data points that make up Final Gather.

Master It   How do you enable visual diagnostics mode to see Final Gather density?

Solution   Here are the steps:

1. Open the Render Setup dialog box.

2. Switch to the Processing tab.

3. Open the Diagnostics portion of the dialog box.

4. Enable the Visual check box within the Diagnostics area, and select the Final Gather radio button.

5. Render your scene.

Cache Final Gather data for still images and animations   Caching Final Gather data for reuse provides many benefits, including the ability to create Final Gather points at a low resolution to save time in a high-resolution rendering, and it allows you to skip frames in lengthy animations and helps prevent flickering during animations.

Master It   Your animation is suffering from long render time and flickering indirect illumination. How do you enable the reuse of Final Gather data and precalculate Final Gather points for your animation?

Solution   Here are the steps:

1. Open the Render Setup dialog box, and switch to the Indirect Illumination tab.

2. Open the Reuse (FG And GI Disk Caching) area.

3. Set the mode to the Single File Only option.

4. Set the Final Gather Map option to the Incrementally Add FG Points To Map Files option. The default filename is `temp.fgm`.

5. Open the drop-down arrow next to the Generate Final Gather Map File Now button, and choose an Nth time interval. The Final Gather Map file is generated.

6. Set the Final Gather Map option to the Read FG Points Only From Existing Map Files option.

7. Render your animation.

Chapter 6: Global Illumination and Caustics

Cache photons for reuse   mental ray provides the Reuse functionality to store and retrieve (cache) Global Illumination and Caustics photons for later reuse.

Master It   You are producing a walk-through animation of an interior space. How would you generate, cache, and reuse Global Illumination photons to render the scene?

Solution   On the Indirect Illumination tab of the Render Setup dialog box are the Reuse options. With Global Illumination enabled, set the Caustics And Global Illumination Photon Map mode to the Read/Write Photons To Map Files option. Click the Generate Photon Map File Now button to create photons and save to a file. Change the cache file to the Read Photons Only From Existing Map Files mode. Render the animation.

Utilize Global Illumination in a scene   Global Illumination, combined with Final Gather, gives the highest-quality renderings in the least amount of time. For interior scenes, the default Global Illumination settings are often useful as is with only the adjustment of the Average GI Photons Per Light setting. For exterior and interior scenes that use a daylight system, Global Illumination photons typically need to be focused around the area of interest to give the best results in a minimum amount of time.

> **Master It**   You are producing an interior rendering with Final Gather and Global Illumination. What are the basic steps to enable and adjust Global Illumination settings in the Render Setup dialog box?

> **Solution**   If using a daylight system, ensure that the Use Photon Target option is set to focus photons into the building. Set Final Gather to a Low or Medium preset and zero Diffuse Bounces. Enable Global Illumination, and adjust the Average GI Photons Per Light setting to ensure good photon coverage.

Utilize Caustics in a scene   Caustics add a great deal of realism to a scene; however, it might take additional setup and a high number of photons to produce a satisfactory Caustics solution.

> **Master It**   You are producing still images of a restaurant dining room table scene including clear glass objects. How do you enable Caustics and adjust settings to ensure a sharp result?

> **Solution**   Ensure that the glass objects have Caustics enabled. In the Render Setup dialog box, enable Caustics, and adjust the Average Caustic Photons Per Light setting until the Caustics are focused in the rendering.

Chapter 7: Importons and Irradiance Particles

Install the plug-in to access Importons and Irradiance Particles   Using importons and irradiance particles requires the installation of the ctrl.ghost plug-in.

> **Master It**   How do you install the ctrl.ghost shader and add the shader to a scene to make it possible to edit the parameters?

> **Solution**   Following the instructions in "Installing the ctrl.ghost Plugin" in this chapter, copy the appropriate files to your copy of 3ds Max/Design. Create a new mr Shader object, and assign a ctrl.ghost shader to the object. Instance the shader into a Material Editor to edit its parameters.

Add importons to a scene   Importons are used to intelligently merge Global Illumination photons to reduce PMAP size and memory requirements and also to position irradiance particles.

> **Master It**   Your rendering with Global Illumination is creating PMAP files too large for your 32-bit machines to render. How do you add importons to a scene to minimize the PMAP file?

> **Solution**   Create an mr Shader object, and assign the ctrl.ghost shader. Instance the shader to a Material Editor. Enable importons, and set Density to 1.0 and Task Size to 128.

Add Irradiance Particles to a scene   Irradiance particles can replace both Final Gather and Global Illumination, along with creating image-based lighting effects.

> **Master It**   You need to create image-based lighting for an outdoor scene. How do you use irradiance particles to accomplish this goal?

Solution Ensure that Final Gather and Global Illumination are disabled. Create an mr Shader object, and assign the ctrl.ghost shader. Instance the shader to a Material Editor to access the parameters. Enable importons, and set Density to 0.8 and Task Size to 64. Enable irradiance particles and the Environment Evaluation option. Add a spherical HDR image to the environment, and render the scene.

Chapter 8: Effects

Use camera lens shaders Camera lens shaders affect how rays are brought in and processed from a camera and include the Depth Of Field/Bokeh, Distortion, mr Physical Sky, Night, Gamma & Gain, and WrapAround shaders. Applying a camera effect is an identical process for each class of effect (lens, output, and volumetric), although each shader has different parameters.

Master It How do you add the Depth Of Field/Bokeh shader to a scene and make it possible to adjust its parameters?

Solution Using the settings and screenshots from this chapter as a reference, perform the following procedure to add shaders to the camera shader and add them to the Compact Material Editor:

1. Set your project folder to the Chapter 8 project on your DVD or local drive, and open the scene file `.\scenes\MasterIt\CameraShaders_2010_Start.max`.

2. Press F10 to open the Render Setup dialog box, and switch to the Renderer tab.

3. Click None next to the Lens shader.

4. In the Material/Map Browser, select the Depth Of Field/Bokeh shader, and click OK (in 3ds Max/Design 2010, you must unhide the DOF/Bokeh shader as described earlier in this chapter and use the Arch: DOF/Bokeh shader listed in the browser).

5. Open the Compact Material Editor, drag the new shader into a sample window, and choose the Instance option.

6. Set Focus Plane to 3′ and Radius Of Confusion to 0.5″.

7. Render Camera05. A completed render with all "Master It" camera effects is available as `.\renderoutput\MasterIt\EffectsXXXX.jpg`, and a completed scene with all "Master It" camera effects is available as `.\scenes\MasterIt\CameraShaders_2010_Finish.max` in the Chapter 8 project.

Use camera output shaders A camera output shader is a post-rendering process applied to an image and includes the Glare and HDR Image Motion Blur effects.

Master It How do you add the HDR Image Motion Blur shader to a scene and make it possible to adjust its parameters?

Solution Using the settings and screenshots from this chapter as a reference, perform the following procedure to add the HDR Motion Blur shader to the camera shader and add it to the Compact Material Editor:

1. Set your project folder to the Chapter 8 project on your DVD or local drive, and open the scene file `.\scenes\MasterIt\CameraShaders_2010_Start.max`.

2. Press F10 to open the Render Setup dialog box, and switch to the Renderer tab.

3. Click the button next to the output shader, and select the HDR Image Motion Blur shader. Click OK to close the dialog box.

4. Drag the new shader into an unused sample window in the Compact Material Editor, and choose the Instance option.

5. Set Background Distance to 10′, and enable the Blur More Objects Near Camera option.

6. In the Render Setup dialog box, click the button next to the volume shader, and select the Mist shader. Click OK to close the dialog box.

7. Drag the new shader into an unused sample window in the Compact Material Editor, and choose the Instance option.

8. Set Transparency to 0.25, enable the Layering option, and set Plane Distance to 3′ and Transition Height to 12.0.

9. Render Camera05. A completed render with all "Master It" camera effects is available as `.\renderoutput\Masterit\Effects*.jpg` where * is an image sequence number, and a completed scene with all "Master It" camera effects is available as `.\scenes\MasterIt\CameraShaders_2010_Finish.max` in the Chapter 8 project.

Use camera volume shaders Camera volume shaders allow you to produce fog and distance-dependent effects and includes the shaders Beam, Mist, mr Physical Sky, Parti Volume, and Submerge.

Master It How do you add the Mist volume shader to a scene and make it possible to adjust its parameters?

Solution Using the settings and screenshots from this chapter as a reference, perform the following procedure to add the Mist shader to the camera shader and add it to the Compact Material Editor:

1. Set your project folder to the Chapter 8 project on your DVD or local drive, and open the scene file `.\scenes\MasterIt\CameraShaders_2010_Start.max`.

2. Press F10 to open the Render Setup dialog box, and switch to the Renderer tab.

3. Click the button next to the volume shader, and select the Mist shader. Click OK to close the dialog box.

4. Drag the new shader into an unused sample window in the Compact Material Editor, and choose the Instance option.

5. Set Transparency to 0.25, enable the Layering option, and set Plane Distance to 3′ and Transition Height to 12.0.

6. Render Camera05. A completed render with all "Master It" camera effects is available as `.\renderoutput\Masterit\Effects*.jpg` where * is an image sequence number, and a completed scene with all "Master It" camera effects is available as `.\scenes\MasterIt\CameraShaders_2010_Finish.max` in the Chapter 8 project.

Chapter 9: mental ray for Architecture

Use a Revit FBX file within 3ds Max Design   The combination of Revit and 3ds Max/Design makes for a powerful partnership. The enhanced file linking capabilities of 3ds Max/Design 2011 allow the artists to maximize the use of materials and lights defined in the Revit model, reducing the time needed to produce rendering and animations.

Master It   You must connect design data in a Revit FBX file export to a scene in 3ds Max Design 2011. How do you use the File Link Manager to attach the FBX file to your scenes?

Solution   Using the procedures outlined in this chapter under "Using the File Link Manager with FBX Files," link your external CAD file to a new scene. Files are provided for you in DWG, FBX, and SAT formats in the .\import folder of the Chapter 9 project.

Create light meters and lighting analysis image overlay   Using lighting analysis in 3ds Max Design can assist architects and lighting designers in validating and improving their designs and assist them with LEED 8.1 design certification.

Master It   You are assisting an architect in producing lighting documentation for a building interior space. How do you add an image overlay and light meter to your scene?

Solution   Using the procedures outlined in this chapter under "Using the Light Meter Object," use the Lighting Analysis Assistant to produce lighting analysis documentation for a scene.

Create nonphotorealistic renderings   Nonphotorealistic renderings help keep the focus on the building and overall massing of a design rather than the details of surface finishes.

Master It   You are in the process of developing a 3D model and rendering a proposed building, and your client wants a progress image. How would you produce a nonphotorealistic rendering using the Material Override and Ambient Occlusion settings?

Solution   Using the procedure outlined in this chapter under "Using Material Override for NPR," convert your scene to use an override material.

Chapter 10: mental ray for Design

Use render studios   Render studios can provide quick, high-quality environments for rendering everything from cell phones to vehicles to buildings.

Master It   You are a design visualization specialist who must create a series of small product renderings for a catalog. The products must have consistent lighting and a solid-colored environment that might vary based on the final catalog page color. How do you create a general-purpose environment for all products?

Solution   Using the steps shown in "Using Solid-Colored Environments" in this chapter, create a single environment with XRefs to the individual products.

Create and use render elements   Render elements allow you to separate different components of a rendering into separate images that can be layered, edited, and combined into a final "beauty" rendering.

Master It   You are a design visualization specialist and must create a rendering where the reflective qualities of the objects might need to be changed while sitting with the client. How do you allow adjustment to the reflectivity in post-processing?

Solution Following the steps in "Creating a Basic Composite" in this chapter, render your product with separate mr A&D Output elements, and combine them in 3ds Max Composite.

Import render-ready solid models Using 3ds Max Design 2011's new SAT and Inventor import options, the resulting Body objects provide models with little or no artifacts that are ready to render.

Master It You are an industrial designer who must produce a high-quality rendering of your product. How do you import your SAT model and use a render studio of your CAD model?

Solution Export your model in the SAT format. Open a render studio from the Chapter 10 .\scenes folder. Rename the scene to your product's name. Import your SAT model, add materials, and render the scene.

Appendix B

About the Companion DVD

Topics in this appendix include:

◆ What You'll Find on the DVD
◆ System Requirements
◆ Using the DVD
◆ Troubleshooting

What You'll Find on the DVD

The following sections summarize the content you'll find on the DVD. If you need help installing the items provided on the DVD, refer to the installation instructions in the "Using the DVD" section.

Projects

The Projects folder contains subfolders organized by chapter. Each folder contains a 3ds Max project .mxp file and associated project subfolders. Example scene files are in the scenes folder and subfolders, rendered images and animations are in the renderoutput folder and subfolders, and bitmaps and precomputed scene data are in the sceneassets folder.

Plug-Ins

The Plugins folder contains files for the ctrl.ghost plug-ins required to use Importons and Irradiance Particles covered in Chapter 7. Files are divided into 3ds Max versions, and you need to copy the correct 32-bit or 64-bit version as described in the book.

Scripts

The Scripts folder contains MAXScript files covered in the book.

3ds Max Design 2009

The 3ds Max Design 2009 folder contains pre-edited mental ray "include files" to enable additional shaders. Be sure to back up your existing files.

3ds Max Design 2010

This 3ds Max Design 2010 folder contains pre-edited mental ray "include files" to enable additional shaders. Be sure to back up your existing files.

Bonus

The Bonus folder contains bonus 2D and 3D material supplied by third-party vendors.

Bonus Videos

BonusVideos includes introduction and overview videos of selected topics in each chapter, along with other related sample video files.

White Papers

The White Papers folder contains links to Autodesk Lighting Analysis white papers on the www.mastering-mentalray.com web site.

System Requirements

Make sure that your computer meets the minimum system requirements shown in the following list. If your computer doesn't match up to most of these requirements, you may have problems using the files on the companion DVD:

◆ A PC running Microsoft Windows XP SP2 or newer or Windows Vista

◆ A Macintosh running Mac OS X or newer

◆ Your computer's processor should be a fast Pentium 4 or newer (or equivalent)

◆ At least 1024MB of RAM

◆ An Internet connection

◆ A DVD-ROM drive

◆ Apple QuickTime 7.0 or later

The minimum system requirements for 3ds Max/Design 2011 are Windows XP SP2 or newer and a 32- or 64-bit operating system with a minimum of 2GB RAM. You will need 5GB of drive space if you want to uncompress and copy all the DVD content to a local drive.

You should have at least 8GB RAM, a 64-bit version of Windows 7 and quad-core processor(s). Using 3ds Max/Design and mental ray is memory- and processor-intensive, and the more memory and speed you have, the better experience you will have with this book.

QuickTime is also required to view or use many of the video clips used in the projects on the disc. If you don't already have QuickTime installed on your computer, you may download it at www.apple.com/quicktime/download.

Using the DVD

To install the items from the DVD to your hard drive, follow these steps:

1. Insert the DVD into your computer's DVD-ROM drive. The license agreement appears.

NOTE   Windows users: The interface won't launch if Autorun is disabled. In that case, click Start ➢ Run (for Windows Vista, click Start ➢ All Programs ➢ Accessories ➢ Run). In the dialog box that appears, type *D*:\Start.exe. (Replace *D* with the proper letter if your DVD drive uses a different letter. If you don't know the letter, see how your DVD drive is listed under My Computer.) Click OK.

2. Read through the license agreement, and then click the Accept button if you want to use the DVD.

The DVD interface appears. The interface allows you to access the content with just one or two clicks.

Alternately, you can access the files at the root directory of your hard drive.

NOTE Mac users: The DVD icon will appear on your desktop; double-click the icon to open the DVD and then navigate to the files you want.

Troubleshooting

Wiley has attempted to provide sample scenes that work on most computers with the minimum system requirements. Alas, your computer may differ, and some sample files may not work properly for some reason.

The two likeliest problems are that you don't have enough memory (RAM) for the programs you want to use or you have other programs running that are affecting installation or running of a program. If you get an error message such as "Not enough memory" or "Setup cannot continue," try one or more of the following suggestions, and then try using the software again:

◆ *Turn off any antivirus software running on your computer*: Installation programs sometimes mimic virus activity and may make your computer incorrectly believe that it's being infected by a virus.

◆ *Close all running programs*: The more programs you have running, the less memory is available to other programs. Installation programs typically update files and programs, so if you keep other programs running, installation may not work properly.

◆ *Have your local computer store add more RAM to your computer*: This is, admittedly, a drastic and somewhat expensive step. However, adding more memory can really help the speed of your computer and allow more programs to run at the same time.

Customer Care

If you have trouble with the book's companion DVD, please call the Wiley Product Technical Support phone number at (800) 762-2974. Outside the United States, call +1 (317) 572-3994. You can also contact Wiley Product Technical Support at http://sybex.custhelp.com. John Wiley & Sons will provide technical support only for installation and other general quality-control items. For technical support on the applications themselves, consult the program's vendor or author.

To place additional orders or to request information about other Wiley products, please call (877) 762-2974.

For potential future updates on this book and DVD, go to www.sybex.com/go/masteringmentalray.

Index

Note to the reader: Throughout this index **boldfaced** page numbers indicate primary discussions of a topic. *Italicized* page numbers indicate illustrations.

Wiley Publishing, Inc. End-User License Agreement